P9-DVF-765

WITHDRAWN
UTSA LIBRARIES

RENEWALS 458-4574
DATE DUE

	M# 19884478		

GAYLORD   PRINTED IN U.S.A.

Developmental Psychobiology of Aggression

This book is the outgrowth of a memorial conference to honor the scientific contributions of Robert B. Cairns, an internationally recognized interdisciplinary developmental scientist. The book is organized around three research themes that were an integral part of Dr. Cairns's theories and research: (1) neural and developmental plasticity; (2) brain–behavior bidirectionality; (3) gene–environment interactions. Throughout this book, these themes are linked together by employing animal models and clinical investigations through a multiple-levels-of-analysis approach to understanding the origins, development, desistance, and prevention of aggression. These studies will add to the compendium of basic knowledge on the developmental psychobiology of aggression and will aid in the ultimate translation of this knowledge to clinical and community settings. This book hopes to foster the legacy of Robert B. Cairns to facilitate the theoretical development and research of a new generation of developmental scientists dedicated to relieving the tragic consequences of aggression on individuals and societies.

David M. Stoff, Ph.D., is chief of the extramural research programs on HIV/AIDS Neuropsychiatry and HIV/AIDS Health Disparities and Director of AIDS Research Training at the Center for Mental Health Research on AIDS of the National Institute of Mental Health (NIMH). Before joining NIMH in 1992, he had a long research career in animal psychopharmacology, the biology of childhood psychiatric disorders, and antisocial behavior. His research was supported by the NIMH through a Research Scientist Development Award and Research Grant. Dr. Stoff is the first editor of two other books in the field: *Aggression and Violence: Neurobiological, Biosocial and Genetic Perspectives* (1996) and *Handbook of Antisocial Behavior* (1997).

Elizabeth J. Susman is the Jean Phillips Shibley Professor of Biobehavioral Health in the Department of Biobehavioral Health at The Pennsylvania State University. She has a long history of programmatic research on the integration of biological and behavioral processes and antisocial behavior. Her work has been supported by the National Institute of Mental Health, the National Institute of Child Health and Human Development, and private foundations. Dr. Susman is president of the Society for Research on Adolescents and serves on a number of scientific journal editorial boards.

Developmental Psychobiology of Aggression

Edited by
DAVID M. STOFF
National Institute of Mental Health

ELIZABETH J. SUSMAN
The Pennsylvania State University

CAMBRIDGE
UNIVERSITY PRESS

Library
University of Texas
at San Antonio

CAMBRIDGE UNIVERSITY PRESS
Cambridge, New York, Melbourne, Madrid, Cape Town, Singapore, São Paulo

Cambridge University Press
40 West 20th Street, New York, NY 10011-4211, USA

www.cambridge.org
Information on this title: www.cambridge.org/9780521826013

© Cambridge University Press 2005

This book is in copyright. Subject to statutory exception
and to the provisions of relevant collective licensing agreements,
no reproduction of any part may take place without
the written permission of Cambridge University Press.

First published 2005

Printed in the United States of America

A catalog record for this publication is available from the British Library.

Library of Congress Cataloging in Publication Data
Developmental psychobiology of aggression / edited by David M. Stoff,
   Elizabeth J. Susman.
       p.   cm.
   "This volume is an outgrowth of a memorial conference to honor the scientific
   contributions and accomplishments of Robert B. Cairns, internationally recognized
   for his pioneering efforts as an interdisciplinary developmental scientist."
   ISBN 0-521-82601-2 (hardback)
   1. Aggressiveness – Physiological aspects.   2. Developmental psychobiology.
   I. Stoff, David M.   II. Susman, Elizabeth J.
   RC569.5.A34D48   2005
   155.2'32 – dc22   2004016030

   ISBN-13   978-0-521-82601-3 hardback
   ISBN-10   0-521-82601-2 hardback

Cambridge University Press has no responsibility for
the persistence or accuracy of URLs for external or
third-party Internet Web sites referred to in this book
and does not guarantee that any content on such
Web sites is, or will remain, accurate or appropriate.

**Library
University of Texas
at San Antonio**

Dedicated to Robert B. Cairns, a pioneering interdisciplinary developmental scientist, for leading the way toward a modern understanding of the interactions among biological, psychological, and environmental influences on development and behavior. His research and theoretical works will be an enduring legacy to outstanding science for current and future generations of scholars.

Robert B. Cairns

Contents

Foreword

Felton Earls, M.D.
Harvard Medical School

In the last quarter of the 20th century, Robert Cairns helped to transform psychology. In doing so, he rescued it from a virulent susceptibility to reductionism. Standing on the shoulders of great psychologists of the first half of that century (James Baldwin and Kurt Lewin most readily come to mind), he created a truly interdisciplinary environment at Chapel Hill. The Carolina Consortium on Human Development became an international crossroad for the establishment of a new synthesis termed developmental science. A legion of graduate students, postdoctoral Fellows, young faculty, and many senior investigators emerged from this oasis with a deeper, more nuanced understanding of human development. By formulating sound theory and exacting the highest standards for basic research, Cairns and his colleagues moved the field into a realm in which social behavior was not reducible: not to motivations or environmental contingencies any more than to neurons or molecules. Behavior was not sacrificed to biology, nor was it glorified to the environment. Rather, a coherence of behavior and biology was refined in a manner that was intellectually robust and scientifically challenging. Evolution, genetics, ontogeny, and social relationships were interwoven with honesty and with appropriate appreciation for the subtleties involved.

In this volume a group of accomplished protégés and admirers of Cairns explore the nature of aggression, an area of social behavior that most intrigued him. How is it that a social species tolerates aggression? For Cairns the species could be mice or humans, the level of analysis could be genes or peer affiliation. What mattered was the capacity to grasp dynamic changes that are reflected in the interplay between organism and the environment.

Cairns was an iconoclast, but his character and the content of his thought were in equilibrium. For anyone who knew him, the words *reciprocity, configuration, novelty, synchrony, correlated constraints* reverberate in the mind. He was simultaneously a theoretician, methodologist, geneticist, and social psychologist. Developmental science emerged from his experiments in mice and his longitudinal studies of humans.

We owe him a great deal, yet in my own experience I would have to say that few people really understood the whole corpus of his work. Along with Urie Bronfenbrenner, Mavis Hetherington, David Magnusson, Bernadette Gray-Little, and Marian Radke-Yarrow, I served on the advisory board of Cairns's research center during the decade leading up to his premature death. In addition to Chapel Hill, we met frequently in the Department of Psychology at Stockholm University and in Chicago as part of the Project on Human Development in Chicago Neighborhoods. Though we saw each other frequently in these places, I had the distinct sense that my discourses with him were nearly always interrupted. It was as if we never completed whatever it was that we intended to talk about. Although there was synchrony in our understanding of the issues, I was not sure if we ever fully agreed. Perhaps the details of these exchanges were not so important. Typically some novel idea arose that displaced the previous theme. Then one day I realized that he was actually carrying on two or three conversations with me all at the same time. The problem was not with him, but with my convergent mind-set. I was trying to focus the conversation while he was adding new data. This insight made me all the more observant of his interactions with others, especially with Urie Bronfenbrenner. Urie had anything but a convergent mind-set. So, I asked myself, what would that encounter look like; Cairns, the multichannel conversant confronting Bronfenbrenner's discourse, which was sure to expand like a Russian novel? The result was not predictable. Cairns never seemed troubled by Urie's flourishes, but Bronfenbrenner did worry about Cairns's lack of coherence.

If one had trouble with Cairns as a conversationalist or lecturer, there was no such problem in his writing. As an author and editor he was eloquent, concise, and brilliant. His unique scientific contributions are packed in a collection of books and papers with two peaks: his 1979 textbook on social development and the longitudinal study he reported with Beverly Cairns published in 1994. This study, *Lifelines and Risks*, is a masterpiece. It is both graceful and rigorous in its exposition. At one point in this book, Cairns and Cairns supply a quote from Baldwin:

The development of the child's personality could not go on at all without the constant modification of his sense of himself by suggestions from others. So he himself, at every stage, is really in part someone else, even in his own thought of himself.

This statement, published in 1897, became the organizing principle for much of his work on social networks and represents a major discovery in the insight that Robert and Beverly Cairns derived from their own empirical work. A century later they showed that self-awareness reflects a dual reality, an internal sense of predictability and an external veridicality that offers more control and restriction than freedom and opportunity.

They, like many before and since, recognized that a fundamental problem was to account for the stability of aggressive behavior, while at the same time understanding how a minority of aggressive persons moved beyond the destructive and handicapping consequences of this behavioral configuration. Their understanding of this is remarkably clear and compelling.

We found in our analyses of social networks that cliques become increasingly segregated as our subjects moved from the 4th and 5th grades to the 7th and 8th grades. Similarly, socioeconomic class became highly salient about the time subjects began to get involved in dating and heterosexual parties. The sociocultural forces of school, home, and the community that were latent in childhood operated like a sledgehammer in adolescence. Rather than a phase of quiescence, middle childhood may be a phase of life where children are permitted to cross boundaries and explore friendships that become closed to them after they enter adolescence.

Their study transcends the specifics of time and place by providing a general truth. Development is conservative and increasingly so as maturation nears. The stereotype of the adolescent bent on taking risks, exploiting new opportunities, and moving beyond the family of origin is seriously challenged by the Cairnses' theory and by their solid evidence.

On the other hand, his experiments in artificial selection in mice demonstrated that aggression in various forms can be turned up or down in a period of a relatively few generations. His contributions to microevolution and behavioral genetics went against the grain of the limit-setting and fateful outcomes that seem inherent in much other work that characterizes the field. He posited that genes act as switches in ontogeny. If the environment supplied the right stimulus and the timing was right, substantial change was possible. Yet, his study of human development revealed the opposite. The social and learning environments shut more doors in the face of growth than they opened. Cairns did not see a contradiction in this. Rather, it represented an invitation to promote health, increase opportunity, and do a better job of fitting our circumstances to the enormous biological potential inherent in our species.

The ultimate value of a colleague is that he or she leaves you with a gem of some sort. It could be an idea, a technique, or an insight, but it has that undeniable quality of shining in the dark. Cairns, as much as anyone, grasped my own reason for being a scientist:

The aim of intensive study of individuals over time is to understand processes in context, not to predict context-free outcomes. Processes and principles, once identified, permit the science to transcend time and place. Specific outcomes and specific predictive equations are necessarily conditioned by and relative to particular contexts, samples, and times. The laws of gravity yield quite different outcomes in rate of descent, depending on whether you watch a pebble fall through the water or air. The scientific task is to specify why contexts make a difference. (p. 253)

The Carolina School of Human Development supplied a foundation on which issues of synchronous patterns, environmental contingencies, and ontogenetic timing represent concepts that must drive the field forward. This book is a wonderful tribute to the rich legacy left by Robert Cairns. In my own lifeline, I can only say that I met him too late and lost him too early.

Reference

Cairns, R. B., and Cairns, B. D. (1994). *Lifelines and risks: Pathways of youth in our time*. New York: Cambridge University Press.

INTRODUCTION

1

Integrated Perspective for Psychobiological Research in Aggression: An Introduction

David M. Stoff
National Institute of Mental Health

Elizabeth J. Susman
The Pennsylvania State University

This volume is an outgrowth of a memorial conference to honor the scientific contributions and accomplishments of Robert B. Cairns, internationally recognized for his pioneering efforts as an interdisciplinary developmental scientist. His theories and research in humans and animals provided a template and direction for future research in the developmental sciences and the psychobiology of aggression. This perspective integrated biology with psychological development, emphasizing the dynamic interactions among biological, psychological, and environmental influences on development and behavior. Cairns described a conception of human developmental processes, characterized by biobehavioral organization and involving reciprocal interactions of bidirectionality, plasticity, and gene–environment relationships. This conceptual framework provided an expanded array of multiple biological and behavioral levels as it applied to aggression, offering a refreshing departure from the very limited unidimensional belief in the deterministic role that unfolding biology exerts on behavior (see Figure 1.1; Cairns, 1996).

In earlier volumes, we presented various research approaches to the biology of aggression (Stoff & Cairns, 1996) and provided a comprehensive review of research on many aspects of antisocial behavior (Stoff, Breiling, & Maser, 1997). This volume updates those works, principally from a developmental psychobiological viewpoint of aggression, emphasizing modern neuroscience approaches that focus not only on "bottom-up" causality (e.g., molecular processes involving genes, cells, and synapses) but also on "top-down" causality (e.g., more molar processes mediated by experiences). Both bottom-up and top-down forms of causality were particularly evident in the propositions by Cairns that explanations are required at

The opinions expressed herein are the views of the authors and do not necessarily reflect the official position of the National Institute of Mental Health or any other part of the U.S. Department of Health and Human Services or The Pennsylvania State University.

Individuals

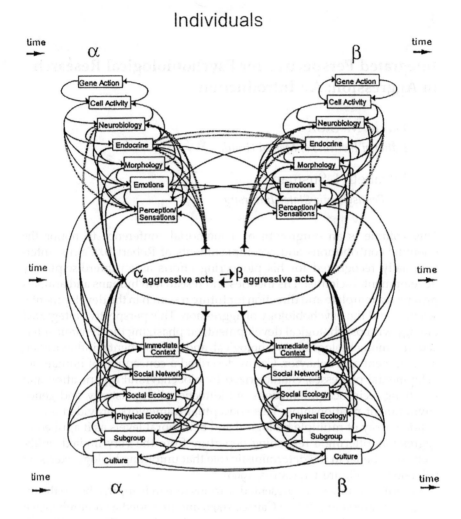

FIGURE 1.1. Models describing two interacting individuals (α, β) in terms of relationships within each individual and with each environment (from Cairns, 1996, p. 50).

multiple levels of analysis from the population level (i.e., epidemiology), through individual and group behavior, neuropathology, and systems-level neurobiology, to cellular and molecular neurobiology. This perspective of aggressive behavior, and, for that matter, any aspect of normal and abnormal behavior development, advocates a multidisciplinary approach that examines biological, psychological, and social–contextual aspects of development. Risk and protective factors cut across multiple levels of analysis, from the molecular and cellular through the psychological and social systems. A focus on multiple levels of analysis requires research designs and strategies that call for the simultaneous assessment of multiple domains of variables both within and outside of the developing person. All levels must be examined and integrated because each level both informs and constrains all other levels of analysis. Cairns most eloquently postulated these interrelationships in his notion that there are "correlated constraints" among variables that can be identified from the multiple sets of causal factors (e.g., genetic, behavioral, cognitive, contextual). As a consequence of these constraints, the major methodological challenge is to employ a holistic approach where individuals and not variables are the focus of analysis. Ideally, multiple levels of analyses should be integrated within the individual and not simply across studies.

Embedded within the holistic, multiple levels of analysis models are three concepts – plasticity, bidirectionality, and gene–environment interactions – that serve as themes around which this volume is structured. The plasticity theme (Part I) is represented in the chapters of Raine, Gendreau and Lewis, Ferris, and Graber, Brooks-Gunn, and Archibald; the bidirectionality theme (Part II) is represented in the chapters of Field, Zahn-Waxler and Usher, Moffitt and Caspi, and Worthman and Brown; the gene–environment theme (Part III) is represented in the chapters of Hood and Suomi. Although these aspects have been presented separately for purposes of communication, in practice they overlap, are interdependent, and often complement one another. Because these themes are pervasive throughout this volume, we found it useful to first elaborate upon them conceptually. We return to these themes in the final chapter illustrating how they are addressed by the findings of the contributing authors with an eye toward integration (Susman & Stoff).

PLASTICITY

The past 20 years of research in developmental neurobiology have raised serious problems for the nativist view, suggesting instead that the primate brain is extraordinarily plastic, and that cortical specialization is largely determined by brain activity and experience. The ramifications of plasticity are profound, indicating that brain structure and function during development, once thought to be deterministic, are now viewed as malleable and at times dependent on stimulation from the environment. Research has shown that the brain demonstrates remarkable plasticity during development, remodeling itself to attain its adult configuration. Such change can occur at many levels, from molecular to neural systems to behavior. We can conceptualize aggression as an integration of approaches at different levels wherein the brain operates in a plastic, self-organizing fashion and, as such, is less constrained by predetermined boundaries than previously thought. The major deterrent to this notion of the brain as plastic was the dogma of biological determinism, which inadequately represents the role of the environment. Both neural plasticity and developmental plasticity have become increasingly important to an understanding of mental health. Gaining knowledge about the mechanisms of plasticity and their patterns of timing across multiple levels of analyses will be challenging and complex.

BIDIRECTIONALITY

Today, the notion of "nature versus nurture" has been set aside in favor of a newer, more integrated model in which processes and outcomes of development are viewed as products of bidirectional interchanges between biology and the environment. Modern research now views brain development and function and their subsequent influence on behavior as possessing self-organizing properties that can, in fact, be altered by experiences at certain sensitive periods of development that occur across the life course. Bidirectionality implies that interactions with the environment have an impact on the course of biological development, which in turn affects behavior and functioning, and these changes in behavior then alter experiences. This model holds to a more integrative and dynamic transactional view of development that stresses the importance of both psychological and neural self-organization. To appreciate the full impact of adopting bidirectional models, research must acknowledge the importance of multiple levels analyses in both biological (molecular, cellular, organs, systems) and behavioral (individual, interaction, groups, and social–cultural) domains.

GENE–ENVIRONMENT INTERACTIONS

For many, the terms *nature* and *nurture* implied a polarity. In his studies emphasizing integration, Cairns taught us of the need for an explicit research focus on the forms of interplay between genes and environment and how this interplay plays out over development and is involved in the causal mechanisms for the origins, persistence, and desistance over time of antisocial behavior. Although many acknowledge that genes endow individuals with certain tendencies regarding their interactions in social settings, it has only recently become accepted how environments are simultaneously essential both for the expression of specific genes and for changing the nature and timing of genetic expression. Although the conventional view is that genes create vulnerability to disease, it is equally likely that they protect against environmental insult. In his early inbreeding studies utilizing the then-new technology of "knockout mice," Cairns pointed to the potential of molecular genetics for understanding environmental risk mechanisms and the interplay between nature and nurture. In general, there has now been a call for a shift from a focus on the relative strength of nature and nurture effects on behavior to a concern for understanding how the interplay between the two comes about and how the interplay affects behavior.

PRINCIPLES OF AGGRESSION RESEARCH

Perhaps more than any other field, the study of aggression has been plagued by certain myths or misconceptions that must be overcome. We discussed some of these myths in our earlier volume on this topic (Stoff & Cairns, 1996), when the field was embroiled in sociopolitical controversy about biological/genetic aggression research (Stone, 1992). Here, we restate these myths in a more positive light, in the form of principles for contemporary psychobiological aggression research. With these rules of research in mind, the biological study of aggression will become more innovative by targeting mechanisms. We reiterate the position of Lederhendler (2003), recently stated in a special issue on the biology of aggression, that the major challenge will be to determine where, when, and how biological events operate in neural and endocrine systems to regulate aggressive behavior, rather than whether neurotransmitters, genes, or hormones "drive" or "cause" aggression.

1. *Aggression research must be interdisciplinary.* The challenging, multidetermined problem of antisocial behavior must be approached through a cooperative effort by a team of investigators, each expert in the use of different methods and concepts, who join together to attack the problem from different vantage points. A breadth of expertise will be needed spanning diverse multiple disciplines including psychology, sociology, criminology, epidemiology and public health, psychiatry, neuroscience, genetics, biomedical science, and developmental sciences. Interdisciplinary collaborations among researchers will lead to a more complete and accurate understanding of the multifaceted biological, psychological, and social issues that are generated by the study of antisocial behavior. An integrated set of multidisciplinary, multimethod, multilevel studies utilizing the powerful newer tools of molecular biology, imaging, and genetics may someday allow us to identify the brain circuits and the neurobiological bases of macrostructural influences (e.g., poverty, familial and societal conditions) on aggression.

2. *Aggression research must be translational.* As a special subset of interdisciplinary research, translational research attempts to integrate information from basic research laboratories to clinical settings and

from clinical settings to practical, real-world environments. Good translational research should operate in both directions with the different domains informing one another. Many barriers will have to be overcome to facilitate the building of bridges among disciplines and settings – among the most important are issues related to communication, attitude, and philosophy and training opportunities. Despite the tremendous technological advances of molecular biology and neuroimaging, we remain mindful of the great knowledge gaps that still exist in translating findings from the basic sciences to psychosocial issues in the development of aggression. Nevertheless, interdisciplinary networks have the potential to integrate basic and clinical studies so that they can simultaneously inform each other and provide information about pathological aggression as well as normative development.

3. *Aggression research must utilize animal models.* Presumed continuity of systems and functions across species is the rationale for animal research on aggression. The use of animal models requires a comparative approach in which the goal is to study the same or a similar phenomenon across multiple species (e.g., rodents, monkeys, humans). An important focus of this approach will be to use specific species in studies for which they are best suited, yet to simultaneously use similar techniques in other species. Although animal aggression research can potentially tell us a great deal about anger, fear, cognition, emotion regulation, temperament, or other behavioral traits related to aggression, it alone is not very revealing about war, terrorism, or other complicated forms of mass violence. Notwithstanding this issue, animal models will undoubtedly make substantial contributions in the analysis of the heterogeneity of aggression to elucidating the underlying neurobiological mechanisms for individual subtypes. The division into offensive and defensive forms of animal aggression has been quite successful, and similar typologies will be needed in applying knowledge from animal models to the human condition.

4. *Aggression research must take a dimensional, phenotypic approach.* Since aggressive behavior is often seen in a group of "antisocial disorders" (e.g., antisocial personality disorder, borderline personality disorder), it may be more fruitful to concentrate on features of a phenotype (i.e., behavioral dimensions) that transcend a specific pathological category and are expressed across different psychiatric diagnoses. The phenotypes that are most relevant for aggression include inhibitory control and affect regulation and involve a wide range of traits, such as impulsivity, fear, anger, and hostility. By breaking apart and dissecting out the component parts of a particular phenotype (e.g., the sensation-seeking component of impulsivity or the

frustration-tolerance, irritability component of affect dysregulation), it may be more possible to link basic neurobiological processes to aggression. Because aggression is not a unitary entity and interacts with a broad range of other behaviors and environmental events (including emotion regulation, information processing, stress, and social activity), biological research should focus on identifying the regulatory brain circuitry for these fundamental components of behavior.

5. *Aggression research must be sensitive to ethical and societal implications of biological and genetic issues.* It is important to recognize that aggression must be viewed as a functional behavior that can only be understood in a social context in which there are multiple causes and potential biological influences. Some have commented on how aggression research has the potential to be viewed as appalling misuses of biological approaches to behavioral "problems," and these examples are sometimes used today to suggest that biology is especially prone to misuse. To prevent misuse, we must be scrupulous in applying modern ethical principles, which should be reexamined and renewed at regular intervals. It is clear that there is no such thing as an aggression or violence gene and there is no biological test that accurately identifies a simple predictor, a "marker," of aggression or violent behavior. Genes or biological events do not cause aggressive or violent behavior; rather, they potentially leave us more or less vulnerable to stressful life experiences or other environmental, social experiences that may precipitate violence. The determinants of human behavior, in particular aggression, are many and complex, and every aspect of our biology is at some level the product of the environment. It is incumbent on the research community to be sensitive to these views in the conduct of genetic and biological research on aggression.

Attention to the foregoing constructs of plasticity, bidirectionality, and gene–environment interactions and to the principles discussed may provide an unprecedented opportunity for a program of research on aggression within an integrated framework of the developmental sciences. It is hoped that the ensuing chapters and a new generation of psychobiological researchers in aggression will help to carry out the legacy of Robert B. Cairns, one of the most distinguished researchers and eloquent advocates of an integrated multilevel approach to the development of aggression.

References

Cairns, R. B. (1996). Aggression from a developmental perspective: Genes, environments and interactions. In G. R. Block & J. A. Goode (Eds), *Genetics of criminal and antisocial behavior* (pp. 45–60). Chichester, UK: John Wiley & Sons.

Lederhendler, I. H. (2003). Aggression and violence: Perspectives on integrating animal and human research approaches. *Hormones and Behavior, 44*(3), 156–160.

Stoff, D. M., Breiling, J. & Maser, J. D. (Eds.). (1997). *Handbook of antisocial behavior.* New York: John Wiley & Sons.

Stoff, D. M., & Cairns, R. B. (Eds.). (1996). *Aggression and violence.* Mahwah, NJ: Lawrence Erlbaum Associates.

Stone, R. (1992). HHS "violence intitiative" caught in a cross-fire. *Science, 258,* 212–213.

PART I

PLASTICITY

2

The Interaction of Biological and Social Measures in the Explanation of Antisocial and Violent Behavior

Adrian Raine

Department of Psychology, University of Southern California

INTRODUCTION

One of the important contributions to the understanding of antisocial and aggressive behavior has come from research that spanned the areas of animal research (Cairns, Hood, & Midlam, 1985), genetic processes (Cairns, McGuire, & Gariepy, 1993), attachment (Cairns, 1966), social interactions (Cairns & Valsiner, 1984), and developmental epistemology (Cairns, 1990). Unlike much other research, this integrative vision of science was not blinded by the interdisciplinary rivalries that have both pervaded and impeded the study of antisocial behavior. Instead, by viewing genetic, biological, psychological, and social influences as equal partners in the explanation of antisocial and aggressive behavior, more significant and lasting advances can be made in this field.

In this context, important progress has been made in delineating replicable psychosocial risk factors for antisocial and violent behavior (Farrington, 2000; Loeber & Farrington, 1998; McCord, 2001; Rutter, Giller, & Hagell, 1998). Within the past 15 years, important progress has also been made in uncovering biological risk factors that predispose to antisocial behavior (Lahey, McBurnett, Loeber, & Hart, 1995; Susman & Finkelstein, 2001). Despite this progress, we know surprisingly little about how these different sets of risk factors *interact* in predisposing to antisocial behavior. Furthermore, although passing heuristic and theoretical references are frequently made to such interactional influences, there

This research was conducted with the support of an Independent Scientist Award (K02 MH01114-01) from the National Institute of Mental Health. It is based on findings reported at the Symposium on Biobehavioral Integration of Aggression and Development, NIH Robert B. Cairns Memorial Conference, Chapel Hill, North Carolina, 14–15 October 2000, at the 10th Scientific Meeting of the International Society for Research in Child and Adolescent Psychopathology, Seattle, 26–30 June 2001, and in Raine (2002c).

are remarkably few investigators who are conducting serious empirical research on this interface in humans (Raine, Brennan, & Farrington, 1997).

The goal of this paper is to further develop the integrative perspective just outlined by reviewing the known facts on biosocial interaction effects in relation to antisocial and violent behavior in order to highlight this important yet underresearched field. The focus is placed on documenting *empirical* examples of interaction effects within the areas of genetics, psychophysiology, obstetrics, brain imaging, neuropsychology and neurology, hormones, neurotransmitters, and environmental toxins, rather than describing heuristic conceptualizations or theoretical perspectives. Only research on humans will be reviewed as perspectives from the animal literature are given in Miczek (2001), Suomi (1999), and Niehoff (1999). Although more complex transactional perspectives are potentially very important (Hinshaw & Anderson, 1996; Susman & Ponirakis, 1997), they are not the focus of this particular review because there are few empirical long-term outcome studies of serious antisocial and violent behavior.

The emphasis is placed on empirical knowledge because research in this area of antisocial behavior is sorely lacking hard empirical data on the nature of interactions, while in contrast speculation is rampant. By documenting these findings at this point in time, it is hoped that the field will be better placed in the future to develop more sophisticated and specific biosocial theories of violence that are empirically testable, as opposed to overly amorphous and all-encompassing. Nevertheless, good theory is also critical for scientific advance, and theoretical perspectives will be returned to in the conclusion section.

GENETICS

There is now clear evidence from twin studies, adoption studies, twins reared apart, and molecular genetic studies to support the notion that there are genetic influences on antisocial and aggressive behavior (Raine, 1993; Rowe, 2001; Rutter, 1997). The more challenging issue now concerns whether genetic processes interact with environmental processes in predisposing to antisocial behavior. There is prima facie evidence that such interactions exist. Twin studies find stronger evidence for heritability of antisocial behavior than do adoption studies (Raine, 1993), and because interaction effects will influence heritability estimates from twin but not adoption designs, it is possible that interaction effects exist. Indeed, it is a truism that genetic processes need an environment in which to become expressed. As such, environmental changes will turn these genetic influences on and off across the life span (Plomin & Rutter, 1998). Genetic factors likely give rise to biological risk factors for antisocial behavior such as low arousal, and if gene × environment interactions are found, this would suggest that interaction effects may well exist at the level of biological influences, a view that will be returned to later.

Gene by Environmental Interactions

One of the most striking examples of gene by environment interactions in genetic studies of crime is a cross-fostering analysis of petty criminality (Cloninger, Sigvardsson, Bohman, & von Knorring, 1982), results of which are illustrated in Figure 2.1. Male Swedish adoptees ($N = 862$) were divided into four groups depending on the presence or absence of (a) a congenital predisposition (i.e., whether biological parents were criminal) and (b) a postnatal predisposition (how the children were raised by their adoptive parents). When both heredity and environmental predispositional factors were present, 40% of the adoptees were criminal compared to 12.1% with only genetic factors present, 6.7% for those with only a bad family environment, and 2.9% when both genetic and environmental factors were absent. The fact that the 40% rate for criminality when both biological and environmental factors are present is greater than the 18.8% rate given by a combination of "congenital only" and "postnatal only" conditions indicates that genetic and environmental factors interact. Further analyses indicated that occupational status of both biological and adoptive parents were the main postnatal variables involved in this nonadditive interaction.

Cloninger and Gottesman (1987) later analyzed data for females to compare with the findings for males. As would be expected, these crime rates in female adoptees are much lower than for males, but the same interactive pattern is present: Crime rates in adoptees are greatest when both heritable and environmental influences are present, with this interaction accounting for twice as much crime as is produced by genetic and environmental influences taken alone (see Figure 2.1).

Evidence for gene × environmental interactions is also provided by Cadoret, Cain, and Crowe (1983), who presented data from three adoption studies. When both genetic and environmental factors are present, they account for a greater number of antisocial behaviors than either of these two factors acting alone. Crowe (1974) also found some evidence for a gene × environment interaction in his analysis of adopted-away offspring of female prisoners, although this trend was only marginally significant ($p < .10$). Cadoret, Yates, Troughton, Woodworth, and Stewart (1995), in an adoption study of 95 male and 102 female adoptees whose parents had either antisocial personality and / or alcohol abuse, showed that parental antisocial personality predicted increased aggression and conduct disorders in the offspring, illustrating evidence for genetic processes. But in addition, an adverse adoptive home environment was found to *interact*

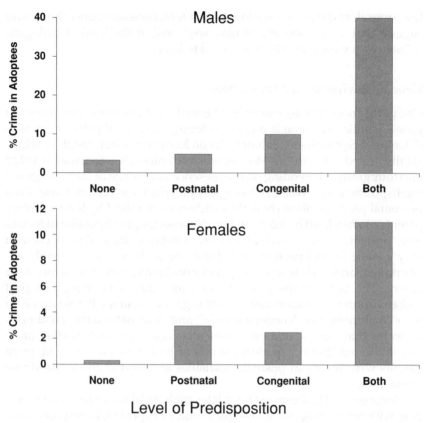

FIGURE 2.1. Increased adult crime in adoptees when both genetic and environmental risk factors are present for both males (Cloninger, Sigvardsson, Bohman, & von Knorring, 1982) and females (Cloninger & Gottesman, 1987).

with adult antisocial personality in predicting increased aggression in the offspring, i.e., a gene by environment interaction effect.

Gene by Environmental Correlation and the Moderating Effects of Demographics

A related but different concept is that of gene–environment correlation. An interesting example is provided in a study by Ge, Conger, Cadoret, and Neiderhiser (1996), who showed that the adopted-away offspring of biological parents who had antisocial personality/substance abuse were more likely to show antisocial and hostile behaviors in childhood, compared to the adopted-away offspring of non-antisocial, non–substance abusing parents. This helps establish genetic transmission of childhood antisocial behavior, but in addition an association was found between antisocial behavior in the *biological* parent and the parenting behaviors of the *adoptive* parents. This can be explained by a transmission pathway in which the biological parent contributes a genetic predisposition toward antisocial behavior in the offspring. The antisocial offspring then in turn elicits negative parenting behaviors in the adoptive parents. This study provides direct evidence of an "evocative" gene–environment correlation and suggests that the association between negative parenting in the adoptive parent and antisocial behavior in the child is mediated by genetic processes. One of the goals of future behavior genetic studies should be to examine further the interplay between genes and environment in this fashion. More generally, there are likely to be future exciting developments with respect to identifying the specific genes that give rise to the risk factors that shape criminal behavior (see later section on neurogenetics).

An interaction of a different kind was also reported by Christiansen (1977) in an analysis of Danish twin data on criminality. Although overall he found significant heritability for crime, he also found that such heritability was greater in (a) those from high socioeconomic backgrounds and (b) those who were rural born. In other words, these sociodemographic variables moderated heritability for criminal behavior. This finding is of interest because, as will be seen later, it has also been found on several occasions with respect to psychophysiological and brain imaging studies. This suggests that stronger biology–antisocial findings can be found in social contexts where social predispositions to crime are minimized.

PSYCHOPHYSIOLOGY

Psychophysiological characteristics are prime candidates for possible interaction effects with psychosocial variables because, as the name implies, they tap the dynamic interface between psychological processes and physiological processes. They also have significant heritability and are likely to provide one of the routes through which genetic influences on antisocial behavior find expression.

Moderating Effect of Benign Home Backgrounds: The Social Push Perspective

A number of studies have found that psychophysiological factors show stronger relationships to antisocial behavior in those from benign social backgrounds that lack the classic psychosocial risk factors for crime. For example, although in general resting heart rate level is lower in antisocial individuals, it is a particularly strong characteristic of antisocial individuals from higher social classes (Raine & Venables, 1984b), those from privileged middle-class backgrounds attending private schools in England (Maliphant, Hume, & Furnham, 1990), and those from intact but not broken homes (Wadsworth, 1976). One prospective study found that low resting heart rate at age 3 years related to aggression at age 11 years in those from high but not low social classes (Raine, Venables, & Mednick, 1997). Increased heart rate variability (indexing increased vagal tone and related to reduced heart rate level) was found to relate positively to aggression in young adults who had not been victims of violence, but not in those who were victims of violence; in this study moderating effects were not observed for resting heart rate (Scarpa, Romero, Fikretoglu, Bowser, & Wilson, 1999). Similarly, with respect to electrodermal classical conditioning, reduced skin conductance activity characterizes antisocial adolescents from high but not low social classes (Raine & Venables, 1981), criminals without a childhood history broken by parental absence and disharmony (Hemming, 1981), and "privileged" (high SES) offenders who commit crimes of evasion (Buikhuisen, Bontekoe, Plas-Korenhoff, & Van Buuren, 1984). In children, reduced skin conductance orienting to neutral tones at age 3 years is related to aggressive behavior at age 11, but only in those from high social class backgrounds. Similarly in adults, schizoid criminals from intact but not broken early home environments show reduced SC orienting (Raine, 1987).

One explanation for this pattern of results is the "social push" hypothesis. Under this perspective, where an antisocial child *lacks* social factors that "push" or predispose him/her to antisocial behavior, then biological factors may more likely explain antisocial behavior (Mednick, 1977; Raine & Venables, 1981). In contrast, social causes of criminal behavior may be more important explanations of antisociality in those exposed to adverse early home conditions. This is not to say that antisocial children from adverse home backgrounds will never evidence biological risk factors for antisocial and violent behavior – they clearly will. Instead, the argument is that in such situations the link between antisocial behavior and biological risk factors will be weaker (relative to antisocial children from benign social backgrounds) because the social causes of crime camouflage the biological contribution. Conversely, in the case of antisocial children from benign home backgrounds, the "noise" created by social influences on antisocial behavior are minimized, allowing the biology–antisocial behavior relationship to shine through.

The importance of this perspective is that biological researchers would be well advised to take into account psychosocial risk factors if they want to uncover stronger biology–antisocial relationships. Reversing the approach, psychosocial researchers may find stronger links between psychosocial influences and antisocial behavior in children who lack biological risk factors for antisocial behavior, although to date no one appears to have tested this proposition.

Interactions Between Psychophysiological and Social Risk Factors

These examples of biosocial interactions are unusual in that the psychophysiological variable is the dependent variable. In these cases, the question that is being asked is whether antisocial individuals with good or bad social backgrounds differ in psychophysiological functioning. When antisocial behavior becomes the dependent variable however, a different conceptual question is posed, namely, is antisocial behavior greatest in those with both social and biological risk factors? Put another way, do psychophysiological factors interact with social factors in explaining the outcome of antisocial behavior?

There have been fewer examples of studies addressing this question in the psychophysiological literature. One particularly thorough analysis is given by Farrington (1997) with respect to statistically significant interactions between resting heart rate and psychosocial variables. Boys with low resting heart rates are more likely to become violent adult offenders if they also have a poor relationship with their parent, and if they come from a large family (Farrington, 1997). Similarly, boys with low heart rates are especially likely to be rated as aggressive by their teachers if their mother was pregnant as a teenager, if they come from a low SES family, or if they were separated from a parent by age 10 (Farrington, 1997). Further research in this area needs to take into account confounds on autonomic functioning. For example, delinquents are more likely to smoke cigarettes, and nicotine consumption increases resting heart rate. As such, the strength of the true relationship between underarousal and antisocial behavior may be artificially suppressed.

Protective Factors

Until recently, nothing was known about biological factors that can protect against antisocial outcome, but there is now some evidence that heightened autonomic arousal may play such a role. Adolescent antisocial behavior is a risk factor for later criminal behavior, but some antisocial adolescents desist from further antisocial behavior. These individuals, compared to both antisocial boys who become criminal and never antisocial controls show increased electrodermal and cardiovascular arousal and orienting in an English sample (Raine, Venables, & Williams, 1995, 1996). In an independent extension of these findings, Brennan et al. (1997) found that Danish boys who had a criminal father but who did not become criminal themselves were characterized by increased electrodermal and cardiovascular orienting compared to both non-antisocial offspring of noncriminal controls, and criminal offspring with criminal fathers. This latter study is particularly interesting because it illustrates how the social risk factor of having a criminal father moderates the protective role of heightened autonomic functioning in relation to crime outcome.

Interpretation of Reduced Autonomic Activity in Antisocial Children

Why should low autonomic activity predispose to antisocial and criminal behavior? There are at least two main theoretical interpretations. Fearlessness theory indicates that low levels of arousal are markers for low levels of fear (Raine, 1993). A fearlessness interpretation of low arousal levels assumes that subjects are not actually at "rest," but that instead the rest period of psychophysiological testing represents a mildly stressful paradigm. Low arousal during this period is taken to indicate lack of anxiety and fear. Lack of fear would predispose to antisocial and violent behavior because such behavior (e.g., fights and assaults) requires a degree of fearlessness to execute; also, lack of fear, especially in childhood, would help explain poor socialization because low fear of punishment would reduce the effectiveness of conditioning. Fearlessness theory receives support from the fact that autonomic underarousal also provides the underpinning for a fearless or uninhibited temperament in infancy and childhood (Kagan, 1994; Scarpa, Raine, Venables, & Mednick, 1997).

A second theory explaining reduced arousal is stimulation-seeking theory (Eysenck, 1977; Quay, 1965; Raine, 1993; Raine, Reynolds, Venables, Mednick, & Farrington, 1998). This theory argues that low arousal represents an unpleasant physiological state, and that antisocial individuals seek stimulation in order to increase their arousal levels back to an optimal or normal level. In line with this perspective, Gatzke-Kopp, Raine, Loeber, Stouthamer-Loeber, and Steinhauer (2002) found both stimulation-seeking and antisocial behavior to be characterized by low autonomic arousal. Antisocial behavior is thus viewed as a form of stimulation-seeking in that committing a burglary, assault, or robbery could be stimulating for some individuals. Stimulation-seeking and fearlessness theories may be complementary perspectives in that a low level of arousal may predispose to crime because it produces some degree of fearlessness, and also because it encourages antisocial stimulation-seeking. Indeed, behavioral measures of stimulation-seeking and fearlessness, both taken at age 3 years in a large sample, predict to aggressive behavior at age 11 years (Raine et al., 1998). The combined effect of these two influences may be more important in explaining antisocial behavior than either influence taken alone.

In contrast to arousal deficits, explanations of reduced orienting activity have centered on attentional and prefrontal dysfunction theories. Raine and Venables (1984a) proposed an attention deficit hypothesis in which it was argued that antisocial individuals were characterized by a fundamental deficit in the ability to allocate attentional resources to environmental events. In discussing this perspective, Fowles (1993) alternatively suggested that there may be two attentional deficits in anti-social individuals, one deficit with respect to attending to neutral stimuli, and one deficit with respect to the anticipation of aversive events.

Reduced skin conductance orienting has also been interpreted with respect to a prefrontal dysfunction hypothesis of antisocial behavior (Raine, 1997). Briefly, this perspective argues that damage to the prefrontal region of the brain leads to psychophysiological abnormalities (reduced orienting and arousal) that predispose to traits and characteristics (e.g., stimulation-seeking, disinhibition, attention deficits) that in turn predispose to anti-social behavior. Support for this model stems from research showing that the prefrontal cortex is involved in the generation of skin conductance orienting responses (Damasio, Tranel, & Damasio, 1990; Williams et al., 2000) and is also involved in arousal regulation and stress responsivity (see Raine, 1997, for further details). Reduced autonomic arousal is in turn associated with increased stimulation-seeking (Gatzke-Kopp, Raine, Loeber, Stouthamer-Loeber, & Steinhauer, 2002), fearlessness (Raine, 1993), and disinhibition (Scarpa, Raine, Venables, & Mednick, 1997), traits that in turn have been associated with antisocial behavior (Raine, Reynolds, Venables, Mednick, & Farrington, 1998).

OBSTETRIC FACTORS

Of all the subfields of biological research on antisocial behavior, obstetric influences show the most compelling evidence for biosocial interactions, with at least 11 studies from five different countries finding evidence for statistical interactions. These obstetric studies fall into three domains: minor physical anomalies, prenatal nicotine exposure, and birth complications.

Pregnancy Complications

(a) Minor Physical Anomalies (MPAs). At least six studies have found an association between increased MPAs and increased antisocial behavior in children (Raine, 1993). Minor physical anomalies have been associated with disorders of pregnancy and are thought to be a marker for fetal neural maldevelopment toward the end of the first 3 months of pregnancy. As such, they may be viewed as an indirect marker of abnormal brain development. MPAs are relatively minor physical abnormalities consisting of such features as low-seated ears, adherent ear lobes, and a furrowed tongue. Although MPAs may have a genetic basis, they may also be caused by environmental factors acting on the fetus such as anoxia, bleeding, and infection (Guy, Majorski, Wallace, & Guy, 1983).

At least three studies have found that MPAs interact with social factors in predicting antisocial and violent behavior. Mednick and Kandel (1988) assessed MPAs in a sample of 129 12-year-old boys seen by an experienced

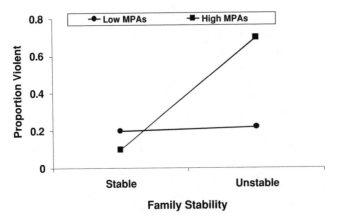

FIGURE 2.2. Interaction between family instability and high minor physical anomalies in the prediction of adult violence (Mednick & Kandel, 1988).

pediatrician. MPAs were found to be related to violent offending as assessed 9 years later when subjects were aged 21 years, although not to property offenses. However, as illustrated in Figure 2.2, when subjects were divided into those from unstable, nonintact homes and those from stable homes, a biosocial interaction was observed. MPAs only predicted violence in those individuals raised in unstable home environments. Similarly, Brennan, Mednick, & Raine (1997) found that those with both MPAs and family adversity had especially high rates of adult violent offending within a sample of 72 male offspring of psychiatrically ill parents. This interaction was again confirmed by Pine, Shaffer, Schonfeld, and Davies (1997), who found that MPAs in 7-year-olds combined with environmental risk in predisposing to conduct disorder at age 17. These findings are similar to those on birth complications reported earlier; in both cases the presence of a negative psychosocial factor is required to "trigger" the biological risk factor, and in both cases the effects are specific to violent offending. In a study confirming specificity of MPAs to violence, Arseneault, Tremblay, Boulerice, Seguin, and Saucier (2000) found that MPAs assessed at age 14 predicted to violent delinquency at age 17 in 170 males, but not to nonviolent delinquency. In this study, effects were independent of family adversity.

(b) Nicotine Exposure. The effect of fetal exposure to alcohol in increasing risk for conduct disorders is well known (e.g., Fast, Conry, & Loock, 1999; Olson et al., 1997; Streissguth, Barr, Bookstein, Sampson, & Olson, 1999), but recently a spate of studies has established beyond reasonable doubt a significant link between smoking during pregnancy and later conduct disorder and violent offending (see Raine, 2002a, for a review). Three of these studies have also observed interactions between nicotine exposure

and psychosocial variables in the prediction of later violent offending, and are impressive in terms of their size, the prospective nature of data collection, long-term outcome, and control for third factors such as antisocial behavior in the parents, other drug use, and low social class. Brennan, Grekin, and Mednick (1999) using a birth cohort of 4,169 males found a twofold increase in adult violent offending in the offspring of mothers who smoked 20 cigarettes a day, and also found a dose–response relationship between increased number of cigarettes smoked and increased violence. However, a *fivefold* increase in adult violence was found when nicotine exposure was combined with exposure to delivery complications – there was no increase in violence in those who were nicotine-exposed but lacking delivery complications. Brennan, Grekin, and Mednick (1999) observed that effects were specific to persistent offending and did not apply to adolescent-limited offending. Similarly, Rasanen et al. (1999) found a twofold increase of violent criminal offending at age 26 in the offspring of women who smoked during pregnancy. In addition, nicotine exposure lead to an 11.9-fold increase in recidivistic violence when combined with single-parent family, and a 14.2-fold increase when combined with teenage pregnancy, single-parent family, unwanted pregnancy, and developmental motor lags. Again, odds ratios were stronger for recidivistic violence than for nonrecidivistic violence and property offending. Gibson and Tibbetts (2000) also found that maternal smoking interacted with parental absence in predicting early onset of offending in a U.S. sample.

Maternal smoking during pregnancy may be an important contributory factor to the brain deficits that have been found in adult offenders. Animal research has clearly demonstrated the neurotoxic effects of two constituents of cigarette smoke – carbon monoxide (CO) and nicotine (see Olds, 1997, for a detailed review). Prenatal nicotine exposure even at relatively low levels disrupts the development of the noradrenergic neurotransmitter system and disrupts cognitive functions (Levin, Wilkerson, Jones, Christopher, & Briggs 1996). Reduction of noradrenergic functioning caused by smoking would be expected to disrupt sympathetic nervous system activity, consistent with evidence outlined earlier for reduced sympathetic arousal in antisocial individuals (Raine, 1996). Pregnant rats exposed to nicotine have offspring with an enhancement of cardiac M2-muscarinic cholinergic receptors that *inhibit* autonomic functions (Slotkin, Epps, Stenger, Sawyer, & Seidler, 1999). This would help to explain the well-replicated finding of *low* resting heart rate in antisocial individuals outlined earlier (Raine, 1993).

Birth Complications

Several studies have shown that babies who suffer birth complications are more likely to develop conduct disorder and delinquency and to commit impulsive crime and violence in adulthood when other psychosocial risk

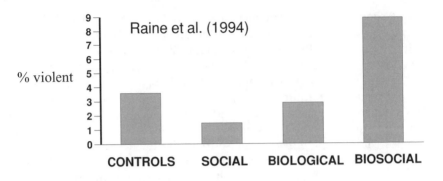

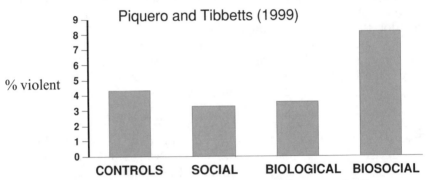

FIGURE 2.3. Interaction between birth complications and negative family outcome in the prediction of adult violence in both Danish (Raine et al., 1994) and U.S. (Piquero & Tibbetts, 1999) samples.

factors are present. Specifically, obstetric factors *interact* with psychosocial risk factors in relation to adult violence. Werner (1987) found that birth complications interacted with a disruptive family environment (maternal separation, illegitimate child, marital discord, parental mental health problems, paternal absence) in predisposing to delinquency. Similarly, Raine, Brennan, and Mednick (1994) prospectively assessed birth complications and maternal rejection at age 1 year in 4,269 live male births in Copenhagen, Denmark. Birth complications significantly interacted with maternal rejection of the child in predicting to violent offending at age 18 years (see Figure 2.3, upper half). Only 4% of the sample had both birth complications and maternal rejection, but this small group accounted for 18% of all the violent crimes committed by the entire sample.

In this latter study, the 4,269 babies were followed up to age 34 when outcome for violent crime was reassessed (Raine, Brennan, & Mednick, 1997). It was found that the biosocial interaction previously observed holds for violent but not nonviolent criminal offending. Furthermore, the interaction was found to be specific to more serious forms of violence and not threats of violence. The interaction held for early-onset but not late-onset violence and was not accounted for by psychiatric illness in the mothers. Rearing in a public care institution in the first year of life and attempt to abort the fetus were the key aspects of maternal rejection found to interact with birth complications in predisposing to violence.

This finding from Denmark has recently been replicated in four other countries (Sweden, Finland, Canada, United States) in the context of a variety of psychosocial risk factors. Piquero and Tibbetts (1999) in a prospective longitudinal study of 867 males and females from the Philadelphia Collaborative Perinatal Project found that those with both pre/perinatal disturbances and a disadvantaged familial environment were much more likely to become adult violent offenders (see Figure 2.3, lower half). Similarly, pregnancy complications interacted with poor parenting in predicting adult violence in a large Swedish sample of 7,101 men (Hodgins, Kratzer, & Mcneil, 2001). In a Canadian sample of 849 boys, Arsenault, Tremblay, Boulerice, and Saucier (2002) found an interaction between increased serious obstetric complications and family adversity in raising the likelihood of violent offending at age 17 years. In a Finnish sample perinatal risk interacted with being an only child in raising the odds of adult violent offending by a factor of 4.4 in a sample of 5,587 males (Kemppainen, Jokelainen, Jaervelin, Isohanni, & Raesaenen, 2001). On the other hand, being an only child is not obviously linked to psychosocial adversity, and the meaning of this interaction requires further elucidation.

A fifth study reported by Brennan, Mednick, and Mednick (1993) and also from Denmark showed that birth complications interacted with parental mental illness in predicting violent crime in the male offspring (see Figure 2.4). On the other hand, no interaction between perinatal insult and family adversity was found for a smaller sample of German children ($N = 322$) where outcome was restricted to follow-up at age 8 years (Laucht et al., 2000). This last failure may be due to the fact that neurological deficits stemming from birth complications may particularly influence the more severe outcome of life-course persistent antisocial behavior rather than the more common outcome of child antisocial behavior (Moffitt, 1993; Moffitt & Caspi, 2001). Indeed, several of the foregoing studies find that interaction effects involving birth complications and family factors show evidence of linkage to what may be broadly termed life-course persistent violent behavior rather than adolescent-limited antisocial behavior. In addition to these interactions with psychosocial variables, low Apgar scores at birth have been found to interact with maternal smoking in the prediction of adult violent offending (Gibson & Tibbetts, 1998).

Birth complications such as anoxia (lack of oxygen), forceps delivery, and preeclampsia (hypertension leading to anoxia) are thought to contribute

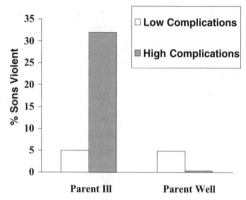

FIGURE 2.4. Interaction between birth complications and parental mental illness in the prediction of violent crime in the offspring (Brennan et al., 1993).

to brain damage, and they may be just one of a number of early sources of brain dysfunction observed in child and adult antisocial groups. On the other hand, as indicated earlier, birth complications may not by themselves predispose to crime, but instead may require the presence of negative environmental circumstance to trigger later adult crime and violence. Furthermore, although they are likely to contribute to prefrontal damage, their effects would not be specific to this brain area but would have an impact on multiple brain sites, including the hippocampus. Interestingly, recent brain imaging studies have shown that the hippocampus shows abnormal functioning in murderers (Raine, Buchsbaum, & LaCasse, 1997) and shows structural abnormalities in psychopaths (Laakso et al., 2001); this brain structure is particularly susceptible to anoxia. In this context, birth complications that are relatively serious and that induce anoxia may be more likely to result in early brain impairments and predispose to later violence in the presence of psychosocal risks than more minor birth complications.

BRAIN IMAGING

Only two brain imaging studies of antisocial, violent behavior appear to have tested for interaction effects with social influences. Nevertheless they are described here because brain imaging is a growing and increasingly influential subarea within biological research on antisocial behavior and because their findings complement those from other areas.

Positron Emission Tomography (PET)

Previous research has indicated that violent offenders have reduced functioning of the prefrontal cortex (Raine, 1993; Volkow et al., 1995). One

PET (positron emission tomography) study addressed the issue of how psychosocial deficits moderate the relationship between prefrontal dysfunction and violence (Raine, Stoddard, Bihrle, & Buchsbaum, 1998). A sample of murderers were divided into those who came from relatively good home backgrounds and those who came from relatively bad homes. Ratings of psychosocial deprivation took into account early physical and sexual abuse, neglect, extreme poverty, foster home placement, having a criminal parent, severe family conflict, and a broken home. Compared to normal controls, deprived murderers showed relatively good prefrontal functioning, whereas nondeprived murderers showed significantly reduced prefrontal functioning. In particular, murderers from good homes had a 14.2% reduction in the functioning of the right orbitofrontal cortex; damage to this brain area results in reduced fear conditioning as well as personality and emotional deficits that parallel criminal psychopathic behavior, or what Damasio and colleagues have termed "acquired sociopathy" (Damasio, 1994). These results extend findings from several psychophysiological studies showing especially reduced autonomic functions in those from benign home backgrounds, and again suggest that biology–violence relationships are potentiated in those lacking psychosocial risk factors for violence.

Functional Magnetic Resonance Imaging (fMRI)

A second brain imaging study found an interaction of a different type in seeking an answer to a different type of question. Although the relationship between physical child abuse and violence is well established (Lewis, Pincus, Bard, & Richardson, 1988; Tarter, Hegedus, Winsten, & Alterman, 1984; Widom, 1997), there appears to be little or no research, biological or social, on factors that differentiate abused victims who go on to perpetrate violence from those who refrain from adult violence. The study in question (Raine et al., 2001) asked two main questions: (a) What are the brain correlates of adults in the community who have suffered severe physical abuse early in life and who go on to perpetrate serious violence in adulthood? (b) What characterizes those who experience severe physical abuse but who refrain from serous violence? Four groups of participants were recruited from the community: (i) nonviolent controls who had not suffered abuse, (ii) severe physical child abuse only (i.e., had suffered severe physical or sexual abuse in the first 11 years, but were not violent), (iii) serious violence only (violence that either caused bodily injury or trauma, or were life-threatening acts), and (iv) severely abused, seriously violent offenders. All underwent functional magnetic resonance imaging (fMRI) while performing a visual/verbal working memory task. Results showed that violent offenders who had suffered severe child abuse show reduced right hemisphere functioning, particularly in the right temporal cortex. Abused individuals who had refrained from serious violence showed relatively lower left, but higher right, activation of the temporal lobe. Abused individuals, irrespective of violence status, showed reduced cortical activation during the working memory task, especially in the left hemisphere. These findings indicate that a biological risk factor (initial right hemisphere dysfunction), when combined with a psychosocial risk factor (severe early physical abuse) predisposes to serious violence. They also suggest that relatively good right hemisphere functioning *protects* against violence in physically abused children. Future brain imaging studies can best build on this beginning research by attempting to identify which specific neural networks, involving multiple brain regions acting in concert, interact with social factors in predisposing to violent and antisocial behavior.

NEUROPSYCHOLOGY AND NEUROLOGY

Neuropsychological and neurological deficits, especially those associated with executive function deficits, are a reasonably well-established risk factor for antisocial behavior in children, adolescents, and adults (Moffitt, 1990a; Morgan & Lilienfeld, 2000; Raine, 1993). Although most neuropsychological and neurological research has not explored the interaction between neuropsychological dysfunction and psychosocial factors in predisposing to violence, a few studies are beginning to suggest that this may be a promising avenue for future research.

Prospective, Longitudinal Findings

Lewis et al. (1989) in a follow-up study of 15-year-old juvenile delinquents found that whereas only having neurocognitive deficits was associated with an average of 2.1 adult violent offenses, and whereas only experiencing child abuse was associated with an average of 1.9 adult offenses, the combination of three neurocognitive indicators combined with child abuse was associated with an average of 5.4 violent offenses in adulthood. Consequently, the combination of neurocognitive and psychosocial risk factors was associated with particularly high rates of violence in adulthood.

Other prospective longitudinal research is broadly consistent with this finding. Moffitt (1990b) reports that boys with both low neuropsychological performance and family adversity had aggression scores four times higher than those of boys with either adversity only or neuropsychological deficits only. Similarly, Raine, Brennan, Mednick, and Mednick (1996) found that those with both early neuromotor deficits (including birth complications) and unstable family environments later went on to have higher rates of teenage behavior problems and adult criminal and violent offending compared to those with only social or only biological risk factors. The biosocial group with both sets of risk factors accounted for 70.2% of all violence committed by the entire cohort.

One nonprospective study of 64 violent juvenile offenders took a different approach by dividing subjects into members of gangs versus non-gang members (Sparling & Cohen, 1997). Non-gang members compared to gang members were much more likely to have neurobehavioral deficits such as history of head injury (57.1% vs. 11.1%) and intermittent explosive disorder (71.4% vs. 11.4%). These pilot findings are intriguing because they suggest that the social variable of belonging to a gang (and the consequent social–affiliative nature of these networks) moderates neurobehavioral–violent relationships. Conceivably, violent offenders with neurobehavioral deficits are less able to sufficiently modulate their aggressive tendencies for good functioning in gangs that value controlled, proactive aggression.

Protective Influence of Stable Home Environment

Although it is reasonable to hypothesize that the negative effects of biological risk factors in predisposing to antisocial behavior may be ameliorated by the benefits of a positive home environment, there appear to be few tests of this hypothesis. Streissguth, Barr, Kogan, and Bookstein (1996), in a study of 473 individuals with fetal alcohol syndrome, found that a stable home environment protected the child from an antisocial outcome. An intriguing case study from Spain of a man who had an iron spike pass through his head, selectively destroying the prefrontal cortex, showed that unlike the case of Phineas Gage, this individual did not have an outcome over the next 60 years of antisocial or criminal behavior (Mataro et al., 2001). Mataro et al. (2001) concluded that prefrontal damage can be followed by stable psychosocial functioning, but a different interpretation can also be made. It is intriguing to note that the subject in question had wealthy parents who owned a family business in which he would be employed for the rest of his life, and that his fiancé (a childhood sweetheart) stood by him after the accident and married him, producing two good children and a family which, in the words of one of the children "protected" him throughout his life. It can be argued that this individual did not develop antisocial behavior and psychosocial dysfunction because his family environment buffered him from these negative outcomes. Without such psychosocial support, a very different outcome may have resulted.

Social Demands of Adolescence Overloading Executive Functions

One interactional neuropsychological model of antisocial behavior concerns the notion that the social and executive function demands of late adolescence overload the late-developing prefrontal cortex, giving rise to prefrontal dysfunction and a lack of inhibitory control over antisocial, violent behavior that peaks at this age (Raine, 2002a). Prior to adolescence, children live in relatively structured environments where complex, life-changing planning and decision-making is not the norm. In contrast, late adolescence is a stage in life where enormous social demands are being placed on the rapidly growing teenager, a load that calls on resources of the frontal cortex and its associated executive functions. Such adolescents need to regulate, control, and inhibit a growing sex drive, juggle the threats and challenges to their social status that arise within their peer groups, deal with the complexities of relations with the opposite sex, increasingly sustain attention at school to maximize chances of academic success, and plan and organize for a future career.

The prefrontal cortex bears the burden of this magnified cognitive load that requires multiple executive functions – sustained attention, behavioral flexibility to changing contingencies, working memory, self-regulation and inhibition, abstract decision-making, planning and organization. Yet this processing load occurs at a time when the prefrontal cortex is still maturing, with myelination of the frontal cortex continuing into the 20s and beyond. A minority of individuals with early damage to or dysfunction of the prefrontal cortex would be particularly likely to suffer an information overload during this time period, resulting in further dysfunction of the prefrontal cortex, less regulatory control, and further lifelong antisocial behavior. Others with a late-maturing but intact prefrontal cortex may be antisocial during childhood and adolescence, but with further maturation of the frontal lobes in early adulthood may eventually discontinue their antisocial behavior. Still others may have frontal dysfunction, but may be protected from antisocial behavior by having more social support or fewer social-transitional demands placed on them, as was argued earlier in the Spanish head trauma case. Yet another group of late-onset offenders (Hamalainen & Pulkkinen, 1996; Ishikawa, Raine, Lencz, Bihrle, & LaCasse, 2001) may have neither significant executive function deficits nor antisocial behavior until early adulthood, when life stressors at this time overload a prefrontal cortex with latent functional impairments.

This theoretical perspective would lead to a number of predictions. In addition to expecting that those with prefrontal dysfunction and poor executive functions would be predisposed to antisocial behavior, this outcome would be most likely in those with a less structured, less stable psychosocial environment. Second, those with significant executive functions who resist becoming antisocial would be expected to have a particularly well-structured, protective social environment or alternatively high intelligence that minimizes the impact of executive function deficits. Third, those with initial early antisocial behavior who desist in life would be expected to show initially poor executive functions but later better executive functioning.

HORMONES, NEUROTRANSMITTERS, AND TOXINS

Hormones

Research on links between hormones and antisocial, aggressive behavior illustrates the complexities of biology–behavior relationships and clearly demonstrates the influence of the social context on biological functioning. Detailed reviews of the bidirectional relationship between hormones and behavior and of the influence of social context on hormones may be found in Dabbs (1992), Mazur and Booth (1999), Susman (1993), Susman and Ponirakis (1997), and Tremblay et al. (1997).

Although links between high testosterone and self-report measures of aggression are relatively weak (Archer, 1991), there is now convincing evidence from a wide number of *behavioral* studies for a link between high testosterone and increased aggressive and violent behavior (see reviews by Archer, 1991; Dabbs, 1992; Harris, 1999; Mazur and Booth, 1999; and Raine, 2002c). Particularly persuasive are experimental randomized, placebo-controlled, crossover trials in normal men that show that testosterone administration increases aggression (Pope, Kouri, & Hudson 2000). Nevertheless, it also appears that although aggression–testosterone links are well established with respect to adult aggressive and violent behavior, this relationship may be absent, or even reversed, with respect to aggression during childhood (Tremblay et al., 1997).

An understanding of why the aggression–testosterone link washes out in childhood may be gained from consideration of social influences on testosterone. It is well established that high testosterone is associated with both high dominance and high socioeconomic status, and while experience of success increases testosterone, failure reduces it (Dabbs, 1992; Mazur and Booth, 1999). Aggressive children are more likely to be rejected by their peers in school (Dodge, Lochman, Harnish, & Bates, 1997), and it may be this social ostracization and failure in academia that artificially reduces their otherwise high testosterone levels. This interpretation is supported by two pieces of evidence. First, Tremblay et al. (1997) report that 13-year-old boys who are both physically tough *and* well liked have high testosterone levels. Second, while Tremblay et al. (1997) found that aggressive boys have low testosterone at ages 13 and 14, follow-up at age 16 after 30% had dropped out of school show them to have substantially higher testosterone than nonaggressive boys. It may be that aggression–testosterone links are found in violent offenders during adulthood because they are better able to use their aggression to raise their dominance status within their antisocial subcultures and achieve some degree of social success.

Despite the clear evidence that contextual and environmental influences alter both testosterone and cortisol, few researchers have tested for biosocial interactions in the way that interactions have been tested for

psychophysiological and obstetric factors. That is, do social variables moderate the relationship between hormones and antisocial behavior? Dabbs
and Morris (1990) found that in low-SES subjects, those with high testosterone had higher levels of childhood and adulthood delinquency, whereas
these effects were not found for high-SES subjects. On the other hand, risk
ratios for some measures of antisocial behavior (military AWOL, marijuana
use, many sex partners) were equally high in both SES groups, and consequently these initial findings should be viewed with caution. Nevertheless,
Scarpa, Romero, Fikretoglu, Bowser, and Wilson (1999) found that children
who gave large cortisol responses to a provocation task and who also had
been physically abused had the highest aggression scores. Both of these
hormonal studies are therefore similar in that biology–antisocial relationships were more marked in those from negative environments (low SES,
abuse) and lie in contrast to studies measuring psychophysiological and
brain imaging risk factors (low heart rate, low skin conductance, increased
vagal tone, low prefrontal activity) that find antisocial–psychophysiology
relationships strongest in those from *benign* home backgrounds. It
remains to be seen whether further hormone studies find stronger
hormone–antisocial links in those from negative rather than positive home
backgrounds.

Neurotransmitters and Toxins

Neurotransmitter and toxin research is also beginning to provide evidence
of interactions with social and environmental processes. Moffitt et al.,
(1997) found that whereas violent offenders had higher blood serotonin
levels than controls, those with both high blood serotonin and a conflicted
family background were over three times more likely to become violent by
age 21 compared to men with only high serotonin or only conflicted family
background. Similarly, Masters, Hone, and Doshi (1998) in an analysis of
violent crime rates in 1,242 counties in the United States, found a three-
way interaction among environmental lead or manganese exposure, high
population density, and alcoholism rates, with highest rates of violence in
counties with high densities, exposure to toxins, and alcoholism. As with
research on hormones, there is a dearth of empirical data to support or
refute a biosocial interaction hypothesis of antisocial and violent behavior
with respect to toxins and further tests of this proposition are required.

CONCLUSIONS AND RECOMMENDATIONS

Summarizing the key findings of this review, there has in recent years been
growing evidence for replicable interactions between biological and social
factors in relation to antisocial and violent behavior. In the last review of
this area, Brennan and Raine (1997), found only nine studies to illustrate

biosocial interactions. In the current review, 39 studies can been outlined that illustrate interaction between biological and social factors in relation to antisocial and violent behavior. Clearly, there is recent, growing evidence that social and biological processes do interact in predisposing to antisocial behavior. To date, the best-replicated biosocial effect appears to consist of birth complications interacting with negative home environments in predisposing to adult violence, and there is also evidence that this effect particularly characterizes life-course persistent antisocial behavior.

Although these findings give reason to take biosocial perspectives on antisocial behavior seriously, study counts and documentation of findings by themselves will not advance knowledge within a field. The establishment of interaction effects is not an end process, but merely the end of a beginning in understanding antisocial behavior. Interaction effects need to be explained with respect to their underlying mechanisms. For example, birth complications consistently interact with negative home environments in predisposing to adult violence, and this effect seems specific to violence, and to violence with an early onset – but why? What are the processes operating in negative home environments that trigger the deleterious effects of birth complications? Do birth complications predispose to violence by mild impairment to brain functioning, or does family adversity instead predispose to both birth complications such as pregnancy-induced hypertension and also childhood conduct disorder? That is, are birth complications merely a marker of a third factor and by themselves unrelated to violence? Although these questions are difficult to answer, the next generation of biosocial research needs to go beyond simple interaction effects and research the fundamental mechanisms and processes underlying the interactions.

Theoretical perspectives are needed to help guide future research on biosocial interaction effects. Moffitt (1993) has argued that life-course persistent offending is a product of early interactions between neuropsychological and family factors and as such would predict early biosocial interaction effects in relation to life-course persistent offending, a prediction that seems to be generally supported by the data. In addition, the social push perspective argues that the link between antisocial behavior and biological risk factors will be weaker in adverse homes because the social predispositions to crime camouflage the biological contribution. In contrast, in benign home environments the role of biological predispositions can be more easily detected. The prefrontal dysfunction–executive overload theory outlined earlier is more specific in identifying conditions under which antisocial behavior will result as a function of the interplay between an immature prefrontal cortex and psychosocial demands. Ultimately, biosocial perspectives of antisocial behavior will be maximally helpful when a complementary and balanced theoretical–empirical approach is developed.

In analyzing the pattern of interaction effects observed earlier, there are two main conclusions that can be drawn and that can guide future hypothesis testing. When the biological and social factors are the grouping variable and antisocial behavior is the outcome, then the presence of both risk factors appears to increase rates of antisocial and violent behavior. When social and antisocial variables are the grouping variables and biological functioning is the outcome, then the social variable invariably (but not always) moderates the antisocial–biology relationship such that these relationships are strongest in those from benign home backgrounds. A question for future biosocial studies is whether these two patterns of findings, which ask different questions, can be substantiated, or whether different patterns emerge. In addition, studies conducted to date are relatively simplistic, and the question of whether these biosocial interactions are carried by conditions comorbid with antisocial behavior such as hyperactivity need to resolved (Hinshaw, Lahey, & Hart, 1993).

There are also statistical as well as theoretical difficulties facing future research into the biosocial bases of antisocial behavior. Statistically speaking, interactions and moderator effects are notoriously difficult to obtain because of problems of measurement error (McClelland & Judd, 1993), with power in the type of studies reviewed above being less than 20% of experimental studies. As such, type II error is frequently more of a problem than type I error in biosocial studies. Even where no statistically significant effect is observed, it would be advisable for researchers to report the means and standard deviations for groups on the biological variable broken down by the social variable (e.g., high vs. low social class) and compute effect sizes so that future meta-analyses can be conducted with the ensuing benefit of increased power.

A practical barrier to future biosocial research is the simple fact that few psychosocial researchers take into account biological variables, and few biological researchers take into account social variables. Even when they do, psychosocial variables are often conceptualized as covariates or nuisance variables by biological researchers rather than as moderators. Researchers need to face the fact that there will likely be diminishing returns from further research on currently known risk factors and that more will be gained from examining interactions between risk factors. Indeed, researchers who do not test for interaction effects that may well exist, and who obtain nonsignificant main effects, will erroneously conclude that the variables in question are of no etiological significance. Although the measurement of biological variables poses significant challenges for psychosocial researchers, low resting heart rate is the best-replicate biological correlate of antisocial behavior in child and adolescent samples (Raine, 1993), takes only 1 minute to assess, and can be measured cheaply and easily using a stethoscope or digital heart rate meter, or by taking a pulse manually.

Incorporating even this simple biological measure into psychosocial longitudinal research would be a step in the right direction.

Finally, biosocial studies of antisocial behavior should not be restricted to risk and protective factors but also need to consider prevention implications at two levels. First, environmental manipulations can be used to alter biological risk factors. For example, an environmental enrichment at ages 3–5 years using a randomized, stratified design resulted in significant increases in psychophysiological arousal and attention 8 years later at age 11 years (Raine et al., 2001). Second, psychosocial influences may moderate the effects of a prevention program on antisocial behavior. As one example, Olds et al. (1998) demonstrated that a prenatal and early postnatal health prevention program was more successful in reducing delinquency at age 15 years in unmarried, low-SES mothers than in less disadvantaged mothers. Biosocial research on risk and protective factors themselves should clearly be a priority for establishing a new generation of more biosocially informed prevention and intervention programs.

Reference List

Archer, J. (1991). The influence of testosterone on human aggression. *British Journal of Clinical Psychology, 82*, 1–28.

Arsenault, L., Tremblay, R. E., Boulerice, B., & Saucier, J. F. (2002). Obstetrical complications and violent delinquency: Testing two developmental pathways. *Child Development 73*, 496–508.

Arseneault, L., Tremblay, R. E., Boulerice, B., Seguin, J. R., & Saucier, J. F. (2000). Minor physical anomalies and family adversity as risk factors for violent delinquency in adolescence. *American Journal of Psychiatry, 157*, 917–923.

Brennan, P. A., Grekin, E. R., & Mednick, S. A. (1999). Maternal smoking during pregnancy and adult male criminal outcomes. *Archives of General Psychiatry, 56*, 215–219.

Brennan, P. A., Mednick, B. R., & Mednick, S. A. (1993). Parental psychopathology, congenital factors, and violence. In S. Hodgins (Ed.), *Mental disorder and crime* (pp. 244–261). Thousand Oaks, CA: Sage.

Brennan, P. A., Mednick, S. A., & Raine, A. (1997). Biosocial interactions and violence: A focus on perinatal factors. In A. Raine, P. A. Brennan, D. Farrington, & S. A. Mednick (Eds.), *Biosocial bases of violence* (pp. 163–174). New York: Plenum.

Brennan, P. A., & Raine, A. (1997). Biosocial bases of antisocial behavior: Psychophysiological, neurological, and cognitive factors. *Clinical Psychology Review, 17*, 589–604.

Brennan, P. A., Raine, A., Schulsinger, F., Kirkegaard-Sorensen, L., Knop, J., Hutchings, B., et al. (1997). Psychophysiological protective factors for male subjects at high risk for criminal behavior. *American Journal of Psychiatry, 154*, 853–855.

Buikhuisen, W., Bontekoe, E. H., Plas-Korenhoff, C., & Van Buuren, S. (1984). Characteristics of criminals: The privileged offender. *International Journal of Law and Psychiatry, 7*, 301–313.

Cadoret, R. J., Cain, C. A., & Crowe, R. R. (1983). Evidence for gene-environment interaction in the development of adolescent antisocial behavior. *Behavior Genetics, 13*, 301–310.

Cadoret, R. J., Yates, W. R., Troughton, E., Woodworth, G., & Stewart, M. A. (1995). Genetic–environmental interaction in the genesis of aggressivity and conduct disorders. *Archives of General Psychiatry, 52*, 916–924.

Cairns, R. B. (1966). Attachment behavior of mammals. *Psychological Review, 73*, 409–426.

Cairns, R. B. (1990). Developmental epistemology and self-knowledge: Towards a reinterpretation of self-esteem. In G. Greenberg & E. Tobach (Eds.), *Theories of the evolution of knowing* (pp. 69–86). Hillsdale, NJ: Lawrence Erlbaum.

Cairns, R. B., Hood, K. E., & Midlam, J. (1985). On fighting in mice: Is there a sensitive period for isolation effects? *Animal Behaviour, 33*, 166–180.

Cairns, R. B., McGuire, A. M., & Gariepy, J. L. (1993). Developmental behavior genetics: Fusion, correlated constraints, and timing. In D. F. Hay & A. Angold (Eds.), *Precursors and causes in development and psychopathology* (pp. 87–122). New York: Wiley.

Cairns, R. B., & Valsiner, J. (1984). Child psychology. *Annual Review of Psychology, 35*, 553–577.

Christiansen, K. O. (1977). A preliminary study of criminality among twins. In S. A. Mednick and K. O. Christiansen (Ed.), *Biosocial bases of criminal behavior* (pp. 89–108). New York: Gardner Press.

Cloninger, C. R., & Gottesman, I. I. (1987). Genetic and environmental factors in antisocial behavior disorders. In *The causes of crime: New biological approaches.* Cambridge, UK: Cambridge University Press.

Cloninger, C. R., Sigvardsson, S., Bohman, M., & von Knorring, A. L. (1982). Predisposition to petty criminality in Swedish adoptees: II. Cross-fostering analysis of gene-environmental interactions. *Archives of General Psychiatry, 39*, 1242–1247.

Crowe, R. R. (1974). An adoption study of antisocial personality. *Archives of General Psychiatry, 31*, 785–791.

Dabbs, J. M. (1992). Testosterone measurements in social and clinical psychology. *Journal of Social and Clinical Psychology, 11*, 302–321.

Dabbs, J. M., & Morris, R. (1990). Testosterone, social class, and antisocial behavior in a sample of 4,462 men. *Psychological Science, 1*, 209–211.

Damasio, A. (1994). *Descartes' error: Emotion, reason, and the human brain.* New York: GP Putnam's Sons.

Damasio, A. R., Tranel, D., & Damasio, H. (1990). Individuals with sociopathic behavior caused by frontal damage fail to respond autonomically to social stimuli. *Behavioural Brain Research, 41*, 81–94.

Dodge, K. A., Lochman, J. E., Harnish, J. D., & Bates, J. E. (1997). Reactive and proactive aggression in school children and psychiatrically impaired chronically assaultive youth. *Journal of Abnormal Psychology, 106*, 37–51.

Eysenck, H. J. (1977). *Crime and personality.* (3rd ed.) St. Albans: Paladin.

Farrington, D. P. (1997). The relationship between low resting heart rate and violence. In A. Raine, P. A. Brennan, D. Farrington, & S. A. Mednick (Eds.), *Biosocial bases of violence* (pp. 89–105). New York: Plenum.

Farrington, D. P. (2000). Psychosocial predictors of adult antisocial personality and adult convictions. *Behavioral Sciences and the Law, 18*, 605–622.

Fast, D. K., Conry, J., & Loock, C. A. (1999). Identifying Fetal Alcohol Syndrome among youth in the criminal justice system. *Journal of Developmental and Behavioral Pediatrics, 20,* 370–372.

Fowles, D. C. (1993). Electrodermal activity and antisocial behavior: Empirical findings and theoretical issues. In J. C. Roy, W. Boucsein, D. C. Fowles, & J. H. Gruzelier (Eds.), *Progress in electrodermal research* (pp. 223–237). New York: Plenum.

Gatzke-Kopp, L., Raine, A., Loeber, R., Stouthamer-Loeber, M., & Steinhauer, S. (2002). Serious delinquent behavior, sensation seeking, and electrodermal arousal. *Journal of Abnormal Child Psychology, 30,* 311–326.

Ge, X., Conger, R. D., Cadoret, R. J., & Neiderhiser, J. M. (1996). The developmental interface between nature and nurture: A mutual influence model of child antisocial behavior and parent behaviors. *Developmental Psychology, 32,* 574–589.

Gibson, C. L., & Tibbetts, S. G. (1998). Interaction between maternal cigarette smoking and Apgar scores in predicting offending behavior. *Psychological Reports, 83,* 579–586.

Gibson, C. L., & Tibbetts, S. G. (2000). A biosocial interaction in predicting early onset of offending. *Psychological Reports, 86,* 509–518.

Guy, J. D., Majorski, L. V., Wallace, C. J., & Guy, M. P. (1983). The incidence of minor physical anomalies in adult male schizophrenics. *Schizophrenia Bulletin, 9,* 571–582.

Hamalainen, M., & Pulkkinen, L. (1996). Problem behavior as a precursor of male criminality. *Development and Psychopathology, 8,* 443–455.

Harris, J. A. (1999). Review and methodological considerations in research on testosterone and aggression. *Aggression and Violent Behavior, 4,* 273–291.

Hemming, J. H. (1981). Electrodermal indices in a selected prison sample and students. *Personality and Individual Differences, 2,* 37–46.

Hinshaw, S. P., & Anderson, C. A. (1996). Conduct and oppositional defiant disorders. In E. J. Mash & R. A. Barkley (Eds.), *Child psychopathology* (pp. 113–149). New York: Guilford Press.

Hinshaw, S. P., Lahey, B. B., & Hart, E. L. (1993). Issues of taxonomy and comorbidity in the development of conduct disorder. *Development and Psychopathology, 5,* 31–49.

Hodgins, S., Kratzer, L., & Mcneil, T. F. (2001). Obstetric complications, parenting, and risk of criminal behavior. *Archives of General Psychiatry, 58,* 746–752.

Ishikawa, S. S., Raine, A., Lencz, T., Bihrle, S., & LaCasse, L. (2001). Autonomic stress reactivity and executive functions in successful and unsuccessful criminal psychopaths from the community. *Journal of Abnormal Psychology, 110,* 423–432.

Kagan, J. (1994). *Galen's prophecy: Temperament in human nature.* New York: Basic Books.

Kemppainen, L., Jokelainen, J., Jaervelin, M. R., Isohanni, M., & Raesaenen, P. (2001). The one-child family and violent criminality: A 31-year follow-up study of the Northern Finland 1966 birth cohort. *American Journal of Psychiatry, 158,* 960–962.

Laakso, M. P., Vaurio, O., Koivisto, E., Savolainen, L., Eronen, M., Aronen, H. J., et al. (2001). Psychopathy and the posterior hippocampus. *Behavioural Brain Research, 118,* 187–193.

Lahey, B. B., McBurnett, K., Loeber, R., & Hart, E. L. (1995). Psychobiology. In G. P. Sholevar (Ed.), *Conduct disorders in children and adolescents* (pp. 27–44). Washington, DC: American Psychiatric Press.

Laucht, M., Esser, G., Baving, L., Gerhold, M., Hoesch, I., Ihle, W., et al. (2000). Behavioral sequelae of perinatal insults and early family adversity at 8 years of age. *Journal of the American Academy of Child and Adolescent Psychiatry, 39*, 1229–1237.

Levin, E. D., Wilkerson, A., Jones, J. P., Christopher, N. C., & Briggs, S. J. (1996). Prenatal nicotine effects on memory in rats: Pharmacological and behavioral challenges. *Developmental Brain Research, 97*, 207–215.

Lewis, D. O., Lovely, R., Yeager, C., & Dellafemina, D. (1989). Toward a theory of the genesis of violence – A follow-up study of delinquents. *Journal of the American Academy of Child and Adolescent Psychiatry, 28*, 431–436.

Lewis, D. O., Pincus, J. H., Bard, B., & Richardson, E. (1988). Neuropsychiatric, psychoeducational, and family characteristics of 14 juveniles condemned to death in the United States. *American Journal of Psychiatry, 145*, 584–589.

Loeber, R., & Farrington, D. P. (1998). Never too early, never too late: Risk factors and successful interventions for serious and violent juvenile offenders. *Studies on Crime and Crime Prevention, 7*, 7–30.

Maliphant, R., Hume, F., & Furnham, A. (1990). Autonomic nervous system (ANS) activity, personality characteristics, and disruptive behaviour in girls. *Journal of Child Psychology and Psychiatry and Allied Disciplines, 31*, 619–628.

Masters, R. D., Hone, B., & Doshi, A. (1998). Environmental pollution, neurotoxicity, and criminal violence. In J. Rose (Ed.), *Environmental toxicology: Current developments* (pp. 13–48). New York: Gordon and Breach.

Mataro, M., Jurado, M. A., Garcia-Sanchez, C., Barraquer, L., Costa-Jussa, F. R., & Junque, C. (2001). Long-term effects of bilateral frontal brain lesion 60 years after injury with an iron bar. *Archives of Neurology, 58*, 1139–1142.

Mazur, A., & Booth, A. (1999). The biosociology of testosterone in men. In D. Franks & S. Smith (Eds.), *Mind, brain, and society: Toward a neurosociology of emotion: Vol. 5.* (pp. 311–338). Stamford; CT: JAI Press.

McClelland, G. H., & Judd, C. M. (1993). Statistical difficulties of detecting interactions and moderator effects. *Psychological Bulletin, 114*, 376–390.

McCord, J. (2001). Psychosocial contributions to psychopathy and violence. In A. Raine & J. Sanmartin (Eds.), *Violence and psychopathy* (pp. 141–170). New York: Kluwer Academic/Plenum.

Mednick, S. A. (1977). A bio-social theory of the learning of law-abiding behavior. In S. A. Mednick & K. O. Christiansen (Eds.), *Biosocial bases of criminal behavior.* New York: Gardner Press.

Mednick, S. A., & Kandel, E. S. (1988). Congenital determinants of violence. *Bulletin of the American Academy of Psychiatry and the Law, 16*, 101–109.

Miczek, K. A. (2001). Research on animal aggression: Emerging successes for understanding determinants of human violence. In M. E. Carroll & J. B. Overmier (Eds.), *Animal research and human health: Advancing human welfare through behavioral science* (pp. 41–61). Washington, DC: American Psychological Association.

Moffitt, T. E. (1990a). The neuropsychology of delinquency: A critical review. In M. Tonry and N. Morris (Eds.), *Crime and justice: A review of research* (pp. 99–169). Chicago: University of Chicago Press.

Moffitt, T. E. (1990b). Juvenile delinquency and Attention Deficit Disorder: Boys' developmental trajectories from age 3 to age 15. *Child Development, 61,* 893–910.

Moffitt, T. E. (1993). Adolescence-limited and life-course-persistent antisocial behavior: A developmental taxonomy. *Psychological Review, 100,* 674–701.

Moffitt, T. E., & Caspi, A. (2001). Childhood predictors differentiate life-course persistent and adolescence-limited antisocial pathways among males and females. *Development & Psychopathology, 13,* 355–375.

Moffitt, T., Caspi, A., Fawcett, P., Brammer, G. L., Raleigh, M., Yuwiler, A., et al. (1997). Whole blood serotonin and family background relate to male violence. In A. Raine, P. A. Brennan, D. P. Farrington, & S. A. Mednick (Eds.), *Biosocial bases of violence* (pp. 231–249). New York: Plenum.

Morgan, A. B., & Lilienfeld, S. O. (2000). A meta-analytic review of the relation between antisocial behavior and neuropsychological measures of executive function. *Clinical Psychology Review, 20,* 113–156.

Niehoff, D. (1999). *The biology of violence.* New York: Free Press.

Olds, D. (1997). Tobacco exposure and impaired development: A review of the evidence. *Mental Retardation and Developmental Disabilities Research Reviews, 3,* 257–269.

Olds, D., Henderson, C. R. J., Cole, R., Eckenrode, J., Kitzman, H., Luckey, D., et al. (1998). Long-term effects of nurse home visitation on children's criminal and antisocial behavior: 15-year follow-up of a randomized controlled trial. *JAMA: Journal of the American Medical Association, 280,* 1238–1244.

Olson, H. C., Streissguth, A. P., Sampson, P. D., Barr, H. M., Bookstein, F. L., & Thiede, K. (1997). Association of prenatal alcohol exposure with behavioral and learning problems in early adolescence. *Journal of the American Academy of Child and Adolescent Psychiatry, 36,* 1187–1194.

Pine, D. S., Shaffer, D., Schonfeld, I. S., & Davies, M. (1997). Minor physical anomalies: Modifiers of environmental risks for psychiatric impairment? *Journal of the American Academy of Child and Adolescent Psychiatry, 36,* 395–403.

Piquero, A., & Tibbetts, S. (1999). The impact of pre/perinatal disturbances and disadvantaged familial environment in predicting criminal offending. *Studies on Crime and Crime Prevention, 8,* 52–70.

Plomin, R., & Rutter, M. (1998). Child development, molecular genetics, and what to do with genes once they are found. *Child Development, 69,* 1223–1242.

Pope, H. G. J., Kouri, E. M., & Hudson, J. I. (2000). Effects of supraphysiologic doses of testosterone on mood and aggression in normal men: A randomized controlled trial. *Archives of General Psychiatry, 57,* 133–140.

Quay, H. C. (1965). Psychopathic personality as pathological stimulation-seeking. *American Journal of Psychiatry, 122,* 180–183.

Raine, A. (1987). Effect of early environment on electrodermal and cognitive correlates of schizotypy and psychopathy in criminals. *International Journal of Psychophysiology, 4,* 277–287.

Raine, A. (1993). *The psychopathology of crime: Criminal behavior as a clinical disorder.* San Diego: Academic Press.

Raine, A. (1996). Autonomic nervous system activity and violence. In D. M. Stoff & R. B. Cairns (Eds.), *Aggression and violence: Genetic, neurobiological, and biosocial perspectives* (pp. 145–168). Mahwah, NJ: Lawrence Erlbaum.

Raine, A. (1997). Antisocial behavior and psychophysiology: A biosocial perspective and a prefrontal dysfunction hypothesis. In D. Stoff, J. Breiling, & J. D. Maser (Eds.), *Handbook of antisocial behavior* (pp. 289–304). New York: Wiley.

Raine, A. (2002a). Annotation: The role of prefrontal deficits, low autonomic arousal, and early health factors in the development of antisocial and aggressive behavior. *Journal of Child Psychology and Psychiatry, 43*, 417–434.

Raine, A. (2002b). The biological basis of crime. In J. Q. Wilson & J. Petersilia (Eds.), *Crime: Public policies for crime control* (pp. 43–74). San Francisco: ICS Press.

Raine, A. (2002c). Biosocial studies of antisocial and violent behavior in children and adults: A review. *Journal of Abnormal Child Psychology, 30*, 311–326.

Raine, A., Brennan, P., & Farrington, D. P. (1997). Biosocial bases of violence: Conceptual and theoretical issues. In A. Raine, P. A. Brennan, D. P. Farrington, & S. A. Mednick (Eds.), *Biosocial bases of violence* (pp. 1–20). New York: Plenum.

Raine, A., Brennan, P., Mednick, B., & Mednick, S. A. (1996). High rates of violence, crime, academic problems, and behavioral problems in males with both early neuromotor deficits and unstable family environments. *Archives of General Psychiatry, 53*, 544–549.

Raine, A., Brennan, P., & Mednick, S. A. (1994). Birth complications combined with early maternal rejection at age 1 year predispose to violent crime at age 18 years. *Archives of General Psychiatry, 51*, 984–988.

Raine, A., Brennan, P., & Mednick, S. A. (1997). Interaction between birth complications and early maternal rejection in predisposing individuals to adult violence: Specificity to serious, early-onset violence. *American Journal of Psychiatry, 154*, 1265–1271.

Raine, A., Buchsbaum, M., & LaCasse, L. (1997). Brain abnormalities in murderers indicated by positron emission tomography. *Biological Psychiatry, 42*, 495–508.

Raine, A., Park, S., Lencz, T., Bihrle, S., LaCasse, L., Widom, C. S., et al. (2001). Reduced right hemisphere activation in severely abused violent offenders during a working memory task: An fMRI study. *Aggressive Behavior, 27*, 111–129.

Raine, A., Reynolds, C., Venables, P. H., Mednick, S. A., & Farrington, D. P. (1998). Fearlessness, stimulation-seeking, and large body size at age 3 years as early predispositions to childhood aggression at age 11 years. *Archives of General Psychiatry, 55*, 745–751.

Raine, A., Stoddard, J., Bihrle, S., & Buchsbaum, M. (1998). Prefrontal glucose deficits in murderers lacking psychosocial deprivation. *Neuropsychiatry, Neuropsychology, and Behavioral Neurology, 11*, 1–7.

Raine, A., & Venables, P. H. (1981). Classical conditioning and socialization – a biosocial interaction. *Personality and Individual Differences, 2*, 273–283.

Raine, A., & Venables, P. H. (1984a). Electrodermal nonresponding, antisocial behavior, and schizoid tendencies in adolescents. *Psychophysiology, 21*, 424–433.

Raine, A., & Venables, P. H. (1984b). Tonic heart rate level, social class and antisocial behaviour in adolescents. *Biological Psychology, 18*, 123–132.

Raine, A., Venables, P. H., Dalais, C., Mellingen, K., Reynolds, C., & Mednick, S. A. (2001). Early educational and health enrichment at age 3–5 years is associated with increased autonomic and central nervous system arousal and orienting at age 11 years: Evidence from the Mauritius Child Health Project. *Psychophysiology, 38*, 254–266.

Raine, A., Venables, P. H., & Mednick, S. A. (1997). Low resting heart rate at age 3 years predisposes to aggression at age 11 years: Evidence from the Mauritius Child Health Project. *Journal of the American Academy of Child and Adolescent Psychiatry, 36,* 1457–1464.

Raine, A., Venables, P. H., & Williams, M. (1995). High autonomic arousal and electrodermal orienting at age 15 years as protective factors against criminal behavior at age 29 years. *American Journal of Psychiatry, 152,* 1595–1600.

Raine, A., Venables, P. H., & Williams, M. (1996). Better autonomic conditioning and faster electrodermal half-recovery time at age 15 years as possible protective factors against crime at age 29 years. *Developmental Psychology, 32,* 624–630.

Rasanen, P., Hakko, H., Isohanni, M., Hodgins, S., Jarvelin, M. R., & Tiihonen, J. (1999). Maternal smoking during pregnancy and risk of criminal behavior among adult male offspring in the northern Finland 1996 birth cohort. *American Journal of Psychiatry, 156,* 857–862.

Rowe, D. C. (2001). *Biology and crime.* Los Angeles: Roxbury Publishing Company.

Rutter, M. L. (1997). Nature–nurture integration: The example of antisocial behavior. *American Psychologist, 52,* 390–398.

Rutter, M., Giller, H., & Hagell, A. (1998). *Antisocial behavior by young people.* Cambridge, UK: Cambridge University Press.

Scarpa, A., Raine, A., Venables, P. H., & Mednick, S. A. (1997). Heart rate and skin conductance in behaviorally inhibited Mauritian children. *Journal of Abnormal Psychology, 106,* 182–190.

Scarpa, A., Romero, N., Fikretoglu, D., Bowser, F. M., & Wilson, J. W. (1999). *Community violence exposure and aggression: Biosocial interactions.* Paper presented at the meeting of the American Society of Criminology, Toronto, Canada.

Slotkin, T. A., Epps T. A., Stenger, M. L., Sawyer, K. J., & Seidler, F. J. (1999). Cholinergic receptors in heart and brainstem of rats exposed to nicotine during development: implications for hypoxia tolerance and perinatal mortality. *Brain Research, 113,* 1–12.

Sparling, Y. A., & Cohen, R. (1997). Neurobehavioral influences on propensity for juvenile violence. *Journal of Neuropsychiatry, 9,* 134–135.

Streissguth, A. P., Barr, H. M., Bookstein, F. L., Sampson, P. D., & Olson, H. C. (1999). The long-term neurocognitive consequences of prenatal alcohol exposure: A 14-year study. *Psychological Science, 10,* 186–190.

Streissguth, A. P., Barr, H. H., Kogan, J., & Bookstein, F. L. (1996). *Understanding the occurrence of secondary disabilities in clients with Fetal Alcohol Syndrome (FAS) and Fetal Alcohol Effects (FAE).* Seattle: Washington Publication Services.

Suomi, S. J. (1999). Developmental trajectories, early experiences, and community consequences: Lessons from studies with rhesus monkeys. In D. P. Keating & Clyde Hertzman (Eds.), *Developmental health and the wealth of nations: Social, biological, and educational dynamics* (pp. 185–200). New York: Guilford Press.

Susman, E. J. (1993). Psychological, contextual, and psychobiological interactions: A developmental perspective on conduct disorder. *Development and Psychopathology, 5,* 181–189.

Susman, E. J., & Finkelstein, J. W. (2001). Biology, development, and dangerousness. In G. F. Pined & L. Pagani (Eds.), *Clinical assessment of dangerousness: Empirical contributions* (pp. 23–46). New York: Cambridge University Press.

Susman, E. J., & Ponirakis, A. (1997). Hormones–context interaction and antisocial behavior in youth. In A. Raine, P. A. Brennan, D. Farrington, & S. A. Mednick (Eds.), *Biosocial bases of violence* (pp. 251–269). New York: Plenum.

Tarter, R. E., Hegedus, A. M., Winsten, N. E., & Alterman, A. I. (1984). Neuropsychological, personality, and familial characteristics of physically abused delinquents. *Journal of the American Academy of Child Psychiatry, 23,* 668–674.

Tremblay, R. E., Schaal, B., Boulerice, B., Arseneault, L., Soussignan, R., & Perusse, D. (1997). Male physical aggression, social dominance, and testosterone levels at puberty: A developmental perspective. In A. Raine, P. A. Brennan, D. P. Farrington, & S. A. Mednick (Eds.), *Biosocial bases of violence* (pp. 271–291). New York: Plenum.

Volkow, N. D., Tancredi, L. R., Grant, C., Gillespie, H., Valentine, A., Nullani, N., et al. (1995). Brain glucose metabolism in violent psychiatric patients: A preliminary study. *Psychiatry Research: Neuroimaging, 61,* 243–253.

Wadsworth, M. E. J. (1976). Delinquency, pulse rate and early emotional deprivation. *British Journal of Criminology, 16,* 245–256.

Werner, E. E. (1987). Vulnerability and resiliency in children at risk for delinquency: A longitudinal study from birth to young adulthood. In J. D. Burchard & S. N. Burchard (Eds.), *Primary prevention of psychopathology* (pp. 16–43). Newbury Park, CA: Sage.

Widom, C. S. (1997). Child abuse, neglect, and witnessing violence. In D. M. Stoff, J. Breiling, & J. D. Maser (Eds.), *Handbook of antisocial behavior* (pp. 159–170). New York: Wiley.

Williams, L. M., Brammer, M. J., Skerrett, D., Lagopolous, J., Rennie, C., Kozek, K., et al. (2000). The neural correlates of orienting: an integration of fMRI and skin conductance orienting. *Neuroreport, 11,* 3011–3015.

3

Social Deprivation, Social–Emotional Behavior, and the Plasticity of Dopamine Function

Paul L. Gendreau
University of Montréal

Mark H. Lewis
University of Florida

BRAIN PLASTICITY AND SOCIAL DEVELOPMENT

The notion of plasticity in relation to biological and behavioral development is not a new one. Even when very little was known about brain
structure and function and long before the advent of modern molecular
and neuroanatomical techniques, scientists recognized that the brain had
the capacity to adapt and change in response to environmental input. Already in 1892, William James stressed the importance of brain plasticity in
the organization of habits:

Plasticity, then, in the wide sense of the word, means the possession of a structure
weak enough to yield to an influence, but strong enough not to yield all at once.
Each relatively stable phase of equilibrium in such a structure is marked by what we
call a new set of habits. Organic matter, especially nervous tissue, seems endowed
with a very extraordinary degree of plasticity of this sort; so that we may without
hesitation lay down as our first proposition the following: that *the phenomena of
habit in living beings are due to plasticity of the organic materials of which their bodies are
composed.* (p. 2, italic original (James, 1892)

James's intuition was confirmed in the 1960s when a group of scientists
provided the first empirical evidence of environmentally induced alterations in brain chemistry and structure (Diamond, Krech, & Rozenzweig,
1964; Krech, Rozenzweig, & Bennett, 1960; Rozenzweig, Krech, Bennett,
& Diamond, 1962). Importantly, it was shown that these neurobiological
alterations were associated with enhanced behavioral and particularly cognitive functions. In the past four decades, an increasing body of evidence
has recognized further the crucial and time-dependent influence of the
environment in shaping the developing brain. Well known is the seminal
work of Wiesel and Hubel, who demonstrated that early monocular deprivation in kittens produced persistent functional alterations in neurons
of the visual cortex (Wiesel & Hubel, 1965). This finding led to the important finding that specific visual input had to be presented during a precise

window of time for vision to develop normally (Hubel & Wiesel, 1970). The notion of critical period for the establishment of normal brain and behavior functions has received a great deal of attention among developmental neurobiologists and behavioral scientists (for a review see Greenough, Black, & Wallace, 1987, and Bornstein, 1989).

With respect to social behavior and the importance of the environment in shaping its development, several important issues are still to be answered. For instance, what environmental factors are most capable of altering social behavior? Are there sensitive periods for the establishment of social behavioral patterns? What altered neurobiological functions are associated with these environmentally induced changes in social behavior? To what extent are the brain structures involved in the development and expression of social behavior malleable?

A first attempt to answer these questions was initiated by the late Robert Cairns at the University of North Carolina at Chapel Hill. Approximately 25 years ago, Cairns set in motion a program of selective breeding of ICR mice based on the animals' propensity to exhibit either high or low levels of aggression following isolation housing (Cairns, MacCombie, & Hood, 1983). Mice were singly caged from 21 days of age to approximately 45–50 days, as this specific period of ontogeny and this particular length of isolation (sensitive period) were shown to produce the highest levels of aggression (Cairns, Hood, & Midlam, 1985). Hence, by altering the social environment during a restricted window of time, two lines of mice that differed markedly in behavioral reactivity were produced: one line of animals that promptly and ferociously attacked and a second line that exhibited high levels of freezing and nonagonistic social approach (for a review see Cairns, Gariépy, & Hood, 1990 or Gariépy, 1995).

In the early 1990s, our research group began to investigate the neurobiological bases of these line differences in isolation-induced social reactivity. Based on a previous study in monkeys that showed enhanced behavioral response to apomorphine in animals that had been socially deprived (Lewis, Gluck, Beauchamp, Keresztury, & Mailman, 1990), we examined the effects of the full-efficacy D_1 dopamine receptor agonist dihydrexidine on the social behavior of these high and low aggressive mice (Lewis, Gariépy, Gendreau, Nichols, & Mailman, 1994). Whereas other ligands (e.g., chlordiazepoxide, phenelzine) failed (Tancer, Gariépy, Mayleben, Petitto, & Lewis, 1992) dihydrexidine drastically altered the expression of social reactivity in both strains. In the high aggressive line, the number of attacks was dose-dependently reduced. In fact, it was almost nonexistent at the highest dose tested (10 mg/kg). In the low aggressive line, it was the frequency of nonagonistic approaches that followed a similar pattern. But above all, the most impressive effect was the large increase in social–emotional reactivity (e.g., escape, startle, kicking, upright defensive posture) that was observed in response to what would be normally mild and nonthreatening social stimulation. By a simple administration of a dopamine agonist, we were basically able to wipe out the effects of 20 generations of selective breeding on isolation-induced aggression and to transform aggressive mice – and to a lesser extent docile mice – into extremely reactive/fearful animals (Gariépy, Lewis, & Cairns, 1996).

These results generated a set of experiments examining in more detail the role of dopamine and its specific receptors in the mediation of isolation-induced behavioral reactivity. Research was conducted not only in these selectively bred mice (e.g., Gariépy, Gendreau, Mailman, Tancer, & Lewis, 1995; Gariépy, Gendreau, Cairns, & Lewis, 1998) but also in other strains of mice in order to assess the generality of our findings (e.g., Gendreau, Gariépy, Petitto, & Lewis, 1997a; Gendreau, Petitto, Gariépy, & Lewis, 1998; Gendreau, Petitto, Petrova, Gariépy, & Lewis, 2000). Briefly, our findings indicated that dopamine played an important role in the mediation of specific forms of social reactivity induced by prolonged social deprivation and suggested that D1-like and D2-like dopamine receptors were differentially involved in the expression of this reactivity.

An impressive amount of work on the effects of isolation housing as well as maternal separation on dopamine function and behavioral development in rats has been coming from Trevor Robbins's laboratory in England (e.g., Hall, Wilkinson, Humby, & Robbins, 1999; Jones, Marsden, & Robbins, 1990; Matthews, Dalley, Matthews, Tsai, & Robbins, 2001). Robbins and his colleagues demonstrated the significant plasticity of dopamine function following maternal separation in young animals and social deprivation in older animals. Altogether these studies in mice and rats indicated an important role for dopamine in mediating the effects of social deprivation on subsequent behavior. Here, we summarize some of the findings related to the plasticity of dopamine function in response to both long-term social deprivation and repeated bouts of maternal separation. Furthermore, we examine how these neurobiological changes are associated with the expression of emotional, more specifically *social*–emotional, behavior.

SOCIAL INFLUENCES ON BEHAVIORAL DEVELOPMENT: BRIEF HISTORICAL PERSPECTIVE

The investigation of the effects of the social environment on neurobehavioral development has relied on two major models or frameworks: the social deprivation paradigm and the early maternal separation paradigm. These two frames of reference have different but related historical starting points. Long-term social deprivation studies have been used extensively to examine the contribution of environmental factors on a variety of behavioral functions. Already in the late 19th century, this paradigm was used by both sides of the nature–nurture controversy to defend the notion

that behavioral development was the result of maturation, independent
of environmental influences; the consequence of postnatal conditioning;
or – more appropriately – the product of a complex interaction between
hereditary (genetic) and environmental factors (Carmichael, 1925). The
effects of prolonged social isolation on behavioral development have
been documented in a considerable number of species, including nonhuman primates, sheep, dog, rat, mouse, duck, chicken, fish, and even
fruit fly! Almost a century ago, Craig (1914) used the social isolation
paradigm to induce abnormal behavioral development in doves. Calvin
Stone (1926) at Stanford University investigated the effects of social deprivation on sexual behavior in rats. Then, even before the influential
studies of Harry Harlow, the effects of prolonged social deprivation in
nonhuman primates had been examined (e.g., Foley, 1934; McCulloch &
Haselrud, 1939).

Parallel to these early studies of social deprivation in animals, revealing but tragic observations were being made in humans at the time of
World War II. In a series of papers published in *The Psychoanalytic Study of
the Child*, René Spitz noted that institutionalized infants were commonly
afflicted by a specific group of physical, emotional, and psychosocial
impairments, a collection of symptoms referred to as the "hospitalism
syndrome" (Spitz, 1945; Spitz & Wolf, 1946). Among the symptoms reported were delayed maturation, diminished reaction to social stimulation, increased sadness, high levels of stereotyped behavior, and social
withdrawal. Although several reports concerning the impact of institu-
tional care upon child development had been published prior to these
observations – reports that revealed the extremely high rates of mortality
among institutionalized infants (Bakwin, 1949) – Spitz was the first to describe systematically this syndrome in infants and to offer a explanation.
Based on the purest psychoanalytic tradition, Spitz suggested that this
developmental abnormality was the result of a disrupted mother–infant
relationship, literally the "loss of the love object." Even though this conclusion was confounded by the fact that the infants were probably more
affected by the general absence of proper care rather than the absence of
the mother per se, these observations initiated an important line of research on the short- and long-term consequences of early, more particularly maternal, deprivation on children's development. Around the time
Spitz published his observations, a number of studies on human attachment and anxiety in relationship to maternal separation were emerging
in Europe (Bowlby, 1940). Subsequently, animal studies of maternal separation were conducted in nonhuman primates (Hinde & Spencer-Booth,
1971; Kaufman & Rosenblum, 1967) and other mammals such as sheep,
dogs, and cats (see Cairns, 1979). During the past three or four decades,
studies of the effects of maternal separation upon her offspring's development have been conducted primarily in rats. This has proved to be a useful

experimental model, as brain and behavior development is rapid in this species.

The social deprivation paradigm and the early maternal separation paradigm differ in many experimental aspects. In social deprivation studies, the animal is without any social contact for a period of time that ranges from one or a few days to several months. In addition, the onset of deprivation usually occurs once weaning is completed, at least in rodents. In nonhuman primates, social deprivation, either partial or "total," has been often conducted as soon as a few hours after birth. Isolation confinement typically prevents tactile (sometimes visual) contact and social interaction with conspecifics. Conversely, maternal separation is performed before weaning, typically within the first few days after parturition, lasts a few minutes to several hours, and is usually repeated several times. In this paradigm, the motherless pup is rarely left alone but remains with other pups in a temperature-controlled incubator. In addition – and this seems to be a key element for the observed effects – the interactions between the mother and the pup are altered following reunion.

SOCIAL DEPRIVATION AND MATERNAL SEPARATION: EFFECTS ON SOCIAL–EMOTIONAL BEHAVIOR

Both maternal separation and prolonged social deprivation are known to alter significantly the expression of social–emotional reactivity in animals. Given the important distinctions both between and within each of these two paradigms, it is not surprising that different behavioral outcomes have been observed. Prolonged individual housing is recognized to produce a set of behavioral abnormalities traditionally referred to as the "social deprivation syndrome" (Goosen, 1981) or more simply "the isolation syndrome" (Hatch et al., 1965; Valzelli, 1973). One of the most constant and robust characteristics of animals that have been socially isolated is their lower threshold for exhibiting high levels of emotional reactivity to stimuli of various modalities (Bernstein & Mason, 1962; Cairns, 1972). Such behavioral hyperreactivity is seen even in response to what would normally be mild and nonthreatening stimuli and is particularly robust when isolated animals are exposed to social stimulation (Gendreau et al., 1997a; Rodgers & Cole, 1993). Depending on genetic/biological predisposition, social deprivation has been shown to increase aggressiveness, social avoidance, depressive symptoms, and defensive or fearlike behavior in different mammalian species, including nonhuman primates (Harlow & Suomi, 1974; Mason & Sponholz, 1963), dogs (Fuller & Clark, 1966), and rodents (Cairns et al., 1985; Krsiak, 1975; Lagerspetz, Tirri, & Lagerspetz, 1968). Isolated animals, particularly nonhuman primates, have been shown also to exhibit stereotyped behavior, learning deficits, self-injurious behavior, and inadequate reproductive and maternal behavior (Gluck & Sackett, 1974; Mason & Berkson, 1975).

Animals that have experienced repeated maternal separation early in ontogeny exhibit a behavioral syndrome in adulthood somehow different from what has been reported for animals that have been deprived of social contact after weaning. Contrary to animals that have undergone prolonged post-weaning social isolation, maternally deprived animals commonly show a higher threshold for emotional responding and blunted emotional reactivity or ahedonia, a set of symptoms that is reminiscent of depression (Sanchez, Ladd, & Plotsky, 2001). This is associated with dysregulation of the hypothalamic–pituitary–adrenal (HPA) axis. This pattern of emotional expression and regulation is opposite to what is observed immediately after removal of the mother as pups react to maternal absence by exhibiting enhanced motor–behavioral arousal (Hofer, 1975). Adult rats that experienced early maternal separation typically show higher locomotor activity in a novel setting but only after an initial period of lower activity (Meaney, Brake, & Gratton, 2002).

It is tempting to suggest that animals separated from their mother exhibit a behavioral syndrome that is opposite to that of animals deprived of social contact after weaning (Hall, 1998). This suggestion, however, is based on a relatively small number of findings as the majority of maternal separation studies have focused on the immediate effects rather than the long-term consequences. In addition, whereas studies on the effects of social deprivation have targeted a wide spectrum of behavioral and neurobiological functions, studies on maternal separation have mainly focused on the effects on neuroendocrine function. The significant procedural differences between the studies (e.g., strain or species, number and duration of separation bouts, age at which separation or deprivation occurs) also make the comparisons delicate. Finally, considering the possibility that early development may be characterized with more precise and more sensitive windows of vulnerability, it is not surprising that studies of maternal separation generally produce more inconsistent results than those performing the social deprivation procedure later in ontogeny.

DOPAMINE FUNCTION IN SOCIALLY AND MATERNALLY DEPRIVED ANIMALS

Since the discovery of dopamine (DA) as a neurotransmitter in the late 1950s (Blaschko, 1957; Carlsson, Lindqvist, Magnusson, & Waldeck, 1958), much has been learned concerning its function and mode of action. Nowadays, DA is known to mediate a variety of behavioral and physiological functions and has been associated with the manifestation of psychosocial disturbances in humans (e.g., schizophrenia, drug abuse). Nevertheless, its role in mediating emotional behavior in animals has been somehow overlooked. This may be due to the fact that traditional animal models of emotional behavior do not allow the expression of a wide range of behaviors, do not produce a sufficient amount of novelty, or do not generate enough emotional stimulation to differentiate the contribution of DA in the expression of emotional behavior from its influence on motor activity (Franklin & Tang, 1995; Gendreau et al., 1997b). In recent years, however, there has been a growing interest in the role of DA in mediating emotional behavior. The discovery of the D_3 (Sokoloff, Giros, Martres, Bouthenet, & Schwartz, 1990) and D_4 (Van Tol et al., 1991) DA receptor subtypes that are primarily expressed within mesolimbic regions of the brain is manifestly related to this new interest.

As mentioned earlier, our studies showed that DA played a significant role in mediating social–emotional reactivity induced by prolonged social isolation. Following postweaning social isolation, a substantial number of mice display aggressive behavior toward a standard group-housed male. It was demonstrated that systemic injection of a DA agonist was very effective in disorganizing this social pattern and in inducing high levels of fearlike behavior. These effects were not observed in mice that had been reared in social groups (Lewis et al., 1994). Several studies have shown that aggressive behavior can be suppressed by dopaminergic compounds, when the motor system is either clearly overactivated or clearly depressed (Baggio & Ferrari, 1980; McMillen, DaVanzo, Song, Scott, & Rodriguez, 1989; Miczek, DeBold, & van Erp, 1994). Accordingly, the dopaminergic system has been postulated to play a nonspecific, regulatory role on behavior by modifying the level of excitability or arousal (Le Moal & Simon, 1991). Our results, however, clearly indicated that pharmacological activation of the dopaminergic system induces specific forms of social-emotional reactivity that are independent of the effects on motor activity (see also Franklin & Tang, 1995). In isolated mice, administration of D2-like DA ligands was shown to depress locomotor activity when testing was conducted in a nonsocial context, but as soon as social interactions were provided, high levels of motor–emotional reactivity reminiscent of fearfulness were commonly observed.

These findings suggest that social deprivation generates its behavioral effects at least partially via alterations in central dopaminergic mechanisms. There are pharmacological and neurochemical studies supporting this hypothesis. Compared to animals that had been reared in social groups, isolated animals have been generally characterized by enhanced sensitivity to the stimulant effects of d-amphetamine, apomorphine, or cocaine (Ahmed, Stinus, Le Moal, & Cador, 1995; Jones et al., 1990; Lewis et al., 1990; Phillips et al., 1994; Wilmot, Vanderwende, & Spoerlein, 1986). Although some studies did not report this effect (Bowling & Bardo, 1994; Hall, Fong, Ghaed, & Pert, 2001; Jones, Hernandez, Kendall, Marsden, & Robbins, 1992; Weiss, Domeney, Heidbreder, Moreau, & Feldon, 2001), these observations suggest that social deprivation heightens social–emotional reactivity by means of alterations in DA sensitivity. Increased sensitivity to DA was observed in the striatum of rats that had been isolated for 3 months following weaning; then, after 12 months of isolation housing, such hypersensitivity was detected in the cortex (Oehler, Jahkel, & Schmidt, 1987). In addition, isolated rats were shown to acquire sensitization to amphetamine at a lower dose than that of animals that have been raised in groups; the behavioral response to amphetamine following a stressor (footshock) was also higher in isolated animals (Ahmed et al., 1995). Then, other studies reported no change in DA receptor affinity following prolonged social deprivation (Gariépy et al., 1995, 1998; Rilke, May, Oehler, & Wolffgramm, 1995; Guisado, Fernandez-Tome, Garzon, & Del Rio, 1980). Furthermore, no differences in the effects of D_1 (SKF 38393) and D_2 (quinpirole) DA agonists on cyclic AMP accumulation in the caudate-putamen was found following isolation (Jones et al., 1992). As isolates were more sensitive to the motor depressant effects of a low dose of apomorphine, the authors concluded that isolation primarily alters presynaptic – therefore D2-like receptor – function.

Increased postsynaptic DA receptor density may be another mechanism explaining the enhanced sensitivity of isolated animals to DA agonists. Although D_1/D_2 interactions are required for the expression of a number of behaviors (Waddington & Daly, 1993), they appear to be differentially malleable by the environment. In comparison with animals that were singly caged, 2-year-old rats that had been exposed to enriched contextual conditions (toys) during 30 days showed an increase in D1-like but not in D2-like receptor density in the striatum (Anderson, Gatley, Rapp, Coburn-Litvak, & Volkov, 2000). Higher density of striatal D1-like but not D2-like DA receptors was also found in mice following postweaning isolation (Gariépy et al., 1995, 1998). In another study, striatal D2-like receptors were also unaffected by 18 months of social isolation (Rilke, Jahkel, & Oehler, 1998). One study reported higher levels of D2-like DA binding sites following postweaning isolation housing, but assessment of D1-like receptors was not conducted (Guisado et al., 1980). On the other hand, no differences in D1-like and D2-like DA receptor density were found between isolated animals, group-housed animals, and animals that were raised in a enriched conditions between 30 and 60 days of age (Bardo & Hammer, 1991). Other studies showed reduced D1-like and D2-like DA receptor density in the striatum and nucleus accumbens of isolated animals (Rilke et al., 1995; Bean & Lee, 1991). Moreover, the downregulation of D2-like DA receptors was blocked by chronic haloperidol treatment (Bean & Lee, 1991).

Contrasting results have also been reported concerning activity of the dopaminergic system. Some findings can be interpreted as evidence for lower (re)activity of the mesocorticolimbic DA system, whereas the opposite conclusion can be drawn from other studies. For instance, isolation housing has been associated with reduced DA turnover in different brain regions (Weinstock, Speiser, & Ashkenazi, 1978), with reduced DA turnover after exposure to a stressor (Miura, Qiao, & Ohta, 2002), and with increased basal level of DA in the nucleus accumbens (Hall et al., 1998; Miura et al., 2002), and prefrontal cortex (Heidbreder et al., 2000; Jones et al., 1992). On the other hand, decreased DOPAC/DA ratio was also found in the cortex of isolated animals, but the reversed pattern was observed in the nucleus accumbens and striatum (Blanc et al., 1980). Higher basal DA turnover was also reported in the amygdala of isolated animals (Heidbreder et al., 2000). In addition, increased DA activity was observed in the nucleus accumbens (Fulford & Marsden, 1998) and in the frontal cortex of isolated animals (Crespi, Wright, & Mobius, 1992; Jones et al., 1992). Finally, neurostructural changes in the nigrostriatal DA pathway and reduced levels of tyrosine hydroxylase (a marker for DA neurons) in the striatum have been found following long-term social deprivation in monkeys (Martin, Spicer, Lewis, Gluck, & Cork, 1991).

The short- and long-term effects of maternal separation on DA function have also been investigated, albeit less extensively than the effects of post-weaning social deprivation. It has been argued that maternal separation alters DA function in a manner opposite to what is observed for post-weaning isolation (Hall, 1998). However, similar to the effects of social deprivation later in ontogeny, adult rats that experienced a single 24-hour period of maternal separation at postnatal day 3 showed enhanced behavioral response (increased stereotypy) to apomorphine (Rots et al., 1996). In addition, both maternal isolation (Hall et al., 1999; Kehoe, Shoemaker, Arons, Triano, & Suresh, 1998) and postweaning social deprivation (Jones et al., 1992) were found to increase amphetamine-induced DA release. One study reported that postweaning social deprivation but not maternal deprivation reduced amphetamine-induced sensitization (Weiss et al., 2001). Adult rats that had been maternally separated did not exhibit enhanced behavioral response to amphetamine but showed higher sensitization to the drug after repeated daily injection of saline (Meaney et al., 2002). The effects of maternal separation can be also observed in younger animals. For instance, in 10-day-old rats, 1-hour maternal separation from the second to the ninth day postnatally produced increased DA turnover in hypothalamus and septum whereas nigrostriatal DA activity was reduced (Kehoe et al., 1998). Finally, maternal separation had no effect on D_1 or D_2 receptor binding in the prefrontal cortex and nucleus accumbens but substantially decreased DA transporter binding in caudate/putamen and accumbens (Meaney et al., 2002).

To understand the age-dependent effects of social influences on DA function, it is essential to examine the ontogeny of the dopaminergic system. In rats, density of D_1, D_2, and D_4 DA receptors in the caudate-putamen and nucleus accumbens peaks around the fourth postnatal week (28 days), then declines by about one third to reach adult levels approximately 3 to 4 weeks later (Tarazi, Tomasini, & Baldessarini, 1998; Tarazi & Baldessarini, 2000; Teicher, Andersen, & Hostetter, 1995). Between the first and the fourth week following birth, there is a three- to four-fold increase of DA receptors in these structures (Tarazi and Baldessarinig 1998). A different developmental pattern is observed in the frontal cortex and hippocampus, where DA receptor density increases gradually to reach adult level at about the eighth postnatal week (Tarazi et al., 1998; Tarazi and Baldessarini, 2000). At 25 months of age, D1-like and D2-like DA receptor densities are about 70% lower than levels observed at 3–4 months of age (Hyttel, 1989; Morelli, Mennini, Cagnotto, Toffano, & Di Chiara, 1990). In general, DA receptors, at least D_1 receptors, are expressed according to a rostral–caudal gradient, with receptors in the more caudal regions being expressed generally prior to those in the more anterior part such as in the frontal cortex (Murrin & Zeng, 1990). Finally, there are important gender differences in the development of DA function, at least in rats. For instance, male rats have been characterized with greater expression of striatal D1 and D2 receptors than females, but the loss being greater, their adult levels are similar (Andersen, Rutstein, Benzo, Hostetter, & Teicher, 1997; Andersen & Teicher, 2000). A gender difference in the ontogeny and expression of DA function is clearly an issue that warrants further examination.

As the development of dopaminergic function shows high levels of variability between structures, genders, and species, it is not surprising that a variety of neurobiological outcomes have been reported following maternal separation or postweaning social deprivation. The differences in the ontogeny of DA function may explain the age-dependent effects of social deprivation on neurobehavioral development. Mapping the normal development of DA function in brain regions associated with the expression of social behavior, particularly those affected by changes in the social environment, is an important step toward understanding the specific and time-dependent effects of social and maternal deprivation on neurobehavioral function.

REVERSIBILITY OF THE EFFECTS OF SOCIAL DEPRIVATION ON SOCIAL BEHAVIOR AND DOPAMINE FUNCTION

Social deprivation and maternal separation studies have shown that when normal patterns of social interactions are altered during ontogeny, adverse long-term consequences on brain and behavior development often occur. Are these consequences irreversible? Concerning visual, auditory, olfactory, and somatosensory functions, it is well established that their development is somehow conditional to the presence of specific experiential stimulation at definite times during ontogeny (Crair, Gillespie, & Stryker, 1998; Kral, Hartmann, Tillein, Heid, & Klinke, 2001; Meisami &

Mousavi, 1981; Stern, Maravall, & Svoboda, 2001). Nevertheless, developmental improvement of these functions is not totally impervious to later environmental influences. In studies of early sensory deprivation during these so-called "critical" periods of development, which produced significant alterations in brain and behavior, functional recovery, albeit at times limited, is indeed achievable (Brainard & Knudsen, 1998; Cynader, Berman, & Hein, 1976).

The notion of critical period and the concept of reversibility of brain processes associated with the expression of *social behavior* are perhaps more controversial. In 1935, Lorenz observed that social bonding or attachment in precocial birds was determined within a very small window of time – "a circumscribed ontogenic phase" (Lorenz, 1981, p. 279) – and that any moving object in proximity would become, for the majority of animals, a sort of permanent "attachment figure." Lorenz, an ethologist with a behaviorist standpoint, argued that the process of imprinting was a simple conditioning response similar to the acquisition of avoidance behavior following a traumatic experience. Furthermore, Lorenz described both conditioning processes as *irreversible* (Lorenz, 1981). This assumption was not accurate as there is evidence that both imprinting (Salzen & Meyer, 1967) and avoidance responses (Myslivecek & Hassmannova, 1979) can be significantly modified by subsequent experience.

The proposition that behavioral patterns are determined during a precise ontogenetic window and do not respond to later environmental input is obviously at odds with the notion of plasticity. Although the extent to which a given biological or behavioral feature can be modified is dependent upon the age, genetic–biological predisposition, and prior experience of the individual, malleability of brain and behavior occurs throughout the life span. For that reason, it is perhaps more appropriate, especially when social processes are implied, to refer to sensitive, rather than critical, periods of development. Thus, contrary to the conclusion of Lorenz on the establishment of species identity in birds, social behaviors are not fixed by early experience and irreversible but highly malleable to subsequent social influences provided through education, rehabilitation, therapy, and other societal efforts. Although there are clearly developmental and individual constraints on plasticity, neural reorganization is not limited to the first few years of life. The brain mechanisms involved in the expression of social behavior may be among the most malleable ones – the most open to change, and therefore not limited to early maturation and development. From an evolutionary point of view, such capacity for reorganization throughout ontogeny is clearly favorable (Cairns et al., 1990).

Is there a sensitive period for the establishment of social behavioral patterns? In 1985, Cairns and his colleagues published one of the first systematic studies aimed at determining whether there was a sensitive period for the establishment of social isolation–induced aggression in male mice (Cairns et al., 1985). A five by five factorial design that included five different onsets of isolation (isolation began at postnatal day 21, 28, 35, 56, or 84) and five different durations (no isolation or isolation lasted 1, 4, 16, 64 days) was used. No fewer than 250 experimental animals and 250 test partners were used for this purpose. It was demonstrated that the earlier the onset and longer the duration of isolation housing, the more pronounced were its effects on the expression of aggressive behavior. A similar conclusion was reached in nonhuman primates (Harlow, Dodsworth, & Harlow, 1965).

Can the effects of social deprivation on behavior be reduced or completely reversed? Again, this depends on the onset and duration of the social deprivation. For instance, monkeys that have been reared in total isolation from birth to 6 months of age and then placed with younger females showed almost complete social–emotional recovery when raised subsequently with younger animals (Suomi & Harlow, 1972). Return to normal levels of sociability is not as robust when the length of social isolation is prolonged (Harlow & Suomi, 1971). Comparable findings have been reported for severely deprived Romanian orphans: recovery of cognitive function was complete when adoption occurred prior to 6 months of age, very extensive for children who were adopted before reaching 24 months of age, but more difficult for those who were adopted after that age (O'Connor, Rutter, Beckett, Keaveney, & Kreppner, 2000). Developmental catch-up was therefore possible for all children, but progress was not as marked when children were placed within a new family home after 2 years of age. These observations in animals and humans indicated that recovery of behavioral and cognitive function is always possible albeit conditional to the age at which transition from adverse to more favorable environmental conditions takes place. Accordingly, "sensitive periods" for the development of normal behavioral patterns can be appreciably extended by providing sufficient environmental enrichment. This rule is also true for the recovery of more basic function such as the development of auditory function (Brainard & Knudsen, 1998).

Experimental studies in animals and clinical observations in humans indicate that the degree of functional recovery after brain lesion generally correlates negatively with the age at which the lesion has occurred. The greater plasticity of the younger brain compared to the more mature one is known as the "Kennard principle" (Finger & Wolf, 1988). This principle is not totally accurate, however. For instance, in children functional recovery is better when cortical injury occurs between 12 and 24 months rather than between birth and 12 months of age (Kolb, Gibb, & Gorny, 2000). Similarly in rats, it was shown that depletion of D_1 and D_2 receptors in the striatum following administration of N-ethoxycarbonyl-2-ethoxy-1,2-dihydroquinoline (EEDQ) was reversed in 16-day-old animals – and to a lesser degree in 39-day-old animals – but not in 10-day-old pups

(Crawford, Rowlett, McDougall, & Bardo, 1994). Also, depletion of striatal DA, which impaired motor function in adults, had no effect in 3-, 15-, and 20-day–old rat pups. Furthermore, whereas motor recovery was observed within a week when depletion was performed at 27 days of age, recovery took 4 to 5 weeks in older animals (Weihmuller & Bruno, 1989). A different time course for the upregulation of striatal DA D_1 and D_2 receptors following 1-methyl-4-phenyl-1,2,3,6-tetrahydropyridine (MPTP) lesion of the nigrostriatal pathway was also shown, with the upregulation of D_1 sites being slower but more enduring than that of D_2 sites (Weihmuller, Bruno, Neff, & Hadjiconstantinou, 1990).

There is also evidence that the DA system is highly sensitive to less invasive pharmacological manipulations. For instance, it was shown that two doses (2 mg) of methamphetamine reduced striatal DA transporter binding by 80% after a week (Harvey, Lacan, Tanious, & Melega, 2000). Interestingly, improvement was substantial but still incomplete 1.5 years later (a 10% reduction was still present). These results indicate that the age at which the injury or trauma comes about will determine the nature and intensity of the effects on DA function. The results also demonstrate the considerable malleability of the dopaminergic system in response to severe and milder forms of brain alterations.

As mentioned previously, we observed altered DA receptor density in mice following social isolation (Gariépy et al., 1995). Can these environmentally induced alterations in DA function be overturned? This seems the case, as the effects of 24 days of postweaning social isolation on DA receptor density were fully reversed by regrouping the isolated animals for an additional 24 days (Gariépy et al., 1998). Importantly, this neurobiological recuperation was coupled with a recovery in social behavior, as behavioral patterns returned to normal levels after a period of "rehabilitation." To our knowledge, this is the only evidence showing reversibility of DA function and DA-dependent behavior after an initial period of social deprivation.

CONCLUDING REMARKS ON SOCIAL DEPRIVATION, DOPAMINE FUNCTION, AND SOCIAL DEVELOPMENT

Studies of the effects of maternal separation and social deprivation on neurobehavioral development have generated a great deal of disparate findings both within and between each experimental model. This is particularly salient at the neurobiological level as contradictory outcomes on a variety of mechanisms have been reported. Based on the evidence reported in this review, however, we can prudently formulate three general statements concerning the effects of social deprivation on DA function: (1) There are variations in social rearing conditions that alter the development of the dopaminergic system; (2) these alterations mediate to some extent the long-term social–emotional disturbances typically observed following social deprivation; and (3) the effects of social deprivation on DA function are dependent upon the period at which it is initiated and terminated.

Based on the pharmacological data presented earlier, a more specific statement can be put forward: Social deprivation augments the sensitivity to dopamine agonists. What remains ambiguous is the neurochemical mechanism accountable for this supersensitivity as contradictory observations were made. Functional supersensitivity of the dopaminergic system can be produced by denervation, chronic pharmacological blockade, or disuse of DA pathways, an effect that may be mediated by an increase in receptor density (Hess, Albers, Le, & Creese, 1986; Ungerstedt, Ljungberg, Hoffer, & Siggins, 1975). Nevertheless, functional supersensitivity can be achieved without an increase in receptor density. For instance, no increase in DA receptor number was observed following bilateral 6-hydroxydopamine lesions of ascending DA pathways (LaHoste & Marshall, 1992). Also, no increase in D1-like and D2-like receptors or in DA transporters was observed in DA-deficient mice, although these mice showed enhanced behavioral reactivity to D1-like and D2-like DA receptor agonists and to L-DOPA (Kim, Szczypka, & Palmiter, 2000). Accordingly, many compensatory mechanisms may occur in response to environmental influences that may explicate the enhanced sensitivity of socially deprived animals to dopamine agonists. These mechanisms (i.e., increased receptor density or affinity, enhanced transmitter release, diminished reuptake, sensitized receptors, or other downstream processes) do not appear to be necessary or sufficient to mediate the effects of social deprivation upon behavioral processes.

Assessing the effects of diverse social moderators on the development of specific neurobiological mechanisms is complicated by a host of factors. Discrepancy in biological assays (in vivo, ex vivo, or in vitro) is unlikely to be the main reason for these inconsistencies. Differences in species or strains, and more particularly variation in the time of onset and duration of the social deprivation period, are unambiguous key elements. Apparently, the sensitivity of the organism – its nervous system – to physical and social stimulation varies greatly, with some structures and functions being more susceptible to specific experiences at specific times in ontogeny, and with perhaps more precise and more sensitive windows of susceptibility occurring early in development. For instance, in examining the effects of 24-hr maternal separation on HPA axis responsiveness, it was observed that 20-day-old animals deprived at postnatal day 3 were hyperreactive, whereas those separated 8 days later at postnatal day 11 had a blunted HPA axis response (van Oers, De Kloet, & Levine, 1997). The specific windows of susceptibility for the development of normal DA system and DA-dependent behavior have not been yet established.

Another critical variable for the contradictory results reported here involves the specific nature of the deprivation. It is already known that the short- and long-term effects of maternal separation on stress response can be prevented by simply stroking the anogenital region of the motherless pups with a fine brush (van Oers, De Kloet, & Levine, 1999). Similarly, it was shown that levels of licking, grooming, and nursing in an arched-back position are key components of maternal behavior for generating important neural and behavioral alterations in the offspring (Liu, Diorio, Day, Francis, & Meaney, 2000). These studies indicate the importance of specific physical–social stimulation provided by the mother for normal neurobehavioral development.

Depriving the pups periodically of maternal nursing behavior does not obviously entail the same significance as preventing juveniles or adult animals from interacting socially with same-age conspecifics. What are the animals undergoing postweaning social deprivation deprived of? In rats, neither daily handling nor cohabitation with conspecifics made less active by daily haloperidol treatment were successful in reversing the effects of isolation housing (Bean & Lee, 1991). In mice, neither daily handling of isolates nor housing one male with females reduced the frequency of intermale fighting (Gariépy, 1995). Although reduced exposure to pheromones may be of significance (Scott, 1966), these results suggest that it is not the amount of tactile stimulation or the passive presence of conspecifics but the level and nature of *social interaction* that may be the crucial factor for the observed effects. Is the absence of play the critical element as suggested by some authors (Einon, Morgan, & Kibbler, 1978)? This may be true for rats and perhaps for mice, as they exhibit rudimentary forms of play behavior (Pellis & Pasztor, 1999) but it is likely that play experience is not the only interactive element missing during prolonged social deprivation (Bekoff, 1976).

A better definition and comprehension of the multiple environmental factors that are manipulated when animals are separated from their mother or deprived from social contact clearly is a necessary step before examining the whole set of brain structures and mechanisms that are associated with the effects of deprivation. As pointed out by Greenough (1988), however: "every change in the environment, no matter how seemingly specific, has nonspecific consequences" (p. 290). With respect to the effects of postweaning social deprivation in mice, heightened aggression may be the specific consequence of not having the opportunity to fight and learn to inhibit aggressive behavior, whereas heightened behavioral reactivity to novelty (not associated with aggressiveness) may be more a matter of lack of social stimulation on the whole. The disruption of prepulse inhibition by social isolation (Robbins, Jones, & Wilkinson, 1996) may also represent a nonspecific outcome of this experimental procedure.

It takes time for the brain to mature and show coherent patterns of activity that support adaptive patterns of behavioral organization. In rats, striatal DA efferent neurons reach their target regions only 1 week after birth (Chesselet et al., 2000). Then, maturation of the DA system, as measured by receptor density, is not complete before at least 8 weeks of age (Tarazi et al., 1998). In humans, at least 5 years are necessary before DA receptor density in the striatum gets to adult levels (Seeman et al., 1987). The development of neurobiological functions is thus characterized with discrete qualitative changes during the course of ontogeny. Processes of brain development such as cell production, migration, and differentiation can be influenced by environmental factors during the prenatal and perhaps early postnatal period. Other ontogenetic processes such as myelination and synaptogenesis, that is, the formation of synaptic links between neurons and the regulation of post- and presynaptic receptors or transporters, are open to environmental influences for a much longer period of time, in reality throughout the life span in the case of synaptogenesis (Rice & Barone, 2000). Functional alterations induced by specific experience (or lack of) may be associated with a reorganization of synaptic circuitry, including increased dendritic arborization, increased spine density, altered receptor density and/or sensitivity, and altered G-protein mechanism.

Much research on brain plasticity has so far focused on the hippocampus and adjacent areas. In recent years, however, increasing evidence indicates that other brain structures – rich in dopaminergic innervations – can be also substantially altered by the environment, even during adulthood. For instance, a high degree of axonal plasticity due to molecular mechanisms different from those occuring in the hippocampus was found in the striatum of adult rats (Chesselet et al., 2000). In addition, long-term potentiation, an important mechanism for synaptic plasticity that persists throughout ontogeny, has been observed in the striatum (Charpier & Deniau, 1997). There is also evidence that alterations in dopaminergic function may induce structural changes at the level of the synapse. For instance, reduction of dopaminergic activity by administration of D_1 and D_2 DA antagonists decreased synaptic density in the prefrontal cortex, whereas administration of a DA agonist increased it (Sugahara & Shiraishi, 1998).

It is important to mention that most studies examining the effects of social deprivation or maternal deprivation on brain function have focused on cognitive and/or nonsocial behavior. This may not be surprising, however, as assessment of emotional reactivity in rodents has been traditionally conducted within nonsocial contexts (e.g., open field, elevated plus-maze). Given that the propensity to be "emotional" in a nonsocial context is not necessarily a good predictor of the level of emotional reactivity exhibited in response to social stimulation (Berton, Ramos, Chaouloff, & Mormede,

1997; Gariépy, Hood, & Cairns, 1988; Gendreau et al., 1997a) and given that what isolated animals are deprived of is mainly social interaction, it would be more informative to test the effects of social deprivation on *social behavior*. Moreover, although it is still common to refer to unitary constructs such as fearfulness, anxiety, fear, depression, and stress without describing the nature of the behavior and the context where it is observed, we believe that it would be beneficial to go beyond the traditional terminology and focus on specific behavior expressed in specific contexts.

All neurobehavioral functions are the result of a complex interaction among genetic, social, and developmental/maturational variables of which it is difficult to control. Animal models afford the unique opportunity of identifying the specific brain structures and neurochemical systems affected by the social environment at specific developmental times. Thanks to the recent advances in molecular biology, pharmacology, and neuroimaging methods, these animal models have provided evidence that alterations in the social environment of the developing organism can induce abnormal behavioral and neurobiological phenotypes, including changes in brain morphology, in neurotransmitter function, and in levels of gene expression. Alteration in dopaminergic function is only one of many processes that can be altered by activity-dependent mechanisms, which are themselves dependent upon the developmental stage of the individual. Although many other neurotransmitter systems (e.g., norepinephrine, serotonin, acetylcholine) have been also shown to be altered by social deprivation, particularly after long-term postweaning social isolation (for a review see Hall, 1998), the DA system appears to be particularly sensitive to environmental influences and to play a very important role in the effects of social deprivation on social–emotional behavior.

Naturally, caution has to be exercised in drawing conclusions based entirely on animal models. The important species differences with respect to social environment and maturation of the neurobiological systems make the interpretation and generalization of the results a very challenging task. Animal models of neurobehavioral development are scientifically relevant when the species-typical effects can be discriminated from those involving more general developmental processes. In this regard, both the maternal separation paradigm and the social deprivation paradigm have contributed to our progress in understanding the general and the specific contribution of social relationships and interactions in the development of neurobehavioral functions.

ACKNOWLEDGMENTS

Preparation of this chapter was supported by a research grant from the "Fonds pour la Formation de Chercheurs et l'Aide à la Recherche du Québec" to PLG.

References

Ahmed, S. H., Stinus, L., Le Moal, M., & Cador, M. (1995). Social deprivation enhances the vulnerability of male Wistar rats to stressor- and amphetamine-induced behavioral sensitization. *Psychopharmacology, 117*, 116–124.

Andersen, S. L., Rutstein, M., Benzo, J. M., Hostetter, J. C., & Teicher, M. H. (1997). Sex differences in dopamine receptor overproduction and elimination. *Neuroreport, 8*, 1495–1498.

Andersen, S. L., & Teicher, M. H. (2000). Sex differences in dopamine receptors and their relevance to ADHD. *Neuroscience and Biobehavioral Reviews, 24*, 137–141.

Anderson, B. J., Gatley, S. J., Rapp, D. N., Coburn-Litvak, P. S., & Volkow, N. D. (2000). The ratio of striatal D1 to muscarinic receptors changes in aging rats housed in an enriched environment. *Brain Research, 872*, 262–265.

Baggio, G., & Ferrari, F. (1980). Role of brain dopaminergic mechanisms in rodent aggressive behavior: influence of (+/−)N-n-propyl-norapomorphine on three experimental models. *Psychopharmacology, 70*, 63–68.

Bakwin, H. (1949). Psychologic aspects of pediatrics. *Journal of Pediatrics, 35*, 512–521.

Bardo, M. T., & Hammer, R. P., Jr. (1991). Autoradiographic localization of dopamine D1 and D2 receptors in rat nucleus accumbens: Resistance to differential rearing conditions. *Neuroscience, 45*, 281–290.

Bean, G., & Lee, T. (1991). Social isolation and cohabitation with haloperidol-treated partners: Effect on density of striatal dopamine D2 receptors in the developing rat brain. *Psychiatry Research, 36*, 307–317.

Bekoff, M. (1976). The social deprivation paradigm: Who's being deprived of what? *Developmental Psychobiology, 9*, 499–500.

Bernstein, S., & Mason, W. A. (1962). The effects of age and stimulus conditions of the emotional responses of Rhesus monkeys: Responses to complex stimuli. *Journal of Genetic Psychology, 101*, 279–298.

Berton, O., Ramos, A., Chaouloff, F., & Mormede, P. (1997). Behavioral reactivity to social and nonsocial stimulations: A multivariate analysis of six inbred rat strains. *Behavior Genetics, 27*, 155–166.

Blanc, G., Herve, D., Simon, H., Lisoprawski, A., Glowinski, J., & Tassin, J. P. (1980). Response to stress of mesocortico-frontal dopaminergic neurones in rats after long-term isolation. *Nature, 284*, 265–267.

Blaschko, H. (1957). Metabolism and storage of biogenic amines. *Experientia, 13*, 12.

Bornstein, M. H. (1989). Sensitive periods in development: Structural characteristics and causal interpretations. *Psychological Bulletin, 105*, 179–197.

Bowlby, J. (1940). The influence of early environment in the development of neurosis and neurotic character. *International Journal of Psycho-Analysis, 21*, 154–178.

Bowling, S. L., & Bardo, M. T. (1994). Locomotor and rewarding effects of amphetamine in enriched, social, and isolate reared rats. *Pharmacology, Biochemistry and Behavior, 48*, 459–464.

Brainard, M. S., & Knudsen, E. I. (1998). Sensitive periods for visual calibration of the auditory space map in the barn owl optic tectum. *Journal of Neuroscience, 18*, 3929–3942.

Cairns, R. B. (1972). Fighting and punishment from a developmental perspective. In J. K. Cole & D. D. Jensen (Eds.), *Nebraska Symposium on motivation* (pp. 59–124). Lincoln: University of Nebraska Press.

Cairns, R. B. (1979). *Social development: The origins and plasticity of interchanges.* San Franscisco: Freeman.

Cairns, R. B., Gariépy, J. L., & Hood, K. E. (1990). Development, microevolution, and social behavior. *Psychological Review, 97,* 49–65.

Cairns, R. B., Hood, K. E., & Midlam, J. (1985). On fighting in mice: Is there a sensitive period for isolation effects? *Animal Behavior, 33,* 166–180.

Cairns, R. B., MacCombie, D. J., & Hood, K. E. (1983). A developmental–genetic analysis of aggressive behavior in mice: I. Behavioral outcomes. *Journal of Comparative Psychology, 97,* 69–89.

Carlsson, A., Lindqvist, M., Magnusson, T., & Waldeck, B. (1958). On the presence of 3-hydroxytyramine in brain. *Science, 127,* 471.

Carmichael, L. (1925). Heredity and environment: Are they antithetical? *Journal of Abnormal and Social Psychology, 20,* 245–260.

Charpier, S., & Deniau, J. M. (1997). In vivo activity-dependent plasticity at cortico-striatal connections: Evidence for physiological long-term potentiation. *Proceedings of the National Academy of Sciences, USA, 94,* 7036–7040.

Chesselet, M. F., Butler, A. K., Napieralski, J. A., Morehouse, W. V., Szele, F. G., & Uryu, K. (2000). Anatomical plasticity in the striatum during development and after lesions in the adult rat. In M. Baudry, J. L. Davis, & R. F. Thompson (Eds.), *Advances in synaptic plasticity* (pp. 167–195). Cambridge, MA: MIT Press.

Craig, W. (1914). Males doves reared in isolation. *Journal of Animal Behavior, 4,* 121–133.

Crair, M. C., Gillespie, D. C., & Stryker, M. P. (1998). The role of visual experience in the development of columns in cat visual cortex. *Science, 279,* 566–570.

Crawford, C. A., Rowlett, J. K., McDougall, S. A., & Bardo, M. T. (1994). Age-dependent differences in the rate of recovery of striatal dopamine D1 and D2 receptors after inactivation with EEDQ. *European Journal of Pharmacology, 252,* 225–231.

Crespi, F., Wright, I. K., & Mobius, C. (1992). Isolation rearing of rats alters release of 5-hydroxytryptamine and dopamine in the frontal cortex: An in vivo electrochemical study. *Experimental Brain Research, 88,* 495–501.

Cynader, M., Berman, N., & Hein, A. (1976). Recovery of function in cat visual cortex following prolonged deprivation. *Experimental Brain Research, 25,* 139–156.

Diamond, M. C., Krech, D., & Rozenzweig, M. R. (1964). The effects of an enriched environment on the histology of the rat cerebral cortex. *Journal of Comparative Neurology, 123,* 111–120.

Einon, D. F., Morgan, M. J., & Kibbler, C. C. (1978). Brief periods of socialization and later behavior in the rat. *Developmental Psychobiology, 11,* 213–225.

Finger, S., & Wolf, C. (1988). The 'Kennard effect' before Kennard. The early history of age and brain lesions. *Archives of Neurology, 45,* 1136–1142.

Foley, J. P. (1934). First year development of a rhesus monkey (Macaca mulatta) reared in isolation. *Journal of Genetic Psychology, 45,* 39–105.

Franklin, S. R., & Tang, A. H. (1995). Dopamine agonists facilitate footshock-elicited locomotion in rats, and suppress level-press responding for food. *Psychopharmacology, 121,* 480–484.

Fulford, A. J., & Marsden, C. A. (1998). Effect of isolation-rearing on conditioned dopamine release in vivo in the nucleus accumbens of the rat. *Journal of Neurochemistry, 70,* 384–390.

Fuller, J. L., & Clark, L. D. (1966). Genetic and treatment factors modifying the postisolation syndrome in dogs. *Journal of Comparative and Physiological Psychology, 61,* 251–257.

Gariépy, J.-L. (1995). The mediation of aggressive behavior in mice: A discussion of approach/withdrawal processes in social adaptations. In K. E. Hood, G. Greenberg, & E. Tobach (Eds.), *Behavioral development: Concepts of approach/withdrawal and integrative levels* (pp. 231–285). New York: Garland Publishing.

Gariépy, J. L., Gendreau, P. L., Cairns, R. B., & Lewis, M. H. (1998). D1 dopamine receptors and the reversal of isolation-induced behaviors in mice. *Behavioural Brain Research, 95,* 103–111.

Gariépy, J. L., Gendreau, P. L., Mailman, R. B., Tancer, M., & Lewis, M. H. (1995). Rearing conditions alter social reactivity and D1 dopamine receptors in high- and low-aggressive mice. *Pharmacology, Biochemistry and Behavior, 51,* 767–773.

Gariépy, J. L., Hood, K. E., & Cairns, R. B. (1988). A developmental–genetic analysis of aggressive behavior in mice (*Mus musculus*): III. Behavioral mediation by heightened reactivity or immobility? *Journal of Comparative Psychology, 102,* 392–399.

Gariépy, J.-L., Lewis, M. H., & Cairns, R. B. (1996). Genes, neurobiology, and aggression: Time frames and functions of social behaviors in adaptation. In M. Stoff & R. B. Cairns (Eds.), *Aggression and violence: Neurobiological, biosocial and genetic perspectives* (pp. 41–63). New York: Lawrence Erlbaum.

Gendreau, P. L., Gariépy, J. L., Petitto, J. M., & Lewis, M. H. (1997a). D1 dopamine receptor mediation of social and nonsocial emotional reactivity in mice: Effects of housing and strain difference in motor activity. *Behavioral Neuroscience, 111,* 424–434.

Gendreau, P. L., Petitto, J. M., Gariépy, J. L., & Lewis, M. H. (1998). D2-like dopamine receptor mediation of social–emotional reactivity in a mouse model of anxiety: Strain and experience effects. *Neuropsychopharmacology, 18,* 210–221.

Gendreau, P. L., Petitto, J. M., Petrova, A., Gariépy, J., & Lewis, M. H. (2000). D(3) and D(2) dopamine receptor agonists differentially modulate isolation-induced social-emotional reactivity in mice. *Behavioural Brain Research, 114,* 107–117.

Gendreau, P. L., Petitto, J. M., Schnauss, R., Frantz, K. J., Van Hartesveldt, C., Gariépy, J. L., et al. (1997b). Effects of the putative dopamine D3 receptor antagonist PNU 99194A on motor behavior and emotional reactivity in C57BL/6J mice. *European Journal of Pharmacology, 337,* 147–155.

Gluck, J. P., & Sackett, G. P. (1974). Frustration and self-aggression in social isolate rhesus monkeys. *Journal of Adolescence, 83,* 331–334.

Goosen, C. (1981). Abnormal behavior patterns in rhesus monkeys: Symptoms of mental disease. *Biological Psychiatry, 16,* 697–716.

Greenough, W. T. (1988). The turned-on brain: Developmental and adult responses to the demands of information storage. In S. C. Easter, K. F. Barald, & B. M. Carlson (Eds.), *From message to mind: Directions in developmental neurobiology* (pp. 288–302). Sunderland, MA: Sinauer Associates.

Greenough, W. T., Black, J. E., & Wallace, C. S. (1987). Experience and brain development. *Child Development, 58*, 539–559.

Guisado, E., Fernandez-Tome, P., Garzon, J., & Del Rio, J. (1980). Increased dopamine receptor binding in the striatum of rats after long-term isolation. *European Journal of Pharmacology, 65*, 463–464.

Hall, F. S. (1998). Social deprivation of neonatal, adolescent, and adult rats has distinct neurochemical and behavioral consequences. *Critical Review in Neurobiology, 12*, 129–162.

Hall, F. S., Fong, G. W., Ghaed, S., & Pert, A. (2001). Locomotor-stimulating effects of indirect dopamine agonists are attenuated in Fawn hooded rats independent of postweaning social experience. *Pharmacology, Biochemistry and Behavior, 69*, 519–526.

Hall, F. S., Wilkinson, L. S., Humby, T., Inglis, W., Kendall, D. A., Marsden, C. A. et al. (1998). Isolation rearing in rats: Pre- and postsynaptic changes in striatal dopaminergic systems. *Pharmacology, Biochemistry and Behavior, 59*, 859–872.

Hall, F. S., Wilkinson, L. S., Humby, T., & Robbins, T. W. (1999). Maternal deprivation of neonatal rats produces enduring changes in dopamine function. *Synapse, 32*, 37–43.

Harlow, H. F., Dodsworth, R. O., & Harlow, M. K. (1965). Total social isolation in monkeys. *Proceedings of the National Academy of Sciences, USA, 54*, 90–97.

Harlow, H. F., & Suomi, S. J. (1971). Social recovery by isolation-reared monkeys. *Proceedings of the National Academy of Sciences, USA, 68*, 1534–1538.

Harlow, H. F., & Suomi, S. J. (1974). Induced depression in monkeys. *Behavioral Biology, 12*, 273–296.

Harvey, D. C., Lacan, G., Tanious, S. P., & Melega, W. P. (2000). Recovery from methamphetamine induced long-term nigrostriatal dopaminergic deficits without substantia nigra cell loss. *Brain Research, 871*, 259–270.

Hatch, A. M., Wiberg, G. S., Zawidzka, Z., Cann, M., Airth, J. M., & Grice, H. C. (1965). Isolation syndrome in the rat. *Toxicology and Applied Pharmacology, 7*, 737–745.

Heidbreder, C. A., Weiss, I. C., Domeney, A. M., Pryce, C., Homberg, J., Hedou, G., et al. (2000). Behavioral, neurochemical and endocrinological characterization of the early social isolation syndrome. *Neuroscience, 100*, 749–768.

Hess, E. J., Albers, L. J., Le, H., & Creese, I. (1986). Effects of chronic SCH23390 treatment on the biochemical and behavioral properties of D1 and D2 dopamine receptors: Potentiated behavioral responses to a D2 dopamine agonist after selective D1 dopamine receptor upregulation. *Journal of Pharmacology and Experimental Therapeutics, 238*, 846–854.

Hinde, R. A., & Spencer-Booth, Y. (1971). Effects of brief separation from mother on rhesus monkeys. *Science, 173*, 111–118.

Hofer, M. A. (1975). Survival and recovery of physiologic functions after early maternal separation in rats. *Physiology and Behavior, 15*, 475–480.

Hubel, D. H., & Wiesel, T. N. (1970). The period of susceptibility to the physiological effects of unilateral eye closure in kittens. *Journal of Physiology, 206*, 419–436.

Hyttel, J. (1989). Parallel decrease in the density of dopamine D1 and D2 receptors in corpus striatum of rats from 3 to 25 months of age. *Pharmacology and Toxicology, 64*, 55–57.

James, W. (1892). In G. Allport (Ed.), *Psychology: The briefer course*. New York: Harper & Brothers.

Jones, G. H., Hernandez, T. D., Kendall, D. A., Marsden, C. A., & Robbins, T. W. (1992). Dopaminergic and serotonergic function following isolation rearing in rats: Study of behavioural responses and postmortem and in vivo neurochemistry. *Pharmacology, Biochemistry and Behavior, 43*, 17–35.

Jones, G. H., Marsden, C. A., & Robbins, T. W. (1990). Increased sensitivity to amphetamine and reward-related stimuli following social isolation in rats: Possible disruption of dopamine-dependent mechanisms of the nucleus accumbens. *Psychopharmacology, 102*, 364–372.

Kaufman, I. C., & Rosenblum, L. A. (1967). Depression in infant monkeys separated from their mothers. *Science, 155*, 1030–1031.

Kehoe, P., Shoemaker, W. J., Arons, C., Triano, L., & Suresh, G. (1998). Repeated isolation stress in the neonatal rat: Relation to brain dopamine systems in the 10-day-old rat. *Behavioral Neuroscience, 112*, 1466–1474.

Kim, D. S., Szczypka, M. S., & Palmiter, R. D. (2000). Dopamine-deficient mice are hypersensitive to dopamine receptor agonists. *Journal of Neuroscience, 20*, 4405–4413.

Kolb, B., Gibb, R., & Gorny, G. (2000). Cortical plasticity and the development of behavior after early frontal cortical injury. *Developmental Neuropsychology, 18*, 423–444.

Kral, A., Hartmann, R., Tillein, J., Heid, S., & Klinke, R. (2001). Delayed maturation and sensitive periods in the auditory cortex. *Audiology and Neurootology, 6*, 346–362.

Krech, D., Rozenzweig, M. R., & Bennett, E. L. (1960). Effects of environmental complexity and training on brain chemistry. *Journal of Comparative Physiology and Psychology, 53*, 509–519.

Krsiak, M. (1975). Timid singly-housed mice: Their value in prediction of psychotropic activity of drugs. *British Journal of Pharmacology, 55*, 141–150.

Lagerspetz, K. Y., Tirri, R., & Lagerspetz, K. M. (1968). Neurochemical and endocrinological studies of mice selectively bred for aggressiveness. *Scandinavian Journal of Psychology, 9*, 157–160.

LaHoste, G. J., & Marshall, J. F. (1992). Dopamine supersensitivity and D1/D2 synergism are unrelated to changes in striatal receptor density. *Synapse, 12*, 14–26.

Le Moal, M., & Simon, H. (1991). Mesocorticolimbic dopaminergic network: Functional and regulatory roles. *Physiological Reviews, 71*, 155–234.

Lewis, M. H., Gariépy, J. L., Gendreau, P. L., Nichols, D. E., & Mailman, R. B. (1994). Social reactivity and D1 dopamine receptors: Studies in mice selectively bred for high and low levels of aggression. *Neuropsychopharmacology, 10*, 115–122.

Lewis, M. H., Gluck, J. P., Beauchamp, A. J., Keresztury, M. F., & Mailman, R. B. (1990). Long-term effects of early social isolation in *Macaca mulatta*: Changes in dopamine receptor function following apomorphine challenge. *Brain Research, 513*, 67–73.

Liu, D., Diorio, J., Day, J. C., Francis, D. D., & Meaney, M. J. (2000). Maternal care, hippocampal synaptogenesis and cognitive development in rats. *Nature Neuroscience, 3*, 799–806.

Lorenz, K. (1981). *The foundations of ethology.* New York: Simon and Schuster.

Martin, L. J., Spicer, D. M., Lewis, M. H., Gluck, J. P., & Cork, L. C. (1991). Social deprivation of infant rhesus monkeys alters the chemoarchitecture of the brain: I. Subcortical regions. *Journal of Neuroscience, 11,* 3344–3358.

Mason, W. A., & Berkson, G. (1975). Effects of maternal mobility on the development of rocking and other behaviors in rhesus monkeys: A study with artificial mothers. *Developmental Psychobiology, 8,* 197–211.

Mason, W. A., & Sponholz, R. R. (1963). Behavior of rhesus monkeys raised in isolation. *Journal of Psychiatric Research, 1,* 299–306.

Matthews, K., Dalley, J. W., Matthews, C., Tsai, T. H., & Robbins, T. W. (2001). Periodic maternal separation of neonatal rats produces region- and gender-specific effects on biogenic amine content in postmortem adult brain. *Synapse, 40,* 1–10.

McCulloch, T. L., & Haselrud, G. M. (1939). Development of an infant chimpanzee during her first year. *Journal of Comparative Psychology, 28,* 437–445.

McMillen, B. A., DaVanzo, E. A., Song, A. H., Scott, S. M., & Rodriguez, M. E. (1989). Effects of classical and atypical antipsychotic drugs on isolation-induced aggression in male mice. *European Journal of Pharmacology, 160,* 149–153.

Meaney, M. J., Brake, W., & Gratton, A. (2002). Environmental regulation of the development of mesolimbic dopamine systems: A neurobiological mechanism for vulnerability to drug abuse? *Psychoneuroendocrinology, 27,* 127–138.

Meisami, E., & Mousavi, R. (1981). Lasting effects of early olfactory deprivation on the growth, DNA, RNA and protein content, and Na-K-ATPase and AchE activity of the rat olfactory bulb. *Brain Research, 254,* 217–229.

Miczek, K. A., DeBold, J. F., & van Erp, A. M. (1994). Neuropharmacological characteristics of individual differences in alcohol effects on aggression in rodents and primates. *Behavioral Pharmacology, 5,* 407–421.

Miura, H., Qiao, H., & Ohta, T. (2002). Attenuating effects of the isolated rearing condition on increased brain serotonin and dopamine turnover elicited by novelty stress. *Brain Research, 926,* 10–17.

Morelli, M., Mennini, T., Cagnotto, A., Toffano, G., & Di Chiara, G. (1990). Quantitative autoradiographical analysis of the age-related modulation of central dopamine D1 and D2 receptors. *Neuroscience, 36,* 403–410.

Murrin, L. C., & Zeng, W. Y. (1990). Ontogeny of dopamine D1 receptors in rat forebrain: A quantitative autoradiographic study. *Brain Research. Developmental Brain Research, 57,* 7–13.

Myslivecek, J., & Hassmannova, J. (1979). Ontogeny of active avoidance in the rat: Learning and memory. *Developmental Psychobiology, 12,* 169–186.

O'Connor, T. G., Rutter, M., Beckett, C., Keaveney, L., & Kreppner, J. M. (2000). The effects of global severe privation on cognitive competence: Extension and longitudinal follow-up. English and Romanian Adoptees Study Team. *Child Development, 71,* 376–390.

Oehler, J., Jahkel, M., & Schmidt, J. (1987). Neuronal transmitter sensitivity after social isolation in rats. *Physiology and Behavior, 41,* 187–191.

Pellis, S. M., & Pasztor, T. J. (1999). The developmental onset of a rudimentary form of play fighting in C57 mice. *Developmental Psychobiology, 34,* 175–182.

Phillips, G. D., Howes, S. R., Whitelaw, R. B., Wilkinson, L. S., Robbins, T. W., & Everitt, B. J. (1994). Isolation rearing enhances the locomotor response to cocaine and a novel environment, but impairs the intravenous self-administration of cocaine. _Psychopharmacology, 115_, 407–418.

Rice, D., & Barone S Jr (2000). Critical periods of vulnerability for the developing nervous system: Evidence from humans and animal models. _Environmental Health Perspectives, 108 (Suppl 3)_, 511–533.

Rilke, O., Jahkel, M., & Oehler, J. (1998). Dopaminergic parameters during social isolation in low- and high-active mice. _Pharmacology, Biochemistry and Behavior, 60_, 499–505.

Rilke, O., May, T., Oehler, J., & Wolffgramm, J. (1995). Influences of housing conditions and ethanol intake on binding characteristics of D2, 5-HT1A, and benzodiazepine receptors of rats. _Pharmacology, Biochemistry and Behavior, 52_, 23–28.

Robbins, T. W., Jones, G. H., & Wilkinson, L. S. (1996). Behavioural and neurochemical effects of early social deprivation in the rat. _Journal of Psychopharmacology, 10_, 39–47.

Rodgers, R. J., & Cole, J. C. (1993). Influence of social isolation, gender, strain, and prior novelty on plus-maze behaviour in mice. _Physiology and Behavior, 54_, 729–736.

Rots, N. Y., de Jong, J., Workel, J. O., Levine, S., Cools, A. R., & De Kloet, E. R. (1996). Neonatal maternally deprived rats have as adults elevated basal pituitary–adrenal activity and enhanced susceptibility to apomorphine. _Journal of Neuroendocrinology, 8_, 501–506.

Rozenzweig, M. R., Krech, D., Bennett, E. L., & Diamond, M. C. (1962). Effects of enviromental compexity and training on brain chemistry and anatomy. _Journal of Comparative Physiology and Psychology, 55_, 429–437.

Salzen, E. A., & Meyer, C. C. (1967). Imprinting: Reversal of a preference established during the critical period. _Nature, 215_, 785–786.

Sanchez, M. M., Ladd, C. O., & Plotsky, P. M. (2001). Early adverse experience as a developmental risk factor for later psychopathology: Evidence from rodent and primate models. _Development and Psychopathology, 13_, 419–449.

Scott, J. P. (1966). Agonistic behavior of mice and rats: A review. _American Zoology, 6_, 683–701.

Seeman, P., Bzowej, N. H., Guan, H. C., Bergeron, C., Becker, L. E., Reynolds, G. P., et al. (1987). Human brain dopamine receptors in children and aging adults. _Synapse, 1_, 399–404.

Sokoloff, P., Giros, B., Martres, M. P., Bouthenet, M. L., & Schwartz, J. C. (1990). Molecular cloning and characterization of a novel dopamine receptor (D3) as a target for neuroleptics. _Nature, 347_, 146–151.

Spitz, R. A., (1945). Hospitalism: An inquiry into the genesis of psychiatric conditions in early childhood. _Psychoanalytic Study of the Child, 1_, 53–74.

Spitz, R. A., & Wolf, K. M. (1946). Anaclitic depression: An inquiry into the genesis of psychiatric conditions in early childhood, II. _Psychoanalytic Study of the Child, 2_, 313–342.

Stern, E. A., Maravall, M., & Svoboda, K. (2001). Rapid development and plasticity of layer 2/3 maps in rat barrel cortex in vivo. _Neuron, 31_, 305–315.

Stone, C. P. (1926). The initial copulatory response of female rats reared in isolation from the age of 20 days to age of puberty. *Journal of Comparative Psychology, 6,* 78–83.

Sugahara, M., & Shiraishi, H. (1998). Synaptic density of the prefrontal cortex regulated by dopamine instead of serotonin in rats. *Brain Research, 814,* 143–156.

Suomi, S. J., & Harlow, H. F. (1972). Social rehabilitation of isolate-reared monkeys. *Developmental Psychology, 6,* 487–496.

Tancer, M. E, Gariépy, J.-L., Mayleben, M. A., Petitto, J. M., & Lewis, M. H. (1992). *NC100 mice: A putative animal model for social phobia.* Washington, DC: Society of Biological Psychiatry.

Tarazi, F. I., & Baldessarini, R. J. (2000). Comparative postnatal development of dopamine D(1), D(2) and D(4) receptors in rat forebrain. *International Journal of Developmental Neuroscience, 18,* 29–37.

Tarazi, F. I., Tomasini, E. C., & Baldessarini, R. J. (1998). Postnatal development of dopamine D4-like receptors in rat forebrain regions: Comparison with D2-like receptors. *Brain Research. Developmental Brain Research, 110,* 227–233.

Teicher, M. H., Andersen, S. L., & Hostetter, J. C., Jr. (1995). Evidence for dopamine receptor pruning between adolescence and adulthood in striatum but not nucleus accumbens. *Brain Research. Developmental Brain Research, 89,* 167–172.

Ungerstedt, U., Ljungberg, T., Hoffer, B., & Siggins, G. (1975). Dopaminergic supersensitivity in the striatum. *Advances in Neurology, 9,* 57–65.

Valzelli, L. (1973). The "isolation syndrome" in mice. *Psychopharmacologia, 31,* 305–320.

van Oers, H. J., De Kloet, E. R., & Levine, S. (1997). Persistent, but paradoxical, effects on HPA regulation of infants maternally deprived at different ages. *Stress, 1,* 249–262.

van Oers, H. J., De Kloet, E. R., & Levine, S. (1999). Persistent effects of maternal deprivation on HPA regulation can be reversed by feeding and stroking, but not by dexamethasone. *Journal of Neuroendocrinology, 11,* 581–588.

Van Tol, H. H., Bunzow, J. R., Guan, H. C., Sunahara, R. K., Seeman, P., Niznik, H. B., et al. (1991). Cloning of the gene for a human dopamine D4 receptor with high affinity for the antipsychotic clozapine. *Nature, 350,* 610–614.

Waddington, J. L., & Daly, S. A. (1993). Regulation of unconditioned motor behaviour by D1:D2 interactions. In J. L.Waddington (Ed.), *D1:D2 dopamine receptor interactions* (pp. 51–78). San Diego: Academic Press.

Weihmuller, F. B., & Bruno, J. P. (1989). Age-dependent plasticity in the dopaminergic control of sensorimotor development. *Behavioural Brain Research, 35,* 95–109.

Weihmuller, F. B., Bruno, J. P., Neff, N. H., & Hadjiconstantinou, M. (1990). Dopamine receptor plasticity following MPTP-induced nigrostriatal lesions in the mouse. *European Journal of Pharmacology, 180,* 369–372.

Weinstock, M., Speiser, Z., & Ashkenazi, R. (1978). Changes in brain catecholamine turnover and receptor sensitivity induced by social deprivation in rats. *Psychopharmacology, 56,* 205–209.

Weiss, I. C., Domeney, A. M., Heidbreder, C. A., Moreau, J. L., & Feldon, J. (2001). Early social isolation, but not maternal separation, affects behavioral sensitization to amphetamine in male and female adult rats. *Pharmacology, Biochemistry and Behavior, 70,* 397–409.

Wiesel, T. N., & Hubel, D. H. (1965). Comparison of the effects of unilateral and bilateral eye closure on cortical unit responses in kittens. *Journal of Neuroscience, 28*, 1029–1040.

Wilmot, C. A., Vanderwende, C., & Spoerlein, M. T. (1986). Behavioral and biochemical studies of dopamine receptor sensitivity in differentially housed mice. *Psychopharmacology, 89*, 364–369.

4

Animal Studies on Inappropriate Aggressive Behavior Following Stress and Alcohol Exposure in Adolescence

Craig F. Ferris

University of Massachusetts Medical School

INTRODUCTION

Violence is a national health problem. Understanding the etiology and pathophysiology that predispose certain individuals to behave in an inappropriate, excessively aggressive way is critical to reducing the incidence of personal violence in the United States. It is clear that traumatic events in early life make children more vulnerable to future stressors and enhance the probability of antisocial behaviors (Luntz & Widom, 1994). Children exposed to early stressful environments and maltreatment prior to kindergarten are more aggressive and have more social problems than control children (Lansford et al., 2002; Sanson, Smart, Prior, & Oberhlaid, 1993). Children exposed to early physical and emotional neglect may develop learning patterns that affect the interpretation of hostile social information, resulting in inappropriate aggressive behavior and general conduct disorder (Dodge, Bates, & Pettit, 1990). Furthermore, children with conduct problems are at risk for alcohol and drug abuse, a predisposition exacerbated by the fact that alcoholism and drug-taking foster antisocial behaviors and violence (Ito, Miller, & Pollock, 1996).

Although psychosocial developmental studies on children have provided insight into the long-term behavioral consequences of early abuse and alcoholism, the biological changes that accompany exposure to these risk factors are not well understood. For ethical reasons, there can be no prospective human studies looking at changes in neurobiology and neuroendocrinology in response to early life traumas. Therefore, biological data must be gleaned from animal studies that try to model certain aspects of the human condition. For example, studies on rodents and monkeys indicate stress and exposure to alcohol during the prenatal and postnatal periods can affect aggressive behavior later in life. Prenatal alcohol exposure increases aggressive behavior in rats (Royalty, 1990). Similarly, male

and female rats exposed to unpredictable, mild physical stress during the
first week of life show enhanced aggressive behavior as adults (Gonzalez
Jatuff, Berastegui, Rodriguez, & Rodriguez Echandia, 1999). These findings
in rodents translate to nonhuman primates, as rhesus monkeys exposed
to the stressors of noise and alcohol in utero display abnormal agonistic
behaviors as adolescents and adults under stressful situations such as
group formation (Schneider, Moore, Kraimer, Roberts, & DeJesus, 2002).
Rhesus monkeys isolated from their mother in early life show monoamine
deficits, altered regulation of the stress response and a dysfunctional
autonomic nervous system as young adults (Clarke, 1993; Higley, Suomi,
& Linnoila, 1991; Kraemer & Clarke, 1990). Often their aggressive behavior is unpredictable, inappropriate, and excessive (Harlow, Harlow,
& Suomi, 1971). Self-injurious behavior is not uncommon (Kraemer &
Clarke, 1990).

Unlike the perinatal and early childhood periods, there is little clinical
and preclinical information on the long-term neurobiological and behavioral consequences of stress during the *peripubertal period* or "adolescence."
The 1978 study of national child abuse and neglect by the American Humane Association reported a high incidence of abuse toward adolescents
between the ages 12 and 17; in fact, data indicate the incidence of adolescent abuse equals or exceeds that of all other age groups (Lourie, 1979;
Schellenbach & Guerney, 1987). Indeed, adolescents have the highest risk of
nonfatal assault of any other age group (U.S. Department of Justice, 1992).
Whereas much attention has been paid to victimization of infants and children, less is known about the behavioral and biological consequences of
abuse during adolescence.

The work discussed here examines the long-term changes in neurobiology and behavior in response to social subjugation and exposure to alcohol in an animal model of adolescence. The resident/intruder paradigm
of offensive aggression is used to socially subjugate adolescent Syrian
golden hamsters (*Mesocrecitus auratus*) and later in adulthood to assess
their agonistic behavior in the context of social conflict. Moreover, the
golden hamster is one of only a few mammals that will spontaneously
drink alcohol after weaning. In this model, adolescent hamsters are allowed to voluntarily consume alcohol with and without the added risk
factor of unpredictable and uncontrollable electrical shock as a stressor. At the end of adolescence, exposure to alcohol and shock stress is
stopped and animals are tested for aggression as young adults in the
resident/intruder paradigm. In particular, this work focuses on (1) the
interaction of serotonin (5-HT) and vasopressin (VP) in the control of
aggression, and (2) how social subjugation and exposure to alcohol in
adolescence alter brain plasticity and behavior in the context of 5-HT
and VP.

USING HAMSTERS TO STUDY THE EFFECTS OF STRESS AND ALCOHOL EXPOSURE IN ADOLESCENCE

In humans, adolescence is defined as a period of pronounced physical, cognitive, and emotional growth. This period usually begins just before puberty and ends in early adulthood with sexual maturity, social awareness, and independence (Ingersoll, 1992). In golden hamsters, there is a developmental period analogous to adolescence. In the wild, hamsters wean around postnatal day 25 (P-25), leave the home nest, forage on their own, establish nest sites, and defend their territory (Dieterlen, 1959; Schoenfeld & Leonard, 1985). Hamsters can begin to establish dominance hierarchies as early as P-35 (Whitsett, 1975) and have a minimal breeding age of 42 days (Festing, 1958). Androgen levels start to rise dramatically between P-28 and P-35 (Miller, Whitsett, Vandenbergh, & Colby, 1977; Vomachka & Greenwald, 1979). Thus between P-25 and P-42, as hamsters achieve independence from the maternal nest, they double their weight and size, reach full sexual maturity and reproductive competence, and establish social relationships. This period between P-25 and P-42 will be designated as adolescence in golden hamsters. Since hamsters in the wild are solitary and live in their own isolated burrows (Dieterlen, 1959; Schoenfeld & Leonard, 1985), animals studied in the laboratory setting can be individually housed after weaning, an experimental feature that eliminates the confounding variable of group interactions. Another added benefit to studying hamsters is their taste for alcohol. Unlike most other mammals, hamsters will readily drink alcohol in a free-choice paradigm (Arvola & Forsander, 1961). Immediately after weaning and following isolation in their own nest site on P-25, adolescent hamsters will drink alcohol in addition to water and food ad libitum (Ferris, Shtiegman, & King, 1998).

The resident/intruder model of aggression relies on the motivation of a resident animal to chase and fight intruders coming into their territory (Miczek, 1974). Residents will show highly specific attack patterns characteristic of offensive aggression, i.e., the initiation of attacks and bites, toward intruders. Golden hamsters are particularly amenable to the study of agonistic behavior because they show a high level of spontaneous aggression toward conspecifics (Grant & MacKintosh, 1963; Lerwill & Makings, 1971). The isolation of hamsters into individual cages as noted earlier only enhances their aggression toward an intruder (Brain, 1972; Payne, 1973). Hamsters are nocturnal and their aggression is greatest during the dark phase of the circadian cycle (Landau, 1975; Lerwill & Makings, 1971). For this reason they are maintained on a reverse light:dark cycle, and their behavior is scored and filmed under the illumination of a red light.

NEUROCHEMICAL CONTROL OF AGGRESSION

Serotonin

Numerous neurochemical signals have been implicated in the facilitation and inhibition of aggressive behavior (for review, see Eichelman 1990). One in particular, serotonin (5-HT), appears to have a seminal role in reducing aggression in all mammals studied including humans (Coccaro & Kavoussi, 1997; Cologer-Clifford, Simon, Richter, Smoluk, & Lu, 1999; Dalta, Miitra, & Bhaattacharya, 1991; Delville, Mansour, & Ferris, 1995; Ferris et al., 1997; Molina, Ciesielski, Gobailles, Insel, & Mandel, 1987; Ogren, Holm, Renyi, & Ross, 1980; Olivier, Mos, Van Der Heyden, & Hartog, 1989; Sanchez & Hyttel, 1994; Villalba, Boyle, Caliguri, & De Vries, 1997). For example, elevation in brain levels of serotonin following treatment with serotonin reuptake inhibitors such as fluoxetine (Prozac) reduce multiple measures of aggression in a wide range of animals. Mice lacking the 5-HT transporter gene have reduced aggression and less activity overall than control mice (Holmes, Murphy, & Crawley, 2002). Conversely, male rats depleted of brain serotonin by treatment with neurotoxins are highly aggressive and assume dominant positions when housed with control animals (Ellison 1976) and enhanced biting attacks toward intruders (Vergnes, Depaulis, Boehrer, & Kempf, 1988). Serotonin appears to reduce aggression by binding to 5-HT$_{1A}$ and 5-HT$_{1B}$ receptors. Several 5-HT$_{1A}$ and 5-HT$_{1B}$ receptor agonists produce a dose-dependent decrease in aggressive behavior (Sijbesma et al., 1991). Mutant mice lacking the 5-HT$_{1B}$ receptor (Saudou et al., 1994) are exceedingly aggressive toward intruders and appear to be more impulsive (Bouwknecht et al., 2001). Mice and rats bred for high and low aggressive behavior show phenotypic differences in 5-HT$_{1A}$ receptors (Korte et al., 1996; van der Vegt et al., 2001).

The relationship between low 5-HT function and high impulsivity has also been reported in nonhuman primates (Mehlman et al., 1994). Adolescent monkeys with the highest aggression and greatest risk taking show the lowest levels of serotonin metabolite 5-hydroxyindoleacetic acid (5-HIAA) concentrations in the CSF. Only monkeys with the most severe forms of aggression and risk taking are correlated with low levels of 5-HIAA metabolite in CSF. These same high-aggression, high-risk phenotypes were discovered to have a variation in the 5-HT transporter associated with decreased serotonergic function (Bennett et al., 2002). In vervet monkeys, impulsivity in response to unfamiliar male intruders is inversely correlated with 5-HIAA levels in cerebrospinal fluid (Fairbanks, Melega, Jorgensen, Kaplan, & McGuire, 2001). Treatment with a 5-HT reuptake inhibitor reduces the impulsivity of male vervets toward intruders.

There is compelling evidence from human studies demonstrating an inverse relation between 5-HT function and impulsivity and aggression. The metabolite of 5-HT, 5-HIAA, is lower in cerebrospinal fluid in violent men as compared to controls (Brown et al., 1982; Linnoila et al., 1983). Children with conduct disorder and operational defiant disorder have low 5-HIAA as compared to other control adolescents (Kruesi, Rapoport, Hamburger, Hibbs, & Potter, 1990). Reduced 5-HT function is inversely correlated with impulsivity in personality disorder adults (Dolan, Anderson, & Deakin, 2001). Treatment with 5-HT reuptake inhibitors reduces inappropriate aggressive behavior in children (Zubieta & Alessi, 1992) and adults with personality disorders characterized by a history of excessive aggressive behavior (Coccaro, Astill, Herbert, & Schut, 1990). Adult males with a history of conduct disorder show reduced measures of aggression and impulsivity when treated with a 5HT reuptake inhibitor or the 5HT releasing agent D-fenfluramine (Cherek and Lane, 2001; Cherek, Lane, Pietras, & Steinberg, 2002).

Vasopressin

Studies on rodents indicate a role for vasopressin (VP) in the modulation of aggression. In hamsters, a VP receptor antagonist, microinjected into the anterior hypothalamus, causes a dose-dependent inhibition of aggression of a resident male toward an intruder (Ferris & Potegal, 1988). Treatment with VP receptor antagonist prolongs the latency to bite an intruder and reduces the number of bites, but does not alter other social or appetitive behaviors. Conversely, microinjection of VP into the anterior hypothalamus of resident hamsters significantly increases the number of biting attacks on intruders (Ferris et al., 1997). Vasopressin receptor antagonist also blocks aggression associated with the development of dominant/subordinate relationships (Potegal, & Ferris, 1990). Treating adolescent hamsters with anabolic steroids increases the density of VP immunoreactive fibers and neuropeptide content in the anterior hypothalamus and enhances VP-mediated aggression as adults (Harrison, Connor, Nowak, Nash, & Melloni, 2000). The ability of VP to modulate offensive aggression is not limited to the anterior hypothalamus. Microinjecting VP into the ventrolateral hypothalamus of the hamster facilitates offensive aggression (Delville et al., 1995). Infusion of VP into the amygdala or lateral septum facilitates offensive aggression in castrated rats (Koolhaas, Moor, Hiemstra, & Bohus, 1991; Koolhaas, Van den Brink, Roozendal, & Boorsma, 1990). In prairie voles, vasopressin injections with the cerebral ventricles increase aggressive behavior (Winslow, Hastings, Carter, Harbaugh, & Insel, 1993), while early postnatal exposure to VP increases aggressive behavior in adult male prairie voles (Stribley & Carter, 1999) In humans and in rats, high indexes of aggressivity correlate with high concentrations of VP in cerebrospinal fluid (Cocarro et al., 1998; Haller et al., 1996). The ability of VP to affect aggression at multiple sites in the CNS and in various mammalian species is evidence that this neurochemical system may have a broad physiological role enhancing arousal and attack behavior during agonistic interactions.

VASOPRESSIN/SEROTONIN INTERACTIONS

Defining the mechanisms and anatomical substrates underlying interactions between functionally opposed neurotransmitter systems is critical for understanding and treating inappropriate aggressive behavior. One working hypothesis is that VP promotes aggression and dominant behavior by enhancing the activity of the neural network controlling agonistic behavior that is normally restrained by 5-HT (Delville, Mansour, & Ferris, 1996; Ferris, 1996, 2000; Ferris et al., 1997; Ferris, Stolberg, & Delville, 1999). The anterior hypothalamus, the primary site of VP regulation of aggression, has a high density of 5-HT binding sites and receives a dense innervation of 5-HT fibers and terminals. The VP neurons in the anterior hypothalamus implicated in the control of aggression appear to be preferentially innervated by 5-HT. Intraperitoneal injection of fluoxetine blocks aggression facilitated by the microinjection of VP in the hypothalamus. Fluoxetine elevates 5-HT and reduces VP levels in hypothalamic tissue in hamsters (Ferris, 1996) and in rats (Altemus, Cizza, & Gold, 1992). Kia and coworkers (1996) reported intense immunocytochemical staining for 5-HT$_{1A}$ receptors in the VP system of rats, supporting the notion that activation of 5-HT$_{1A}$ receptors can influence the activity of VP neurons. However, the present data suggest 5-HT can also block the activity of VP following its release in the hypothalamus as evidenced by the dose-dependent diminution of aggression with injections combining VP and 5-HT$_{1A}$ receptor agonist. Enhanced aggression caused by activation of AVP V$_{1A}$ receptors in the hypothalamus is suppressed by the simultaneous activation of 5-HT$_{1A}$ receptors in the same site. It is not clear whether a common neuronal phenotype in the hypothalamus shares both receptor subtypes, or VP and 5-HT act on separate neurons in the hypothalamus.

These preclinical studies examining the interaction between VP and 5-HT are particularly relevant since Cocarro and coworkers (1996) reported a similar reciprocal relationship in human studies. Personality disordered subjects with a history of fighting and assault show a negative correlation for prolactin release in response to D-fenfluramine challenge, indication of a hyposensitive 5-HT system. Moreover, these same subjects show a positive correlation between CSF levels of VP and aggression. Thus, in humans, a hyposensitive 5-HT system may result in enhanced CNS levels of VP and the facilitation of aggressive behavior.

SOCIAL SUBJUGATION IN ADULT ANIMALS

Social subjugation is a very significant and natural stressor in the animal kingdom. Animals defeated and subjugated during establishment of dominance heirarchies or territorial encounters can be highly submissive in future agonistic interactions. For example, defeated mice display less aggression and more submissive behavior (Frishknecht, Siegfreid, & Waser, 1982; Williams & Lierle, 1988). Rats consistently defeated by more aggressive conspecifics show a behavioral inhibition characterized by less social initiative and offensive aggression, as well as an increase in defensive behavior (Van de Poll, DeJonge, Van Oyen, & Van Pelt, 1982). Repeatedly defeated male hamsters respond in a submissive manner when confronted by a nonaggressive intruder (Potegal, Huhman, Moore, & Meyerhoff, 1993). However, following repeated defeat by a dominant conspecific, a resident hamster will be defensive or fearful of equal-sized nonaggressive intruders (Potegal et al., 1993). The generalization of submissive behavior toward nonthreatening, novel stimulus animals is an example of "conditioned defeat" (Potegal et al., 1993). Conditioned defeat in adult hamsters is not permanent, as the flight and defensive behaviors disappear over many days. This disappearance of overt conditioned defeat appears time-dependent and not a function of repeated exposure to novel nonaggressive intruders. Adult male rhesus monkeys will fight for dominance status when forming a social group with breeding females. When two such established groups are brought together to form one, the dominant or alpha male from each will fight for dominance. The loser is relegated to the lowest social rank in the male hierarchy, displaying highly submissive behavior (Rose, Berstein, & Gordon, 1975). Chronic social subjugation in male talapoin monkeys reduces social activity and sexual behavior even in the absence of dominant conspecifics (Eberhart, Yodyingyuad, & Keverne, 1985).

Could social subjugation, that is, repeated defeat by more aggressive opponents, result in changes in the VP and 5-HT systems that could predispose subjugated animals to be less aggressive in subsequent social encounters? In support of this notion are reports that the development of submissive behavior is accompanied by an increase in the activity of the 5-HT system (Yodyingyuad, de la Riva, Abbott, Herbert, & Keverne, 1985). Stress is associated with an activation of 5-HT release and/or turn over in the brain (Adell, Garcia-Marquez, Armario, & Gelpi, 1988; Blanchard, Sakai, McEwen, Weiss, & Blanchard, 1993; De Souza & Van Loon, 1986). Conversely the increase in the density of 5-HT immunoreactive boutons in the anterior hypothalamus (Delville, Melloni, & Ferris, 1998) may suggest an increased release of this neurochemical signal. With more 5-HT release there is a downregulation of the 5-HT_{1A} receptor. The downregulation of serotonin receptors in response to social stress has been reported previously (Bolanos-Jimenez et al., 1995; McKittrick, Blanchard, Blanchard,

McEwen, & Sakai, 1995). In addition, a decrease in VP immunoreactivity has been observed within select populations of neurons in the hypothalamus in continuously defeated, castrated hamsters (Ferris, Axelsor, Martin, & Roberge, 1989). This depletion of VP immunoreactivity in subjugated animals is associated with a decrease in fighting. However, changes in the VP system were only observed in subjugated animals; no effect was recorded in dominant animals.

SOCIAL SUBJUGATION IN ADOLESCENCE

Recent studies on social subjugation in adolescent hamsters revealed unique neurobiological and behavioral outcomes as compared to adult animals (Delville et al., 1998). Male golden hamsters were weaned at P-25, were exposed daily to aggressive adults from P-28 to P-42, and were tested for offensive aggression as young adults several days later after the cessation of stress. Animals with a history of social subjugation show a context-dependent alteration in their aggressive behavior. They show typical conditioned defeat, fleeing from nonaggressive intruders of comparable age and size. In this respect, they are similar to socially subjugated adult male hamsters. However, when confronted by a smaller, weaker intruder they are exceedingly aggressive, displaying short attack latencies and high number of bites as compared to sibling controls that are not subjugated during adolescence.

This exaggerated aggressive response in animals displaying conditioned defeat was unexpected. Equally surprising, the basal testosterone levels in young adult hamsters exposed to the daily stress of threat and attack throughout adolescence are comparable to those in control siblings (unpublished observation). Moreover, following an agonistic encounter with an aggressive, larger conspecific, animals stressed in adolescence show much lower cortisol levels than their sibling controls. Hence the anticipated decrease in circulating levels of testosterone and increase in glucocorticoids with repeated defeat reported in many studies on adult animals (Bronson & Eleftheriou, 1964; Eberhart, Keverne, & Meller, 1980, 1983; Rose, Berstein, & Gordon, 1975) including hamsters (Huhman, Moore, Ferris, Mougey, & Meyerhoff, 1991) do not replicate in adolescent hamsters.

Young adult hamsters with a history of adolescent stress also have changes in the neurochemical systems regulating aggressive behavior. In addition to the decrease in VP levels in adult hamsters as mentioned previously, there is an increase in 5-HT innervation to the anterior hypothalamus as compared to their sibling controls (Delville et al., 1998). As noted, 5-HT decreases aggressive behavior, in part, by inhibiting the activity of the VP system at the level of the anterior hypothalamus. Thus it is possible that the stress of threat and attack in adolescence alters the interaction between the VP/5-HT systems affecting the regulation of aggression and possibly the context-dependent nature of the aggressive response.

VOLUNTARY ALCOHOL CONSUMPTION IN ADOLESCENCE

Adults diagnosed with antisocial behavior usually have a history of several risk factors contributing to their negative outcome. In many cases, teenage use of alcohol and drugs of abuse can be identified as contributing factors. Therefore, it was of interest to look at the behavioral and biological consequence of exposing adolescent hamsters to alcohol with and without the added risk of stress.

The pattern of voluntary alcohol consumption in adolescent hamsters is most interesting (Ferris et al., 1998). Animals will readily drink from a 10% alcohol solution on P-25, their first day of isolation from the maternal nest site. The daily intake of alcohol increases steadily over the adolescent period with a mean blood ethanol concentration of approximately 53 mg%. There are no physical signs of intoxication. The growth and body weight are not significantly different from those of sibling controls "yoked" to a regimen of voluntary sucrose consumption. Alcohol consumption peaks around P-35 to P-36, the time of puberty and activation of the hypothalamic–pituitary–gonadal axis. Indeed, the peak in adolescent alcohol consumption of almost 19 g/kg/day is correlated with the first rise in blood levels of testosterone. After this critical pubertal period, the daily consumption of alcohol levels off to around 11 g/kg/day and persists into young adulthood. What is most striking about the relationship between puberty and drinking is the early and enhanced release of testosterone in hamsters exposed to alcohol. Chronic and acute exposure to alcohol in adult animals including humans consistently lower plasma testosterone levels (Cicero, Meyer, & Bell, 1978; Frias, Torres, Miranda, Ruiz, & Ortega, 2002; Mello, Mendelsohn, Bree, Ellingboe, & Skupny, 1985). Nonetheless, on P-35 and P-36 hamsters exposed to alcohol have twice the blood levels of testosterone compared to their sibling controls. However, the difference in circulating testosterone levels between alcohol- and sucrose-exposed hamsters is short-lived as the levels of steroid hormone rise in the control animals to equal those of the alcohol animals by young adulthood. One interpretation of these data is that the consumption of alcohol in adolescence "jump starts" the hypothalamic–pituitary–gonadal axis, exposing the hamsters to elevated levels of testosterone during puberty. This alcohol-induced change in adolescent neuroendocrinology also appears to have long-term behavioral consequences. Several days after the cessation of alcohol exposure, hamsters show exaggerated attack behavior toward smaller intruders as compared to their sibling controls.

Could the pattern of alcohol consumption by adolescent hamsters and the resulting behavioral and neuroendocrine changes be altered by stress? To test this notion, animals were exposed to unpredictable/uncontrollable foot shock for several minutes each day from PN-25 to PN-38. This stressor was chosen because it is more potent than the resident/intruder paradigm in producing "conditioned defeat." Rodents exposed to electrical shock are highly submissive toward conspecifics (Williams, 1982). It was hypothesized that adolescent hamsters exposed to shock stress would not defend their territory as young adults in the resident/intruder paradigm. Adolescent hamsters exposed to shock drink almost twice as much of a 30% alcohol solution as sibling controls (Ferris & Brewer, 1996). Again peak drinking occurs around P-35 and P-36 in both stressed and nonstressed hamsters. Unfortunately, blood samples were not collected in these studies for the evaluation of steroid hormones. However, when tested in a resident/intruder paradigm several days after the cessation of stress and alcohol, animals exposed to the combination of both risk factors were more aggressive toward smaller intruders than sibling controls exposed to alcohol alone.

The common denominator in both the social subjugation and alcohol studies was the stability of the blood levels of testosterone. Gonadal hormones are critical in brain development and neuronal plasticity. As transduction factors they can turn on and off genes affecting the proteins involved in different signaling pathways. For instance, testosterone has pronounced effect on the limbic VP system. The level of immunoreactive VP in neurons of the bed nucleus of the stria terminalis and amygdala and their fiber projections to the septum are dramatically reduced following castration (De Vries & Al-Shamma, 1990; De Vries, Buijs, & Swaab, 1981; De Vries, Buijs, Van Leeuwen, Caffe, & Swaab, 1985). Accompanying the fall in VP is a reduction in VP mRNA in the bed nucleus (Miller, Urban, & Dorsas, 1989). Following castration, testosterone replacement increases levels of nuclear primary transcripts in the bed nucleus and amygdala with 3 hours of treatment (Szot & Dorsa, 1994). Hence the genetic expression of this neurochemical signal in adult animals is affected by testosterone. Interestingly, in the golden hamster VP receptor binding within the ventrolateral hypothalamus is androgen dependent (Delville et al., 1996). Castration essentially eliminates VP binding sites in this area of the hamster brain, raising the possibility that the diminished aggression noted in castrated hamsters (Ferris et al., 1989; Payne & Swanson, 1972; Vandenbergh 1971; Whitsett 1975) is caused by a loss of VP responsiveness in this hypothalamic area. Testosterone also has a significant effect on 5-HT_{1A} and 5-HT_{1B} receptor sensitivity in the mouse, altering aggressive response (Cologer-Clifford et al., 1999). Hence the maintenance of testosterone during social subjugation in adolescence and its actual enhancement with alcohol could be contributing to a sensitized vasopressin system leading to context-dependent heightened aggression in adulthood.

SUMMARY

Serotonin and VP appear to play significant roles in the regulation of impulsivity and aggression. Serotonin reduces aggressive response while VP enhances arousal and aggression in a context-dependent manner. There are compelling neuroanatomical, pharmacological, and molecular data supporting an interaction between 5-HT and VP in the control of aggression. Serotonin may act, in part by reducing the activity of the VP system. The preclinical studies discussed in this work provide evidence of a highly plastic nervous system in adolescence. The 5-HT and VP systems are affected by the daily stress of threat and attack by older conspecifics. As young adults, animals with a history of adolescent stress show inappropriate and excessive aggressive behavior. In the presence of adult hamsters, they can be very submissive; however smaller, younger hamsters elicit intense biting attacks. These findings underscore the context-dependent nature of aggressive behavior and the neurobiological and behavioral consequences of stress in adolescence.

It is interesting that testosterone is spared in adolescents exposed to chronic social subjugation since adults have a very predictable loss of gonadal hormone following defeat. Similarly, adult animals and humans exposed to alcohol show a very predictable diminution in testosterone levels, but again adolescent hamsters show no such suppression of gonadal hormone. Indeed, they actually show an enhanced activation of the hypothalamic gonadal axis with alcohol exposure. It would seem that nature has set up mechanisms for protecting the reproductive neuroendocrine status of adolescent hamsters and perhaps humans. There would seem to be adaptive value in this protective mechanism since adolescence is a period of heightened social conflict both in animals and in humans. Smaller, peripubertal, immature males are not fully able to defend territories and compete for mates. While they have to wait their turn, they are imbued with a resistance to risk factors that can be devastating to their adult counterparts. Learning and a sustained, if not augmented, gonadal neuroendocrine system may be contributing factors to the inappropriate, excessive offensive aggression displayed by adult hamsters with a history of adolescent social subjugation and alcohol exposure. Whether this particular interaction between brain and environment during rodent adolescence translates to human adolescence is purely speculation. However, these data in rodent studies clearly demonstrate that the developmental period analogous to human adolescence is unique in its response to stress and exposure to alcohol. Further studies in both monkeys and humans may show adolescence to be a very resilient period in developmental psychology and biology.

ACKNOWLEDGMENTS

These experiments were supported by grants MH 52280 from the NIMH. The contents of this review are solely the responsibility of the authors and do not necessarily represent the official views of the NIMH.

References

Adell, A., Garcia-Marquez, C., Armario, A., & Gelpi, E. (1988). Chronic stress increases serotonin and noradrenaline in rat brain and sensitize their responses to a further acute stress. *Journal of Neurochemistry, 50,* 1678–1681.

Altemus, M., Cizza, G., & Gold, P. W. (1992). Chronic fluoxetine treatment reduces hypothalamic vasopressin secretion in vitro. *Brain Research, 593,* 311–313.

American Humane Association (1978). *National analysis of official child neglect and abuse reporting.* Denver: American Humane Association.

Arvola, A., Forsander, O. (1961). Comparison between water and alcohol consumption in six animal species in free choice experiments. *Nature* 4790: 814.

Bennett, A. J., Lesch, K. P., Heils, A., Long, J. C., Lorenz, J. G., Shoaf, S. E., et al. (2002). Early experience and serotonin transporter gene variation interact to influence primate CNS function. *Molecular Psychiatry, 7,* 118–122.

Blanchard, D. C., Sakai, R. R., McEwen, B., Weiss, S. M., & Blanchard, R. J. (1993). Subordination stress: Behavioral, brain and neuroendocrine correlates. *Behavioral Brain Research, 58,* 113–121.

Bolanos-Jimenez, F., Manhaes de Castro, R. M., Cloez-Tarayani, I., Monneret, V., Drieu, K., & Fillion, G. (1995). Effects of stress on the functional properties of pre- and postsynaptic 5-HT_{1B} receptors in the rat brain. *European Journal of Pharmacology, 294,* 531–540.

Bouwknecht, J. A., Hijzen, T. H., van der Gugten, J., Maes, R. A. A., Hen, R., & Olivier, B. (2001). Absence of 5-HT1B receptors is associated with impaired impulse control in male 5-HT1B knockout mice. *Biological Psychiatry, 49,* 557–568.

Brain, P. F. (1972). Effects of isolation/grouping on endocrine function and fighting behavior in male and female golden hamsters (*Mesocricetus auratus* Waterhouse). *Behavioral Biology* 7, 349–357.

Bronson, F. H., & Eleftheriou, B. F. (1964). Chronic physiological effects of fighting in mice. *General and Comparative Endocrinology, 4,* 9–14.

Brown, G. L., Ebert, M. H., Goyer, P. F., Jimerson, D. C., Klein, W. J., Bunney, W. E., et al. (1982). Aggression, suicide, and serotonin: Relationship to CSF amine metabolites. *American Journal of Psychiatry, 139,* 741–746.

Cherek, D. R., & Lane, S. D. (2001). Acute effects of D-fenfluramine on simultaneous measures of aggressive escape and impulsive responses of adult males with and without a history of conduct disorder. *Psychopharmacology, 157,* 221–227.

Cherek, D. R., Lane, S. D., Pietras, C. J., & Steinberg, J. L. (2002). Effects of chronic paroxetine administration on measures of aggressive and impulsive responses of adult males with a history of conduct disorder. *Psychopharmacology, 159,* 266–274.

Cicero, T. J., Meyer, E. R., & Bell, R. D. (1978). Effects of ethanol and on the hypothalamic pituitary–luteizing hormone axis and testicular steroidogenesis. *J. Pharmacol. Exp. Ther.* 208: 210–215.

Clarke, A. S. (1993). Social rearing effects on HPA axis activity over early development and response to stress in young rhesus monkeys. *Developmental Psychobiology, 26,* 433–447.

Coccaro, E. F., Astill, J. L., Herbert, J. L., & Schut, A. G. (1990). Fluoxetine treatment of impulsive aggrerssion in DSM-III-R personality disorder patients. *Journal of Clinical Psychopharmacology, 10,* 373–375.

Coccaro, E. F., & Kavoussi, R. J. (1997). Fluoxetine and impulsive aggressive behavior in personality-disordered subjects. *Archives of General Psychiatry, 54,* 1081–1088.

Coccaro, E. F., Kavoussi, R. J., Hauger, R. L., Cooper, T. B., & Ferris, C. F. (1998). Cerebrospinal fluid vasopressin levels correlates with aggression and serotonin function in personality-disordered subjects. *Archives of General Psychiatry, 55,* 708–714.

Cologer-Clifford, A., Simon, N. G., Lu, S. F., & Smoluk, S. A. (1997). Serotonin agonist-induced decreases in intermale aggression are dependent on brain region and receptor subtype. *Pharmacology Biochemistry and Behavior, 58:* 425–430.

Cologer-Clifford, A., Simon, N. G., Richter, M. L., Smoluk, S. A., & Lu, S.-F. (1999). Androgens and estrogens modulate 5-HT_{1A} and 5-HT_{1B} agonist effects on aggression. *Physiology & Behavior, 65,* 823–828.

Dalta, K. P., Mitra, S. K., & Bhattacharya, S. K. (1991). Serotonergic modulation of footshock induced aggression in paired rats. *Indian Journal of Experimental Biology, 29,* 631–635.

Delville, Y., Mansour, K. M., & Ferris, C. F. (1995). Serotonin blocks vasopressin-facilitated offensive aggression: Interactions within the ventrolateral hypothalamus of golden hamsters. *Physiology & Behavior, 59,* 813–816.

Delville, Y., Mansour, K. M., & Ferris, C. F. (1996). Testosterone facilitates aggression by modulating vasopressin receptors in the hypothalamus. *Physiology & Behavior, 60,* 25–29.

Delville, Y., Melloni, R. H., Jr., & Ferris, C. F. (1998). Behavioral and neurobiological consequences of social subjugation during puberty in golden hamsters. *Journal of Neuroscience, 18,* 2667–2672.

De Souza, E. B., & Van Loon, G. R. (1986). Brain serotonin and catecholamine responses to repeated stress in rats. *Brain Research, 367,* 77–86.

De Vries, G. J., & Al-Shamma, H. A. (1990). Sex differences in hormonal responses of vasopressin pathways in the rat brain. *Journal of Neurobiology, 21,* 686–693.

De Vries, G. J., Buijs, R. M., & Swaab, D. F. (1981). Ontogeny of the vasopressinergic neurons of the suprachiasmatic nucleus and their extrahypothalamic projections in the rat brain – presence of a sex difference in the lateral septum. *Brain Research, 218,* 67–78.

De Vries, G. J., Buijs, R. M., Van Leeuwen, F. W., Caffe, A. R., & Swaab, D. F. (1985). The vasopressinergic innervation of the brain in normal and castrated rats. *Journal of Comparative Neurology, 233,* 236–254.

Dieterlen, F. (1959). Das Verhalten des Syrischen Goldhamsters (*Mesocricetus auratus* Waterhouse). *Zeitschrift für Tierpsychologic, 16,* 47–103.

Dodge, K. A., Bates, J. E., & Pettit, G. S. (1990). Mechanisms in the cycle of violence. *Science, 250,* 1678–1683.

Dolan, M., Anderson, I. M., & Deakin, J. F. (2001). Relationship between 5-HT function and impulsivity and aggression in male offenders with personality disorders. *British Journal of Psychiatry, 178,* 352–359.

Eberhart, J. A., Keverne, E. B., & Meller, R. E. (1980). Social influences on plasma testosterone levels in male talapoin monkeys. *Hormones and Behavior, 14,* 247–266.

Eberhart, J. A., Keverne, E. B., & Meller R. E. (1983). Social influences on circulating levels of cortisol and prolactin in male talapoin monkeys. *Physiology & Behavior, 30,* 361–369.

Eberhart, J. A., Yodyingyuad, U., & Keverne, E. B. (1985). Subordination in male talapoin monkeys lowers sexual behaviour in the absence of dominants. *Physiology & Behavior, 35,* 673–677.

Eichelman, B. S. (1990). Neurochemical and psychopharmacologic aspects of aggressive behavior. *Annual Review of Medicine, 41,* 147–158.

Ellison, G. (1976). Monoamine neurotoxins: Selective and delayed effects on behavior in colonies of laboratory rats. *Brain Research, 103,* 81–92.

Fairbanks, L. A., Melega, W. P., Jorgensen, M. J., Kaplan, J. R., & McGuire, M. T. (2001). Social impulsivity inversely associated with CSF 5-HIAA and fluoxetine exposure in vervet monkeys. *Neuropsychopharmacology, 24,* 370–378.

Ferris, C. F. (1996). Serotonin inhibits vasopressin facilitated aggression in the Syrian hamster. In C. F. Ferris & T. Grisso (Eds.), Understanding aggressive behavior in children [Special issue]. *New York Academy of Sciences, 794,* 98–103.

Ferris, C. F. (2000). Adolescent stress and neural plasticity in namsters: A vasopressin-serotonin model of inappropriate aggressive behavior. *Exp. Physiol.* 85 Spec No 855–905.

Ferris, C. F., Axelson, J. F., Martin, A. M., & Roberge, L. R. (1989). Vasopressin immunoreactivity in the anterior hypothalamus is altered during the establishment of dominant/subordinate relationships between hamsters. *Neuroscience, 29,* 675–683.

Ferris, C. F., & Brewer, J. (1996). Adolescent stress alters ethanol ingestion and agonistic behavior in male golden hamsters. In T. Grisso & C. F. Ferris (Eds.), Understanding aggressive behavior in children [Special issue]. *Annals of the New York Academy of Sciences, 794,* 348–351.

Ferris, C. F., Melloni, R. H., Jr., Koppel, G., Perry, K. W., Fuller, R. W., & Delville, Y. (1997). Vasopressin/serotonin interactions in the anterior hypothalamus control aggressive behavior in golden hamsters. *Journal of Neuroscience, 17,* 4331–4340.

Ferris, C. F., & Potegal, M. (1988). Vasopressin receptor blockade in the anterior hypothalamus suppresses aggression in hamsters. *Physiology & Behavior, 44,* 235–239.

Ferris, C. F., Shtiegman, K., & King, J. A. (1998). Voluntary ethanol consumption in male adolescent hamsters increases testosterone and aggression. *Physiology & Behavior, 63,* 739–744.

Ferris, C. F., Stolberg, T., & Delville, Y. (1999). Serotonin regulation of aggressive behavior in male golden hamsters (*Mesocricetus auratus*). *Behavioral Neuroscience, 113,* 804–815.

Festing, M. F. W. (1958). Hamsters. In Universities Foundation for Animal Welfare (Ed.), *The UFAW handbook on the care and management of laboratory animals* (4th ed., pp. 242–256). Baltimore: Williams & Wilkins.

Frias, J., Torres, J. M., Miranda, M. T., Ruiz, E., & Ortega, E. (2002). Effects of acute alcohol intoxication on pituitary–gonadal axis hormones, pituitary–adrenal axis hormones, beta-endorphin and prolactin in human adults of both sexes. *Alcohol and Alcoholism, 37,* 169–173.

Frishknecht, H. R., Seigfreid, B., & Waser, P. G. (1982). Learning of submissive behavior in mice: A new model. *Behavioural Processes, 7,* 235–245.

Gonzalez Jatuff, A. S., Berastegui, M., Rodriguez, C. I., & Rodriguez Echandia, E. L. (1999). Permanent and transient effects of repeated preweaning stress on social and sexual behaviors of rats. *Stress, 3,* 97–106.

Grant, E. C., & Mackintosh, J. H. (1963). A comparison of the social postures of some common laboratory rodents. *Behavior, 21,* 246–259.

Haller, J., Makara, G. B., Barna, I., Kovacs, K., Nagy, J., & Vecsernyes, M. (1996). Compression of the pituitary stalk elicits chronic increases in CSF vasopressin, oxytocin as well as in social investigation and aggressiveness. *Journal of Neuroendocrinology, 8,* 361–365.

Harlow, H. F., Harlow, M. K., & Suomi, S. J. (1971). From thought to therapy: Lessons from a primate laboratory. *American Scientist, 59,* 538–549.

Harrison, R. J., Connor, D. F., Nowak, C., Nash, K., & Melloni, R. H., Jr. (2000). Chronic anabolic–androgenic steroid treatment during adolescence increases anterior hypothalamic vasopressin and aggression in intact hamsters. *Psychoneuroendocrinology, 25,* 317–338.

Higley, J. D., Suomi, S. J., & Linnoila, M. (1991). CSF monamine metabolite concentrations vary according to age, rearing, and sex, and are influenced by the stressor of social separation in rhesus. *Psychopharmacology, 103,* 551–556.

Holmes, A., Murphy, D. L., & Crawley, J. N. (2002). Reduced aggression in mice lacking the serotonin transporter. *Psychopharmacology, 161,* 160–167.

Huhman, K. L., Moore, T. O., Ferris, C. F., Mougey, E. H., & Meyerhoff, J. L. (1991). Acute and repeated exposure to social conflict in male golden hamsters: Increases in plasma POMC-peptides and cortisol and decreases in plasma testosterone. *Hormones and Behavior, 25,* 206–216.

Ingersoll, G. (1992). Psychological and social development. In E. R. McAnarney, R. E. Kreipe, D. P. Orr, & G. D. Comerci (Eds.), *Textbook of adolescent medicine* (pp. 91–98). Philadelphia: Saunders.

Ito, T. A., Miller, N., & Pollock, V. E. (1996). Alcohol and aggression: A meta-analysis on the moderating effects of inhibitory cues, triggering events, and self-focused attention. *Psychological Bulletin, 120,* 60–82.

Joppa, M. A., Rowe, R. K., & Meisel, R. L. (1997). Effects of serotonin 1A or 1B receptor agonists on social aggression in male and female syrian hamsters. *Pharmacology; Biochemistry; and Behavior, 58,* 349–353.

Kia, H. K., Miquel, M. C., Brisorgueil, M. J., Daual, G., Riadm, Elmestikawy, S., Namon, M., & Verge, D. (1996). Immunocytochemical localization of serotonin 1A receptions in the rat central nervous system. *J. Comp. Neurol., 271,* 3052–3057.

Koolhaas, J. M., Moor, E., Hiemstra, Y., & Bohus, B. (1991). The testosterone-dependent vasopressinergic neurons in the medial amygdala and lateral septum: Involvement in social behaviour of male rats. In S. Jard & R. Jamison (Eds.), *Vasopressin* (pp. 213–219). London: John Libbey Eurotext.

Koolhaas, J. M., Van den Brink, T. H. C., Roozendal, B., & Boorsma, F. (1990). Medial amygdala and aggressive behavior: Interaction between testosterone and vasopressin. *Aggressive Behaviors, 16,* 223–229.

84   Craig F. Ferris

Korte, S. M., Meijer, O. C., De Kloet, E. R., Buwalda, B., Keijser, J., Sluyter, F., et al. (1996). Enhanced 5-HT$_{1a}$ receptor expression in forebrain regions of aggressive house mice. *Brain Research, 736,* 338–343.

Kraemer, G. W., & Clarke, A. S. (1990). The behavioral neurobiology of self-injurious behavior in rhesus monkeys. *Progress in Neuro-psychopharmacology & Biological Psychiatry, 14*(Suppl), S141–S168.

Kruesi, M. J., Rapoport, J. L., Hamburger, S., Hibbs, E., & Potter, W. Z. (1990). Cerebrospinal fluid monoamines metabolites, aggression and impulsivity in disruptive behavior disorders of children and adolescents. *Archives of General Psychiatry, 47,* 419–426.

Landau, I. T. (1975). Light–dark rhythms in aggressive behavior of the male golden hamster. *Physiology & Behavior, 14,* 767–774.

Lansford, J. E., Dodge, K. A., Pettit, G. S., Bates, J. E., Crozier, J., & Kaplow, J. (2002). A 12-year prospective study of the long-term effects of early child physical maltreatment on psychological, behavioral, and academic problems in adolescence. *Archives of Pediatrics & Adolescent Medicine, 156,* 824–830.

Lerwill, C. J., & Makings, P. (1971). The agonistic behavior of the golden hamster *Mesocricetus auratus* (Waterhouse). *Animal Behaviour, 19,* 714–721.

Linnoila, M., Virkkunen, M., Scheinin, M., Nuutila, A., Rimon, R., & Goodwin, F. K. (1983). Low cerebrospinal fluid 5-hydroxyindoleacetic acid concentration differentiates impulsive from nonimpulsive violent behavior. *Life Science, 33,* 2609–2614.

Lourie, I. S., Campiglia, P., James, L. R., & Dewitt, J. (1979). Adolescent abuse and neglect: The role of runaway youth programs. *Child Today, 8,* 27–29.

Luntz, B. K., & Widom, C. S. (1994). Antisocial personality disorder in abused and neglected children gown up. *American Journal of Psychiatry, 151,* 670–674.

McKittrick, C. R., Blanchard, D. C., Blanchard, R. J., McEwen, B. S., Sakai, R. R., (1995). Serotonin receptor binding in a colony model of chronic social stress. *Biological Psychiatry, 37,* 383–393.

Mehlman, P. T., Higley, J. D., Faucher, I., Lilly, A. A., Taub, D. M., Vickers, J., et al. (1994). Low CSF 5-HIAA concentration and severe aggression and impaired impulse control in nonhuman primates. *American Journal of Psychiatry, 151,* 1485–1491.

Mello, N. K., Mendelson, J. H., Bree, M. P., Ellingboe, J., & Skupny, A. S. T. (1985). The effects of ethanol on luteinizing hormone and testosterone in male macaque monkeys. *Journal of Pharmacology and Experimental Therepeutics, 233,* 588–596.

Miczek, K. A. (1974). Intraspecies aggrression in rats: Effects of d-amphetamine and chlordiazepoxide. *Psychopharmacologia, 39,* 275–301.

Miller, L. L., Whitsett, J. M., Vandenbergh, J. G., & Colby, D. R. (1977). Physical and behavioral aspects of sexual maturation in male golden hamsters. *Journal of Comparative Physiology B: Journal of Comparative Psychology, 91,* 245–259.

Miller, M. A., Urban, J. H., & Dorsa, D. M. (1989). Steroid dependency of vasopressin neurons in the bed nucleus of the stria terminalis by *in situ* hybridization. *Endocrinology, 125,* 2335–2340.

Molina, V., Ciesielski, L., Gobailles, S., Insel, F., & Mandel, P. (1987). Inhibition of mouse killing behavior by serotonin mimetic drugs: Effects of partial alteration of serotonin neurotransmission. *Pharmacology, Biochemistry; and Behaviors, 27,* 123–131.

Mos, J., Olivier, B., Poth, M., & van Aken, H. (1992). The effects of intraventricular administration of eltoprazine 1-(3-trifluoromethylphenyl)piperazine hydrochloride and 8-hydroxy-2-(di-*n*-propylamino)tetraline on resident intruder aggression in the rat. *European Journal of Pharmacology, 212*, 295–298.

Ogren, S. O., Holm, A. C., Renyi, A. L., & Ross, S. B. (1980). Anti-aggressive effect of zimelidine in isolated mice. *Acta Pharmacologica Toxicologica, 47*, 71–74.

Olivier, B., Mos, J., Van der Heyden, J., & Hartog, J. (1989). Serotonergic modulation of social interactions in isolated male mice. *Psychopharmacology, 97*, 154–156.

Payne, A. P. (1973). A comparison of the aggressive behavior of isolated intact and castrated male golden hamsters towards intruders introduced into the home cage. *Physiology & Behavior, 10*, 629–631.

Payne, A. P., & Swanson, H. H. (1972). The effect of sex hormones on the agonistic behavior of the male golden hamster (*Mesocricetus auratus* Waterhouse). *Physiology, Behavior, 8*, 687–691.

Potegal, M., & Ferris, C. F. (1990). Intraspecific aggression in male hamsters is inhibited by vasopressin receptor antagonists. *Aggressive Behavior, 15*, 311–320.

Potegal, M., Huhman, K., Moore, T., & Meyerhoff, J. (1993). Conditioned defeat in the Syrian golden hamster (*Mesocricetus auratus*). *Behavioral and Neural Biology, 60*, 93–102.

Rose, R. M., Berstein, I. S., & Gordon, T. P. (1975). Consequences of social conflict on plasma testosterone levels in rhesus monkeys. *Psychosomatic Medicine, 37*, 50–61.

Royalty, J. (1990). Effects of prenatal ethanol on juvenile play-fighting and postpubertal aggression in rats. *Psychological Reports, 66*, 551–560.

Sanchez, C., & Hyttel, J. (1994). Isolation-induced aggression in mice: Effects of 5-hydroxytryptamine uptake inhibitors and involvement of postsynaptic 5-HT_{1A} receptors. *European Journal of Pharmacology, 264*, 241–247.

Sanson, A., Smart, D., Prior, M., & Oberklaid, F. (1993). Precursors of hyperactivity and aggression. *Journal of the American Academy of Child and Adolescent Psychiatry, 32*, 1207–1216.

Saudou, F., Amara, D. J., Dierich, A., LeMeur, M., Ramboz, S., Segu, A., et al. (1994). Enhanced aggressive behavior in mice lacking 5-HT_{1B} receptor. *Science 265*, 1875–1878.

Schellenbach, C. J., & Guerney, L. F. (1987). Identification of adolescent abuse and future intervention prospects. *J Adol Abuse, 10*, 1–2.

Schneider, M. L., Moore, C. F., Kraimer, G. W., Roberts, A. D., & DeJesus, O. T. (2002). The impact of prenatal stress, fetal alcohol exposure, or both on development: Perspectives from a primate model. *Psychoneuroendocrinology, 27*, 285–298.

Schoenfeld, T. A., & Leonard, C. M. (1985). Behavioral development in the Syrian golden hamster. In H. I. Siegel (Ed.), *The hamster: Reproduction and behavior*. New York: Plenum.

Sijbesma, H., Schipper, J. J., de Kloet. E. R., Mos, J., Van Aken, H., & Olivier, B. (1991). Postsynaptic 5-HT1 receptors and offensive aggression in rats: A combined behavioral and autoradiographic study with eltoprazine. *Pharmacology Biochemistry, and Behavior, 38*, 447–458.

Stribley, J. M., & Carter, C. S. (1999). Developmental exposure to vasopressin increases aggression in adult prairie voles. *Proceedings of the National Academy of Science, USA, 96*, 12601–12604.

Szot, P., & Dorsa, D. M. (1994). Expression of cytoplasmic and nuclear vasopressin RNA following castration and testosterone replacement: Evidence for transcriptional regulation. *Molecular and Cellular Neurosciences, 5,* 1–10.

Vandenbergh, J. G. (1971). The effects of gonadal hormones on the aggressive behaviour of adult golden hamsters. *Animal Behavior, 19,* 589–594.

Van de Poll, N. E., DeJonge, F., Van Oyen, H. G., & Van Pelt, J. (1982). Aggressive behaviour in rats: Effects of winning or losing on subsequent aggressive interactions. *Behavior Processes, 7,* 143–155.

van der Vegt, B. J., de Boer, S. F., Bulwalda, B., de Ruiter, A. J. H., de Jong, J. G., & Koolhaas, J. M. (2001). Enhanced sensitivity of postsynaptic serotonin-1A receptors in rats and mice with high trait aggression. *Physiology & Behavior, 74,* 205–211.

Vergnes, M., Depaulis, A., Boehrer, A., & Kempf, E. (1988). Selective increase of offensive behavior in the rat following intrahypothalamic 5,7-DHT-induced serotonin depletion. *Behavioural Brain Research, 29,* 85–91.

Villalba, C., Boyle, P. A., Caliguri, E. J., & De Vries, G. J. (1997). Effects of the selective serotonin reuptake inhibitor fluoxetine on social behaviors in male and female prairie voles (*Microtus ochrogaster*). *Hormones and Behavior, 32,* 184–191.

Vomachka, A. J., & Greenwald, G. S. (1979). The development of gonadotropin and steroid hormone patterns in male and female hamsters from birth to puberty. *Endocrinology, 105,* 960–966.

Whitsett, J. M. (1975). The development of aggressive and marking behavior in intact and castrated male hamsters. *Hormones and Behavior, 6,* 47–57.

Williams, J. (1982). Influence of shock controllability by dominant rats on subsequent attack and defensive behaviors toward colony intruders. *Animal Learning & Behavior* 10, 305–314.

Williams, J., & Lierle, D. M. (1988). Effects of repeated defeat by a dominant conspecific on subsequent pain sensitivity, open-field activity, and escape learning. *Animal Learning & Behavior, 16,* 477–485.

Winslow, J., Hastings, N., Carter, C., Harbaugh, C., & Insel, T. (1993). A role for central vasopressin in pair bonding in monogamous prairie voles. *Nature, 365,* 545–548.

Yodyingyuad, U., de la Riva, C., Abbott, D. H., Herbert, J., & Keverne, E. B. (1985). Relationship between dominance hierarchy, cerebrospinal fluid levels of amine transmitter metabolites (5-hydroxyindole acetic acid and homovanillic acid) and plasma cortisol in monkeys. *Neuroscience, 16,* 851–858.

Zubieta, J. A., & Alessi, N. E. (1992). Acute and chronic administration of trazodone in the treatment of disruptive behavior disorders in children. *Journal of Clinical Psychopharmacology, 12,* 346–351.

5

Links Between Girls' Puberty and Externalizing and Internalizing Behaviors: Moving from Demonstrating Effects to Identifying Pathways

Julia A. Graber
University of Florida

Jeanne Brooks-Gunn
Teachers College and College of Physicians and Surgeons, Columbia University

Andrea B. Archibald
Teachers College, Columbia University

Adolescence has fascinated developmental scholars because the transition into adolescence involves biological, psychological, and social changes (Graber & Brooks-Gunn, 1996). At the same time, adolescence has been a focus for research on psychopathology as rates of several disorders increase dramatically during this time period. Most notably, the past few decades have witnessed volumes of studies and theories on adolescent depression, conduct disorder, and subclinical psychopathology (Steinberg & Morris, 2001). Many of these studies have sought to understand the confluence of bio-psychosocial developmental factors that result in the emergence of serious behavioral and emotional problems. In this chapter, we consider several bio-psychosocial models that have been used to explain changes in internalizing and externalizing behaviors during adolescence. Examples from our own work highlight the role of pubertal development in understanding behavioral plasticity during adolescence.

Discussions of plasticity in developmental processes have frequently focused on early development and gene–environment interactions in understanding development and behavior (Baltes, Lindenberger, & Staudinger, 1998). Despite a focus on the early periods of development, the notion that adaptation occurs in neural and behavioral development throughout life

The research reported in this paper was funded by the National Institutes of Health and the W. T. Grant Foundation. Reprint requests may be addressed to Julia A. Graber, Department of Psychology, University of Florida, P. O. Box 112250, Gainesville, FL 32611-2250; Tel: (352) 392-0601 x235; Fax: (352) 392-7985; jagraber@ufl.edu.

has been a cornerstone of life span developmental perspectives (Baltes et al., 1998; Cairns, 1998). Recent studies in neuroscience have demonstrated that new neural connections continue to be made across the life span (e.g., Bruer & Greenough, 2001) and specific changes in the prefrontal cortex and limbic regions of the brain occur during adolescence (see Spear, 2000 for a review). Certainly, over the course of development, there are increasing constraints on the range of plasticity; however, these advances in developmental neuroscience suggest that discussions of plasticity need not be limited to early development but are salient in understanding functional changes in brain and behavior across the life course.

However, at the same time that plasticity in developmental processes is thought to be at the heart of understanding individual differences in behavioral outcomes, Cairns (1998) pointed out that it has been more challenging to developmental scientists to explain continuity or stability of behavior over the life span (or significant periods thereof). That is, "*if plasticity and change are inevitable in social development, how can continuity and stability be achieved?*" (Cairns, 1998, p. 153). Notably, Cairns identifies some seemingly paradoxical problems in development. First, developmental models, especially the bio-psychosocial models applied to adolescent development, postulate bidirectionality of effects (e.g., biological factors influence the psychological, psychological factors influence biology), yet continuity in behavioral patterns is observed. Second, plasticity in behavior over the life span should not be expected if early gene–environment interactions resulted in canalization. Thus, the challenge for developmental scientists, as we and others have noted (e.g., Graber & Brooks-Gunn, 1996; Rutter, 1994), is to explain individual differences in behavior not only in terms of who does or does not exhibit the behavior, but also in terms of when a behavioral course begins, if it is maintained, and what predicts the absence of the behavior.

In the case of the transition into adolescence, these questions are particularly salient as behavioral systems are challenged to adapt in nearly every arena of development. Specifically, this transition is marked by pubertal development; the physiological changes of puberty alter nearly every system of the body (e.g., neural, cardiovascular, muscular, skeletal) and result in reproductive capacity. At the individual or psychological level, not only are adolescents challenged to adapt to their changing bodies by altering their body image (Brooks-Gunn & Reiter, 1990; Steiner-Adair, 1986), but they must also cope with their family's and peers' responses to their maturing bodies. Additionally, increases in cognitive capacities and social cognitions result in more advanced reasoning, decision making, and thinking than at prior times of development (Keating, 1990). Such abilities also encompass emotional and social reasoning and afford shifts to greater intimacy in peer relationships (e.g., Berndt, 1996). At the social or broader contextual level, the majority of adolescents will make one or more school transitions during this same time period with multiple structural and inter-personal changes occurring in this context (e.g., grading systems become more stringent, students change classes, and teachers, more frequently during the day, the size of the school increases; see Eccles et al., 1993). The social context at home also undergoes substantial change as this period of development is further marked as a time of increased parent-adolescent conflict (Paikoff & Brooks-Gunn, 1991; Steinberg, 2001). At the general level, nearly all youth experience each of these challenges. Thus, either nearly all should have dramatic shifts in behavior and potentially damaging effects from the experience of simultaneous and cumulative risks, or, alternatively, these changes are endemic to the developmental process and all youth should have the appropriate resources to adapt and sustain adaptive behavioral patterns. Rather, as Cairns (1998) points out, both stability and change occur in social behaviors during this period. The goal then must be to move from the general level to understand how navigating the transition into adolescence results in individual differences in behavioral outcomes.

In addition, within the study of adolescent psychopathology, gender has been a consistent individual difference. Much of this work has focused on why and when the gender difference in depression emerges. In particular, the goal has been to explain the differential factors in development that result in an approximately 2:1 gender difference in rates of major depressive disorder that is commonly reported in adults. Moreover, the marked gender difference emerges during adolescence such that there are minimal differences in rates of depression in childhood, before age 12, with rates of depression varying consistently by gender by age 14 (e.g., Birmaher et al., 1996; Lewinsohn, Rohde, & Seeley, 1998). As such, substantial attention has been given to explaining *"Why more girls?"* (e.g., Brooks-Gunn & Petersen, 1991) and hence more studies have focused either only on development of internalizing behaviors in girls or on comparative studies of processes in boys and girls.

In contrast, for conduct disorder and more global externalizing behaviors, much more attention has been given to boys. The scarcity of girls in the literature until fairly recently has in part been due to the notion that serious conduct problems were not substantial problems among girls (see Pajer, 1998, for a discussion of this issue). For example, in examinations of juvenile crime rates, boys do account for substantially more of the problem than do girls. At the same time, an issue that is important to understanding pathways to behavioral outcomes and individual differences in these pathways, specifically, is that the general heading of externalizing problems or symptoms encompasses a range of behaviors in severity and type. Involvement in the juvenile justice system can be an identifier of severe behavioral problems; but, at the same time, other less serious behaviors may have developmental consequences (Pajer, 1998).

As Cairns and Cairns (2000) have delineated, discussions of aggression have suffered from the problem of "overinclusion" in that too often qualitatively and quantitatively distinct behaviors are included into a unitary construct based on fitting into a fairly general outcome (i.e., aggression). For example, as Cairns and Cairns (2000) suggest, numerous distinctions have been made between verbal and physical aggression, as well as incorporating the context (e.g., relational aggression) into the distinction, and other behavioral constructs (e.g., overt versus covert). These behaviors range in the potential severity or impairment in functioning that the individual may experience in families, schools, peer groups, and society. From this perspective, understanding the range of behaviors and when and why individual differences in these behaviors occur is informative for understanding a broader spectrum of adolescent adjustment.

The more serious end of the aggression or externalizing behavior spectrum is actual diagnosable conduct disorder. A caveat of the literature on conduct disorder has been that early-onset (childhood) conduct disorder is more likely to be life-course persistent (Moffitt, 1993) and that late-onset (adolescent) conduct disorder has less prediction to adult criminal outcomes. During adolescence and possibly late childhood, more sizable numbers of girls with these problems can be identified. Interestingly, in an examination of conduct disorder across studies, youth who met criteria for adolescent onset of conduct disorder were more likely to be girls and had lower reports of physical aggression than those who had earlier onset of conduct disorder (Lahey et al., 1998). If the adolescent onset pattern of conduct disorder is associated with fewer adult impairments and if girls are more likely to exhibit this pattern of onset, this provides support for the assertion that the more serious conduct problems are more common among boys. Thus, the focus of research would be on models that explain conduct disorder pathways for boys, and more specifically, life-course persistent pathways.

Part of the assumption underlying the focus on conduct disorders in adolescence, especially when actual criminal behavior in part of the symptoms exhibited, is that these identify pathways to longer-term criminal behavior and poor adult outcomes. Again, women make up a much smaller percentage of the adult criminal population, especially for violent crime. Therefore, the focus on the most deviant and harmful behaviors to society based on a focus on criminal activity results in greater attention to boys and the desire to explain pathways for boys. Certainly, this particular set of developmental outcomes is indisputably important. However, Pajer (1998) has suggested that the adult outcomes for adolescent girls who are diagnosed with a conduct disorder or were considered delinquent are also of importance; moreover, these girls are not free from pathology and problems in adulthood. In a review of the studies that have followed girls who were delinquent or had conduct disorder as adolescents into adulthood,

Pajer noted severe difficulties in adulthood including increased mortality rates for these women in comparison to the general population, higher rates of adult criminal activity in comparison to the general population and in comparison to psychiatric controls, psychiatric difficulties including substance abuse and suicidal behavior, dysfunctional interpersonal relationships (e.g., marriage to abusive spouses), and higher rates of impaired parenting as evidenced by percentage of offspring removed from the mother's care (in comparison to psychiatric controls and the general population) or history of involvement with family court. At the most severe end of the spectrum of externalizing or aggressive behaviors, girls who have these problems during adolescence appear to have important lifelong difficulties that have intergenerational effects. Thus, for adolescent girls with serious externalizing problems, there may be more stability in these behavioral patterns than would be found when only one source of information is examined (i.e., criminal records).

At the same time, it has been suggested that developmental transitions may serve as potential "turning points" for behavioral pathways that afford behavioral change. In particular, Pickles and Rutter (1991) present examples from key transitions such as marriage. In this example, choice of partner was salient to outcomes. For young women with histories of deviant behaviors, young women who chose partners who did not have comparable histories did not persist in their own externalizing problems, whereas young women who chose partners with comparable backgrounds demonstrated continuity in their pathways from adolescence to adulthood. Some of the adult outcomes for conduct-disordered girls identified by Pajer (1998) are in part associated with making relationship choices that maintain behavioral patterns rather than promote change (e.g., high rates of marriage to abusive spouses). Of course, such choices in adulthood no doubt stem from relationship patterns formed across development, and impaired social interactions are likely co-occurring symptoms of externalizing problems for adolescent girls.

From a developmental perspective for aggression and externalizing behaviors, numerous studies have identified childhood predictors to pathways to persistent problems in boys (see Loeber, Farrington, Stouthamer-Loeber, & Van Kammen, 1998, and Moffitt, 1993, for reviews). Notably, it is questionable whether or not girls fit the same developmental progression in that it is possible to identify only a very few girls with early onset for externalizing/conduct problems in the preschool or early elementary school-age years (e.g., Stormshak, Bierman, & the Conduct Problems Prevention Research Group, 1998). Yet as previously discussed, rates of adolescent-onset conduct disorder have not been found to vary substantially by gender in a cross-study comparison (Lahey et al., 1998); or, it may be that rates vary less by gender than previously thought. Based on the literature discussed, the logical question is where these girls came from and what it is about the transition into adolescence that may account for individual differences among girls in pathways to psychopathology.

In particular, our own work has focused on the pubertal transition and how a normative developmental process that is experienced by all youth sets individuals on different trajectories for adjustment, in terms of internalizing and externalizing behaviors, during adolescence and possibly beyond. In this chapter we will review some of the models that have connected puberty with changes in adjustment in early adolescence, especially for girls. As part of this chapter, we will present highlights of findings of a series of studies by our group. These studies exemplify the importance of understanding behavioral and adjustment pathways and the interaction of individual and contextual factors that shape these pathways during the transition to adolescence. In keeping with Cairns and Cairns's work on "lives in progress" (Cairns & Cairns, 1994), we focus on how the interaction of individuals within contexts during the pubertal transition set girls on different pathways for externalizing, internalizing, and healthy adjustment during the adolescent decade.

PUBERTY AND ADJUSTMENT: DEMONSTRATING EFFECTS

As indicated, puberty has been identified as a potentially important period of development, as adjustment pathways may demonstrate stability or change during this period of the life course, in part depending upon the dramatic changes that occur at this time. Although all youth will go through puberty, several aspects of the pubertal experience may differ among individuals. Obviously, the primary individual differences factor at this time is gender, in that the species has two genders with distinct reproductive capacities in adulthood. In addition, as part of differences in the course of pubertal development, girls begin puberty about 2 years earlier than their male counterparts, usually between 8 and 10 years of age (see Grumbach & Styne, 1998 and Kaplowitz et al., 1999, for recent reviews). As we and others have discussed previously (Brooks-Gunn, Graber, & Paikoff, 1994; Buchanan, Eccles, & Becker, 1992; Graber, Brooks-Gunn, & Warren, in press), there are at least three main categories of models that have been proposed that link puberty and adjustment. These main domains are hormonal models, status models, and timing models. Hormonal models propose that the hormonal changes of puberty either have direct influence on emotions or interact with other factors resulting in increases in negative affect such as depressive or aggressive symptoms. Status models suggest that attaining a particular level of physical development is associated with behavioral change. Such models rely on the social interpretation, either by the self or others, that a behavior is expected or typical for someone who has reached a certain level of development; otherwise, the individual may have a negative response or receive negative feedback from others about her or his development. Timing models suggest that it is not level per se that matters but being in synch or out of synch with one's peers in development; that is, developing earlier or later than most other children or adolescents is associated with negative adjustment outcomes.

Within each, the literature has been dominated by the examination of direct effect models. At the same time, we and others (Brooks-Gunn et al., 1994; Susman, 1997) have delineated more elaborated models for understanding puberty within the context of social and psychological development. The goal of the present discussion is not to review the literature to date in these areas. Rather, a brief summary is provided; our focus will be on recent empirical work that is examining more elaborated models for linking puberty and adjustment. Across this work, competing demands have existed. The first goal is to document that effects occur, and then it is necessary to determine why or how effects are found.

Hormone Effects on Adjustment

In general, examinations of hormonal influences on behavior at puberty, have focused on the dramatic increases in testosterone and estradiol during the course of puberty, with much of this literature examining links to aggressive behavior and feelings and depressive affect (e.g., see Buchanan et al., 1992, for review); a literature also links hormones and sexual behavior (e.g., Halpern, Udry, & Suchindran, 1997; Udry & Campbell, 1994). Across the literature, effects for aggressive or depressive symptoms or affect vary across study, by gender, by hormone, and by outcome.

Evidence suggests that increases in negative affect or variability in emotions is in part associated with hormonal factors (Archibald, Graber, Brooks-Gunn, & Warren, 2004; Brooks-Gunn et al., 1994; Buchanan et al., 1992; Susman et al., 1985). For example, Susman and her colleagues (1985) investigated associations between hormone levels and adjustment difficulties cross-sectionally in girls and boys who ranged in age from 9 to 14; the sample covered all levels of pubertal development from no pubertal development to completed pubertal development as indexed by Tanner stages. These researchers also assessed numerous hormones (i.e., luteinizing hormone, follicle stimulating hormone, testosterone, estradiol, and adrenal androgens, DHEA and DHEAS). One of the most consistent findings from this study on associations between hormones and affect was that associations were more often found for boys than for girls. For girls, high-for-age levels of FSH, but not LH, were associated with reports of sad affect and symptoms of psychopathology. However, having high-for-age levels suggests that the effect was accounted for by maturational timing; and in fact, after accounting for timing differences, hormones did not predict girls' adjustment in this study (Susman et al., 1985). Subsequent examination of aggressive and externalizing symptoms in this sample also demonstrated

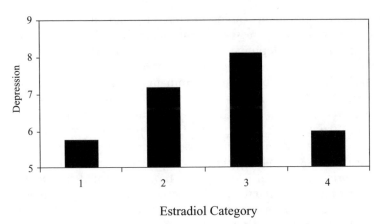

Estradiol Category

FIGURE 5.1. Significant quadratic effect of estradiol categories on depressive symptoms in girls. From "Mood and Behavior at Adolescence: Evidence for Hormonal
Factors," by M. P. Warren and Brooks-Gunn, 1989, *Journal of Clinical Endocrinology
and Metabolizing, 69*, pp. 77–83. Copyright 1989 by the Endocrine Society. Adapted
with permission.

few effects for girls (Susman et al., 1987). In this case, higher levels of androgens were related to acting-out problems in boys.

In work that focused on hormone-symptom associations in girls only,
Brooks-Gunn and her colleagues (Brooks-Gunn & Warren, 1989; Paikoff,
Brooks-Gunn, & Warren, 1991; Warren & Brooks-Gunn, 1989) sought to
test the hypothesis that "associations between negative emotional expression and hormonal changes will occur when the endocrine system is being
'turned on,' in the sense of moving from prepubertal to postpubertal levels"
(Brooks-Gunn & Warren, 1989, p. 41). Similarly to the work of Susman and
her colleagues, several hormones were assayed from a blood draw (specifically, FSH, LH, estradiol, DHEAS, and testosterone). Girls were then divided into four categories based on their levels of estradiol; estradiol levels
show the most dramatic increases during puberty, and many of the other
hormone levels correlate strongly with estradiol. Furthermore, the categories were based on ranges that reflected different levels of impact on
reproductive organs and functioning of the reproductive system. In comparisons of girls by these categories cross-sectionally, there was a significant
quadratic effect for girls' depressive symptoms (see Figure 5.1). The highest levels of depressive symptoms were found in the group that demonstrated onset (group 2) or rapid rise (group 3) in hormones (Brooks-Gunn
& Warren, 1989; Warren & Brooks-Gunn, 1989). In this study, DHEAS levels
also had a negative association with aggressive symptoms. When viewed
in isolation of other factors, hormones accounted for a small but significant percentage of the variance in negative affect. Longitudinal follow-up

of the same sample produced similar findings (Paikoff et al., 1991). Moreover, additional analyses that examined the prediction of aggressive and depressive symptoms by hormonal versus social factors found that social factors accounted for a greater percentage of the variance in symptoms (Brooks-Gunn & Warren, 1989).

In general, linear models do not capture the links between hormones and internalizing and externalizing symptoms for girls. Notably, recent work by Susman and her colleagues (Finkelstein et al., 1997; Susman et al., 1998) has used experimental methods to test such effects in a clinical sample. Specifically, adolescents with delayed pubertal development (due to medical condition) were enrolled in a double-blind, placebo-controlled study of the effects of hormone exposure. In this work, they demonstrate that sex steroids predicted increased physical aggression when testosterone (for boys) or estrogen (for girls) was administered at puberty (Finkelstein et al., 1997); negligible effects were found on mood (Susman et al., 1998). If hormonal influences are most pronounced when levels change rapidly, such changes may result in perturbations in mood as young adolescents adapt to new physiological input that they may have difficulty identifying or labeling. In this case, hormones at puberty may have an arousal effect on emotions, and then, in the process of labeling or along with other events, these changes lead to increases in aggressive or depressive moods (Brooks-Gunn et al., 1994; Buchanan et al., 1992; Graber et al., in press). This issue will be discussed in more detail in a subsequent section.

Status Effects on Adjustment, or Teasing Apart Status and Hormonal Effects

The literature on pubertal hormones and behavior is comparable to examinations of pubertal status effects in many ways. First, examinations of pubertal status links to adjustment focus on comparisons of outcomes among individuals at different levels or stages of key external signs of pubertal development (e.g., breast growth, pubic hair, testicular changes); staging is usually indexed by some measure of Tanner stages that range from no signs of development to development completed. In general, status has been thought to be important in that it demonstrates to oneself and others that the individual is more adultlike in appearance, and hence results in new responses from others in an adolescent's social world. As such, status effects seem to be salient for sexual behaviors or engagement in problem behaviors (e.g., drinking), as visual cues of looking more mature are likely used by others in determining "attractiveness" or appropriateness of sexual advances and other behaviors (Udry & Campbell, 1994). To date, limited effects of stage of pubertal development and aggressive or depressive affect have been found.

In both hormone and status models, the focus is frequently on adjustment correlates of being at a particular level of development, in terms of hormone levels or external signs of development. In part, the challenge has been to disentangle hormonal and status effects, as hormonal increases are the cause of the changes in physical growth and development. For example, in a study of early and mid-adolescent girls, Angold and colleagues (Angold, Costello, & Worthman, 1998) have found that depressive disorder was predicted by pubertal status; specifically, reaching Tanner Stage 3 of pubertal status was associated with increased levels of depression in girls. Subsequently, in testing hormonal effects on depressive disorder, Angold and colleagues (Angold, Costello, Erkanli, & Worthman, 1999) found that elevated estradiol and testosterone levels were predictive of girls' depression, and that these effects eliminated effects due to secondary sexual characteristics. Thus, considering both status and hormones demonstrated hormonal influences rather than status effects on the clinical end of the internalizing symptom spectrum.

In our own work, we have recently undertaken an investigation of girls' entry into puberty in order to examine how initial pubertal changes may be affecting girls' internalizing and externalizing in the mid to late childhood years. Via examination of both some initial hormonal changes and ratings of external markers of puberty (Tanner stages), it is possible to attempt to disentangle status from hormones and see what the affective experiences are of girls when they are in the early stages of puberty. In this study, we (Archibald et al., 2004) assessed hormone levels for LH and FSH over 3 consecutive days when girls were 8–9 years of age and again, about nine months later. Girls also completed daily diaries of their moods on these same days. We found that increases in concentration of LH relative to FSH over a 9-month period in middle to late childhood were significantly associated with girls' reports of more intense anger over time. Moreover, this relationship remained significant after accounting for secondary sexual characteristics as tapped by Tanner stages of breast and pubic hair development (i.e., visible signs of pubertal development). These are the first longitudinal findings of effects of the earliest hormone changes on preadolescent girls' daily mood states. In addition, in looking at pubertal status over the 9-month period, it was clear that girls were progressing at different rates through the Tanner stages. When girls were classified by amount of change, beginning pubertal development and experiencing greater change in level was associated with increased sadness and decreased positive mood (in comparison to girls who began puberty but progressed very little over the span of the study). As this study only examined changes in mood variability and intensity, it does not speak to internalizing and externalizing symptoms directly, but is consistent with the prior studies by Brooks-Gunn and Warren (1989; Warren & Brooks-Gunn, 1989) which found that girls experiencing rapid increases in hormones had higher depressive and aggressive symptoms. In the Archibald et al. (2004)

study, what seems to be salient in terms of pubertal status is actually perhaps best thought of as an effect of *rate* of pubertal change. Tanner (1970)
had for some time noted that adolescents vary not only in the timing of the
onset of puberty but also in the rate of progression through stages. Also,
Brooks-Gunn, Petersen, and Eichorn (1985) 20 years ago suggested that
psychological impact of rate of pubertal development merited investigation. Yet, we have found few studies that have examined rate as a factor in
change in affect during puberty.

Timing Effects on Adjustment

However, just as it has been difficult to disentangle hormonal and status
effects, it has also been a challenge to disentangle effects of level of development from differences in timing in development. As noted, there is
substantial variability among normally developing individuals in when
puberty begins and how it progresses (Tanner, 1962, 1970). Examinations
of the effects of timing of puberty on adjustment make comparisons among
individuals in terms of going through puberty earlier, at about the same
time, or later than one's peers. Although the notion that timing was important to adolescent adjustment and possibly personality was originally
proposed nearly 50 years ago by Jones and her colleagues (Jones & Bayley,
1950; Jones & Mussen, 1958), in the past 5–10 years a surge of studies have
documented the importance of timing to the development of psychopathology during adolescence (e.g., Graber, Lewinsohn, Seeley, & Brooks-Gunn,
1997; Hayward et al., 1997). The early maturation and the deviancy hypotheses are the two main hypotheses that have been the foundation of
these studies (Brooks-Gunn et al., 1985). The early maturation hypothesis
suggests that being earlier than one's peers results in individuals entering
into more "adultlike" behaviors commensurate with their physical appearance but before developing the skills needed to negotiate these situations.
The result is that early maturers, potentially both girls and boys (Huddleston & Ge, 2003), may engage in more problem behaviors and experience
greater distress during adolescence. As per the deviation hypothesis, being
out of synch with one's peers results in poor mental health; in this case,
early-maturing girls and late-maturing boys should be at risk for negative
outcomes as their development is the most out of synch or off time given
the relative gender difference in puberty.

As indicated, recent studies have demonstrated important effects of
timing on adjustment. Much of the evidence is in line with what would
be expected from both the deviation and early maturation hypotheses.
Thus, these global hypotheses have not been particularly informative in
understanding why pubertal timing influences the course of development.
Or rather, studies have not been designed to test fully the mechanisms
underlying timing effects. For the early maturation hypothesis, it is not
clear which developmental processes have been interrupted or curtailed

by puberty. Is it that once a girl looks older, she is more often in situations that demand social cognitive expertise (e.g., better decision making) or emotion regulation (e.g., regulating sexual feelings) that is typical for someone of her physical appearance rather than typical for someone of her age? For the deviancy hypothesis, how does being "deviant" from peers result in subsequent problems? It may be that the individual's perception of being deviant from peers results in negative emotions that stem from feeling different (Graber, Petersen, & Brooks-Gunn, 1996). For girls, it has been suggested that the experience of gaining weight and being larger than other girls, and often one's same-age boys, leads to poor self-evaluations and subsequent problems for early maturers. At the same time, late-maturing boys are smaller and shorter than all their same-age peers; again, gender norms for physical appearance would place these boys at risk for negative self-evaluations. However, tests of the specific pathways that might be predicted from each hypothesis have not been extensively made.

To date, early maturation in girls has been linked to both diagnosable disorders and subclinical symptoms including depression; alcohol, tobacco, and substance use; disruptive behaviors/conduct disorder; eating disorders and symptoms; and suicide attempts (e.g., Dick, Rose, Kaprio, & Viken, 2000; Ge, Conger, & Elder, 2001a; Graber, Brooks-Gunn, Paikoff, & Warren, 1994; Graber et al., 1997; Hayward et al., 1997; Lanza & Collins, 2002; Stice, Presnell, & Bearman 2001; Wichstrom, 2001). For example, Figure 5.2 shows the effect of pubertal timing on life-time history of depression (Figure 5.2a) and life-time history of disruptive behavior disorder (Figure 5.2b) in the high school years in the Oregon Adolescent Depression Project (OADP; Graber et al., 1997). In the OADP (see Figure 5.2a), late maturation was associated with higher rates of lifetime history of depression for girls in mid-adolescence; this is one of the few negative effects of late maturation that has been found for girls. Notably, rates of conduct disorder for early-maturing girls in the OADP are equivalent to rates of conduct disorder for boys, overall. Perhaps what has been most striking in the literature are the consistent associations of early maturation with disorders (as per DSM criteria) rather than just a range of symptoms. And, early maturation in girls is linked to both internalizing and externalizing types of problems or disorders rather than just one or the other.

Several studies of timing effects have been limited to samples of girls and thus, less is known about associations between timing and psychopathology in boys. In the emerging literature on boys, effects of timing on subclinical psychopathology for both early- and late-maturing boys during young and mid-adolescence have also been demonstrated. For boys, early maturation has been linked with elevated depressive symptoms, alcohol use and abuse, and delinquent and externalizing behaviors (Ge, Conger, & Elder, 2001b; Wichstrom, 2001; Williams & Dunlop, 1999). No identified studies

2a Depression

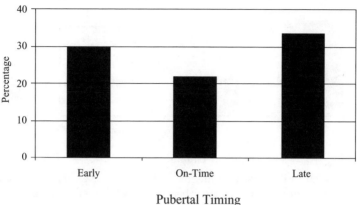

Pubertal Timing

2b Disruptive Behavior Disorder

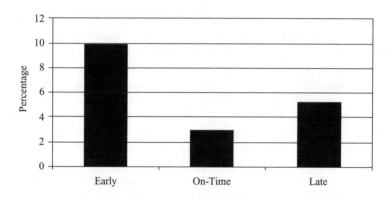

Pubertal Timing

FIGURE 5.2. Pubertal timing effect on lifetime history of depression (2a) and disruptive behavior disorder (2b) in the OADP (Graber et al., 1997). In 2a, rates for early-maturing and late-maturing girls are significantly higher than for on-time maturers. In 2b, rates for early-maturing girls are significantly higher than for on-time maturers.

have linked early maturation in boys with diagnosable disorders, only subclinical symptoms. Late maturation has also been linked to elevated psychological distress during mid adolescence (Graber et al., 1997) and increased alcohol use in young adulthood (Andersson & Magnusson, 1990).

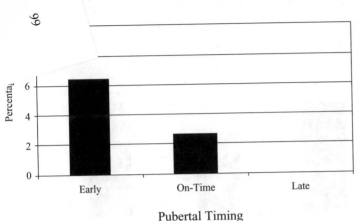

FIGURE 5.3. Pubertal timing effect on lifetime history rates of elevated antisocial personality traits in the OADP at age 24 (Graber et al., 2004). Rates for young women who were early maturers are significantly higher than for young women who were on-time maturers. No late-maturing women had elevated antisocial personality traits.

In regionally and nationally representative samples (Graber et al., 1997; Lanza & Collins, 2002), race was not a significant covariate in links between disorders or substance use and pubertal timing for girls; however, only Lanza and Collins (2002) had sufficient sample size for nonwhite youth for these to be meaningful analyses. Specific links within racial groups between timing and adjustment are just beginning to be studied. Ge and colleagues (Ge, Brody, Conger, Simons, & Murry, 2002) report similar effects of early maturation in both boys and girls on internalizing and externalizing behaviors and symptoms in a community sample of African-American young adolescents. Although the empirical base is still quite limited, the emerging evidence is that early maturation is a risk for adjustment problems for white and African-American youth and possibly other groups.

Most recently, in our own work with the Oregon Adolescent Depression Project (OADP; Graber, Seeley, Brooks-Gunn, & Lewinsohn, 2004), we have examined the longer-term consequences of pubertal timing on psychopathology in young adulthood. Of note, is that early timing effects for girls were maintained into young adulthood in that young women who had been earlier maturers continued to have higher lifetime prevalence rates of major depression, anxiety, disruptive behavior disorders, and hence any Axis I psychiatric disorder, as well as higher lifetime rates of attempted suicide in comparison to other women. By young adulthood, early maturing women also had higher rates of antisocial personality traits in comparison to their on-time counterparts (see Figure 5.3). As demonstrated previously in the examination of disorder in the high school years, early maturation was a risk for both internalizing and externalizing problems at the disorder end of the spectrum. Over time, other girls or young women do not simply have later onset of disorder; that is, the timing difference would disappear if the on-time and late maturers developed disorders at the same rate as early maturers but at later times in the course of adolescence. Instead, on-time and late maturers do not "catch up" in rates of disorder (at least by age 24) and differences in lifetime prevalence rates are maintained into adulthood.

In young men, late maturers had higher lifetime rates of disruptive behavior disorder and higher current rates of substance use than their on-time counterparts. Early maturation in boys resulted in daily tobacco use rates at age 24 for these young men that were nearly twice the national average for men ages 25–34 (40% versus 26.6%, respectively). In the OADP analyses, the disruptive behavior disorders category included ADHD, conduct, and oppositional defiant disorder; ADHD did not account for any of the effects.

Notably, the extant literature on conduct disorders has identified childhood and adolescent onset of disorders as the two patterns that are predominant in the course of development. In a recent cross-sample comparison (Lahey et al., 1998), girls were more likely to exhibit adolescent onset rather than onset in childhood in only one of the samples under comparison. However, Lahey and colleagues note that gender differences in age at onset have been consistently found in other studies. It is clear from work in projects that screen for children with high risk for subsequent development of conduct disorder and aggression in the earlier school years that boys greatly outnumber girls in possessing these characteristics (e.g., Moffitt, 1993; Stormshak et al., 1998). From our work with the OADP, pubertal timing appears to be an important factor in conduct disorder among girls at adolescence. Also from this work, it is clear that late-maturing males seem to fit a different pattern for onset of conduct problems and substance use; it may be that their disorders are comparable in precursors and behavioral expression to adolescent-onset cases, but that the onset occurs during the transition into adulthood (between the ages of 19 and 23 in this sample). That is, late maturers may follow the same progression of adolescent onset, but the process is delayed. Or it may be that the experience of late maturation results in increased symptomatology in young adulthood.

Based on the literature and our own studies, pubertal timing appears to be salient to the onset of both depression and conduct-related disorders for early-maturing girls and to conduct-related disorders among late-maturing boys. The data for girls, moreover, indicate the severity and uniqueness of this association. That is, other girls do not eventually catch up to early maturers in terms of rates of disorders, but rather these individuals persist in higher lifetime prevalence rates. How timing confers these risks has been the other focal point of research on timing and adjustment.

IDENTIFYING PATHWAYS TO EXPLAIN WHY PUBERTAL HORMONE,
STATUS, AND TIMING EFFECTS OCCUR

From the prior discussion, some issues emerge that need to be addressed in
identifying mechanisms and pathways of timing effects. In several studies, examinations of pubertal effects have been conducted in young to
mid-adolescent samples. From the perspective of understanding adolescent transitions, this approach worked well. However, such an approach
misses the beginning of puberty for many girls and some boys. Thus, studies have rarely followed individuals through the full range of pubertal
development for both girls and boys. (See Susman et al., 1985, 1987, for
exceptions; in this case, participants were recruited by pubertal stage rather
than by age.)

Moreover, although there has been substantial discussion of why various aspects of pubertal development (e.g., timing or hormones) influence
adjustment, examination of pathways has been somewhat limited. In part,
the process of identifying an effect has not been straightforward. At the
same time, several key hypotheses have been discussed frequently with
more or less substantive evidence in support of these. In addition, new
models are being developed to explain effects that have also begun to
emerge. In this section we examine a few of these models with highlights
from some of our work.

"Arousal" as a Pathway to Increased Symptomatology

As noted, hormonal links to behavior have been demonstrated for both
increased internalizing and externalizing symptoms. Many of these studies have considered hormonal influences in isolation of other factors. In
contrast, when looking at the effects of stressful life events and hormonal
influences simultaneously, Brooks-Gunn and Warren (1989) demonstrated
that stressful events explained a greater proportion of the variance in depressive symptoms in young adolescent girls. In this case, hormonal and
social factors were examined independently of one another.

Another approach has focused on arousal rather than stressful life events
(Buchanan et al., 1992; Brooks-Gunn et al., 1994). That is, new physiological
patterns may stimulate an emotional response that is subsequently labeled
negatively by the adolescent. Thus, a social–cognitive process may mediate the association of hormonal changes on adolescent outcome. In this
case, aroused emotional states may be indicated by increased moodiness,
sudden mood changes, feelings of self-consciousness, or elevated intensity
of moods that, if interpreted negatively, would then lead to internalizing
symptoms or emotional outbursts (i.e., acting out) and externalizing symptoms. Comparably, an important issue in understanding pubertal timing

effects is considering individual differences within timing group. In this case, early timing among girls has been linked to serious psychopathology, as described, but not all early-maturing girls develop disorders. Again, some type of individual differences factor or characteristic may interact with the experience of pubertal timing (e.g., peer group affiliation).

In order to test pathways from pubertal factors to symptoms, we examined these issues in a study of 100 young adolescent girls; both depressive and aggressive symptoms were examined (Graber et al., in press). In this study, we focused on two hormones, estradiol and DHEAS, in identifying pathways from hormonal levels to symptoms. For girls, estradiol levels and changes have commonly been the focus of investigation, and in this sample, rapidly changing levels of estradiol had previously been found to be predictive of symptom levels (Warren & Brooks-Gunn, 1989; as shown in Figure 5.1). DHEAS taps adrenal androgen activity; DHEAS and other adrenal androgens have demonstrated associations with aggression, in particular (Susman et al., 1987; Warren & Brooks-Gunn, 1989) and depressive symptoms (Angold et al., 1998; Susman et al., 1997). In addition to the two hormonal influences, we also examined the effects of early timing on aggressive and depressive symptoms.

As indicated the primary purpose of the investigation, though, was to examine pathways. In order to test pathways, we examined emotional arousal, attention difficulties, and stressful life events. Emotional arousal was tapped by mood changes and increased intensity of moods (tension, self-consciousnes). Models tested whether each of these factors mediated the association between the pubertal factor (estradiol, DHEAS, or timing) and depressive or aggressive symptoms. For depressive symptoms, the effect of early pubertal timing was mediated by emotional arousal (see Figure 5.4). Estradiol (collapsed into categories) was associated with depressive affect as previously discussed (Brooks-Gunn & Warren, 1989; Warren & Brooks-Gunn, 1989) but mediation was not found for any of the constructs tested. In predicting aggressive symptoms, for both estradiol and DHEAS, the effects on symptom levels were mediated by stressful life events; early maturation was not associated with aggressive symptoms.

From these analyses, the question remained why early maturation was mediated by emotional arousal, especially as hormonal links to the outcome variables were not mediated by arousal as we had predicted. We conducted additional analyses to determine if early maturation was associated with "hormonal arousal" that might be an underlying factor in emotional arousal. Because this sample of girls was drawn from several age groups, early maturation was not confounded with hormonal levels; that is, if girls were older and at later stages of pubertal development (and hence, higher hormonal levels), they could be on-time or later maturers and need not be early maturers. As it has been suggested that adrenal response

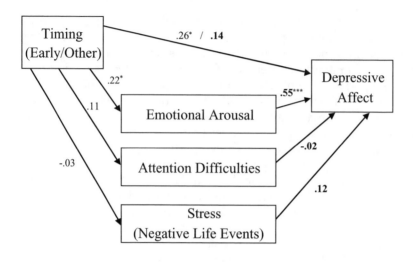

$R^2 = .37$; $\underline{F}(5, 90) = 9.89$, $\underline{p} < .0001$;   **Mediated Pathway via Arousal**

FIGURE 5.4. Path model for early pubertal timing and depressive affect. On the left side of the model, the β values were calculated separately for the pathway for timing to depressive affect and to each potential mediator. The β coefficients on the right side of the model (shown in bold type) were calculated with all variables (predictor and mediators) entered simultaneously into the model; there are two β coefficients for the timing predictor to the outcome.

is linked to stress responses (e.g., cortisol response to stress), we focused on DHEAS levels in connection to early maturation. The upper third of the distribution of DHEAS was considered to be high hormonal arousal. Interestingly, the interaction of DHEAS (high versus low arousal) and timing (early versus other) was predictive of depressive symptoms with a trend for the interaction to predict the emotional arousal construct. As shown in Figure 5.5, girls who were early maturers and who had high arousal as tapped by higher levels of DHEAS had the highest reports of depressive symptoms. (A similar pattern is seen for the emotional arousal variable.) These moderator models were not predictive of aggressive symptoms.

These findings are suggestive of the complexity of the pathways from pubertal processes to adolescent outcomes. For depressive symptoms, direct hormonal effects seemed to have some predictive power; however, what is perhaps most striking is the identification of a moderating effect that may shed light on why early maturational timing leads to higher rates of depression by mid-adolescence. In particular, a subgroup of girls at about age 12 had increased levels of DHEAS and early maturation. This pattern was associated with elevated emotional arousal (mood changes and mood intensity) and depressive symptoms. At the same time, DHEAS levels did

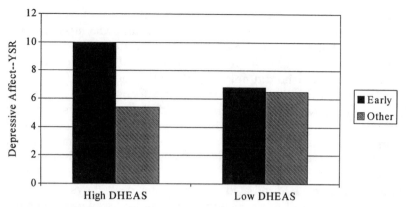

FIGURE 5.5. The interaction of high DHEAS levels (as an index of high adrenal activity) and early maturation on girls' depressive affect.

not vary by timing group; as indicated, the age range of the sample meant that timing and status or hormonal levels were not confounded. The fact that DHEAS is an adrenal hormone is also of interest. Goodyer and his colleagues (Goodyer, Herbert, Tamplin, & Altham, 2000) have found that DHEAS levels were predictive of onset of a depressive disorder over a 1-year period in a sample of postpubertal adolescents. Unfortunately, they did not examine puberty or timing in this work.

At the same time, even though pubertal timing has also been linked to increased rates of conduct disorder among girls during mid-adolescence (Graber et al., 1997) and externalizing symptoms at young adolescence (e.g., Ge et al., 2002), a comparable subgroup of early maturers with different levels of DHEAS, or other hormonal characteristics, was not identified in our study of pathways to aggressive symptoms. There are several future directions that need to be explored in this area. As previously discussed, "aggression" or "externalizing symptoms" are not unitary constructs. Our study used a measure that essentially tapped verbal aggression. Timing has been linked to conduct disorder. It may be that elevated verbal aggression is predictive of conduct disorder at later points in time; however, it is probably more likely that other forms of aggression, oppositional behaviors, or delinquency are stronger developmental precursors to this disorder in girls. In addition, pathways to externalizing problems for early-maturing girls may have little to do with hormone levels or changes but more to do with social factors – a point that merits further elaboration.

Social Relations as Pathways to Increased Symptomatology

An important caveat of early maturation is that these children look different, specifically older, than same-age peers. As such, they likely see themselves differently and are often treated differently by adults (e.g., Crockett & Petersen, 1987) and by peers. Stattin and Magnusson (1990) demonstrated that early-maturing girls who associated with older peers were more likely to engage in problem behaviors at younger ages than early-maturing girls who did not associate with older peers. The subsequent elaboration on this finding has been to focus on early-maturing girls' associations with deviant peers or associations with boys. Drawing upon the Stattin and Magnusson findings (1990), the hypotheses have been that, first, "older" peers were likely to engage in problem behaviors, and second, that "older" peers were likely to be older boys, that is, romantic partners.

Recent studies have found evidence that older peers, boys, or deviant peers are a correlate of externalizing behaviors for younger adolescent girls. Early maturation along with dating can result in increased symptom levels for eating problems for young adolescent girls (Cauffman & Steinberg, 1996; Gargiulo, Attie, Brooks-Gunn, & Warren, 1987). In another study, early maturational timing was only associated with problem behaviors or externalizing symptoms for girls who attend schools with boys in comparison to girls in single-sex educational environments (Caspi, Lynam, Moffitt, & Silva, 1993). In yet another example of contextual factors that influence the outcomes for early maturers, Ge and his colleagues (2002) found that early maturers living in disadvantaged neighborhoods were more likely to associate with deviant peers than other youth and, in general, as seen in other studies, affiliation with deviant peers was linked to increased externalizing symptoms.

In some sense, the underlying mechanism for why these relationships lead to difficulties for early-maturing girls is that these girls are less mature than the peers with whom they are associating, and as such, may have more difficulty managing the situations that arise. Another interpretation may be that older youth who associate with early-maturing girls, especially boys, are likely less socially competent than other youth and, as such, these youth model and encourage deviant behaviors. Interestingly, in our work with the OADP sample, along with the striking rates of depressive and conduct disorders among early-maturing girls, these girls also consistently report lower levels of social support from family and friends in mid-adolescence and young adulthood (Graber et al., 1997; Graber et al., 2004). By young adulthood, women who had been early maturers had higher rates of traits of Antisocial Personality disorder, a disorder associated with serious impairments in interpersonal relationships. Such findings further elaborate a pattern of relationship difficulties not just in terms of who these girls associate with but also in terms of the quality of the relationships. Deficits in social interactions thus may be a pathway from early maturation to subsequent externalizing symptoms and serious disorders for girls. This hypothesis requires more detailed examinations

of the quality of relationships for early-maturing girls and th
through which they find themselves with deviant peers or old

Deficits in Social Skills as Pathways to Symptomatology

Whereas the literature on pubertal timing effects on adjustment in girls
has hypothesized that social relationships may be an explanatory factor or
mechanism for effects, it has also been suggested, as previously mentioned,
that early maturation may curtail the normative development of social
skills. One of the original tenets of the stage-termination hypothesis, or
early maturation hypothesis was that experiencing puberty earlier than
one's peers resulted in less time for developing adaptive skills needed to
meet the challenges of adolescence. There are no studies that examine this
aspect of the hypothesis, as no studies of pubertal effects on adjustment
have specifically measured social competence skills – anger management,
decision making, or communication skills.

However, there is a literature on normative social skill development
and there is a strong focus on teaching social skills in prevention programming that targets aggression and violence. To date, as we discussed at the
beginning of this chapter, the study of prevention programming for externalizing behaviors has focused more often on boys. Thus, in a separate
line of research on prevention of violence, we have recently examined gender differences in a range of aggressive behaviors, anger levels, and how
adolescent skills or competencies are associated with aggression over time
(Nichols, Graber, Brooks-Gunn, & Botvin, 2004). Interestingly, in this investigation of urban, minority middle school students, whereas boys' reports
of anger levels are stable from sixth to seventh grade, girls' anger levels
are slightly higher than boys' levels in sixth and increase dramatically by
seventh grade. For both boys and girls, anger was predictive of aggressive behaviors. From our studies of pubertal change, anger increases with
changes in hormones (Archibald et al., 2004; Warren & Brooks-Gunn, 1989).
Taken together, there is an emerging picture of girls' anger increasing with
puberty or age; age, though, may be tapping puberty. In our ongoing work
on anger and aggression, we are examining how anger management skills
influence this process. Such findings are potentially quite important in developing violence prevention programs that would be effective for both
boys and girls and in suggesting avenues for subsequent research.

As is clear from the prior discussion, even in our own work, we seemed
to have addressed the etiology of social competence skills and aggression,
and the links between puberty and anger and aggression in separate studies. Because of the separation of the various fields of inquiry, our conclusions on social skills are essentially hypotheses that we hope merit future
research.

CONCLUSIONS

We began with the hypothesis that the period of puberty was particularly important in understanding issues of behavioral change, or plasticity in behavior at adolescence. In the course of this discussion, we have frequently intermixed studies and findings that relate to externalizing and internalizing symptoms and problems. Because of the specific focus of the present volume, somewhat greater attention has been paid to externalizing symptoms in girls. Much of the work described has often considered both types of symptoms, and effects have sometimes been found more often for one than another problem. Notably, serious problems associated with early maturation, especially for girls, are found in conduct disorder and depression as well as other disorders. Pathways to specific outcomes may vary, but only through continuing to test multiple types of outcomes will specificity be determined.

In addition, there are undoubtedly other models that would explain pubertal effects on externalizing and internalizing behaviors. Caspi and Moffitt (1991) have demonstrated that preexisting problems are accentuated for girls who are early maturers. In this study, girls with behavior problems in childhood who were not early maturers in fact did not increase in severity of symptoms by mid-adolescence in comparison to their early-maturing counterparts. Such findings demonstrate that the direction of change in behavior at puberty may not simply be toward worsening of symptoms or emergence of new symptoms. Studies that continue to examine pathways across puberty incorporating multiple dimensions of puberty (e.g., hormones, social factors) are still necessary. At the same time, testing of particular pathways, such as those outlined, is likely achievable with designs that focus on specific segments of development both proximal and distal to puberty. For example, pubertal timing effects seem to emerge in the middle-school to high-school years, and focused studies of this period will likely be useful for testing pathways even though most early-maturing girls are at the end of puberty in middle school and most girls have completed puberty by mid-adolescence. In an effort to understand better "lives in progress," considering transitional periods and in particular puberty is likely to afford a window on the range of behavioral plasticity that exists during this transition. Moreover, this work also speaks to developing and enhancing prevention and intervention initiatives with children and youth.

References

Andersson, T., & Magnusson, D. (1990). Biological maturation in adolescence and the development of drinking habits and alcohol abuse among young males: A prospective longitudinal study. *Journal of Youth and Adolescence, 19,* 33–41.

Angold, A., Costello, E. J., Erkanli, A., & Worthman, C. M. (1999). Pubertal changes in hormone levels and depression in girls. *Psychological Medicine, 29,* 1043–1053.

Angold, A., Costello, E. J., & Worthman, C. M. (1998). Puberty and depression: The roles of age, pubertal status, and pubertal timing. *Psychological Medicine, 28,* 51–16.

Archibald, A. B., Graber, J. A., Brooks-Gunn, J., & Warren, M. P. (2004). *Effects of the earliest pubertal and hormonal changes on pre-adolescent girls' mood: A short-term longitudinal study.* Submitted for publication.

Baltes, P. B., Lindenberger, U., & Staudinger, U. M. (1998). Life-span theory in developmental psychology. In W. Damon (Series Ed.), & R. M. Lerner (Vol. Ed.), *Handbook of child psychology: Vol. 1. Theoretical models of human development* (pp. 939–991). New York: Wiley.

Berndt, T. J. (1996). Transitions in friendship and friends' influence. In J. A. Graber, J. Brooks-Gunn, & A. C. Petersen (Eds.), *Transitions through adolescence: Interpersonal domains and context.* Mahwah, NJ: Lawrence Erlbaum Associates.

Birmaher, B., Ryan, N. D., Williamson, D. E., Brent, D. A., Kaufman, J., Dahl, R. E., et al. (1996). Childhood and adolescent depression: A review of the past 10 years. Part I. *Journal of the American Academy of Child and Adolescent Psychiatry, 35,* 1427–1439.

Brooks-Gunn, J., Graber, J. A., & Paikoff, R. L. (1994). Studying links between hormones and negative affect: Models and measures. *Journal of Research on Adolescence, 4*(4), 469–486.

Brooks-Gunn, J., & Petersen, A. C. (Eds.). (1991). The emergence of depression and depressive symptoms during adolescence [Special issue]. *Journal of Youth and Adolescence, 20.*

Brooks-Gunn, J., Petersen, A. C., & Eichorn, D. (1985). The study of maturational timing effects in adolescence. *Journal of Youth and Adolescence, 14*(3), 149–161.

Brooks-Gunn, J., & Reiter, E. O. (1990). The role of pubertal processes in the early adolescent transition. In S. Feldman & G. Elliott (Eds.), *At the threshold: The developing adolescent* (pp. 16–53). Cambridge, MA: Harvard University Press.

Brooks-Gunn, J., & Warren, M. P. (1989). Biological contributions to affective expression in young adolescent girls. *Child Development, 60,* 372–385.

Bruer, J. T., & Greenough, W. T. (2001). The subtle science of how experience affects the brain. In D. B. Bailey, Jr., J. T. Bruer, F. J. Symons, & J. W. Lichtman (Eds.), *Critical thinking about critical periods* (pp. 3–26). Baltimore, MD: Brookes Publishing Co.

Buchanan, C. M., Eccles, J. S., & Becker, J. B. (1992). Are adolescents the victims of raging hormones: Evidence for activational effects of hormones on moods and behavior at adolescence. *Psychological Bulletin, 111,* 62–107.

Cairns, R. B. (1998). Developmental plasticity and continuity in social interactions: Attachment and aggression. In National Institute of Mental Health, *Advancing research on developmental plasticity: Integrating the behavioral science and neuroscience of mental health* (pp. 153–163; NIH Pub. No. 98–4338). Bethesda, MD: National Institutes of Health.

Cairns, R. B., & Cairns, B. D. (1994). *Lifelines and risks: Pathways of youth in our time.* New York: Cambridge University Press.

Cairns, R. B., & Cairns, B. D. (2000). The natural history of developmental functions of aggression. In A. J. Sameroff, M. Lewis & S. M. Miller (Eds.), *Handbook of developmental psychopathology* (2nd ed., pp. 403–429). New York: Plenum Press.

Caspi, A., Lynam, D., Moffitt, T. E., & Silva, P. A. (1993). Unraveling girls' delinquency: Biological, dispositional, and contextual contributions to adolescent misbehavior. *Developmental Psychology, 29,* 19–30.

Caspi, A., & Moffitt, T. E. (1991). Individual differences are accentuated during periods of social change: The sample case of girls at puberty. *Journal of Personality and Social Psychology, 61,* 157–168.

Cauffman, E. & Steinberg, L. (1996). Interactive effects of menarcheal status and dating on dieting and disordered eating among adolescent girls. *Developmental Psychology, 32,* 631–635.

Crockett, L. J., & Petersen, A. C. (1987). Pubertal status and psychosocial development: Findings from the Early Adolescence Study. In R. M. Lerner & T. T. Foch (Eds.), *Biological–psychosocial interactions in early adolescence: A life-span perspective* (pp. 173–188). Hillsdale, NJ: Erlbaum.

Dick, D. M., Rose, R. J., Kaprio, J., & Viken, R. J. (2000). Pubertal timing and substance use: Associations between and within families across late adolescence. *Developmental Psychology, 36,* 180–189.

Eccles, J. S., Midgley, C., Wigfield, A., Buchanan, C. M., Reuman, D., Flanagan, C., et al. (1993). Development during adolescence: The impact of stage-environment fit in young adolescents' experiences in schools and in families. *American Psychologist, 48,* 90–101.

Finkelstein, J. W., Susman, E. J., Chinchilli, V. M., Kunselman, S. J., D'Arcangelo, M. R., Schwab, J., et al. (1997). Estrogen or testosterone increases self-reported aggressive behaviors in hypogonadal adolescents. *Journal of Clinical Endocrinology and Metabolism, 82,* 2433–2438.

Gargiulo, J., Attie, I., Brooks-Gunn, J., & Warren, M. P. (1987). Girls' dating behavior as a function of social context and maturation. *Developmental Psychology, 23* (5), 730–737.

Ge, X., Brody, G. H., Conger, R. D., Simons, R. L., & Murry, V. M. (2002). Contextual amplification of pubertal transition effects on deviant peer affiliation and externalizing behavior among African American children. *Developmental Psychology, 38,* 42–54.

Ge, X., Conger, R. D., & Elder, G. H., Jr. (2001a). Pubertal transition, stressful life events, and the emergence of gender differences in adolescent depressive symptoms. *Developmental Psychology, 37,* 404–417.

Ge, X., Conger, R. D., & Elder, G. H., Jr. (2001b). The relationship between puberty and psychological distress in adolescent boys. *Journal of Research on Adolescence, 11,* 49–70.

Goodyer, I. M., Herbert, J., Tamplin, A., & Altham, P. M. E. (2000). First-episode major depression in adolescents: Affective, cognitive and endocrine characteristics of risk status and predictors of onset. *British Journal of Psychiatry, 176,* 142–149.

Graber, J. A., & Brooks-Gunn, J. (1996). Transitions and turning points: Navigating the passage from childhood through adolescence. *Developmental Psychology, 32*(4), 768–776.

Graber, J. A., Brooks-Gunn, J., Paikoff, R. L., & Warren, M. P. (1994). Prediction of eating problems: An eight year study of adolescent girls. *Developmental Psychology, 30,* 823–834.

Graber, J. A., Brooks-Gunn, J., & Warren, M. P. (in press). Pubertal effects on adjustment in girls: Moving from demonstrating effects to identifying pathways. *Journal of Youth & Adolescence.*

Graber, J. A., Lewinsohn, P. M., Seeley, J. R., & Brooks-Gunn, J. (1997). Is psychopathology associated with the timing of pubertal development? *Journal of the American Academy of Child and Adolescent Psychiatry, 36,* 1768–1776.

Graber, J. A., Petersen, A. C., & Brooks-Gunn, J. (1996). Pubertal processes: Methods, measures, and models. In J. A. Graber, J. Brooks-Gunn, & A. C. Petersen (Eds.), *Transitions through adolescence: Interpersonal domains and context* (pp. 23–53). Mahwah, NJ: Lawrence Erlbaum & Associates.

Graber, J. A., Seeley, J. R., Brooks-Gunn, J., & Lewinsohn, P. M. (2004). Pubertal timing and psychopathology: Are effects maintained in young adulthood? *Journal of the American Academy of Child and Adolescent Psychiatry* 43(6), 718–726.

Grumbach, M. M., & Styne, D. M. (1998). Puberty: Ontogeny, neuroendocrinology, physiology, and disorders. In J. D. Wilson, D. W. Fostor, & H. M. Kronenberg (Eds.), *Williams textbook of endocrinology* (pp. 1509–1625). Philadelphia, PA: W. B. Saunders.

Halpern, C. T., Udry, J. R., & Suchindran, C. (1997). Testosterone predicts initiation of coitus in adolescent females. *Psychosomatic Medicine, 59,* 161–171.

Hayward, C., Killen, J. D., Wilson, D. M., Hammer, L. D., Litt, I. F., Kraemer, H. C., et al. (1997). Psychiatric risk associated with early puberty in adolescent girls. *Journal of the American Academy of Child and Adolescent Psychiatry, 36,* 255–262.

Huddleston, J., & Ge, X. (2003). Boys at puberty: Psychosocial implications. In C. Hayward (Ed.), *Gender differences at puberty* (pp. 113–134). New York: Cambridge University Press.

Jones, M. C., & Bayley, N. (1950). Physical maturing among boys as related to behavior. *Journal of Educational Psychology, 41,* 129–148.

Jones, M. C., & Mussen, P. H. (1958). Self-conceptions, motivations, and interpersonal attitudes of early- and late-maturing girls. *Child Development, 29,* 491–501.

Kaplowitz, P. B., Oberfield, S. E., & The Drug and Therapeutics and Executive Committees of the Lawson Wilkins Pediatric Endocrine Society. (1999). Reexamination of the age limit for defining when puberty is precocious in girls in the United States: Implications for evaluation and treatment. *Pediatrics, 104,* 936–941.

Keating, D. P. (1990). Adolescent thinking. In S. Feldman & G. Elliott (Eds.), *At the threshold: The developing adolescent* (pp. 54–90). Cambridge, MA: Harvard University Press.

Lahey, B. B., Loeber, R., Quay, H. C., Applegate, B., Shaffer, D., Waldman, I., et al. (1998). Validity of DSM-IV subtypes of conduct disorder based on age of onset. *Journal of the American Academy of Child and Adolescent Psychiatry, 37,* 435–442.

Lanza, S. T., & Collins, L. M. (2002). Pubertal timing and the onset of substance use in females during early adolescence. *Prevention Science, 3,* 69–82.

Lewinsohn, P. M., Rohde, P., & Seeley, J. R. (1998). Major depressive disorder in older adolescents: Prevalence, risk factors, and clinical implications. *Clinical Psychology Review, 18,* 765–794.

Loeber, R., Farrington, D. P., Stouthamer-Loeber, M., & Van Kammen, W. B. (1998). *Antisocial behavior and mental health problems: Explanatory factors in childhood and adolescence.* Mahwah, NJ: Erlbaum Associates.

Moffitt, T. E. (1993). Adolescence-limited and life-course persistent antisocial behavior: A developmental taxonomy. *Psychological Review, 100,* 674–701.

Nichols, T. R., Graber, J. A., Brooks-Gunn, J., & Botvin, G. J. (2004). *Gender differences in aggression and delinquency among urban minority middle school students.* Submitted for publication.

Paikoff, R., & Brooks-Gunn, J. (1991). Do parent–child relationships change during puberty? *Psychological Bulletin, 110*(1), 47–66.

Paikoff, R. L., Brooks-Gunn, J., & Warren, M. P. (1991). Effects of girls' hormonal status on depressive and aggressive symptoms over the course of one year. *Journal of Youth and Adolescence, 20,* 191–215.

Pajer, K. A. (1998). What happens to "bad" girls? A review of the adult outcomes of antisocial adolescent girls. *The American Journal of Psychiatry, 155,* 862–870.

Pickles, A., & Rutter, M. (1991). Statistical and conceptual models of 'turning points' in developmental processes. In D. Magnusson, L. R. Bergman, G. Rudinger, & B. Torestad (Eds.), *Problems and methods in longitudinal research: Stability and change.* Cambridge, England: Cambridge University Press.

Rutter, M. (1994). Continuities, transitions and turning points in development. In M. Rutter & D. F. Hay (Eds.), *Development through life: A handbook for clinicians* (pp. 1–25). London: Blackwell Scientific Publications.

Spear, L. P. (2000). The adolescent brain and age-related behavioral manifestations. *Neuroscience and Biobehavioral Reviews, 24,* 417–463.

Stattin, H., & Magnusson, D. (1990). *Paths through life: Vol. 2. Pubertal maturation in female development.* Hillsdale, NJ: Erlbaum.

Steinberg, L. (2001). We know some things: Parent–adolescent relationships in retrospect and prospect. *Journal of Research on Adolescence, 11,* 1–19.

Steinberg, L., & Morris, A. S. (2001). Adolescent development. *Annual Review of Psychology, 52,* 83–110.

Steiner-Adair, C. (1986). The body politic: Normal adolescent development and the development of eating disorders. *Journal of the American Academy of Psychoanalysis, 14,* 95–114.

Stice, E., Presnell, K., & Bearman, S. K. (2001). Relation of early menarche to depression, eating disorders, substance abuse, and comorbid psychopathology among adolescent girls. *Developmental Psychology, 37,* 608–619.

Stormshak, E. A., Bierman, K. L., and The Conduct Problems Prevention Research Group. (1998). The implications of different developmental patterns of disruptive behavior problems for school adjustment. *Development and Psychopathology, 10,* 451–467.

Susman, E. J. (1997). Modeling developmental complexity in adolescence: Hormones and behavior in context. *Journal of Research on Adolescence, 7,* 283–306.

Susman, E. J., Finkelstein, J. W., Chinchilli, V. M., Schwab, J., Liben, L. S., D'Arcangelo, M. R., et al. (1998). The effect of sex hormone replacement therapy on behavior problems and moods in adolescents with delayed puberty. *Journal of Pediatrics, 133,* 521–525.

Susman, E. J., Inoff-Germain, G. E., Nottelmann, E. D., Loriaux, D. L., Cutler, G. B., Jr., & Chrousos, G. P. (1987). Hormones, emotional dispositions, and aggressive attributes in early adolescents. *Child Development, 58,* 1114–1134.

Susman, E. J., Nottelmann, E. D., Inoff-Germain, G. E., Dorn, L. D., Cutler, G. B., Loriaux, D. L., et al. (1985). The relation of relative hormone levels and physical development and social–emotional behavior in young adolescents. *Journal of Youth and Adolescence, 14,* 245–264.

Tanner, J. M. (1962). *Growth at adolescence.* New York: Lippincott.

Tanner, J. M. (1970). Physical growth. In P. H. Mussen (Ed.), *Carmichael's manual of child psychology* (pp. 77–155). New York: Wiley.

Udry, J. R., & Campbell, B. C. (1994). Getting started on sexual behavior. In A. S. Rossi (Ed.), *Sexuality across the life course. The John D. and Catherine T. MacArthur Foundation series on mental health and development: Studies on successful midlife development* (pp. 187–207). Chicago: University of Chicago Press.

Warren, M. P., & Brooks-Gunn, J. (1989). Mood and behavior at adolescence: Evidence for hormonal factors. *Journal of Clinical Endocrinology and Metabolism, 69,* 77–83.

Wichstrom, L. (2001). The impact of pubertal timing on adolescents' alcohol use. *Journal of Research on Adolescence, 11,* 131–150.

Williams, J. M., & Dunlop, L. C. (1999). Pubertal timing and self-reported delinquency among male adolescents. *Journal of Adolescence, 22,* 157–171.

PART II

BIDIRECTIONALITY

6

Touch Deprivation and Aggression Against Self Among Adolescents

Tiffany Field

Touch Research Institutes, University of Miami School of Medicine

INTRODUCTION

Increasing trends for suicidal ideation and attempts among adolescents highlight the need for identifying risk factor profiles and interventions. In a recent survey study we reported that depression, anger, number of friends, and marijuana contributed to 66% of the variance on suicidal ideation in adolescents. In other studies with depressed adolescents we were able to reduce depression and suicidal ideation by massage therapy. The model explored in this paper on adolescents' suicidal ideation and suicidal attempts is (1) that depression, aggression, and body dissociation (physical anhedonia and higher thresholds to stimulation and pain) that may have derived from early touch deprivation/abuse may mediate suicidal ideation and attempts; and (2) that suicidal ideation and attempts might be reduced by massage therapy, a treatment that has already been effective with depressed adolescents. Underlying the risk factors for suicidal ideation and attempts are abnormal physiological factors including EEG alpha asymmetry and biochemical imbalances including depressed serotonin and elevated cortisol levels. Thus, some of the intervening mechanisms between touch deprivation/abuse and suicide may be the physiological (EEG asymmetry) and biochemical imbalances (depressed serotonin and elevated cortisol levels) that accompany depression and self-destructive behavior. Massage therapy may reduce suicidal ideation/behavior via reducing depression and cortisol levels and elevating serotonin levels and thereby reducing self-destructive behavior.

This research was supported by an NIMH Senior Research Scientist Award (MH#00331) and an NIMH merit award (MH#46586) to Tiffany Field and funding by Johnson and Johnson.

TOUCH DEPRIVATION AND AGGRESSION AGAINST
SELF (SUICIDE) AMONG ADOLESCENTS

The critical importance of researching adolescent suicide is underscored
by the fact that suicide is the biggest killer of adolescents in the United
States (Madge & Harvey, 1999), and the United States has one of the highest suicide rates among industrialized countries (Weissman et al., 1999).
Several different literatures converge to suggest that an early childhood
experience of abusive touch or the lack of nurturant touch may contribute
to several risk factors for adolescent suicide. The risk factors include becoming aggressive toward self or others (Stein, Apter, Ratzoni, Har-Even,
& Avidan, 1998) and related factors that lead to impulsive aggression including drugs and risk-taking behavior (Fombonne, 1998). A second risk
factor that may result from abusive touch or lack of nurturant touch in
early childhood is depression (Field, 1998). A third is negative body image (Orbach & Mikulincer, 1998) and associated body dissociation. Related
to these characteristics are abnormal physiological factors including EEG
alpha asymmetry (Graae et al., 1996) and biochemical imbalances including elevated cortisol and depleted serotonin levels (Goodwin, 1999; Mann,
Oquendo, Underwood, & Arango, 1999). These risk factors, of course, are
highly interrelated, and most of the data are derived from adolescents who
have suicidal thoughts rather than those who have actually attempted suicide. Without a large sample longitudinal study, of course, the link between
early touch deprivation/abuse and later suicide risk factors would be impossible to assess. However, some suggestive evidence is reviewed here.

Early Touch Deprivation and Later Aggression

A cross-cultural study conducted in 49 different primitive societies
(Prescott, 1990) revealed that in cultures in which there was more physical

1 High Infant Physical Affection ---------------------- Low Adult Physical Violence			2 Low Infant Physical Affection ---------------------- High Adult Physical Violence	
Andamanese	Lau	Tikopia	Alorese	Kaska
Arapesh	Lesu	Timbria	Aranda	Marquesan
Balinese	Maori	Trobriand	Araucanians	Masai
Chagga	Murngin	Wogeo	Ashanti	Navaho
Chenchu	Nuer	Woleaians	Aymara	Ojibwa
Chuckchee	Papago	Yahgan	Azande	Thonga
Cuna	Siriono		Comanche	
Hano	Tallensi		Fon	

FIGURE 6.1. Societies of high and low physical affection.

TABLE 6.1. *Teacher Touch Behavior with Infants and Toddlers*

Teacher Behavior	% Time	
	Infants	Toddlers
Holding	4.0	1.0
Hugging	3.0	0.8
Stroking	7.0	1.5
Kissing	3.0	0.7

affection toward infants there were lower rates to virtually no incidence of adult physical violence (including suicide) and, in contrast, in cultures where there was limited physical affection toward infants, there were significant rates of adult physical violence (see Figure 6.1). These data are relevant in light of the recent mandate that American teachers are not allowed to touch young children because of potential accusations of sexual abuse following increased publicity about sexual abuse in schools. In a recent study on model preschools, we observed very low rates of teachers hugging and kissing infants and progressively lower rates of this physical affection toward toddlers and preschoolers (Field et al., 1994) (see Table 6.1).

Touch deprivation may be contributing to the significant increases in violence and suicide noted in children and adolescents in the United States, which has not only the highest suicide rate but also the highest rate of homicide of all industrialized nations. In a 1994 report of the Center for Disease Control and Prevention (National Center for Injury Prevention and Control International Comparisons of Homicide Rates in Males 15–24 Years of Age, 1988–1991) the homicide rate per 100,000 population was 32% in the United States, which far exceeded 25% in the year 1991 (see Figure 6.2). In contrast, cultures such as France had a homicide rate as low as 1% per 100,000 population. It is interesting in this light that an anthropological study revealed that the highest touch culture was France (110 times touching in a café per 30 minutes) and the United States was the lowest (2 times per 30 minutes) (Jourard, 1966). Combining the cross-cultural data of Prescott (1990) on touch deprivation and violence in the 49 primitive cultures and the café touching behavior by Jourard (1966) suggests the possibility that the low incidence of violence in France may be related to high levels of touching in that culture and, conversely, in the United States, the high levels of violence may be related to low levels of touching.

Being interested in the question of whether touch deprivation in early childhood contributes to aggression in children and adolescents, we conducted studies in these two cultures (United States and France) with the expectation that greater amounts of touching and less aggression may

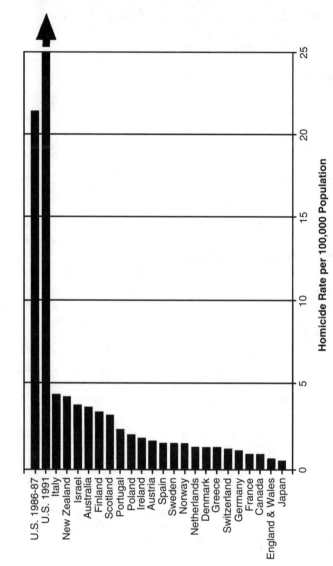

Homicide Rate per 100,000 Population

U.S. 1986-87
U.S. 1991
Italy
New Zealand
Israel
Australia
Finland
Scotland
Portugal
Poland
Ireland
Austria
Spain
Sweden
Norway
Netherlands
Denmark
Greece
Switzerland
Germany
France
Canada
England & Wales
Japan

0   5   10   15   20   25

FIGURE 6.2. International Comparisons of Homicide Rates Males, 15–24 Years of Age, 1988–1991.

TABLE 6.2. *Preschooler and Parent Play on Playgrounds in France and U.S. (% time)*

	France	U.S.
Parent Behavior		
Doing own thing	5	23
Watching child	64	48
Talking to child	23	18
Touching	35	11
Preschooler		
Playing	72	37
Talking to parent	11	5
Touching parent	19	3
Aggression to parent	1	19

occur in France versus the United States. In our study on preschoolers, the parents and their children were observed at McDonalds restaurants and on preschool playgrounds (Field, 1999). For the Paris parents and children, touching occurred 35% of the time as opposed to 11% of the time for Florida parents and children (see Table 6.2). Affectionate touch occurred during 23% of the playground observation time in France and only 7% of the time on the American playground. The French children also showed more physical affection and touching behaviors and less aggression toward their peers than the American children (see Table 6.3).

A similar picture derived from pilot data on young adolescents who were "hanging out" at McDonalds restaurants in Paris versus at McDonalds restaurants in Florida (Field, 2000). In the Paris restaurants the adolescents were noted to show significantly more touching while "hanging out" such as physically leaning on a peer, casually back rubbing while talking, hanging an arm around another's shoulder, and leaning a head on another's shoulder (see Table 6.4). In contrast, the Florida sample exhibited more self-stimulation behavior such as twirling rings on fingers, wringing hands, twirling hair, rubbing one's own limbs, wrapping arms around self, cracking knuckles, and biting lips. We also observed more verbal and

TABLE 6.3. *Preschooler Play with Peers on Playgrounds in France and U.S. (% time)*

Preschooler Behavior	France	U.S.
Touching	66	32
Grabbing	6	15
Aggression	1	29
Fussing	4	30

TABLE 6.4. *Adolescents Interacting at McDonalds*
Restaurants in France and U.S. (% time)

Adolescent Behavior	France	U.S.
Leaning	52	20
Stroking	26	8
Kissing	23	6
Hugging	7	2
Location on body		
Head and shoulders	45	21
Arms and hands	25	38
Purpose of touch		
Affection	43	11
Self-stimulation	8	41
Self-stimulation		
Hair	21	38
Hands	11	29

physical aggression among the American adolescent peers than among the French peers.

We have observed more extreme aggressive behavior in the children of depressed mothers (Field et al., 1987). These children had been videotaped during interactions with their mothers across infancy and early childhood in laboratory play situations. Significant touch deprivation had been noted in these observations, and the children's negative responses to their mothers' unavailability for interaction were often responded to by their mothers' abusive touch. The children scored two standard deviations above the mean on the Tactile Aversiveness Scale.

In a more recent longitudinal study on children of depressed mothers, we noted similar levels of touch deprivation and physical aggression (Jones, Field, & Davalos, 2000). The children's tactile aversiveness scores were again elevated in this study. In addition, an empathy situation in which the mother feigns being hurt consistently elicited aggressive, nonempathetic behaviors from the children. They typically screamed at the mothers, pushed them, and kicked them as the mothers were feigning being hurt.

Early Touch Deprivation and Later Depression

In our studies on depressed adolescents hospitalized for their depression (Field et al., 1992) and depressed adolescent mothers (Field, Grizzle, Scafidi, & Schanberg, 1996) strong relationships were noted between reports of early childhood abuse and scores on the Touch Aversiveness Scale and depression scales as well as suicidal thoughts. We observed the transmission of this profile from depressed adolescent mothers to their infants across infancy and early childhood (Field, 1998). From birth the depressed adolescent mothers did not show the normal exploring-the-baby-by-touch pattern seen in mothers across cultures immediately after the infant's birth (Lundy et al., 1996). During early infancy the depressed mothers showed one of two patterns of stimulation, a withdrawn understimulating pattern where the infant is clearly deprived of tactile, facial, and verbal stimulation, and a pattern of intrusive overstimulation where the infant is bombarded with particularly aversive poking in the facial region (Jones et al., 1997). The infants of these mothers showed a pattern of "depression" themselves. Their activity levels were low, their facial expressions were flat, and their facial and vocal expressions were very infrequent. Their sleep patterns were disorganized, their vagal tone was lower, and their EEG patterns, typically right frontal EEG activation, were similar to those of their mothers (a pattern shown by chronically depressed adults) (Jones, Field, & Davalos, 1998). In addition, their catecholamine and stress hormone profiles were similar to their mothers' profiles (elevated norepinephrine and cortisol levels and lower dopamine and serotonin levels) (Lundy et al., 1999). In our developmental follow-up of these infants to childhood these characteristics persisted, and the children were diagnosed as having internalizing (depression) or externalizing (conduct disorder) or more often comorbidity problems (both internalizing and externalizing problems) (Field et al., 1987).

Another illustration of the close relationship between touch deprivation, in this case touch abuse, depression, and suicidal ideation is provided in a study of sexually abused children (Wozencraft, Wagner, & Pellegrin, 1991). Depression and suicidal ideation occurred more often in victims who had been molested by a family member.

Early Touch Deprivation and Later Negative Body Image and Body Dissociation

Several investigators have suggested that body image initially develops during infancy and childhood in response to empathic behavior of parents including physical affection. Gupta and his colleagues (Gupta & Schork, 1995; Gupta, Madhulika, Gupta, Schork, & Watteel, 1995) conducted interviews of people while they were shopping to survey early touch experiences and body image. The yes/no questions they asked included the statements "I have fond memories of being hugged and/or cuddled by my parents/caregivers during my early childhood years," "I wish I had been hugged or cuddled more during my childhood," "At the present time, I often wish I could get more hugs from others." Their results indicated that adults with early touch deprivation had a poor body image.

In studies we conducted on adolescents with eating disorders we noted negative body image, touch aversiveness, depression, and suicidal thoughts. Adolescent bulimic inpatients had high anxiety levels, depression, and stress hormones (cortisol and norepinephrine) (Field et al., 1998). Elevated levels were also noted in our sample of young anorexic women (Hart et al., 2000). Both groups reported a strong desire for more tactile nurturance.

In similar studies Orbach and his colleagues revealed a strong relationship between negative body image and suicidal thoughts (Orbach, Lotem-Peleg, & Kedem, 1995). They suggested that "negative touch experiences" in early childhood may lead to pathology, self-destructive behavior (Putnam & Stein, 1985), tactile defensiveness, or a tendency to avoid touch stimulation by people or objects (Royeen & Fortune, 1990), as well as an inability to enjoy touch or an indifference to it (less reactivity) (Orbach, 1998). In operational terms, they suggest that the suicidal youngster feels more body dissociation, more physical numbness, more physical anhedonia, less responsiveness to stimulation, less sensitivity to pain, and more distortions and physical sensations of external and internal stimuli. In addition, suicidal individuals are less likely to take care of their body and protect it, and more likely to have negative feelings, attitudes and beliefs about the body. They then said,

We cautiously suggest that altered body experiences combined with negative feelings and attitudes toward the body may help the suffering suicidal person relinquish the body, as he or she has little to lose in terms of body pleasures and satisfaction. Body sensations (pains and pleasures) may inhibit self-destruction, and their absence may facilitate (not cause) such behavior. (Orbach, 1998)

Data to substantiate their claims include their study in which suicidal adolescents were compared with depressed nonsuicidal and nonsuicidal normal adolescents on their attitudes toward their bodies (Orbach, Lotem-Peleg, & Kedem, 1995). Data from scales on suicidal tendencies and dissociative tendencies showed more negative feelings toward the body and greater dissociation for the suicidal group. Suicide attempters have also been noted to have negative attitudes and feelings about their bodies (Petrie, Chamberlain, & Clarke, 1988). In that study, a negative body image predicted future suicide in a sample of suicide attempters.

Higher sensory and pain thresholds have also been noted in suicide attempters (Orbach et al., 1996), and they have also shown faster habituation to noise (Thorell, 1987). In one of these studies (Thorell, 1987), differences occurred in electrodermal reactivity (skin conductance level) during habituation experiments with auditory stimulation among depressed inpatients grouped according to suicidality. Patients who committed suicide compared with the nonsuicidal depressed patients had significantly reduced habituation scores.

Taken together, these data suggest higher pain thresholds and different sensory processing mechanisms. The lesser enjoyment of touch or the anhedonia associated with touch was further documented by Orbach and his colleagues. For example, Orbach and Mikulincer (1996) found that suicidal inpatients enjoyed touch to a lesser degree and showed a greater degree of physical anhedonia than nonpsychiatric inpatients and normal participants.

Retrospective Data Linking Early Touch Deprivation and Suicidal Ideation

A group of investigators in South Australia assessed adolescents' perceptions of how frequently they experienced pleasant (positive) and unpleasant (negative) touch from family and friends (Pearce, Martin, & Wood, 1995). Suicidal ideation was correlated with negative touch experience. In another study, abuse and neglect and their relationships to suicidal behavior (attempts and ideation) were assessed in hospitalized psychiatric adolescents (Lipschitz et al., 1999). Suicide attempters were significantly more likely to report sexual, physical, and emotional abuse and emotional neglect. In multivariate analyses, female gender, sexual abuse, and emotional neglect were significant predictors of suicidal ideation. In still another study attempters were significantly more likely than ideators and nonsuicidal youth to have experienced abuse (Yoder, 1999). In a study on suicidality in college women who were sexually and physically abused and physically punished by their parents, the women who reported sexual abuse were more suicidal than all other groups, and those physically abused were more suicidal than those nonabused/nonpunished (Bryant & Range, 1995). In a multiple regression, sexual abuse accounted for the most variance in suicidality (Bryant & Range, 1995). In at least one study negative touch experiences were related to suicidal ideation as well as the risk factors depression and aggression (Pearce, Martin, & Wood, 1995). A recent review paper, while critical of the methods used in many of these studies, suggested that there is compelling evidence for the link between early physical and sexual abuse and later adolescent suicide (Wagner, 1997).

Data supporting the lack of nurturant touch during early childhood in adolescents who have suicidal thoughts or commit suicide are more difficult to find, of course, because the absence of touch is not typically documented in the same way that abusive touch is documented. In one study from Canada (Adam, Keller, West, Larose, & Gossamer, 1994), adolescents referred to treatment for suicidal ideation were given the parental bonding instrument. Suicidal adolescents reported lower care and greater overprotection in relations with their mothers. Although female subjects reported this pattern for their fathers as well, these data suggest not only that this pattern may be stronger in females than males, but also that maternal influences may be stronger than paternal influences. The pattern, typically referred to as "affectionless control," was reported in several studies on risk factors for adolescent suicide.

These very distant relationships between touch problems in early childhood and suicidal thoughts in later adolescence are not only tenuous because they rely on retrospective self or other reports based on long-term memory, but also because they are biased by the need and inclination to find early precursors for later problems. Further, the incidence based on retrospective report would be expected to be greater than an incidence figure derived from prospective data. Certainly, most individuals who are touch deprived or touch abused in early childhood do not have suicidal thoughts during adolescence. More proximal relationships between adolescents' sense of physical intimacy with their parents, the mediating risk factors (aggression, depression, and negative body image) and suicidal thoughts could be considered more credible because those risk factors are being experienced concurrently and do not rely on long-term memory.

Mediating Risk Factors for Adolescent Suicide

Very few multivariate/multivariable studies have been conducted to determine relationships between adolescent suicidal thoughts and behaviors and mediating risk factors, probably because of the need for very large samples to conduct those studies. Multivariate studies are particularly critical inasmuch as the risk for suicide is clearly a multivariate problem with converging risk factors affecting the adolescents who themselves are "multivariate" type individuals. For example, in a larger sample of 3000 inner-city adolescents, Robins, Helzer, Croughan, & Ratcliff (1981) noted that while 9% with conduct problems and 20% with depression had attempted suicide, as many as 46% who experienced both conduct problems and depression had tried to kill themselves. Thus, the combination of depression and conduct problems appears to be much more lethal than either internalizing or externalizing problems alone.

At least two large sample multivariate studies have been conducted on a compilation of suicidal risk variables. In the first of these (Kandel, Raveis, & Davies, 1991), the interrelationships of depression and suicide with adolescent drug use, delinquency, eating disorders, and the risk factors for these different problems were investigated among 597 9th- and 11th-graders in an urban high school. Causal models indicated that poor interpersonal interactions with parents and peers led to depression, which in turn led to suicidal ideation. Depressive symptoms were the strongest predictors of suicidal ideation.

TABLE 6.5. *Psychological Variables and Intimacy Scores*

Psychological Variables	Intimacy Scores		
	Mother	Father	Friends
Self-Esteem			
Low (<44)	25.0_a^2	21.0_a^2	30.8_a
High (>45)	27.0_b	23.5_b	31.3_a
Depression			
Low (<15)	27.0_a	24.1_a	30.9_a
High (>23)	23.4_b^2	19.1_b^2	31.0_a
Suicidal Thoughts			
Regularly	35.3_a^2	28.4_a^2	31.2_a
Occasionally	37.3_{ab}	31.4_{ab}	31.3_a
Rarely	38.2_{ab}	31.0_{ab}	31.0_a
Never	43.2_b	37.4_b	31.0_a
Drug Use			
Low (<7)	24.3_a	21.7_a	30.0_a
High (>8)	26.0_a	22.4_a	31.7_a
Danger Risk-Taking			
Low (<17)	27.0_a	22.2_a	31.4_a
High (>18)	24.3_b^2	22.5_a	30.4_a

Different subscripts (to be read vertically) indicate group differences. Superscript [1](p < .05) and [2](p < .01) appear by statistically different values.

In the second study levels of negative emotions – anxiety, depression, aggression, and impulsivity – were compared in hospitalized adolescents with a history of either a single or multiple suicide attempts (Stein et al., 1998). Both single and multiple suicide attempt groups demonstrated higher levels of negative emotions than both the normal controls and the nonsuicidal inpatients. When the first attempters were compared with the multiple attempters, similarly high levels were noted for most dimensions of anxiety and depression. A trend toward increased aggression was noted among the multiple suicide attempters on all parameters evaluated. These findings suggest that, in already highly anxious and depressed suicidal inpatients, a high level of aggression might significantly increase the risk of recidivism.

We conducted a survey with 455 adolescents with the focus being on intimacy with parents (physical affection) and its relationship to depression and problem behaviors including drug use, risk-taking, and suicidal thoughts (Field, Lang, Yando, & Bendell, 1995) (see Table 6.5). Intimacy with parents differentiated those students who had risk factors for suicide including depression, drug use, risk-taking, and suicidal thoughts. This was particularly true for intimacy with mothers, as the greatest

TABLE 6.6. *Mean Scores (and Standard Deviations) for Suicidal Ideation Groups*

Variable	No Suicidal Ideation	Suicidal Ideation	t	p
Relationship with Mother	28.8 (5.7)	22.2 (9.4)	3.59	.001
Intimacy with Parents	15.8 (2.8)	13.3 (4.7)	2.79	.01
Closeness to Siblings	3.6 (0.8)	2.9 (1.3)	2.91	.005
Maternal Depression*	1.4 (0.6)	2.1 (1.2)	−3.61	.001
Peer Relations	30.8 (6.8)	27.0 (11.5)	1.72	.05
Popularity	3.2 (0.7)	2.2 (1.1)	4.27	.000
Number of Friends	4.5 (0.8)	3.4 (1.6)	4.28	.000
Well-being*	1.6 (0.6)	2.5 (1.1)	−5.02	.001
Happiness*	1.4 (0.6)	2.5 (1.1)	−5.31	.000
Anger	1.3 (0.4)	0.4 (0.5)	−3.25	.005
Depression (CES-D)*	21.7 (11.0)	34.1 (10.0)	−3.87	.000
Cigarettes*	2.0 (1.2)	3.1 (1.2)	−3.18	.005
Marijuana*	2.2 (1.1)	3.2 (1.0)	−3.25	.005
Cocaine*	1.2 (0.6)	2.2 (1.3)	−4.45	.000
GPA	3.2 (0.7)	2.5 (1.4)	3.06	.005

* Lower score is optimal.

number of significant correlations involved the "intimacy with mother" variable.

More recently we explored the relationship between suicidal ideation and other variables by a questionnaire given to 88 high school seniors (Field, Diego, & Sanders, 2001) (see Table 6.6). Eighteen percent responded positively to the statement "Sometimes I feel suicidal." Positive versus negative responders were inferior on a number of variables including quality of relationships with their mothers, physical affection from parents, closeness to siblings, and family history of depression (maternal depression). They were also inferior on peer relations (quality of peer relationships, popularity, number of friends), feelings (unhappiness, anger and depression), drug use (cigarette use, marijuana and cocaine), and grade point average. In a stepwise regression, unhappiness explained 46% of the variance on suicidal ideation and number of friends, anger, and marijuana use added 20% for a total of 66% of the variance.

Potential Underlying Neurological and Biochemical Dysfunction

In addition to touch deprivation and touch abuse leading to a constellation of internalizing symptoms such as depression, anxiety, and suicidal ideation and externalizing symptoms such as aggressive behavior, substance use, and risk-taking behavior, some degree of neurological dysfunction has also resulted. Studies on suicide and aggression in animals and humans have implicated various biochemical imbalances associated with aggression toward self or others.

EEG Abnormalities

Soft neurological signs and nonspecific EEG abnormalities have been noted in as many as 77% of physically abused children without known head trauma (Davies, 1979; Green et al., 1981). In another study EEG abnormalities were present in 55% of children with physical or sexual abuse histories (Ito et al., 1993). The EEG abnormalities associated with touch deprivation/abuse have been attributed to overstimulation of the developing limbic system (Teicher, Glod, Surrey, & Swett, 1993) including the amygdala, and excessive stimulation may then lead to neurological abnormalities resulting in aggression and suicidality. The amygdala has also been implicated in the emergence of dissociative phenomena and is noted to be markedly affected by elevated cortisol. The prefrontal cortex and dopamine projections to the prefrontal cortex can be specifically activated by stress and contribute to impulsivity.

In the Teicher et al. (1993) study on the Limbic System Checklist-33, which measures semantic, sensory, behavioral, and memory symptoms suggestive of limbic system disturbance, physical abuse was associated with a 38% increase in the scores on the symptom checklist, sexual abuse with a 49% increase, and combined abuse with a 113% increase. The authors suggested that their findings are consistent with the results of previous studies reporting an association between early childhood trauma and the presence of EEG abnormalities (Davies, 1979; Green et al., 1981; Ito et al., 1993). Physical abuse can lead to amygdaloid kindling and the emergence of neurological abnormalities, aggression, and suicidality. The hippocampus can also be markedly affected by high levels of cortisol, which can produce cell death and lead to dissociative phenomena, and involvement of the prefrontal cortex can affect impulsivity.

Brain activity as reflected in alpha waves related to "approach affect" processing was also different in suicidal adolescents (Graae et al., 1996). Normal adolescents had greater alpha (less activation) over the right than the left hemisphere, whereas suicidal adolescents had a nonsignificant asymmetry in the opposite direction. Nondepressed attempters were distinguished from depressed attempters in that they accounted for abnormal asymmetry in the posterior regions. Alpha asymmetry over the posterior regions was related to ratings of suicidal intent, but not depression severity. The alpha asymmetry in suicidal adolescents resembled that seen for depressed adults in its abnormal direction, although it was in the posterior rather than the anterior region. Thus it would appear that reduced left posterior activation, which is not related to depression (which features less left frontal activation), may relate to suicidal or aggressive behavior.

Lower Serotonin Levels

In addition, it is possible that this EEG pattern may be related to the serotonin abnormalities that have been found in suicide victims and in aggressive behavior disorders. People attempting suicide and those committing acts of aggression may share a common disorder involving lower than normal levels of serotonin (Kreusi & Rapaport, 1990; Linnoila et al., 1983; Plizka, Rogeness, Renner, Sherman, & Broussard, 1988; Van Heeringen, 2003). Aratto et al. (1991) have suggested a linkage between abnormal serotonin function in suicide and abnormal laterality. In their study, suicide victims had the reverse pattern of serotonin laterality seen in normal adults; although others have failed to find evidence of serotonin asymmetry (e.g., Arora & Meltzer, 1991).

Several studies have reported lower levels of the major metabolite of serotonin (5HIAA) in suicide victims (Goodwin, 1999; Malone et al., 1995; Mann et al., 1999). These authors have also reported that prolactin release in response to the serotonin-releasing drug fenfluramine is more blunted in suicide attempters than in nonattempters.

In an extensive review of abnormalities in central serotonogic mechanisms, the most consistent finding was a decrease in serotonin (5-HT) and its major metabolite (5-HIAA) in suicide victims compared with controls (Golden et al., 1991; Lin, & Tsoi, 2004; Lindstrom et al., 2004). Suicide victims had lower concentrations of 5-HT or 5-HIAA in the subcortical areas in the brainstem region where the Raphe Nuclei are located. In addition, low concentrations of the dopamine metabolite (homovanillic acid) were frequently noted.

Aggression and suicide have been linked together from several different perspectives including the psychodynamic perspective whereby depression and suicide are viewed as inwardly directed aggressive drives. From an epidemiological perspective, murder is one of the predictors of suicide, with a 30% suicide rate found among murderers (West, 1965). From a clinical perspective, excessive hostilities are characteristic of suicidal depressed patients (Weissman, Fox, & Klareman, 1973). Increased overtly aggressive behavior has been reported in patients who have made suicide attempts (Brown et al., 1982). For more than 30 years animal studies have explored the role that serotonin plays in regulating aggressive behavior (Eichelman, 1987; Soubrie, 1989). Animal paradigms have demonstrated an inverse relationship between central serotonergic activity and aggressive behavior including isolation-induced aggression (Soubrie, 1989; Valzelli & Bernasconi, 1979).

Data from the literature on psychopathology in adolescents (Rogeness et al., 1986) suggest an interaction of high dopamine, low norepinephrine, and low serotonin as a potential model for suicidal behavior. High dopamine would be expected to lead to aggressive behavior, low norepinephrine to underinhibited behavior, and low serotonin to poor impulse control and high aggression. Because neurotransmitter systems do not function in isolation, the interactions among noradrenergic, dopaminergic, and serotonergic systems have been explored. Coccaro (1989) suggested that impulsive aggressive behavior such as suicidal behavior resulted from an interaction of inhibiting (mediated by norepinephrine and serotonin systems) and activating neuronal systems (mediated by dopamine). The work of Sapolsky, Hideo, Rebert, & Finch (1990) suggests a strong interaction between the HPA system and the serotonergic neurotransmitter system. In their corticosteroid cascade model they demonstrate the cortisol damaging effects on the serotonergic neurotransmitter system.

HPA Axis Dysfunction

Several lines of evidence have implicated hypothalamic–pituitary–adrenal (HPA) axis dysfunction in suicidal behavior (Goodwin, 1999; Van Heeringen, 2003). In one study, for example, the weight and morphology of postmortem adrenal glands were compared between suicide victims and sudden-death, nonpsychiatric controls (Szigethy, Conwell, Forbes, Cox, & Caine, 1994). The mean adrenal weight of the combined left and right glands was significantly higher in the suicidal group. This difference was accounted for specifically by an increase in left adrenal weight of the suicidal compared with the control group. A positive correlation between adrenal weight and cortical thickness in both left and right glands provided direct evidence that increased adrenal weight in suicide victims was due to cortical hypertrophy. The finding of left–right adrenal weight asymmetry in suicide victims is consistent with the hypothesis of abnormal lateralized input from higher control centers of the HPA axis. To our knowledge cortisol levels have not been assayed in suicidal ideators or attempters.

A Potential Model for Suicidal Thoughts

In summary, abusive touch or lack of nurturant touch during early childhood might contribute to suicidal behavior in adolescents. We have noted in our own and other studies the potential relationships between abusive touch or lack of nurturant touch in infancy and the development of aggression, depression, and negative body image. Underlying EEG abnormalities and biochemical dysfunction in the HPA axis and the serotonergic and noradrenergic neurotransmitter systems appear to be related to aggression, depression, and negative body image, which in turn may contribute to suicidal ideation.

The model suggested by this group of data appears in Figure 6.3. As can be seen in Figure 6.3, suicidal thoughts are related to (1) decreased serotonin (increased aggression and poor impulse control); (2) increased

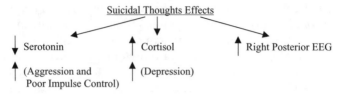

FIGURE 6.3. A Potential Model for Suicidal Thoughts.

cortisol (increased depression); and (3) increased relative right posterior EEG activation.

Interventions

Psychosocial and Behavioral Interventions. Suicide prevention and intervention have become important areas of public health concern because of recent increases in suicide rates internationally. In a review of clinical predictors of adolescent suicide and several related prevention strategies, the method of suicide prevention that was the most effective was a systematic, direct-screening procedure (Shaffer & Craft, 1999). Although several official guidelines recommend screening for suicidal behavior in primary care settings, only 23% either frequently or always screen adolescent patients for suicide risk factors (Frankenfield et al., 2000). Of primary concern to the providers is the time constraint during a well visit and confidentiality issues. The development of a short, easily administered, reliable, and valid screening tool is recommended as one solution to increase screening among primary care providers (Frankenfield et al., 2000). In a review of 103 families whose children made an emergency department visit for mental health assessment or treatment, 5 of 8 parents whose households contained firearms and received injury prevention education took new action to limit access, in contrast to the seven families who did not receive injury prevention education and took no new action to limit firearm access (Kruesi, Grossman, Pennington, et al., 1999). The importance of injury prevention education is highlighted by the significant association found between this education and the action of parents after training to limit access to lethal means, such as firearms.

Another method of intervention is school-based programs. The three types of school based programs currently being used are (1) curriculum-based programs presented to students; (2) in-service presentations to school staff; and (3) student self-report screening measures. A random sample of secondary school principals were given The Suicide Prevention Program Rating Profile (SPPRP), and the results indicated that the curriculum-based and staff in-service programs were significantly more acceptable to principals than was the schoolwide student screening program

(Miller, Eckert, DuPaul, & White, 1999). However, an overview of unpublished literature by Ploeg and colleagues (1996) found insufficient evidence to support curriculum-based suicide prevention programs based on the beneficial and harmful effects of the programs on the students. Most studies showed an improvement in knowledge related to suicide, but they also found increased hopelessness and maladaptive coping for males following the intervention, suggesting that the programs needed closer evaluation (Ploeg et al., 1996).

Psychosocial and behavioral interventions have focused primarily on cognitive and behavioral family training such as the SNAP outpatient treatment program (Rotheram-Borus et al., 1996), problem-solving therapy, and dialectical behavior therapy with varying degrees of treatment adherence (Hawton et al., 1998). Rotheram-Borus and her colleagues (1996), however, found that the implementation of a specialized care program in the emergency room aimed at enhancing positive interactions among family members and emergency room staff and providing realistic expectations about outpatient treatment to the families resulted in a significant improvement in treatment adherence for the attempters in comparision to those in standard aftercare. Programs with various degrees of access to therapists (e.g., intensive intervention plus outreach, home-based treatment, emergency card) have been utilized and compared to standard aftercare, reporting a tendency toward less repetition of self-harm but with summary odds ratios that were not significant because of a small sample size (Hawton et al., 1998).

Assessment using DSM criteria diagnoses found more than 80% of suicidal adolescents to be suffering from major depression with melancholic features, approximately 75% of these adolescents receiving antidepressants as an intervention (Haliburn, 2000). Suicidal adolescents who receive pharmaceutical treatments are more adherent to this form of intervention (68%) than to individual therapy (51%), with the poorest follow-through being in parent guidance/family therapy (33%) (King et al., 1998). The use of antidepressants with suicidal adolescents is a controversial intervention because it has not been found to be generally effective in preventing the repetition of self-harm behavior and has been implicated as a possible cause for their attempting or committing suicide (Edwards, 1995; Healy, Langmaak, & Savage, 1999; King et al., 1998; Poldinger & Holsboer-Trachsler, 1989). In contrast, other researchers propose the lack of adequate treatment for depression before and after the suicide attempt as the most important factor. They suggest that a more accurate understanding of suicidal adolescents is necessary, leading to an improved therapeutic relationship and a reduction in self-harm behavior (Haliburn, 2000). Because of the lack of effectiveness of any single behavioral or cognitive treatment for suicide, and the side effects of psychotropic drugs, complementary therapies are currently being investigated.

Standard treatment of adolescents with suicidal ideation and suicidal attempts has been group psychotherapy. Although positive effects have been noted for group psychotherapy, this therapy is limited to a verbal intimacy experience and does not treat the hypothesized physical contact deprivation experienced by suicidal ideation and suicidal attempt adolescents.

Massage Therapy

We have conducted massage therapy studies on adolescents who have aggression, depression, negative body image, and suicidal ideation problems as well as abnormal EEG asymmetry and elevated cortisol and depressed serotonin levels. These include studies on (1) children and adolescents hospitalized for depression and conduct disorder; (2) depressed adolescent mothers; (3) adolescents hospitalized for bulimia and (4) anorexia; (5) adolescents who have been sexually abused; and (6) violent adolescents. In all of these studies the adolescents experienced lower levels of these problems and lower stress hormones following massage therapy.

1. Hospitalized depressed and conduct disorder children and adolescents who received back massages for a week versus a control group who viewed relaxing videotapes were less depressed and anxious, had lower stress hormones (salivary cortisol, urinary cortisol, and norepinephrine), and had less sleep disturbance; significantly fewer patients in the massage group expressed suicidal ideation (Field et al., 1992).
2. Depressed adolescent mothers showed effects similar to these experienced by the depressed children and adolescents following twice-weekly massage therapy for a month including lower depression scores and a lower percentage expressing suicidal ideation by the last day of the study as well as lower urinary cortisol levels (Field et al., 1996).
3. Bulimic women had fewer symptoms of depression and lower anxiety and stress hormone (urinary cortisol) levels following 1 month of massage. Their eating habits improved and their body image was less distorted. Their dopamine and serotonin levels increased, and the incidence of suicidal ideation decreased (Field et al., 1998).
4. Anorexic patients reported improved attitudes on the Eating Disorder Inventory, and lower depression and anxiety levels, and they exhibited less anxious behavior and more positive affect following a month of massage. At that time they also showed lower cortisol and increased dopamine levels. Once again, a lower incidence of the adolescents who received massage therapy reported suicidal ideation by the end of the study (Hart et al., 2000).

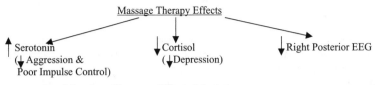

FIGURE 6.4. Massage Therapy Effects Model.

5. Sexually abused adolescent women experienced decreased depression and touch aversion after 1 month of massage therapy. Once again, a lower percentage of the massaged women expressed suicidal ideation (Field et al., 1997).
6. Violent adolescents were given a chair massage twice weekly for a 2-month period (Diego, Field, & Hernandez-Reif, 2000). By the end of the study they were rated by their parents and therapists as being less aggressive, less depressed, and less suicidal. Their cortisol levels also decreased.

The positive effects of massage therapy can be depicted in the model presented in Figure 6.4. Here, massage therapy is predicted to reduce suicidal thoughts by the reduction in cortisol (and depression) and right posterior EEG activity and an increase in serotonin (and decrease in aggression and impulse control).

Summary and Future Directions

In summary, the models explored in this chapter suggest that (1) depression, aggression, and body dissociation (physical anhedonia and higher thresholds to stimulation and pain) that may have derived from early touch deprivation/abuse may mediate suicidal ideation and attempts; and (2) that suicidal ideation and attempts might be reduced by massage therapy, a treatment that has already been effective with depressed adolescents. Underlying the risk factors for suicidal ideation and attempts are abnormal physiological factors including EEG alpha asymmetry and biochemical imbalances including depressed serotonin and elevated cortisol levels. Massage therapy may reduce suicidal ideation by reducing depression and the related biochemical imbalance of depressed serotonin and elevated cortisol levels.

The hypothesized link between early touch deprivation/abuse and later suicide risk factors would be impossible to assess without a large sample longitudinal study. Cross-cultural studies are also needed to explore relationships between negative touch experiences and destructive behavior.

References

Adam, K. S., Keller, A., West, M., Larose, S., & Gossamer, L.B. (1994). Parental representation in suicidal adolescents: A controlled study. *Australian & New Zealand Journal of Psychiatry, 284,* 418–425.

Aratto, M., Frecska, E., Maccrimmon, D., Guscott, R., Saxena, B., Tekes, K., et al. (1991). Serotonergic interhemispheric asymmetry: Neurochemical and pharmaco-EEG evidence. *Progress in Neuropsychopharmacology & Biological Psychiatry, 15,* 759–764.

Arora, R. C., & Meltzer, H. Y. (1991). Laterality and H-imipramine binding: Studies in the frontal cortex of normal controls and suicide victims. *Biological Psychiatry, 29,* 1016–1022.

Brown, G. L., Goodwin, F. K., Ballenger, J. C., et al. (1982). Aggression, suicide, and serotonin: Relationships to CSF amine metabolites. *American Journal of Psychiatry, 139,* 741–746.

Bryant, I., & Range, L. M. (1995). Suicidality in college women who were sexually and physically abused and physically punished by parents. *Violence & Victims. 1.0, 3,* 195–201.

Coccaro, E. F. (1989). Central serotonin and impulsive aggression. *British Journal of Psychiatry, 155, 18,* 52–62.

Davies, R. K. (1979). Incest: Some neuropsychiatric findings. *International Journal of Psychiatry Medicine, 2,* 117–121.

Diego, M. A., Field, T., & Hernandez-Reif, M. (2002). Aggressive adolescents benefit from massage therapy, *Adolescence, 37,* 599–607.

Edwards, J. G. (1995). Suicide and antidepressants. *British Medical Journal, 310,* 205–206.

Eichelman, B. (1987). Neurochemical and psychopharmacologic aspects of aggressive behavior. In H. Y. Meltzer (Ed.), *Psychopharmacology: The third generation of progress* (pp. 697–704). New York: Raven Press.

Field, T. (1998). Maternal depression effects on infants and early interventions. *Preventive Medicine, 27,* 200–203.

Field, T. (1999). Preschoolers in America are touched less and are more aggressive than preschoolers in France. *Early Childhood Development & Care, 151,* 11–17.

Field, T. (1999). American adolescents touch each other less and are more aggressive toward their peers as compared with French adolescent. *Adolescence, 34,* 753–758.

Field, T., Diego, M., & Sanders, C. (2001). Adolescent suicidal ideation. *Adolescence, 36,* 241–248.

Field, T., Grizzle, N., Scafidi, F., & Schanberg, S. (1996). Massage and relaxation therapies' effects on depressed adolescent mothers. *Adolescence, 31,* 903–911.

Field, T., Harding, J., Soliday, B., Lasko, D., Gonzalez, N., & Valdeon, C. (1994). Touching in infant, toddler & preschool nurseries. *Early Child Development and Care, 100,* 101–109.

Field, T., Hernandez-Reif, M., Hart, S., Quintino, O., Drose, L., Field, T., et al. (1997). Sexual abuse effects are lessened by massage therapy. *Journal of Bodywork and Movement Therapies, 1,* 65–69.

Field, T., Lang, C., Yando, R., & Bendell, D. (1995). Adolescents' intimacy with parents and friends. *Adolescence, 30,* 133–140.

Field, T., Morrow, C., Valdeon, C., Larson, S., Kuhn, C., & Schanberg, S. (1992). Massage reduces anxiety in child and adolescent psychiatric patients. *The Journal of the American Academy of Child and Adolescent Psychiatry, 31,* 125–131.

Field, T., Schanberg, D., Goldstein, S., Garcia, R., Vega-lahr, N., Porter, K., et al. (1987). Play interactions and interviews of depressed and conduct disorder children and their mothers. *Child Psychiatry & Human Development, 17,* 213–233.

Field, T., Schanberg, W., Kuhn, C., Fierro, K., Henteleff, T., Mueller, C., et al. (1998). Bulimic adolescents benefit from massage therapy. *Adolescence, 33,* 555–563.

Fombonne, E. (1998). Suicidal behaviors in vulnerable adolescents: Time trends and their correlates. *British Journal of Psychiatry, 173,* 154–159.

Frankenfield, D. L., Keyl, P. M., Gielen, A., Wissow, L. S., Werthamer, L., & Baker, S. P. (2000). Adolescent patients – healthy or hurting? Missed opportunities to screen for suicide risk in the primary care setting. *Archive of Pediatrics & Adolescent Medicine, 154,* 162–168.

Golden, R. N., Gilmore, J. H., Corrigan, M. H. N., Ekstrom, R. D., Knight, B. T., & Garbutt, J. C. (1991). Serotonin, suicide, and aggression: Clinical studies. *Journal of Clinical Psychiatry, 52,* 12, 61–69.

Goodwin, F. K. (1999). Anticonvulsant therapy and suicide risk in affective disorders. *Journal of Clinical Psychiatry, 60,* 89–93.

Graae, F., Tenke, C., Bruder, G., Rotheram, M. J., Piacentini, J., Castro-Blanco, D., et al. (1996). Abnormality of EEG alpha asymmetry in female adolescent suicide attempters. *Society of Biological Psychiatry, 10,* 706–713.

Green, A., Voeller, K., Gaines, R., et al. (1981). Neurological impairment in maltreated children. *Child Abuse and Neglect, 5,* 129–134.

Gupta, M., Madhulika, A., Gupta, A., Schork, N., & Watteel, G. (1995). Perceived touch deprivation and body image: Some observations among eating disordered and non-clinical subjects. *Journal of Psychosomatic Research, 39,* 459–464.

Gupta, M. A., & Schork, N. J. (1995). Touch deprivation has an adverse effect on body image: Some preliminary observations. *International Journal of Eating Disorders, 17,* 185–189.

Haliburn, J. (2000). Reasons for adolescent suicide attempts. *Journal of the American Academy of Child & Adolescent Psychiatry, 39,* 13–14.

Hart, S., Field, T., Hernandez-Reif, M., Shaw, S., Schanberg, S., & Kuhn, C. (2000). Anorexia nervosa symptoms are reduced by massage therapy. Manuscript submitted for publication.

Hawton, K., Arensman, E., Townsend, E., Bremner, S., Feldman, E., Goldney, R., et al. (1998). *British Medical Journal, 317,* 441–447.

Healy, D., Langmaak, C., & Savage, M. (1999). Suicide in the course of the treatment of depression. *Journal of Psychopharmacology, 13,* 94–99.

Ito, Y., Teicher, M., Glod, C., Harper, D., Magnus, E., & Gelbard, H. (1993). Increased prevalence of electrophysiological abnormalities in children with psychological, physical, and sexual abuse. *Journal of Neuropsychiatry, 5,* 401–408

Jones, N. A., Field, T., & Davalos, M. (1998). Massage therapy attenuates right frontal EEG asymmetry in one-month-old infants of depressed mothers. *Infant Behavior and Development, 21,* 527–530.

Jones, N. A., Field, T., & Davalos, M. (2000). Right frontal EEG asymmetry and lack of empathy in preschool children of depressed mothers. *Child Psychiatry and Human Development, 30,* 189–204.

Jones, N. A., Field, T., Fox, N. A., Davalos, M., Malphurs, J., Carraway, K., et al. (1997). Infants of intrusive and withdrawn mothers. *Infant Behavior and Development, 20,* 177–189.

Jourard, S. (1966). An exploratory study of body accessibility. *British Journal of Social and Clinical Psychology, 5,* 221–231.

Kandel, D. B., Raveis, V. H., & Davies, M. (1991). Suicidal ideation in adolescence: Depression, substance use, and other risk factors. *Journal of Youth and Adolescence. 2–0, 2,* 113–121.

King, C. A., Hovey, J. D., Brand, E., et al. (1998). Suicidal adolescents after hospitalization: Parent and family impacts on treatment follow-through. *Year Book of Psychiatry and Applied Mental Health, 3,* 58–59.

Kreusi, M. J. P., & Rapaport, J. L. (1990). Cerebrospinal fluid monoamine metabolites, aggression, and impulsivity in disruptive behavior disorders of children and adolescents. *Archives of General Psychiatry, 47,* 419–426.

Lin, P. Y., & Tsai, E. (2004). Association between serotonin transporter give promoter polymorphism and suicide: Results of a meta-analysis. *Biological Psychiatry, 55,* 1023–1030.

Lindstrom, H. B., Ryding, E. Bisson, P., Ahnlidr, J. A., Roen, S., & Troshman-Bentz, L. (2004). Singularity related to brain serotonin transporter binding capacity in suicide attempters. *European Neuropsychopharmacology, 14,* 295–300.

Linnoila, M., Virkkunen, M., Scheinin, M., Nuutila, A., Rimon, R., & Goodwin, F. K. (1983). Low cerebrospinal fluid 5-hydroxyindoleacetic acid concentration differentiates impulsive from non-impulsive violent behavior. *Life Science, 33,* 2609–2614.

Lipschitz, D. S., Winegar, R. K., Nicolaou, A. L., Hartnick, E., Wolfson, M., & Southwick, S. M. (1999). Perceived abuse and neglect as risk factors for suicidal behavior in adolescent inpatients. *Journal of Nervous and Mental Disease, 187,* 32–39.

Lundy, B. L., Field, T., Cuadra, A., Nearing, G., Cigales, M., & Hashimoto, M. (1996). Mothers with depressive symptoms touching newborns. *Early Development and Parenting, 5,* 129–134.

Lundy, B. L., Jones, N. A., Field, T., Nearing, G., Davalos, M., Pietro, P., et al. (1999). Prenatal depression effects on neonates. *Infant Behavior & Development, 22,* 121–137.

Madge, N., & Harvey, J. G. (1999). Suicide among the young: The size of the problem. *Journal of Adolescence, 22,* 145–155.

Malone, K., Haas, G., Sweeney, J. A., et al. (1995). Major depression and the risk of attempted suicide. *Journal of Affective Disorders, 34,* 173–185.

Mann, J., Oquendo, M., Underwood, M. D., & Arango, V. (1999). The neurobiology of suicide risk: A review for the clinician. *Journal of Clinical Psychiatry, 60,* 7–11.

Miller, D. N., Eckert, T. L., DuPaul, G. J., & White, G. P. (1999). Adolescent suicide prevention: Acceptability of school-based programs among secondary school principals. *Suicide & Life Threatening Behavior, 29,* 72–85.

Orbach, I. (1998). The role of the body experience in suicidal behavior. *Child Psychology and Psychiatry, 1,* 609–621.

Orbach, I., Kedem, P., Herman, L., & Apter, A. (1995). Dissociative tendencies in suicidal, depressed, and normal adolescents. *Journal of Social and Clinical Psychology, 14*, 393–408.

Orbach, I., Lotem-Peleg, M., & Kedem, P. (1995). Attitudes toward the body in suicidal, depressed, and normal adolescents. *Suicide and Life-Threatening Behavior, 5*, 211–21.

Orbach, I., & Mikulincer, M. (1996). The architecture of emotions in repressors and nonrepressors: Is it that simple? *British Journal of Social Psychology.*

Orbach, I., & Mikulincer, M. (1998). The body investment scale: Construction and validation of a body experience scale. *Psychological Assessment, 10*, 415–425.

Orbach, I., Stein, D., Palgi, Y., Asherov, J., Har-Even, D., & Elizur. (1996). Perception of physical pain in accident and suicide attempt patients: Self-preservation vs. self-destruction. *Journal of Psychiatric Research, 30*, 307–320.

Pearce, C. M., Martin, G., & Wood, K. (1995). Significance of touch for perceptions of parenting and psychological adjustment among adolescents. *Journal of the American Academy of Child & Adolescent Psychiatry, 34*, 160–167.

Petrie, K., Chamberlain, K., & Clarke, D. (1988). Psychological predictors of future suicidal behavior in hospitalized suicide attempters. *British Journal of Clinical Psychology, 27*, 247–257.

Plizka, S. R., Rogeness, G. A., Renner, P., Sherman, J., & Broussard, T. (1988). Plasma neurochemistry in juvenile offenders. *Journal of the American Academy of Child & Adolescent Psychiatry, 27*, 588–594.

Ploeg, J., Ciliska, D., Dobbins, M., Hayward, S., Thomas, H., & Underwood, J. (1996). A systematic overview of adolescent suicide prevention programs. *Canadian Journal of Public Health, 87*, 319–324.

Poldinger, W. J., & Holsboer-Trachsler, E. (1989). Psychopathology and psychodynamics of self destruction. *Schweizerische Rundschau fur Medizin Praxis, 78*, 214–218.

Prescott, J. W. (1990). Affectional bonding for the prevention of violent behaviors: Neurobiological, psychological and religious/spiritual determinants. In L. J. Hertzberg, G. F. Ostrum, & J. R. Field (Eds.), *Violent behavior* (Vol. 1, pp. 95–124), Great Neck, NY: PMA Publishing.

Putnam, N., & Stein, M. (1985). Self-inflicted injuries in childhood: A review and diagnostic approach. *Clinical Pediatrics, 24*, 514–518.

Robins, L., Helzer, J., Croughan, J., & Ratcliff, K. (1981). National Institute of Mental Health Diagnostic Interview Schedule. *Archives of General Psychiatry, 38*, 381–390.

Rogeness, G. A., et al. (1986). Near-zero plasma dopamine-B-hydroxylase and conduct disorder in emotionally disturbed boys. *Journal of the American Academy of Child Psychiatry, 25*, 521–527.

Rotheram-Borus, M. J., Piacentini, J., Van Rossem, R., Graae, F., Cantwell, C., & Castro-Blanco, D. (1996). Room program for adolescent suicide attempters. *Journal of the American Academy of Child & Adolescent Psychiatry, 35*, 654–663.

Royeen, C. B., & Fortune, J. C. (1990). Touch inventory for elementary-school aged children. *American Journal of Occupational Therapy, 44*, 155–159.

Sapolsky, R., Hideo, U., Rebert, C., & Finch, C. (1990). Hippocampal damage associated with prolonged glucocorticoid exposure in primates. *Journal of Neuroscience, 10*, 2897–2902.

Shaffer, D., & Craft, L. (1999). Methods of adolescent suicide prevention. *Journal of Clinical Psychiatry, 60*, 70–74, 75–76, 113–116.

Soubrie, P. (1989). Reconciling the role of central serotonin neurons in human and animal behavior. *Behavioral Brain Research, 2*, 319–364.

Stein, D., Apter, A., Ratzoni, G., Har-Even, D., & Avidan, G. (1998). Association between multiple suicide attempts and negative affects in adolescents. *Journal of the American Academy of Child and Adolescent Psychiatry, 37*, 488–494.

Szigethy, E., Conwell, Y., Forbes, N. T., Cox, C., & Caine, E. D. (1994). Adrenal weight and morphology in victims of completed suicide. *Biological Psychiatry, 16*, 374–380.

Teicher, M., Glod, C., Surrey, J., & Swett, C. (1993). Early childhood abuse and limbic system ratings in adult psychiatric outpatients. *Journal of Neuropsychiatry, 5*, 301–306.

Thorell, L. H. (1987). Electrodermal activity in depressive patients: Its relationship to symptomatology, suicidal behavior, cortisol dysregulation and clinical recovery. Unpublished doctoral dissertation, Department of Psychiatry, University of Sweden, Linkoping, Sweden.

Valzelli, L., & Bernasconi, S. (1979). Aggressiveness by isolation and brain serotonin turnover changes in different strains of mice. *Neuropsychobiology, 5*, 129–135.

Van Heeringen, K. (2003). The neurobiology of suicider and suicidality. *Canadian J. of Psychiatry, 48*, 292–300.

Wagner, B. M. (1997). Family risk factors for child and adolescent suicidal behavior. *Psychological Bulletin, 121*, 246–298.

Weissman, M. M., Bland, R. C., Canino, G. J., Greenwald, S., Hwu, H. G., Joyce, P. R., et al. (1999). Prevalence of suicide ideation and suicide attempts in nine countries. *Psychological Medicine, 29*, 9–17.

Weissman, M., Fox, K., & Klareman, G. L. (1973). Hostility and depression associated with suicide attempts. *American Journal of Psychiatry, 130*, 450–455.

West, D. J. (1965). *Murder followed by suicide*. London: Heinemann.

Wozencraft, T., Wagner, W., & Pellegrin, A. (1991). Depression and suicidal ideation in sexually abused children. *Child Abuse & Neglect, 15*, 505–511.

Yoder, K. A. (1999). Comparing suicide attempters, suicide ideators and nonsuicidal homeless and runaway adolescents. *Suicide and Life Threatening Behavior, 29*, 25–36.

7

Intersections of Biology and Behavior in Young Children's Antisocial Patterns: The Role of Development, Gender, and Socialization

Carolyn Zahn-Waxler & Barbara Usher
National Institute of Mental Health

Stephen Suomi
National Institute of Child Health and Human Development

Pamela M. Cole
The Pennsylvania State University

A BIOSOCIAL PERSPECTIVE ON AGGRESSION

Problem aggression in young children is viewed as more biologically driven than antisocial patterns that appear in adolescence and thought to be influenced mainly by peer socialization (Moffitt, 1993). Early-onset aggression is more chronic, serious, and linked to long-term maladaptive outcomes. By virtue of disposition or temperament, some young children are more likely than others to behave in ways that reflect disregard for the rights and welfare of others. Several constitutional factors have been implicated in early externalizing problems. These include neuropsychological problems, hyperactivity, and difficult temperament. Different antecedents and outcomes of early versus delayed onset of antisocial behavior have been identified (e.g., Moffitt & Caspi, 2001). Even early-onset aggression has poor parenting correlates, however, suggesting a complex interplay of biological and environmental processes from the start.

In this chapter we focus on early-appearing aggression and the ways in which socialization and child sex interact with it to alter forms of expression and developmental course. We consider, as well, early-appearing prosocial behaviors that may deter aggression. We draw on two high-risk longitudinal studies that have benefited from the teachings of Robert Cairns. He and his colleagues have been at the forefront in guiding the development of theories, research designs, and analytic approaches that illuminate biosocial interactions in different species and at different points in human development (Cairns, 1997, 2000; Cairns, Cairns, Neckerman, Ferguson, & Gariépy, 1989; Magnusson & Cairns, 1996). Their work has emphasized the modifying roles of socialization, context, and sex on aggression, and the importance of a developmental perspective.

Bidirectional influences have been studied in a number of different ways. Microanalytic approaches focus on moment-to-moment changes, typically in dyadic interactions, over a relatively short period of time and often within a given assessment session. This allows tracking of momentary influences of change, but in isolation is not well suited to understanding developmental patterns of continuity and change. Age cross-sectional research designs can provide information about developmental processes that characterize groups of individuals, but not about the interplay of endogenous and exogenous factors that influence the development of individuals over time. Longitudinal designs that assess both biological and environmental factors are required to uncover dynamic, bidirectional processes. The research designs are most effective in illuminating interactive processes if they are based on multivariate and multi-informant assessments, reflect an interdisciplinary approach, and combine both naturalistic and experimental methods. Robert Cairns has played a major role in advancing this point of view.

A summary of studies of antisocial and violent behavior in children and adults (Raine, 2002) documents several examples of biosocial interactions. This is encouraging because interactions are notoriously difficult to detect and their presence is often underestimated (McClelland & Judd, 1993). Raine concludes that psychosocial risk factors exponentially increase rates of antisocial and violent behavior when biological risk is already present. Psychosocial risk factors were measured in terms of very global constructs such as low SES, family adversity, abuse, neglect, and homes that were unstable/nonintact. Typically these environmental factors are measured retrospectively and do not include specific measures of child-rearing, discipline, and parent–child relationship. More specific socialization measures and longitudinal designs are needed to extend knowledge of biosocial interactions in the etiology of aggression.

A number of negative parenting factors contribute to aggression and delinquent behaviors (Keenan, Loeber, & Green, 1999; Loeber & Stouthamer-Loeber, 1986). These include poor supervision or lack of monitoring, lack of parental warmth, and discipline styles that are either overly permissive or overly harsh and coercive. Based on meta-analysis, Loeber and Stouthamer-Loeber (1986) proposed four aspects of parenting relevant to conduct problems: neglect, conflict, deviant attitudes, and disruptions in parenting. Recently, some of the negative child-rearing practices have been identified as *predictors* of later child antisocial behaviors (e.g., Campbell, Shaw, & Gilliom, 2000; Shaw, Bell, & Gilliom, 2000; Shaw, Owens, Giovannelli, & Winslow, 2001). For the most part, these more specific psychosocial factors have not been studied in terms of how they interact with biological risk. Moreover, few studies focus on the predictive power of socialization over time, taking into account the initial level of child problems. The work of Shaw and colleagues, which examines temperament and early, more biologically based aggression, is one of the important exceptions.

Also with few exceptions (e.g., Wakschlag & Hans, 1999), the risk literature has emphasized both global and more specific (e.g., child-rearing practices) *negative* psychosocial contributions that *increase* the likelihood of aggression or *maintain* existing high levels. There is a need to investigate interactive effects under socialization conditions that could *diminish* antisocial behavior over time. A different research literature within developmental psychology has considered positive aspects of parenting associated with more constructive and fewer destructive child behavior patterns. Although these studies have been conducted mainly with normative samples, the concepts and paradigms are clearly relevant to the study of more serious antisocial problems. That is, they have the potential to address more directly those aspects of parenting that make antisocial activities less attractive and alternative prosocial behaviors more inviting.

Parental responsiveness, involvement, and reciprocity are linked to fewer negative behaviors in offspring (Maccoby & Martin, 1983). Proactive maternal involvement (anticipatory guidance, supportiveness, and affectively positive, educative exchanges between mother and child) has been associated with fewer behavior problems in 4-year-olds (Pettit & Bates, 1989) and fewer problems in preschool children and adolescents (Miller, Cowan, Cowan, Hetherington, & Clingempeel, 1993). In this chapter we examine these more proactive, anticipatory, child-centered approaches that could reduce antisocial patterns over time in young children with externalizing problems.

Other aspects of socialization may discourage aggression and related activities in offspring, such as when caregivers clearly show disapproval of these behaviors but not in the ways associated with negative parenting. Here, too, the work has been done with more normative samples, but it has relevance for understanding etiology of antisocial behavior. This literature also begins to provide ideas of why boys and girls begin to diverge at an early age in expressions of overt aggression. Boys and girls show similar rates of externalizing behavior problems until about age 4, or shortly before (Keenan & Shaw, 1997). After that, many forms of antisocial behavior are more prevalent in males than females (Eme & Kavanaugh, 1995), particularly aggression that is overt, physical, and violent. Some forms of aggression more common to females than males are indirect, subtle, and occur in the context of interpersonal relationships (Cairns et al., 1989; Crick, Casas, & Mosher, 1997; Zahn-Waxler, 1993).

Observational studies of parents' interactions with boys and girls at ages prior to the emergence of sex differences in aggression support the inference that parental disapproval is linked to lower levels of expression.

Parents often treat anger and aggression differently in young boys and girls (see review by Zahn-Waxler, 2000), discouraging girls but tolerating, and sometimes encouraging, more extreme behaviors in their boys. Girls are judged more harshly than boys for showing physical aggression. Anger and retaliation are more accepted in boys, while girls are encouraged to resolve anger and conflict by working on damaged relationships (Fivush, 1989, 1991). Psychological induction is more often used with girls than boys (Smetana, 1989). Induction involves pointing out the harmful consequences for others of the child's aggressive behavior. As early as infancy, parents are less accepting of anger expressions by their girls than by their boys (Malatesta & Haviland, 1982). In addition, by fostering sex-stereotyped ways of behaving, that is, differentially encouraging expressions of "masculine" and "feminine" traits, sometimes in the extreme, parents may wittingly or unwittingly elicit aggression in their sons and prosocial behaviors in their daughters. Differential socialization could help explain why girls, more often than boys, anticipate negative consequences of their aggression (even though they show less of it), whereas boys more often find aggression rewarding and ego-enhancing (Perry, Perry, & Weiss, 1989).

Psychosocial and socialization risk and protective factors must, as noted, be considered against the backdrop of biological factors associated with aggression. It becomes essential to consider the sex of the child, not only because of differential early socialization, but also because of possible biological processes that may contribute to differences in the child's (anti)social behaviors. Many of the biological factors associated with antisocial behavior are more characteristic of males than females (Zahn-Waxler, 1993), such as high testosterone, low autonomic arousal, low serotonin, difficult temperament, hyperactivity, and large physical size and muscle mass. Although only some of these factors distinguish very young boys and girls it is important to consider how early physical, physiological, cognitive, social, and emotional differences in boys and girls may be relevant to developmental differences in aggression.

Early biological advantage in girls may facilitate greater self-regulation that enables them to engage in less disruptive behavior than boys (see reviews by Keenan & Shaw, 1997: Zahn-Waxler, 2000). Girls are more advanced in physical maturation. Because boys develop more slowly, they may be more vulnerable to environmental stressors or mild genetic abnormalities. Boys are at greater risk for early learning problems and their language development is less advanced. Delays in language production and comprehension would decrease the ability to resolve problems and conflicts by verbal means. In addition to showing greater empathy and prosocial behavior from a very early age, girls are more susceptible to feelings of guilt and likely to take responsibility for their action following transgressions. Girls are more advanced than boys in ability to understand their own and others' emotions. These differences may contribute both to how boys and girls are socialized with respect to aggression and how they respond to socialization, indicating the complex reciprocal processes involved.

In summary, two longitudinal studies designed to address some of the gaps in the existing research literature are reviewed here. The goal of this work was to focus on the early development of antisocial behavior, thought to be more biologically based in its origins. We examined (1) protective as well as risk factors in socialization that might alter developmental course, (2) physiological processes not typically studied in young children that might heighten or diminish antisocial behavior, and (3) child sex in relation both to aggression and prosocial patterns that may mitigate against disregard for others. One study focused on young children at risk for behavior problems by virtue of parental psychopathology, the other on preschool children identified as aggressive and disruptive.

ANTECEDENTS OF EXTERNALIZING PROBLEMS IN CHILDREN OF DEPRESSED MOTHERS

We examined the emotional and behavioral functioning of children of depressed and well mothers, first as toddlers and then in kindergarten and first grade. Children with depressed mothers are at known risk for externalizing as well as internalizing problems (Goodman & Gotlib, 1999; Zahn-Waxler, 2002). The children and their mothers were studied in laboratory sessions that included both naturalistic observations and experimental probes (Cummings, Iannotti, & Zahn-Waxler, 1985, 1989; Zahn-Waxler, Iannotti, Cummings, & Denham, 1990). They were observed with mothers, testers, and a same-age playmate. From this study we learned that serious aggression can be seen in 2-year-old children and that it can persist over time. Moreover, two factors could disrupt this process, namely, positive socialization experiences and being a girl, particularly an aggressive girl.

Aggression and Child-Rearing Practices at 2 Years

Two basic types of aggression were seen in the toddlers. Normative aggression consisted of typical object struggles and rough-and-tumble play. Maladaptive aggression consisted of behavior that was disregulated, out of control, and inappropriate in form of expression, such as hitting an adult. Maladaptive aggression was more common in children of depressed mothers than in those whose mothers were well, and in boys than in girls. The presence of sex differences in the aggression of 2-year-olds is earlier than others have found, possibly due to the fact that many mothers had experienced clinical depression.

The observed and self-reported child-rearing practices of depressed and well mothers did not differ, except that guilt induction and anxiety arousal was more common in depressed mothers. A different (nonparental) aspect of socialization also was examined in the form of background anger during peer play (Cummings et al., 1985). In two play sessions, the child and a same-age peer partner observed two adults during a loud, intense verbal conflict, followed by reconciliation. Boys were more aggressive than girls following exposure to background anger, whereas girls showed more distress than boys. There were stable individual differences across sessions in frequencies of aggression and distress. Qualitative differences in aggression also were seen: Children (mostly boys) who showed frequent aggression also instigated aggression that was intense, emotional, escalated, and extended in duration. Thus, although a conflictual environment elicited aggression in toddlers, some children were more consistently aggressive, suggesting that they are (very) early starters (Shaw, Bell, & Gilliom, 2000).

We assume here that the highly aggressive toddlers (more often males) were constitutionally disposed toward these behaviors. This is suggested not only by the early appearance of their aggression but also by its form of expression that included disorganization, poor impulse control, low frustration tolerance, and high activity levels. These are aspects of temperament, known to have constitutional (Rothbart, Ahadi, Hersey, & Fisher, 2001) and genetic bases, and shown to be associated with attentional problems/hyperactivity diagnosed somewhat later, often with comorbid aggression. Notably, all of these problems are more common in males than females.

Prediction of Externalizing Problems and Psychiatric Symptoms at 5 and 6 Years

Longitudinal analyses reiterated the entrenched nature of early behavior problems. Early disregulated aggression (but not normative aggression) predicted (a) externalizing problems based on mothers' CBCL reports when children were 5 years old, and (b) emotional and behavioral symptoms based on children's reports during a structured psychiatric interview at age 6. Problems were more frequent and stable over time in children of depressed than well mothers.

The Moderating Role of Socialization on Later Externalizing Problems

Positive socialization experiences observed at age 2 were found to moderate or "interrupt" the stability of externalizing problems over time (Zahn-Waxler et al., 1990). Although maternal depression had been associated with more early aggression, depressed mothers who had used proactive child-rearing practices had children who showed fewer externalizing problems 3 years later. Proactive parenting included anticipating the child's point of view; exerting modulated, respectful control; and providing structure and organization during peer play – all in the context of a warm relationship. Positive parenting was found to reduce later levels of externalizing problems, even after controlling for children's initial levels of problem aggression. This was the first indication, to our knowledge, that environmental factors could have a beneficial effect in reducing later behavior problems in children with early serious aggression.

The Moderating Role of Child Sex on Later Observed Aggression

In addition to the externalizing problems reported at ages 5 and 6, aggression was assessed during peer interactions at age 5 using procedures parallel to age 2 observations. For this measure of aggression, stability over time was moderated by sex of child (Cummings et al., 1989). Stability of aggression over the 3-year period was most evident for physical and overall aggression, suggesting an aggressive disposition, and was greater for boys than girls. Correlations for boys were substantial (as high as 0.76). Strong continuity patterns were not seen for girls, and some forms of early aggression showed *inverse* relations with their later aggression. For example, young girls who showed more intense aggression and higher overall aggression were *unlikely* to show physical aggression 3 years later. Seen in the context of the socialization studies reviewed, one might speculate that there had been greater discouragement of aggression in girls than boys in the interim period.

These findings are consistent with our other studies of children in the first years of life. In one study (Cummings, Hollenbeck, Iannotti, Radke-Yarrow, & Zahn-Waxler, 1986), aggression in girls (but not boys) was linked to reparation for their misconduct. That is, the more often girls engaged in harm-doing, the more likely they were to try to make amends or repair the damage. In another study, anger and aggression were more often associated with anxiety, guilt, and shame in girls than in boys (Zahn-Waxler, Cole, and Barrett, 1991: Zahn-Waxler & Robinson, 1995). The gender paradox of comorbidities refers to the fact that although girls are less likely than boys to have externalizing problems, when they do engage in serious aggression and misconduct they are also more likely to have internalizing problems such as depression and anxiety (Loeber & Keenan, 1994). The ease with which internalizing emotions such as guilt, shame, and remorse in very young girls become linked to (and possible outcomes of) anger and aggression suggests that precursors of their later comorbidity may reside both in innate factors and in early socialization into the

148   *Carolyn Zahn-Waxler et al.*

female role. Their strong interpersonal orientation may "facilitate" this process.

PRESCHOOL CHILDREN WITH EARLY EXTERNALIZING PROBLEMS

We continued to pursue similar questions about the protective role of supportive, proactive parenting and the moderating role of the child's sex in a sample of 4-year-old children with high (clinical), moderate (subclinical), and low (non-problem) levels of aggressive, disruptive behaviors. Clinical and subclinical cases were selected based on mother and/or teacher reports, using nationally normed instruments with established cutoffs (Achenbach CBCLs and TRFs). While we again assumed that the early presence of serious aggression reflected some underlying biological predisposition, this time we also assessed physiological and neurohormonal processes hypothesized to be associated with externalizing problems. Specifically, we measured autonomic nervous system activity during mood inductions and HPA-axis function in terms of early morning cortisol. We also studied the role of empathy and prosocial behavior in this sample of children with a range of disruptive behavior problems. The children were seen at four time points: 4–5 years, 6–7 years, 9–10 years, and 12–14 years.

Socialization and Antisocial Development

We examined child-rearing practices at the onset of the study, as predictors of continuity and change in the development of children's externalizing problems (Denham et al., 2000). Both mothers and fathers were observed interacting with their children during a series of challenging and pleasurable situations that also varied in degree of structure. Challenging contexts, such as playing a complicated game that is difficult for the child to win, allowed examination of interactions in situations that were likely to involve frustration. Nonchallenging situations, such as having a snack or unstructured time for play, allowed examination of interactions where externally imposed emotional demands were minimal. Child-rearing styles also were reported. Children's antisocial behavior was assessed using Achenbach reports from teachers (TRF), mothers (CBCL), and children (YSR).

Externalizing problems showed strong continuity 2 and 4 years later. Observed, proactive parenting (i.e., supportive presence, clear instruction, and appropriate limit setting) led to a *decrease* in externalizing problems over time, after controlling for initial problems. This facilitative role of proactive parenting, seen especially for the most troubled children, was found for both observed parental behaviors and self-reported styles. Reported styles consisted of a nurturant, child-centered approach and a deemphasis on harsh (restrictive, reactive) methods of child-rearing. Observed parental anger, in contrast, predicted continued difficulties for children. Separate, independent effects were found for fathers and mothers. These findings on proactive socialization replicate and extend those found in the first study, by showing the interactive effects for fathers as well as mothers in reducing children's aggression over time.

Two types of analytic approaches were used. One was the more standard variable-centered approach, which focuses on the variable as the main theoretical and analytical unit. The other was a person-centered approach, advocated by Cairns, which focuses on the individual in identifying different developmental pathways for different antisocial children (i.e., improvement, worsening, no change). Because there is little evidence that externalizing problems increase in middle childhood, the salient distinction is between children who do and do not continue to have problems, that is, those who improve and those who do not change. By using both person-oriented and variable-centered approaches, we were able to identify different socialization processes that contributed to different patterns of change in externalizing problems for the two subgroups of antisocial children.

The socialization influences did not differ for boys and girls. However, in more recent longitudinal work with this sample (Cole, Teti, & Zahn-Waxler, 2003), an aspect of parenting did predict different outcomes. Analyses focused on mother–preschooler regulation of anger during a frustration task where the child had to wait for a prize with nothing interesting to do in the interim (fathers did not participate in this task). Mothers' felt emotions were self-reported, and their emotional responses to children's negative emotions were observed. Mothers' felt anger was related to their observed anger only with their daughters. Yet maternal anger was predictive of stable conduct problems only for sons, particularly boys with conduct problems at school. There were indications of greater authenticity and less ambivalence in mothers' expressions of anger toward their girls than toward their boys. Faced with a son's angry distress, mothers may not communicate their actual feelings, or they may communicate anger that is not really felt.

Ambivalent, mixed emotions in response to child negative control are associated with young children's aggression (Dumas, LaFreniere, & Serketich, 1995). In our study, parents often expressed concern about a son's poorly regulated anger but confusion as to how to handle it because they did not want him to be a wimp or sissy. Our findings suggest that more fine-grained analyses of socialization may be needed in order to understand how it interacts with sex of child in the development of aggression. In the Denham et al. (2000) study, parental anger was coded more globally, using 5-minute intervals to rate parental anger. In the Cole et al. (2003) study, a microanalytic approach was used to code each emotion exchange during the wait.

Biological Processes and Antisocial Development

From the inception of the study a primary interest was in whether the patterns of physiological underarousal more common to antisocial individuals (e.g., Lahey, Hart, Pliszka, Applegate, & McBurnett, 1993; Raine, 2002) would be seen in this sample of young antisocial children. We used two paradigms to study these processes in young children. They included autonomic nervous system activity (heart rate, vagal tone, skin conductance) in a mood-induction task and hypothalamic–pituitary–adrenal axis function as assessed by salivary cortisol. Low arousal of these systems has been hypothesized to reflect low levels of fear, which could predispose to antisocial and violent behavior and reduce the effectiveness of positive socialization practices. Another theory is that low arousal represents an unpleasant physiological state, and antisocial individuals seek stimulation to reduce this negative state. Both processes may operate to heighten aggression. Although fearlessness has traitlike features, it could also be subject to socialization, e.g., in contexts where one becomes conditioned to environmental adversity.

Early generalizations about biological bases of antisocial behavior were based on studies of adolescent and adult males. This ignored the possibility that physiological underarousal might develop over time and possibly be subject to modification by socialization or intervention (Raine, 2002), rather than reflect an inherent deficit. The failure to study females also left unanswered the question of whether their antisocial behavior showed similar biological correlates. We found no evidence, for either young boys or girls, that externalizing problems were *directly* associated with ANS physiological underarousal (Cole, Zahn-Waxler, Fox, Usher, & Welsh, 1996; Zahn-Waxler, Cole, Welsh, & Fox, 1995). However, a subgroup of children who overtly expressed angry, negative emotions also showed low heart rates, high vagal tone, and large ANS change. Whereas children with externalizing problems were overrepresented in this group, some other less troubled children showed these patterns as well. Moreover, children with externalizing problems were overrepresented in another subgroup with a very different affective and physiological profile. These children were highly inexpressive of emotion and showed high heart rate, low vagal tone, and small ANS change. Thus relations between underarousal and aggression are complexly determined and not necessarily directly linked to children's behavior problems. Further evidence of this complexity was seen in skin conductance patterns of young disruptive boys and girls. The most aggressive girls (but not boys) showed high electrodermal activity during an empathy mood induction task. This is opposite to predictions from earlier theory and research and illustrates the limitations of generalizations about biological bases of antisocial behavior using only male samples.

TABLE 7.1. *Correlations Between Salivary Cortisol and Behavior Problems at 6–7 Years*

	Mother (CBCL)			Teacher (TRF)		
	Cortisol			Cortisol		
Achenbach Scales: 6–7 years	Total	Boys	Girls	Total	Boys	Girls
Somatic	.19	−.04	.31	.05	.09	.10
Anxious/Depressed	.18	−.04	.40*	.08	.14	.04
Social Problems	.10	.22	−.01	.24$^+$	.21	.24
Attention	.27*	.32*	.24	.14	.12	−.03
Delinquent	.10	.09	.14	.19	.11	.37$^+$
Aggression	.19	.09	.35$^+$	.24$^+$	.13	.43*
Internalizing	.20	−.03	.36$^+$	.09	.10	.11
Externalizing	.18	.10	.33$^+$	.24$^+$	.13	.43*
Total	.24*	.17	.32	.23$^+$	.17	.31

$^+ p < .10$; $^* p < .05$; $^{**} p < .01$

More recently we have examined relations between cortisol and antisocial behavior. Based on the aforementioned literature, one would also have predicted lower cortisol for highly aggressive children. However, given that high cortisol is associated with reactivity to stress and internalizing symptoms, and given that externalizing problems are commonly comorbid with internalizing problems, predictions are less clear. When children were 6–7 years old, saliva samples were obtained to assess cortisol levels. One saliva sample was taken at the home between 6:30 and 7:30 A.M. on a day just prior to a laboratory visit. Another sample was taken on the morning of a visit, prior to arrival and before a physical examination. A third sample was taken following the exam. There were no differences between boys and girls on any of these measures.

Only early morning cortisol on the day prior to the visit showed associations with child problems (Tables 7.1 and 7.2). Behavior problems were not associated with low cortisol levels. An interesting pattern emerged when analyses were conducted separately for boys and girls and when specific subscales of problems that also included different internalizing symptoms were examined. For boys, relations are mainly between high cortisol and attention problems. For girls, high cortisol is more often linked with anxiety, depression, and antisocial patterns. One might speculate that the physiological links to both internalizing and externalizing problems for girls are also reflective of a greater underlying comorbidity. One way in which our research differed from other studies showing associations between aggression and low cortisol in children (e.g., McBurnett, Lahey, Rathouz, & Loeber, 2000; Raine, Venebles, & Mednick, 1997) is that our children came

TABLE 7.2. *Prediction of Behavior Problems at 9–10 Years from Salivary Cortisol at 6–7 Years*

Achenbach Scales: 9 years	Mother (CBCL) Cortisol			Teacher (TRF) Cortisol			Child (YSR) Cortisol		
	Total	Boys	Girls	Total	Boys	Girls	Total	Boys	Girls
Somatic	.25*	.01	.44*	.13	.12	.27	.09	.22	−.02
Anxious/Depressed	.12	−.08	.31	.22	.32+	.15	.15	.15	.14
Social Problems	.24+	.26	.25	.04	.21	−.13	.33**	.30+	.36+
Attention	.29*	.31+	.29	.15	.46**	−.14	.27*	.35*	.22
Delinquent	.21	.06	.40*	.29*	.22	.58**	.07	−.06	.20
Aggression	.14	.12	.19	.21	.33+	.16	.16	.11	.25
Internalizing	.19	−.05	.38+	.20	.34+	.08	.16	.17	.15
Externalizing	.16	.11	.24	.23+	.32+	.29	.17	.08	.27
Total	.25*	.16	.34+	.24+	.43*	.06	.21	.22	.19

$+ p < .10;$ * $p < .05;$ ** $p < .01$

from middle- and upper-class families. Higher social class status, in general, creates protection and buffering, which may help antisocial children maintain reactivity as they have fewer opportunities to become jaded and habituated or inured to distress and danger.

Empathy and Prosocial Development

Although not part of formal diagnostic criteria, a diminished capacity for empathy and caring behaviors is prominent in descriptions of externalizing problems (American Psychiatric Association, 1987). Again, what is not known is whether antisocial children are deficient in concern for others even in early life, or whether this lack of sensitivity evolves over time. We observed children's responses to others in distress at 4–5 years and 6–7 years of age. At 6–7 years we also obtained mothers', teachers', and children's reports of their empathy and prosocial behaviors (Zahn-Waxler et al., 1995: Hastings, Zahn-Waxler, Robinson, Usher, & Bridges, 2000).

At 4–5 years aggressive, disruptive preschool children, on average, did not differ from nonproblem children on empathic, prosocial behaviors. At both ages girls showed more caring behaviors than boys, irrespective of behavior problems. There was one interesting exception, seen in an interaction of sex and risk status. While disruptive boys showed as much caring and concern for distress victims as did other children, they simultaneously showed more callous and avoidant behaviors toward the injured persons, suggesting more complicated, ambivalent patterns. By 6–7 years the children identified in preschool as having clinical levels of externalizing problems decreased in their observed concern for others. The other children, in contrast, maintained the levels they had shown 2 years earlier. The decrease in observed prosocial behavior in aggressive children is consistent with separate reports from mothers, teachers, and the children, indicating that this group of children was lower on their expressions of concern for others. Concern for others also played a moderating role in the development of externalizing problems from early to middle childhood. Greater concern at 4–5 years predicted decreases in the stability and severity of externalizing problems by 6–7 years, and greater concern at 6–7 years predicted decreases in the stability of problems by 9–10 years.

Environmental factors also played a moderating role in the development of aggressive children's concern for others. Mothers who were strict and punitive, who did not tend to reason or establish fair and consistent rules, and who showed anger and disappointment in their children were likely to impede their children's prosocial development. Negative parenting may have indirect effects on aggression by undermining related competent behaviors. Children who are aggressive *and* who experience forceful, angry parenting may be unable to maintain their concern for others, thus further disinhibiting their aggressive tendencies. In other normative longitudinal studies of children in the first 2 years of life, we have demonstrated the roles of (a) positive parenting in facilitating children's concern for others over time (Zahn-Waxler, Radke-Yarrow, & King, 1979 and (b) negative parenting in diminishing their empathy over time (Robinson, Zahn-Waxler, & Emde, 1994). Positive parenting included warmth, modeling prosocial behavior, and use of firm, clear explanations about others' feelings of distress when they have been harmed. Negative parenting consisted of a family climate with low cohesion, marital dissatisfaction, and conflict.

CONCLUSIONS AND RECOMMENDATIONS

The studies reviewed point to the challenges of trying to understand the early development of serious antisocial behavior, particularly in how biology and environment interact to influence aggression in male and female children. In Raine's biosocial model of violence (2002), he stresses the importance of identifying the influences of genetic and environmental processes in giving rise to social and biological risk and protective factors that both individually and interactively predispose toward and away from antisocial behavior. He reminds us that what we label as a biological variable or a social variable is open to question. Environmental factors (e.g., an accident) can create a biological vulnerability (e.g., brain dysfunction) and biological factors can alter how a child is socialized (e.g., genetic factors that contribute to poor parenting). These terms, then, when applied in the extreme represent a false dichotomy. However, they should be retained at this point in order to further define and refine constructs important to advancing knowledge of the many interwoven processes within and outside the organism that underlie antisocial development.

We have concentrated on early development when serious forms of aggression begin to emerge in some children, particularly boys, and on aspects of positive parenting that can disrupt this process. The evidence is fairly compelling in that externalizing problems were shown to decrease over time even after taking into account children's initial levels of problems. Proactive parenting predicted positive change in two different samples of children who showed early onset of aggressive, antisocial behaviors. Interactions with biological processes were inferred based on the assumption that early aggression has biological bases that can be interrupted by positive socialization. Specific biological factors (and "feminine" traits) also were identified, some of which interacted with sex of child and were related to lower levels of aggression.

What is difficult in this type of research, however, is the ability consistently to demonstrate all main effects and higher order interactions within the same analytic frameworks. Information must be pieced together from different places and sources. There are inevitable trade-offs in approaches used, and no one way is fully satisfactory. Our in-depth measurement of many variables necessarily restricted sample size, and some biosocial interactions undoubtedly went undetected. However, this will also be true when larger sample sizes are used, because both fewer relevant constructs are measured and measurement often is more imprecise. Replication across approaches becomes essential, as do intervention designs based on naturalistic studies. For example, would teaching parents to use proactive techniques alter children's developmental trajectories?

In this research we have emphasized the early years of life. Traditionally this has been viewed as a period of great plasticity and malleability, and we have shown some of the ways in which this is true for antisocial development. However, Cairns emphasized the dynamic properties of processes associated with development, with major shifts possible at any time. He noted the multiple opportunities for influencing the developing system in childhood, adolescence, and beyond. Longitudinal research with adolescents (Ge, Best, Conger, & Simons, 1996) has shown parenting effects on externalizing problems after taking into account initial levels of problems. Subsequent research could include specific biological measures thought to interact with socialization.

The study of biological factors in adolescence has emphasized neurohormones associated with pubertal development and reproduction. Testosterone is a hormone known to be related to aggression in humans and nonhuman animals. In a study of problems in developing adolescents at risk we examined associations with testosterone (Granger et al., 2003). Externalizing problems were not related to high testosterone for boys or girls. For boys, anxiety–depression and attention problems were associated with low testosterone. For girls no direct effects were observed for absolute levels of testosterone. However, girls with disruptive behavior problems showed steeper declines in testosterone across the day.

In follow-up longitudinal analyses we will examine whether (a) testosterone predicts changes in problems over time and (b) quality of parenting also interacts with testosterone such that the combination of influences further enhances prediction. Mazur & Booth (1998) propose that testosterone affects adolescent behavior mostly through indirect social responses elicited by maturation rather than through direct activation of target receptors in organs of the nervous system. In support of such a biosocial explanation, Booth and colleagues (Booth, Johnson, Granger, Crouter, & McHale, 2003) found no evidence of direct testosterone–behavior effects; rather, the expression of testosterone-related behavior was dependent on parent–child relations. When parent–child relations were poor, high-testosterone sons were more likely to engage in risky behaviors (substance use, destruction of property, and trouble with authorities), and low-testosterone sons were more likely to report symptoms of depression. Low-testosterone girls who had poor relations with their mothers were more likely to manifest risky behaviors. But low-testosterone girls with poor relations with their fathers were more likely to manifest depressed affect. Our longitudinal study of adolescents will provide an opportunity to further pursue these issues within a developmental framework.

Findings for female reproductive hormones such as estradiol have not demonstrated consistent patterns. Neuroendocrine evidence (in animals) implicates oxytocin in conjunction with female reproductive hormones and endogenous opioid peptide mechanisms with behaviors incompatible with aggression. Oxytocin is a hormone that enhances relaxation, reduces fearfulness, and decreases sympathetic activity, all of which are antithetical to the fight-or-flight response. Hence it is thought to be adaptive for physical and mental health. Shelley Taylor and her colleagues (Taylor et al., 2000) have questioned the universal applicability of Cannon's original construal of fight–flight as *the* human stress response.

While fight-flight responses to stress are likely to stimulate physical aggression and are more common in males than females, human females' responses often reflect a pattern that Taylor et al. (2000) refer to as tend-and-befriend. Tending involves nurturant activities that protect the self and offspring, promote safety, and reduce distress. Befriending creates and maintains social networks that are also protective. The biobehavioral mechanism that underlies the tend-and-befriend process appears to be linked to the attachment/caregiving system. Including measures of oxytocin could significantly advance future research on individual differences and sex differences in aggression. The strong interpersonal orientation that appears to be rooted in biological processes would be expected to protect against aggression because the consequences of one's behavior toward others matter to the individual.

The value females place on social bonds is important not only to how aggression is conveyed (e.g., social aggression, which is the dark side) but also to the ability to inhibit it in the first place, especially physical aggression. As we have seen, from early childhood girls express more empathy, guilt, and prosocial behaviors than boys. They are also less assertive, more affiliative, compliant, and likely to be influenced by the wishes, emotions, and expectations of authority figures. These qualities of caring for and being influenced by others should function to minimize serious aggression. It is probably no coincidence that these same qualities have been used to establish operational definitions of feminine sex role for purposes of assessment (Bem, 1978).

Although this broad-based interpersonal orientation may be rooted in biological processes associated with bearing and raising children, it is undoubtedly also amenable to socialization influences and social contexts. Interpersonal bonds have been hypothesized to act as a social control against norm violation and rule-breaking. The formation of positive social bonds may turn out to be the central explanation for desistance from bringing harm to others, their property, and society in general. There also may be costs associated with a strong interpersonal orientation, which could under some circumstances create risk for depression and anxiety (Zahn-Waxler et al., 1991).

The studies we have reviewed were selected in an effort to illustrate developmental science principles advocated by Robert Cairns – research that is developmental/longitudinal, multivariate, multimethod, and interdisciplinary and offers the potential for understanding reciprocal, dynamic interactive processes implicated in the development of aggressive, antisocial behavior in males and females. It has been a challenging, humbling, and ultimately reassuring process. It is possible, though not without difficulty, to identify some of those processes.

The varieties of aggression and other antisocial behaviors, each with multiple determinants, virtually ensure that any given research program will provide only a partial picture. Only sustained interdisciplinary, longitudinal research that includes many different investigative teams who study humans and other animals can ultimately provide better answers for how aggression develops, why some are at greater risk than others, and what accounts for continuity and change over time. Artful integration of research findings from diverse literatures is also requisite to establishing this important knowledge base. Robert Cairns indelibly forged recognition of these facts onto developmental scientists, altering how we study aggression and violence and providing important tools for inquiry. He has left a legacy of ideas, challenges, and opportunities that, if followed with the wisdom, rigor, and commitment that he modeled, will help to decipher some of the complexities of the humane and inhumane ways in which we treat one another.

References

American Psychiatric Association. (1987). *Diagnostic and statistical manual of mental disorders* (3rd ed.). Washington, DC: Author.

Bem, S. L. (1978). *Bem Sex Role Inventory: Manual*. Palo Alto, CA: Mind Garden.

Booth, A, Johnson, D., Granger, D. A., Crouter, A., & McHale, S. (2003). Testosterone and child and adolescent adjustment: the moderating role of parent-child relationships. *Developmental Psychology, 39*(1), 85–98.

Cairns, R. B. (1997). Socialization and sociogenesis. In D. Magnusson (Ed.), *The lifespan development of individuals: Behavioral, neurobiological, and psychosocial perspectives: a synthesis*. Cambridge, UK: Cambridge University Press, 277–295.

Cairns, R. B. (2000). Developmental science: Three audacious implications. In L. Bergman, R. Cairns, L. Nilsson, & L. Nystedt (Eds.), *Developmental science and the holistic approach*. Mahwah, NJ: Lawrence Erlbaum Associates, 49–62.

Cairns, R. B., Cairns, B. D., Neckerman, H. J., Ferguson, L. L., & Gariépy, J.-L. (1989). Growth and aggression: I. Childhood to early adolescence. *Developmental Psychology, 25*(2), 320–330.

Campbell, S. B., Shaw, D. S., & Gilliom, M. (2000). Early externalizing behavior problems: Toddlers and preschoolers at risk for later maladjustment. *Development and Psychopathology, 12*(3), 467–488.

Cole, P. M., Teti, L. O., & Zahn-Waxler, C. (2003). Mutual emotion regulation and the stability of conduct problems between preschool and early school age. *Development and Psychopathology, 15*(1), 1–18.

Cole, P. M., Zahn-Waxler, C, Fox, N. A., Usher, B. A., & Welsh, J. D. (1996). Individual differences in emotion regulation and behavior problems in preschool children. *Journal of Abnormal Psychology, 105*, 518–529.

Crick, N. R., Casas, J. F., & Mosher, M. (1997). Relational and overt aggression in preschool. *Developmental Psychology, 33*, 579–588.

Cummings, E. M., Hollenbeck, B., Iannotti, R. J., Radke-Yarrow, M., & Zahn-Waxler, C. (1986). Early organization of altruism and aggression: Developmental patterns and individual differences. In C. Zahn-Waxler, E. M. Cummings, & R. J. Iannotti (Eds.), *Altruism and aggression: Biological and social origins*. New York: Cambridge University Press, 165–188.

Cummings, E. M., Iannotti, R. J., & Zahn-Waxler, C. (1985). Influence of conflict between adults on the emotions and aggression of young children. *Developmental Psychology, 21*, 495–507.

Cummings, E. M., Iannotti, R. J., & Zahn-Waxler, C. (1989). Aggression between peers in early childhood: Individual continuity and developmental change. *Child Development, 60*(4), 887–895.

Denham, S. A., Workman, E., Cole, P. M., Weissbrod, C., Kendziora. K. T., & Zahn-Waxler, C. (2000). Prediction of externalizing problems from early to middle childhood: The role of parental socialization and emotion expression. *Development and Psychopathology, 12*(12), 23–45.

Dumas, J. E., LaFreniere, P. J., & Serketich, W. J. (1995). "Balance of power": A transactional analysis of control in mother–child dyads involving socially competent, aggressive, and anxious children. *Journal of Abnormal Psychology, 104,* 104–113.

Eme, R. F., & Kavanaugh, L. (1995). Sex differences in conduct disorder. *Journal of Clinical Psychology, 24,* 406–426.

Fivush, R. (1989). Exploring sex differences in the emotional context of mother–child conversations about the past. *Sex Roles, 20,* 675–691.

Fivush, R. (1991). Gender and emotion in mother–child conversations about the past. *Journal of Narrative and Life History, 1*(4), 325–341.

Ge, X., Best, K. M., Conger, R. D., & Simons, R. L. (1996). Parenting behaviors and the co-occurrence of adolescent depressive symptoms and conduct problems. *Developmental Psychology, 32*(4), 717–731.

Goodman, S., & Gotlib, I. H. (1999). Risk for psychopathology in the children of depressed mothers: A developmental model for understanding mechanisms of transmission. *Psychological Review, 106*(33), 458–490.

Granger, D., Shirtcliff, E. A., Zahn-Waxler, C., Usher, B., Klimes-Dougan, B., & Hastings, P. (2003). Salivary testosterone diurnal variation and psychopathology in adolescent males and females: Individual differences and developmental effects. *Development and Psychopathology, 15*(2), 431–449.

Hastings, P. D., Zahn-Waxler, C., Robinson, J., Usher, B., & Bridges, D., (2000). The development of concern for others in children with behavior problems. *Developmental Psychology, 36*(5), 531–546.

Keenan, K., Loeber, R., & Green, S. (1999). Conduct disorder in girls: A review of the literature. *Clinical and Child Family Psychology Review, 2,* 3–19.

Keenan, K., & Shaw, D. (1997). Development and social influences on young girls' early problem behavior. *Psychological Bulletin, 121,* 95–113.

Lahey, B. B., Hart, E. L., Pliszka, S., Applegate, B., & McBurnett, K. (1993). Neurophysiological correlates of conduct disorder: A rationale and review of research. *Journal of Clinical Child Psychology, 22*(2), 141–153.

Loeber, R., & Keenan, K. (1994). The interaction between conduct disorder and its comorbid conditions: Effects of age and gender. *Clinical Psychology Review, 14,* 497–523.

Loeber, R., & Stouthamer-Loeber, M. (1986). Family factors as correlates and predictors of juvenile conduct problems and delinquency. In M. Tonry & N. Morris (Eds.), *Crime and justice: An annual review of research* (pp. 29–149). Chicago: University of Chicago Press.

Maccoby, E. E., & Martin, J. A. (1983). Socialization in the context of the family: Parent child interaction. In P. H. Mussen (Series Ed.) & E. Hetherington (Vol. Ed.), *Handbook of child psychology: Vol. 4 Socialization, personality, and social development* (4th ed., pp. 1–101). New York: Wiley.

Magnusson, D., & Cairns, R. B. (1996) Developmental science: Toward a unifying framework. In R. D. Cairns, G. H. Elder, & E. Jane Costello (Eds.), *Developmental science.* New York: Cambridge University Press, 7–30.

Malatesta, C. Z., & Haviland, J. (1982). Learning display rules: The socialization of emotion expression in infancy. *Child Development, 53,* 991–1003.

Mazur, A., & Booth, A. (1998). Testosterone and dominance in men. *Behavioral and Brain Sciences, 21,* 353–363.

McBurnett, K., Lahey, B. B., Rathouz, P. J., & Loeber, R. (2000). Low salivary cortisol and persistent aggression in boys referred for disruptive behavior. *Archives of General Psychiatry, 57*(1), 38–43.

McClelland, G. H., & Judd, C. M. (1993). Statistical difficulties of detecting interactions and moderator effects. *Psychological Bulletin, 114,* 376–390.

Miller, N. B., Cowan, P. A., Cowan, C. P., Hetherington, E. M., & Clingempeel, W. G. (1993). Externalizing in preschoolers and early adolescents: A cross-study replication of a family model. *Developmental Psychology, 29,* 3–18.

Moffitt, T. E. (1993). Adolescent-limited and life-course persistent antisocial behavior: A developmental taxonomy, *Psychological Review, 100*(4), 674–701.

Moffitt, T. E., & Caspi, A. (2001). Childhood predictors differentiate life-course persistent and adolescent-limited antisocial pathways among males and females. *Development and Psychopathology, 13*(2), 355–375.

Perry, D. G., Perry, L. C., & Weiss, R. J. (1989). Sex differences in the consequences that children anticipate for aggression. *Developmental Psychology, 25,* 312–319.

Pettit, G. S., & Bates, J. E. (1989). Family interaction patterns and children's behavior problems from infancy to four years. *Developmental Psychology, 25,* 413–420.

Raine, A. (2002). Biosocial studies of antisocial and violent behavior in children and adults: A review. *Journal of Abnormal Child Psychology, 30*(4), 311–326.

Raine, A., Venebles, P. H., & Mednick, S. A. (1997). Low resting heart rate at age 3 years predisposes to aggression at age 11 years: Evidence from the Mauritius Child Health Project. *Journal of the American Academy of Child and Adolescent Psychiatry, 36,* 1457–1464.

Robinson, J. L., Zahn-Waxler, C., & Emde, R. N. (1994). Patterns of development in early empathic behavior: Environmental and child constitutional influences. *Social Development,* 125–145.

Rothbart, M., Ahadi, S. A., Hersey, K. L., & Fisher, P. (2001). Investigations of temperament at three to seven years. The child behavior questionnaire. *Child Development, 72*(5), 1394–1408.

Shaw, D. S., Bell, R. Q., & Gilliom, M. (2000). A truly early starter model of antisocial behavior revisited. *Clinical Child and Family Psychology Review, 3,* 155–172.

Shaw, D. S., Owens, E. B., Giovannelli, J., & Winslow, E. B. (2001). Infant and toddler pathways leading to early externalizing disorders. *Journal of the American Academy of Child and Adolescent Psychiatry, 40*(1), 36–43.

Smetana, J. G. (1989). Toddlers' social interactions in the context of moral and conventional transgressions in the home. *Developmental Psychology, 25*(4), 499–509.

Taylor, S. E., Klein, L. C., Lewis, B. P., Gruenwald, T. L., Gurung, R. A. R., & Updegraff, J. A. (2000). Biobehavioral responses to stress in females: Tend and befriend, not fight-or-flight. *Psychological Review, 107*(3), 411–429.

Wakschlag, L. S., & Hans, S. L. (1999). Relations of maternal responsiveness during infancy to the development of behavior problems in high-risk youths. *Developmental Psychology, 35,* 569–579.

Zahn-Waxler, C. (1993). Warriors and worriers: Gender and psychopathology. *Development and Psychopathology, 5,* 79–89.

Zahn-Waxler, C. (2000). The development of empathy, guilt, and internalization of distress: Implications for gender differences in internalizing and externalizing problems. In R. J. Davidson (Ed.), *Anxiety, depression, and emotion* (pp. 222–265). Oxford, UK: Oxford University Press.

Zahn-Waxler, C. (2002). Children of depressed mothers. In B. S. Zuckerman, A. F. Lieberman, & N. A. Fox (Eds.), *Emotion regulation and developmental health: infancy and early childhood* (Johnson & Johnson Pediatric Roundtable Monographs, Johnson & Johnson Pediatric Institute, L.L.C., pp. 203–219).

Zahn-Waxler, C., Cole, P. M., & Barrett, K. C. (1991). Guilt and empathy: Sex differences and implications for the development of depression. In K. Dodge & J. Garber (Eds.), *Emotional regulation and dysregulation* (pp. 243–272). New York: Cambridge University Press.

Zahn-Waxler, C., Cole, P. M., Welsh, J. D., & Fox, N. A. (1995). Psycho-physiological correlates of empathy and prosocial behaviors in preschool children with behavior problems. *Development and Psychopathology, 8,* 103–122.

Zahn-Waxler, C., Iannotti, R. R. J., Cummings, E. M., & Denham, S. A. (1990). Antecedents of problem behaviors in children of depressed mothers. *Development and Psychopathology, 2,* 271–291.

Zahn-Waxler, C., Radke-Yarrow, M., & King, R. A. (1979). Childrearing and children's prosocial initiations toward victims of distress. *Child Development, 50,* 319–330.

Zahn-Waxler, C., & Robinson, J. (1995). Empathy and guilt: Early origins of feelings of responsibility. In K. Fischer & J. Tangney (Eds.), *Self-conscious emotions: Shame, guilt, embarrassment, guilt and pride.* Guilford Press, 143–173.

8

Life-Course Persistent and Adolescence-Limited Antisocial Males: Longitudinal Followup to Adulthood

Terrie E. Moffitt & Avshalom Caspi

University of Wisconsin, Madison; Institute of Psychiatry, London; University of Otago, New Zealand

This chapter tests and refines a developmental taxonomy of antisocial behavior, which proposed two primary hypothetical prototypes: life-course persistent offenders whose antisocial behavior begins in childhood and continues worsening thereafter, versus adolescence-limited offenders whose antisocial behavior begins in adolescence and desists in young adulthood (Moffitt, 1993). Two of our previous reports have described clinically defined groups of childhood-onset and adolescence-onset antisocial youths in the Dunedin birth cohort during childhood (Moffitt & Caspi, 2001) and at age 18 (Moffitt, Caspi, Dickson, Silva, & Stanton, 1996). Recently we followed up the cohort at age 26, and here we describe how the two groups of males fared in adulthood. In so doing we test a hypothesis *critical to the theory*: that childhood-onset, but not adolescent-onset, antisocial behavior is associated in adulthood with antisocial personality, violence, and continued serious antisocial behavior that expands into maladjustment in work life and victimization of partners and children (Moffitt, 1993).

THE TWO PROTOTYPES AND THEIR PREDICTED ADULT OUTCOMES

According to the theory, life-course persistent antisocials are few, persistent, and pathological. Adolescence-limited antisocials are common, relatively temporary, and near normative. The developmental typology hypothesized that childhood-onset versus adolescent-onset conduct

We thank the Dunedin Study members, their peer informants, the Dunedin Unit research staff and investigators, the Dunedin Police, the New Zealand Health Research Council, and the U.S. National Institute of Mental Health (MH45070, MH49414, MH56344). An extended report of many of the data analyses in this chapter has been published elsewhere (Moffitt et al., 2002).

problems have different etiologies. In addition, the typology differed from other developmental crime theories by predicting different outcome pathways for the two types across the adult life-course (Caspi & Moffitt, 1995; Moffitt, 1993, 1994, 1997). In a nutshell, we suggested that "life-course persistent" antisocial behavior originates early in life, when the difficult behavior of a high-risk young child is exacerbated by a high-risk social environment. The child's risk emerges from inherited or acquired neuropsychological variation, initially manifested as subtle cognitive deficits, difficult temperament, or hyperactivity. The environment's risk comprises factors such as inadequate parenting, disrupted family bonds, and poverty. The environmental risk domain expands beyond the family as the child ages, to include poor relations with people such as peers and teachers, then later with partners and employers. Over the first two decades of development, transactions between individual and environment gradually construct a disordered personality with hallmark features of physical aggression and antisocial behavior persisting to mid-life. The theory invokes the developmental principle of cumulative continuity to predict that antisocial behavior will infiltrate multiple adult life domains: illegal activities, problems with employment, and victimization of intimate partners and children (Moffitt et al., 1996; Moffitt, Caspi, Harrington & Milne, 2002).

In contrast, we suggested that "adolescence-limited" antisocial behavior emerges alongside puberty, when otherwise healthy youngsters experience dysphoria during the relatively role-less years between their biological maturation and their access to mature privileges and responsibilities, a period we called the maturity gap. While adolescents are in this gap it is virtually normative for them to find the life-course persistent youths' delinquent style appealing and mimic it as a way to demonstrate autonomy from parents, win affiliation with peers, and hasten social maturation. However, because their predelinquent development was normal and healthy, most young people who become adolescence-limited delinquents are able to desist from crime when they age into real adult roles, turning gradually to a more conventional lifestyle. This recovery may be delayed if the antisocial activities of adolescence-limited delinquents attract factors we called snares, such as a criminal record, incarceration, addiction, truncated education without credentials, becoming a teen parent, sexually transmitted disease, or injury. Such snares can compromise the ability to make a successful transition to adulthood, impair health, and lead to social disadvantage.

DIFFERENTIAL CHILD AND ADOLESCENT RISK FACTORS FOR MALES ON THE LIFE-COURSE PERSISTENT VERSUS ADOLESCENCE-LIMITED PATHS IN THE DUNEDIN STUDY

Our studies of childhood predictors measured between ages 3 and 13 for males in the Dunedin cohort have shown that the life-course persistent path is differentially predicted by difficult temperament, neurological abnormalities, low intellectual ability, reading difficulties, hyperactivity, poor scores on neuropsychological tests, and slow heart rate (Jeglum-Bartusch, Lynam, Moffitt, & Silva, 1997; Moffitt, 1990; Moffitt & Caspi, 2001; Moffitt, Lynam, & Silva, 1994). In contrast, study members on the adolescence-limited path, despite being involved in delinquency to the same extent as their counterparts on the life-course persistent path, tended to have backgrounds that were normative, or sometimes better than the average Dunedin child's (Moffitt & Caspi, 2001).

Our studies of adolescent outcomes measured at ages 15 and 18 have shown that the life-course persistent path is differentially associated in males with weak bonds to family, early school leaving, and psychopathic personality traits of alienation, impulsivity, and callousness (Moffitt et al., 1996), and with conviction for violent crimes (Jeglum-Bartusch et al., 1997; Moffitt et al., 1996). In contrast, the adolescence-limited path is differentially associated with delinquent peers (Jeglum-Bartusch et al., 1997; Moffitt & Caspi, 2001), a tendency to endorse unconventional values and a personality trait called social potency (Moffitt et al., 1996), and with nonviolent delinquent offenses (Jeglum-Bartusch et al., 1997).

Our findings about differential childhood risk for childhood-onset versus adolescent-onset offenders are generally in keeping with findings reported from several samples in eight countries. More than 20 publications by different research groups who have tested the theory are reviewed in Moffitt (2003). Despite this body of research, no prior study had followed the two types from preschool to adulthood to test the theory's predictions about differential adult adjustment, as we report here.

ARE TWO GROUPS ENOUGH? FOLLOWING UP
"RECOVERIES" AND "ABSTAINERS"

The original theoretical taxonomy asserted that two prototypes, life-course persistent and adolescence-limited offenders, account for the preponderance of the population's antisocial behavior, and thus warrant the preponderance of attention by theory and research. Researchers testing for the presence of the two types have since uncovered a third type, labeled "low-level chronics" because they offend persistently, but at a low rate, from childhood to adolescence (Fergusson, Horwood; & Nagin, 2000) or from adolescence to adulthood (Nagin, Farrington, & Moffitt, 1995). We previously reported a small group of Dunedin study males who had exhibited extreme, pervasive, and persistent antisocial behavior problems during childhood, but who surprisingly engaged in only low to moderate delinquency during adolescence, thus failing to meet our criterion for life-course persistent group membership. In that report we optimistically labeled this group "recoveries" (Moffitt et al., 1996). However, persuaded by the findings about low-level chronics in other samples, we follow up the "recovery" group at age 26 to uncover whether they indeed had recovered, or instead had become low-level-chronic offenders.

A final group followed up here are the rare males who manage to avoid virtually all antisocial behavior during childhood and adolescence. We earlier labeled this small group "abstainers" (Moffitt et al., 1996). Dunedin abstainers described themselves at age 18 on personality measures as extremely over-controlled, fearful, interpersonally timid, and socially inept, and they also remained virgins. Nonetheless, they were staying the course to pursue higher education at 18, and thus we follow them here to uncover whether they developed into healthy or problematic adults.

THE DUNEDIN BIRTH COHORT

Participants are male[1] members of the Dunedin Multidisciplinary Health and Development Study, a longitudinal investigation of health and behavior (Silva & Stanton, 1996). The cohort of 1,037 children (52% male, 48% female) was constituted at age 3 when the investigators enrolled 91% of the consecutive births between April 1972 and March 1973 in Dunedin, New Zealand. Cohort families represent the full range of socioeconomic status in the general population of New Zealand's South Island, and they are primarily white. Assessments have been conducted at ages 3 ($n = 1037$), 5, 7, 9, 11, 13, 15, 18, 21, and, most recently, at age 26 ($n = 980$, 499 males, 96% of living cohort members). For documentation supporting generalization from the Dunedin cohort to other countries, see Moffitt, Caspi, Rutter, & Silva (2001).

MEASURES OF ADULT OUTCOMES

We compared males on the adolescence-limited versus life-course persistent pathways on 79 measures taken at age 26. The measures were selected to represent five domains of adult outcome implicated by the theory: criminal offending (property crimes, rule violations, drug crimes, and

---

[1] This report focuses on males only. Including females introduces a confound between the sexes' mean-level differences on measures and the groups' differing sex compositions. This confound cannot be disentangled statistically because the group of LCP females is so small that it has no statistical power. In a previous report (Moffitt & Caspi, 2001), we found that only six Dunedin females could be said to be on the LCP path (a male to female ratio of 10:1) whereas 78 females were on the AL path (a ratio of 1.5:1), a sex pattern also reported by others (Fergusson et al., 2000; Kratzer and Hodgins, 1999; Tibbetts and Piquero, 1999). Moreover, the adult life domains affected by an antisocial history are different for men and women, arguing for studying them separately (Moffitt et al., 2001). Adult outcomes of conduct-disordered girls in the Dunedin cohort are reported in other publications (Bardone, Moffitt, Caspi, Dickson, & Silva, 1996; Bardone et al.,1998; Moffitt, Caspi, Rutter, & Silva, 2001).

violence, 24 measures), personality (8 measures), psychopathology (substance abuse and mental disorders, 19 measures), personal life (relationships with women and children; 12 measures) and economic life (education, occupation, income, unemployment and work problems, 16 measures). Each of the five domains was measured via at least two sources of data: personal interviews, official records, or questionnaires completed by informants who knew the study member well. The 79 measures are described in detail in Moffitt et al. (2002). The results of our look at 79 outcome variables, to be described in the following pages of this chapter, attested that antisocial disorders have a very wide nomothetic net and reinforced the usefulness of heterotypic continuity as a developmental concept.

THE COMPARISON GROUPS OF THE TAXONOMY

This chapter compares groups of males already defined and described in earlier reports. To operationalize the theory of two types, comparison groups were designated on the basis of individual life histories from age 5 to 18. The scales measuring antisocial behavior at each age and the procedures for using them to define the groups are described in detail in earlier reports about these groups (Moffitt et al., 1996, 2002; Moffitt & Caspi, 2001). Study members who met criteria for extreme antisocial behavior across both childhood and adolescence were designated on the *life-course persistent path*, hereafter referred to as the LCP path (47 males, 10%). Study members who met criteria for extreme antisocial behavior as adolescents, but who had not been extremely antisocial as children, were designated on the *adolescence-limited path*, hereafter called the AL path (122 males, 26%). The LCP- and AL-path males were well matched on offending, showing virtually identical and statistically indistinguishable scores at their 18th birthdays on self-reported delinquency, parent-reported conduct problems, police arrests, and court convictions (Moffitt et al., 1996; Moffitt & Caspi, 2001).

Three additional groups were defined, using the criteria described in detail in Moffitt et al. (1996, 2002). Study members who met criteria for extreme antisocial behavior in childhood but whose delinquency was not extreme enough in adolescence to warrant assignment to the LCP path were designated on the *recovery* path (40 males, 8%). The few study members who had not engaged in antisocial behavior from age 5 to 18 according to parent, teacher, or self-reports were designated as *abstainers* (25 males, 5%). Males not meeting our criteria for any of the four clinical comparison groups were designated as *unclassified*; as a group their antisocial behavior was approximately normative, never differing significantly from the cohort's mean score on any of the antisocial measures from age 5 to 18 (243 males, 51%). The percentage of study members who were successfully followed up at age 26 did not differ significantly among the five taxonomy groups (Moffitt et al., 2002).

HOW TO INTERPRET THE STATISTICAL ANALYSES IN TABLES 8.1 THROUGH 8.6

Tables 8.1 through 8.6 show two types of group comparisons. First, stars in the column of data under each group show whether or not that group differed from the unclassified comparison group, as tested in multiple regression analyses (OLS for continuously distributed outcomes; logistic for dichotomously scored outcomes). Each regression equation contained four dummy variables to represent the Abstainers, the Recoveries, the LCP group, and the AL group. The contrast or reference group in each regression equation was the Unclassified group. In view of the large number of tests, alpha was set at $p < .01$.

Second, the far right column of each table shows the hypothesis test of particular interest for the taxonomy: the LCP group was predicted to fare worse as adults than the AL group. Specific tests of this hypothesis were conducted using planned contrasts for continuously distributed outcomes (e.g., months in prison), and by calculating the odds ratio from a cross-tabulation of groups on dichotomous outcomes (e.g., percent convicted). Odds ratios (OR) are significant if their 95% confidence intervals (CI) do not include 1.

The tables show many outcome variables plotted as Z scores standardized on the full cohort of males with a mean of 0 and SD of 1. Each group's mean Z score indicates how far that group deviates from the mean for the representative sample (0), a mean that can be interpreted as the normative standard for 26-year-old males. The distance in SD units between a group's mean and the normative zero, or between the means of two groups, may be interpreted as an effect size, where .2 SD is a small effect, .5 SD is a medium effect, and .8 SD is a large effect (Cohen, 1988).

FINDINGS ABOUT CRIME PARTICIPATION

Table 8.1 presents the men's self-reports of offending in the year prior to their age-26 interview. Broadly speaking, both LCP and AL men offended more than others, but LCP men tended to be more frequent and serious offenders than AL men. Men on the LCP and AL paths reported a similar variety of different types of offenses, but LCP men reported a significantly higher mean number of offenses, accounting for 2.2 times more than their share of the cohort's total self-reported offenses. Breaking down the offenses by type revealed that AL and LCP groups did not differ on participation in self-reported property crimes (theft, fraud, vandalism) or rule violations (e.g., driving without a license, public drunkenness), but

TABLE 8.1. *Self-Reported Offending: Comparisons among Male Groups at Age 26, on Self-Reported Measures of Past-Year Offending, and Informants' Reports of Fighting*

	Group					LCP-AL difference
	Unclassified	Abstainer	Recovery?	LCP-path	AL-path	
N with interview data	233	25	39	42	119	
All types of offenses combined						
Mean variety of offenses (SD)	3.3(2.4)	1.4(1.5)	2.9(2.9)	6.6*(5.8)	6.4*(4.8)	ns
Mean number of offenses (SD)	101(195)	21(47)	95(228)	397*(591)	277*(443)	p = .04
Ratio of a group's share of the cohort's total 76,909 offenses to the group's N	0.6	0.2	0.6	2.2	1.6	—
Property offenses						
% reporting any offense	41%	24%*	28%	60%	58%*	ns
Mean number of offenses Z-score (SD)	−.09(.3)	−.13(.2)	−.08(.4)	−.07(.2)	.14*(1.3)	ns
Rule-violation offenses						
% reporting any offense	87%	56%*	77%	93%	92%	ns
Mean number of offenses Z-score (SD)	−.04(.9)	−.33(.1)	−.08(.7)	.25(1.8)	.13(.9)	ns
Drug offenses						
% reporting any offense	60%	16%*	44%	76%	79%*	ns
Mean number of offenses Z-score (SD)	−.21(.5)	−.36(.1)	−.22(.5)	.72*(1.8)	.29*(1.2)	p = .01
Violent offenses						
% reporting any offense	11%	0%	21%	43%*	34%*	ns
Mean number of offenses Z-score (SD)	−.18(.2)	−.24(0)	.07(1.2)	.62*(2.5)	.20*(1.0)	p = .01
Violence, informants' reports						
Gets into fights Z-score (SD)	−.21(.6)	−.39(.1)	−.05(.8)	.81*(1.7)	.21*(1.1)	p = .001

* This group differs significantly from the unclassified comparison group. *df* = 452 for planned contrasts, *p* < .01.

TABLE 8.2. *Court Convictions: Comparisons among Male Groups at Age 26, on Cumulative Adult Court Records of Criminal Convictions*

	Group					LCP-AL difference
	Unclassified	Abstainer	Recovery?	LCP-path	AL-path	
N with record search	234	25	39	45	121	
All types of crimes combined						
% convicted in adult court	17%	4%	28%	55%*	34%*	OR = 2.2(1.1–4.5)
Mean no. of convictions (SD)	0.6(3.1)	0(.2)	1.2(4.5)	6.9*(11.5)	3.5*(10.8)	p = .006
Ratio: group's share of the cohort's total 935 convictions to group N	0.3	0	0.6	3.4	1.7	—
Mean no. months sentenced to prison (SD)	.01(.1)	0(0)	.15(.9)	11.6*(44.3)	7.4*(34.4)	ns
Property convictions						
% convicted	6%	0%	18%	44%*	25%*	OR = 2.4(1.1–4.9)
Mean number of convictions, Z-score (SD)	-.14(.6)	-.22(0)	-.10(.4)	.41*(1.1)	.20*(1.5)	ns
Court-order-violation convictions						
% convicted	3%	0%	3%	31%*	11%*	OR = 3.4(1.4–8.0)
Mean number of convictions, Z-score (SD)	-.14(.1)	-.17(0)	-.02(.9)	.52*(1.3)	.16*(1.7)	p = .04
Drug convictions						
% convicted	3%	0%	5%	22%*	14%*	ns
Mean number of convictions, Z-score (SD)	-.17(.3)	-.22(0)	-.16(.3)	.74*(2.0)	.21*(1.4)	p = .002
Violent convictions						
% convicted	5%	0%	10%	38%*	14%*	OR = 3.7(1.6–8.1)
Mean no. of convictions, Z-score (SD)	-.17(.2)	-.22(0)	-.12(.3)	.79*(2.2)	.15*(1.3)	p = .001

* This group differs significantly from the unclassified comparison group. $df = 458$ for planned contrasts, $p < .01$

TABLE 8.3. *Personality: Comparisons among Male Groups at Age 26, Mean Standardized Z-scores (with SD in parentheses) on Measures of Personality Traits from the Men's Self-Reports and from Reports by Informants Who Knew Them Well.*

	Group					LCP-AL difference
N with interview data[a]	Unclassified	Abstainer	Recovery?	LCP-path	AL-path	
	233	25	39	42	119	
Stability ↔ Neuroticism						
Self, Negative emotionality	−.20(.8)	−.68*(.6)	.08(1)	.67*(1.2)	.31*(1)	p = .03
Informant, Neuroticism	−.18(.9)	−.36(.7)	.27*(1.2)	.43*(1.1)	.13*(1)	p = .09
Callousness ↔ Agreeableness						
Self, Communion	.07(.9)	.14(.9)	−.11(1)	−.39*(1.3)	−.02(1)	p = .04
Informant, Agreeableness	.20(.8)	.47(.9)	−.04(.9)	−.59*(1.2)	−.18*(1.1)	p = .02
Impulsivity ↔ Conscientiousness						
Self, Constraint	.07(1)	.88*(.7)	.03(.8)	.09(.8)	−.38*(1)	p = .005
Informant, Conscientiousness	.21(.9)	.40(.9)	−.16(1)	−.19(1.1)	−.27*(1)	ns
Introversion ↔ Extraversion						
Self, Agency	.03(1)	−.02(1)	−.13(.9)	−.08(.9)	.03(1)	ns
Informant, Extraversion	.06(.9)	−.48*(1)	−.20(1.1)	−.09(1.1)	.09(1)	ns

[a] Interview N = 458, but informant report N = 438.

* This group differs significantly ($p < .01$) from the unclassified comparison group; in planned contrasts $df = 453$ for self-reports and $df = 433$ for informant reports.

Note: Informants completed a brief checklist measuring the Big 5 personality traits, whereas study members themselves completed the longer Multidimensional Personality Questionnaire.

TABLE 8.4. *Psychopathology: Comparisons among Male Groups at Age 26, on Measures of Mental Disorder from Reports by Their Informants and from Self-Reports in Diagnostic Interviews*

	Group					
	Unclassified	Abstainer	Recovery?	LCP-path	AL-path	LCP-AL difference
N with interview data[a]	233	25	39	42	119	
Informants' report of mental health problems						
Alcohol problems, Z score (SD)	−.15(.8)	−.45(0)	−.16(.6)	.72*(1.6)	.19*(1.1)	$p = .002$
Drug problems, Z score (SD)	−.26(.6)	−.40(.2)	−.21(.6)	.68*(1.6)	.46*(1.3)	ns
Antisocial personality, Z score (SD)	−.31(.7)	−.56(.4)	.18*(1)	.77*(1.3)	.30*(1.1)	$p = .006$
Schizophreniform, Z score (SD)	−.19(.7)	−.36(.4)	.15(1)	.53*(1.3)	.21*(1.3)	$p = .06$
Depression, Z score (SD)	−.20(.7)	−.19(.7)	.52*(1.4)	.45*(1.3)	.11*(1.1)	$p = .05$
Anxiety, Z score (SD)	−.18(.8)	−.11(.9)	.32*(1.3)	.32*(1.3)	.16*(1.1)	ns
Social isolation, Z score (SD)	−.13(.8)	.17(1)	.48*(1.4)	.13(.9)	.00(1.1)	ns
Past-year DSM-IV Diagnoses from Interviews						
Alcohol dependence	16%	0%	10%	19%	27%*	ns
Cannabis dependence	8%	0%	10%	29%*	22%*	ns
Other drug dependence	2%	0%	0%	12%*	14%*	ns
Antisocial personality	2%	0%	3%	19%*	13%*	ns
Schizophreniform	3%	0%	5%	6%	5%	ns
Manic episode	3%	0%	3%	5%	5%	ns
Depressive episode	12%	4%	28%*	17%	19%	ns
Anxiety disorder	17%	8%	33%*	29%	25%	ns
Lifetime PTSD	4%	0%	11%	17%*	12%*	ns
Social/agoraphobia	9%	8%	31%*	17%	10%	ns
Official attention for mental health problems						
Treated in past year	17%	0%	31%	29%	26%	ns
Convicted for driving legally intoxicated	2%	0	3%	20%*	8%*	OR = 2.7(1.0–7.3)

[a] Interview $N = 458$, but informant report $N = 438$.

* This group differs significantly ($p < .01$) from the unclassified comparison group; in planned contrasts $df = 453$ for self-reports and $df = 433$ for informant reports.

TABLE 8.5. *Personal Life: Comparisons among Male Groups at Age 26, on Measures of Relationships with Women and Children, from Court Records and the Men's Self-Reports*

	Group					
	Unclassified	Abstainer	Recovery?	LCP-path	AL-path	LCP-AL difference
N with interview data	233	25	39	42	119	
Relationships with women						
% married	17%	24%	0	14%	9%	ns
% in a relationship or dating in the past year	97%	88%	90%	93%	94%	ns
% unhappy in his past-year relationship	26%	0%	28%	34%	36%	ns
% with any physical abuse of partner past year	9%	4%	10%	24%*	15%	ns
Physical partner abuse past year, Z-score (SD)	−.14(.7)	−.30(.3)	−.09(.7)	.48*(1.4)	.24*(1.4)	ns
Controlling partner abuse past year, Z-score (SD)	−.13(.7)	−.41(.2)	−.01(.8)	.65*(1.8)	.12(1.1)	$p = .004$
% convicted of violence against women (rape, assault)	0%	0%	5%	11%*	1%	OR = 15(1.7–132)
Relationships with children						
% fathering children	13%	16%	10%	45%*	23%	OR = 2.8(1.3–5.9)
% fathering multiple children	5%	8%	5%	29%*	9%	OR = 4(1.6–9.9)
% who hit child in anger	3%	0%	5%	10%*	5%	ns
Frequency of hitting child, Z-score (SD)	−.04(.1)	−.05(0)	−.04(.1)	.49*(3.4)	−.04(.1)	$p = .004$

* This group differs significantly ($p < .01$) from the unclassified comparison group; in planned contrasts $df = 453$ for self-reports and $df = 458$ for conviction records.

TABLE 8.6. *Economic Life: Comparisons among Male Groups at Age 26, on Measures of Schooling, Work-Life, and Income, Taken from Records, the Men's Self-Reports, and Informants' Reports*

	Group					
	Unclassified	Abstainer	Recovery?	LCP-path	AL-path	LCP-AL Difference
N with interview data	233	25	39	42	119	
Education						
Education completed, Z score (SD)	.27(.9)	.46(.8)	−.27*(.9)	−.93*(1)	−.07*(1)	p = .000
% with no high school certificate (left age 15–16)	9%	4%	21%	57%*	20%*	OR = 5.3(2.5–11.3)
% with college degree	25%	32%	10%	2%*	15%	ns
Occupation and income						
Status of occupation, Z score (SD)	.22(1)	.41(1.1)	−.42*(.9)	−.54*(.9)	−.09*(.9)	p = .01
Mean past-year gross income (SD)	$34,669(19015)	$28,900(12850)	$27,948(12379)	$30,369(16186)	$31,220(19704)	ns
% with illegal income	10%	4%	10%	41%*	39%*	ns
Mean past-year illegal income (SD)	$67(472)	$1(0)	$938(5762)	$3,071(9386)	$4,052*(14517)	ns
% supported by public benefits past year[b]	22%	12%	36%	43%*	33%	ns
Number of public benefits past year, Z score[b] (SD)	−.10(.9)	−.29(.8)	.14(.9)	.43*(1.1)	.04(.9)	p = .02
Unemployment and work problems						
Has problems making ends meet, Z score (SD)	−.17(.9)	−.36(.5)	.26*(1.3)	.38*(1.2)	.18*(1)	ns
Informant-reported financial probs, Z score (SD)	−.26(.8)	−.39(.6)	.36*(1.1)	.45*(1.1)	.27*(1.1)	ns
Mean months registered unemployed age 21–26 (SD)	2(5)	3(7)	5(10)	9*(16)	4(9)	p = .004
Informant-reported work problems, Z score (SD)	−.11(.9)	−.46(.4)	.28(1.2)	.49*(1.3)	.02(1)	p = .01
Staff rating, first impression in interview situation, Z score (SD)	.08(.9)	.33(1)	−.05(1)	−.42*(1.2)	−.14(1)	ns
% believing a criminal record has harmed chances for employment	2%	0%	13%*	22%*	19%*	ns
Expectations for getting ahead in future, Z score (SD)	.23(.8)	.24(.7)	−.44*(1)	−.31*(1)	−.17*(1)	ns

[a] Interview N = 458, but informant report N = 438.

* This group differs significantly (p < .01) from the unclassified comparison group; in planned contrasts df = 453 for self-reports and df = 433 for informant reports.

[b] Government support for the man himself, i.e., excludes support for dependent children.

LCP men reported a significantly higher mean frequency of drug-related offenses (e.g., use, trafficking) and violent offenses (e.g., assault, robbery) than AL men. The greater violence of LCP men was corroborated by informants, who reported that getting into fights was a significantly worse problem for LCP than AL men. The AL group accounted for about twice their share of the cohort's self-reported property and drug offenses, whereas the LCP group accounted for three times their share of drug offenses and five times their share of violent offenses (for details see Moffitt et al., 2002).

Table 8.1 shows that the abstainer group generally reported little offending, whereas the recovery group generally reported moderate offending (near the mean of the unclassified group or sample norm).

Table 8.2 presents the men's cumulative court conviction records. Overall, both LCP and AL men were convicted more than others, but LCP men's convictions tended to be more frequent and serious than AL men's. Significantly more LCP men than AL men had been convicted as adults; LCP men accounted for 3.4 times more than their share of the cohort's total convictions. Breaking down the offenses by type revealed that LCP men had worse conviction records than AL men for property crimes, court-order violations (e.g., failing to pay fines, breaching probation, escaping prison), drug trafficking, and violent crimes. As was the case for self-reports (Table 8.1), the effect sizes for the difference between LCP and AL men's frequency of conviction tended to grow wider as the type of crime grew more serious. The AL group accounted for about twice their share of the cohort's 882 convictions, but the LCP group accounted for about three to four times their share of the cohort's convictions.

Table 8.2 shows that the abstainer group had virtually no convictions (one individual had one conviction), whereas the recovery group generally had moderate levels of convictions (near the mean of the unclassified group or sample norm) with 28% of the so-called recovery group having been convicted as an adult.

PERSONALITY

Table 8.3 presents the groups' mean scores on personality measures obtained from self-reports and informants' reports. Both LCP and AL men had significantly elevated neuroticism scores, but the LCP men scored significantly worse than the AL men. LCP men also scored significantly worse than AL men on callousness. These two group differences replicated across self-reports and informants' reports and the LCP men's personality scores were extreme, about one-half *SD* from the male norm. LCP men were not particularly impulsive, but the AL men viewed themselves as significantly more impulsive than LCP men and AL men were also considered impulsive by informants.

Table 8.3 shows that the abstainer group had significantly and extremely low neuroticism, high conscientousness, and low extraversion, all more than one half SD from the male norm. The recovery group had significantly elevated neuroticism, according to their informants.

PSYCHOPATHOLOGY

Table 8.4 presents psychopathology outcomes. In general, both LCP and AL men had more mental health problems than others, but according to the informants, the LCP men had more of every type of mental health problem than the AL men. Compared to AL men, LCP men were rated by their informants as having significantly worse problems with alcohol, symptoms of antisocial personality disorder, symptoms of schizophreniform disorder (bizarre paranoid beliefs, hearing things), and symptoms of depression. In striking contrast to the informants' perceptions, the men's self-reports during the standardized diagnostic interview generated approximately equal rates of diagnosed disorder for LCP and AL groups. Both groups had elevated rates of past-year substance dependence and antisocial personality disorder, as well as lifetime post traumatic stress disorder, when compared to the unclassified control men. Nearly one-third of both the LCP and AL groups said they had sought or experienced treatment for a mental disorder in the past year (GP, psychiatrist, emergency room, drug rehabilitation clinic, prescribed psychiatric medication, or hospitalized). However, the AL group accounted for about one and one-half times their share of the cohort's 513 months of psychiatric disability, whereas the LCP group accounted for two and one-half times their share.

Table 8.4 shows that the abstainer group had virtually no mental disorder. The recovery group were said by their informants to have particular problems of depression and anxiety; one-third were diagnosed with anxiety disorders and one-third had been treated. Of particular relevance for the recovery group were indicators of social isolation; informants described them as having unique difficulty making friends and 31% met diagnostic criteria for social phobia or agoraphobia.

PERSONAL AND FAMILY RELATIONSHIPS

Table 8.5 presents outcomes in relationships with women and children. In this life domain, the LCP men tended to be significantly worse than the unclassified controls, but the AL men were not. One-third of both the LCP and AL groups were unhappy in their relationships; the two groups were not significantly different on variety of abusive physical acts they reported using against partners in the past year; and LCP and AL men had similar opportunity to abuse women (percentage married, in a relationship, or dating). However, the LCP men were significantly distinguished from unclassified and AL men on the extent of controlling abuse they used against women (humiliating, restricting, intimidating, or stalking; .65 *SD* above the male norm), and on court conviction for violence against women (11% of LCP men), suggesting LCP men's abuse was more serious. The AL group accounted for fewer than their share of the cohort's 13 convictions for rape and woman-battering, whereas the LCP group accounted for six times their share. Table 8.5 reveals that LCP males fathered a uniquely large number of children by age 26. The AL group accounted for about their share of the cohort's 136 babies fathered, whereas the LCP group accounted for two and one-half times their share. Table 8.5 also shows that LCP men were uniquely likely to hit a child in anger.

Finally, Table 8.5 shows that the abstainer group had virtually no problems in the domain of relationships with women and children, whereas the recovery group generally fared about the same as the average male in this life domain (near the mean of the unclassified group or sample norm, though two individuals in the recovery group were convicted of crimes against women).

ECONOMIC LIFE

Table 8.6 presents outcomes in economic life. Both LCP and AL men had more economic difficulties than others, but the LCP group (and the recovery group) tended to have the poorest outcomes. LCP men had significantly less education than AL men; more than half of LCP men had no high school qualification. Only one LCP man attended college. LCP men's current/most recent jobs (e.g, sheep shearer, fisherman, car painter, logger, petrol station attendant, taxi driver) were significantly lower status than AL men's jobs (e.g., sheep farmer, fishing boat captain, car salesman, carpenter, florist, salon manager, musician).

Although all five groups of men reported a similar amount of gross income from all sources in the past year, about NZ$30,000, the nature of their economic lives varied greatly. For LCP and AL men, a significant amount of that income was unearned: made up of illegal income (mainly from fencing stolen goods and drug trafficking and in a few cases, the sex trade) and social welfare benefits (unemployment benefits, injury compensation, and disability payments). LCP men were significantly more likely than AL men to receive more than one of these public benefits. Despite having incomes similar to the other men, LCP and AL men felt they had problems making ends meet. Their informants agreed, noting that they were poor money managers and appeared to lack sufficient money.

Regarding problems with work, as compared to the AL men, LCP men had spent significantly more time unemployed, and their informants reported that they experienced more problems at work (conflicts with coworkers and supervisors, difficulty keeping jobs). The AL group accounted for about their share of the cohort's 1,589 months of unemployment, whereas the LCP group accounted for twice their share. Table 8.6 shows that our staff observer rated the LCP men as making the poorest impression on their assessment day; relative to other men, LCP men seemed threatening, suspicious, irritable, not cheerful or friendly. Both LCP and AL men said they believed a criminal record has prevented them from getting employment, and both had pessimistic expectations about getting ahead in the future.

Finally, Table 8.6 shows that the abstainer group had virtually no problems in the domain of economic life. For example, their occupations were the highest status in the cohort by age 26 (wool buyer, ship's purser, agricultural pilot, computer programmer, clergyman, electrician, librarian, nurse, sports coach, undertaker), and they made the best impression of all the men, as rated by our staff observer. The recovery group had significant difficulties in the economic life domain; they resembled the LCP men in having significantly little education, unskilled low-status jobs, and financial problems, and they had the most pessimistic expectations about getting ahead of all men in the cohort.

CUMULATIVE INDEX OF ADJUSTMENT PROBLEMS

We also compared the groups on a composite index of 10 problems in adult adjustment (one point each was summed for a violent conviction record, a nonviolent conviction record, a substance-dependence diagnosis, a psychiatric diagnosis, partner abuse, child abuse, no high school qualification, out-of-wedlock fatherhood, government welfare benefits, and long-term unemployment more than 6 months; for details see Moffitt et al., 2002). The clear majority of unclassified men had only 1 or 2 of these problems. Most abstainers were problem-free or had only 1 problem. Only 15% of the recovery group was free from adjustment problems, and most had numerous problems, emphasizing that our earlier "recovery" label was a misnomer. Likewise, only 15% of LCP men were free of problems; moreover, two-thirds of the LCP men had 3 or more problems; four times more LCP than AL men scored at the extreme by suffering 7 to 10 life problems, and 70% of the cohort men with these extreme problems were LCP men. In contrast, two-thirds of AL men had 2 or fewer problems.

WHAT DID WE LEARN ABOUT THE ABSTAINER GROUP: THEY
GREW UP TO BE SUCCESSFUL YOUNG ADULTS

Abstainers were originally defined as males with no more than one antisocial problem at any assessment age from 5 to 18 years, according to all reporters in the Dunedin Study. Abstainers so defined comprised 5% of cohort males. The theory anticipated that abstainers would be this rare because it argued that some delinquency is virtually normative for contemporary adolescents. According to the theory, if adolescence-limited delinquency is normative, adaptational social behavior, then the existence of teens who abstain from delinquency requires explanation. The theory speculated that teens committing no antisocial behavior must have structural barriers that prevent them learning about delinquency, no experience of the maturity gap because of early access to adult roles, or personal characteristics that exclude them from peer networks (Moffitt, 1993; predictions are found on pp. 689, 695). Our earlier study of the Dunedin abstainers as teens suggested that the last might be true; as 18-year-olds they were overcontrolled, timid, and socially awkward, unusually good students, and latecomers to heterosexual relationships (Moffitt et al., 1996). Dunedin abstainers also fit the profile of the compliant good student who during adolescence becomes unpopular with peers (Bukowski, Sippola, & Newcomb, 2000).

In our 1996 paper we speculated that Dunedin abstainers might as adults be late-bloomers. Age-26 data show that they have bloomed. From adolescence they retained their personality profile of unusually strong self-constraint, but in adulthood this style seems to have become successful. As adults the abstainer men had virtually no crime or diagnosable mental disorders, and a count of 10 possible adjustment problems showed they were virtually free of these. According to their informants they had the least problem behaviors of all men in the cohort. As a group they were the most likely to have settled into marriage and to have a happy relationship, and they were delaying children (a desirable strategy for a generation needing prolonged education to succeed). They held the highest status jobs in the cohort, though their incomes were not the highest, probably because they pursued postgraduate studies or held entry-level white-collar jobs. They were the most likely to be college educated and financially responsible, the least likely to have problems in their work lives, and they expressed optimism about their own futures. We share that optimism.

WHAT WE LEARNED ABOUT THE RECOVERY GROUP: THEY WERE MISNAMED EARLIER, AND THEY GREW UP TO SUFFER "INTERNALIZING" PROBLEMS

The so-called recovery group was originally defined as males with stable, pervasive and extreme antisocial problems in childhood, but whose participation in delinquency during adolescence was only moderate, and not extreme enough to meet criteria for membership in the LCP group. Recoveries so defined comprised 8% of cohort males. This group was something of a surprise to the theory, because it argued that early-onset antisocial behavior initiates a chain of cumulative disadvantage that perpetuates disordered behavior, and on that basis it predicted that "false positive subjects, who meet criteria for a stable and pervasive antisocial childhood history and yet recover (eschew delinquency) after puberty, should be extremely rare" (Moffitt, 1993, p. 694). The age-26 data suggest that, as predicted, true recoveries are extremely rare. Recovery was clearly a misnomer we prematurely assigned to some group members, because more than one quarter of them subsequently engaged in illegal behavior as adults. Their offending pattern may fit an oft-observed pattern referred to as "intermittency" or "suspension," in which some offenders are not convicted for a period but then reappear in the courts (Laub & Sampson, 2001). The group's self-reported offending at age 26 is at the cohort norm, 28% had been convicted of crimes as adults (10% for violent crimes), and the group accounted for approximately its share of offenses and convictions of all types. Regarding illegal activities, this group of antisocial children participated at low levels as adolescents and as adults. Over time, the Dunedin recovery group's offending pattern closely resembles that of the "low-level chronic offenders," first identified in trajectory analyses of a British cohort (Nagin et al., 1995).

Researchers have been curious about this group since it was described in our 1996 paper, speculating optimistically that recoveries might be children who experienced some strong protective factor(s). Anticipating true recoveries to be extremely rare, the theory had proffered no specific explanation for what sort of people they would be. However, the theory had broadly argued that teens who engage in less delinquency than expected might have off-putting personal characteristics that excluded them from the peer groups in which most delinquency happens. Thus, to keep faith with the theory, we were obliged to consider whether boys in the recovery group might be social isolates. Our earlier study of the recoveries revealed no protective factors; they had extremely under-controlled temperaments as 3-year-olds, and as teens they had unremarkable scores on most measures (Moffitt et al., 1996). (Unpublished analyses showed that they shared with the LCP males low IQ and family adversity in childhood.)

This in-depth age-26 follow up reveals more, suggesting that this group is unique from the other males in suffering from internalizing forms of psychopathology. As many as one-third of this group had diagnosed depression or anxiety disorders, their personality profile showed elevated neuroticism, and their informants rated them as the most depressed and anxious men in the cohort. Members of this group, unlike other cohort men, were often social isolates; their informants reported that they had difficulty making friends, none had married, and many had diagnoses of agoraphobia and/or social phobia. Almost all adults with social phobia meet criteria for comorbid avoidant, dependent, and/or schizotypal personality disorders (Alnaes & Torgersen, 1988). Thus, although these personality disorders have not been diagnosed in the Dunedin study, we speculate that men in this group may suffer from them. This pattern in which formerly antisocial little boys develop into depressed, anxious, and socially isolated men resembles closely a finding from a British longitudinal study of males followed from ages 8 to 32. In that study, boys at high risk who were as adults "false positives" (committing less crime than predicted based on age-8 risk factors) were found to have few or no friends, had low-paid jobs, lived in dirty home conditions, and had been described in case records as withdrawn, highly strung, obsessional, nervous, or timid (Farrington, Gallagher, Morley, St. Ledger, & West, 1988). If we look to this Dunedin group of high-risk boys to reveal what protective factors prevented them from involvement in serious crime, our findings and Farrington's are not uplifting. To the extent that much delinquency is a group activity, the members of the recovery group may have been "protected" by their social isolation. Consistent with this hypothesis, they were at age 26 quite unlikely to be involved with drugs or alcohol (also a finding in the British study), perhaps the most social among the problem behaviors we measured.

There was good evidence that the men in the recovery group suffered life impairment. One-third had experienced treatment for mental health problems in the past year. As a group they had completed less education than average and few had attended college. They had low-status occupations and many financial difficulties, and they expressed the least hope for their futures. Robins (1966) is often quoted as having said that one-half of conduct-problem boys do not grow up to have antisocial personalities. Such quotations have been used to argue that early conduct problems are fully malleable and need not be a cause for pessimism. However, less often quoted is Robins' (1966) other observation, that conduct-problem boys who do not develop antisocial personalities generally suffer other forms of maladjustment as adults. Our count of 10 adjustment problems showed that only 15% of Dunedin's 87 young boys with childhood-onset conduct problems (i.e., 47 LCP and 40 recoveries) truly "recovered," escaping all adjustment problems. Farrington et al. (1988, p. 158) noted about the conduct problem boys in their longitudinal study, "There seemed to be no real success stories." This finding is consistent with our theory's emphasis on the importance of childhood adjustment for adult adjustment. It also suggests that prevention programs targeting antisocial children will not be wasted on the half who are not on course to become life-course persistent criminal offenders.

WHAT WE LEARNED ABOUT THE LIFE-COURSE PERSISTENT GROUP: THEY GREW UP TO BE THE MOST VIOLENT AND LEAST LIKELY TO REFORM

The life-course persistent group comprised males with stable, pervasive, and extreme antisocial behavior in childhood plus extreme delinquent involvement in adolescence. The males so defined comprised 10% of cohort males. The theory predicted that these males would still be antisocial when they reached adulthood and would have worse outcomes than their adolescence-limited counterparts. In the year prior to age 26, Dunedin LCP men compared to AL men were significantly more involved as a group in serious criminal offending according to self-reports. They were two to three times more likely than AL men to have been convicted as adults, which attests to the relatively greater seriousness of their offenses. A comparison of specific offenses suggested that LCP men tended to specialize in serious offenses (carrying a hidden weapon, assault, robbery, violating court orders) whereas AL men specialized in nonserious offenses (theft less than $5, public drunkenness, giving false information on application forms, pirating computer software). According to their informants' reports, LCP men had significantly more symptoms of antisocial personality disorder than AL men. As predicted by the theory, LCP men as a group particularly differed from AL men in the realm of violence, including violence against women and children. LCP men accounted for five times their share of the cohort's violent offenses. This violence difference was corroborated by all three data sources (self-reports, informant reports, official records) with large effect sizes. In addition, compared to AL men, LCP men had a more psychopathic personality profile (present since 18, see Moffitt et al., 1996), and the informants who knew them well viewed them as having more serious psychiatric and behavior problems. Our count of 10 possible adjustment problems showed that most of the LCP men were heavily burdened by problems in multiple life domains.

The theory predicted that life-course persistent offenders would have difficulty desisting from crime at turning-point opportunities such as marriage or employment, because unlike adolescence-limited delinquents, life-course persistent delinquents would selectively get undesirable jobs and partners, and their limited behavioral repertoire would lead them to express antisocial behavior at work and at home (Moffitt, 1993, pp. 683, 684, 695). This article did not examine within-individual change in response to turning-point opportunities, but several findings suggest that the LCP men are unlikely to benefit in the near future from the reforming effects of a good job. At age 26, relative to their peers, they had poor work histories in low-status unskilled jobs, lacked the minimum education qualifications needed to get a good job, made a poor interpersonal impression in an interview-type situation, and had official conviction records for serious crimes that may deter employers from hiring them. LCP men's substance-dependence problems and tendency to get into conflicts at work are likely to prevent advancement in the low-skill jobs they are able to get. They are also unlikely to benefit in the near future from the reforming effects of a good woman and family, in view of their extreme personality traits of negative emotionality and callousness, their tendency to use abuse to control women, and their inclination to father unusually large numbers of children but not stay around to help rear them.

At first, our assertion that opportunities for change will often be turned by LCP men into opportunities for continuity seems at odds with the work of Sampson and Laub's turning-point theory (1993). These sociologists have generated the compelling theory, and much empirical evidence, that desistance from crime is due to salient life events at key points in the life-course (e.g., a good marriage, a stable job, new opportunities in the military). The life events engender social bonds that exert informal social controls on criminals and help them to reform. However, our theory and our findings here question whether LCP men typically develop such bonds. At age 26, we see mainly evidence of transactions between LCP men's undesirable behavior and negative reactions to it from courts, employers, women, and informants who know them well. Such person–environment transactional processes have been shown to promote persistence of antisocial behavior (Caspi, Bem, & Elder, 1989).

WHAT WE LEARNED ABOUT THE ADOLESCENCE-LIMITED GROUP: THEIR PROBLEMS ARE NOT LIMITED TO ADOLESCENCE

Males on the adolescence-limited trajectory were originally defined as males with unremarkable antisocial behavior in childhood but extreme delinquent involvement in adolescence. The males so defined comprised 26% of cohort males. The theory predicted that these males would have better outcomes when compared to their life-course persistent counterparts. This particular prediction was supported for 68 of the 79 outcome measures, albeit only 33 with statistical significance (the previous section summarized the significant differences between AL and LCP men).

The theory also predicted that "before taking up delinquency adolescence-limited offenders have ample years to develop a repertoire of pro-social behaviors and basic academic skills that make them eligible for post-secondary education, good marriages, and desirable jobs" (Moffitt, 1993, p. 690). This prediction also found support. At age 26, AL men as a group stand a better chance than LCP men of benefitting from a good job; they had better work histories and skilled occupations, 80% of them had the high school qualifications needed to get a good job, they made a reasonable if not salutary impression in an interview-type situation, and fewer of them had conviction records to deter employers. Not surprisingly, at age 26 they held higher status jobs than LCP men. As children and adolescents AL men had average or better scores on factors known to predict labor-market success; they had normal IQ scores and were good readers (Moffitt & Caspi, 2001), and they had elevated scores on a personality trait called social potency (Moffitt et al., 1996).

AL men also stand a better chance than LCP men of benefitting from the reforming effects of a good woman. They described themselves as being about as agreeable (not callous) and extraverted as the average male, they had engaged in some physical conflict with partners but were not inclined to be unusually controlling of them. As children and adolescents AL men had average or better scores on factors thought to predict relationship success; they had average family relationships, average temperaments, and were not rejected by peers (Moffitt & Caspi, 2001), and they had close attachments to their parents and elevated scores on a personality trait called social closeness (Moffitt et al., 1996). The findings at age 26 are consistent with the theory's note that "Adolescence-limited delinquents can profit from opportunities for desistence, because they retain the option of resuming a conventional lifestyle" (Moffitt, 1993, p. 695).

Despite all this promise, the AL men at 26 were still in trouble. Although AL men fared better overall than the LCP men, they fared poorly relative to the "unclassified" men (who represented males with only an ordinary, unremarkable juvenile delinquency history). AL men accounted for twice their share of the property and drug convictions accumulated by the cohort during adulthood, and they also self reported an impressive number of past-year property and drug-related offenses at age 26. Our count of 10 possible adjustment outcomes revealed that it was usual for AL men to suffer one to three of those. As many AL men as LCP men self-reported symptoms sufficient to earn a psychiatric diagnosis, but their informants said they had few mental health problems. This discrepancy between the AL men and informants who knew them well suggests that the AL men believed themselves to have symptoms, but the symptoms had not brought about enough impairment to be noticed by friends and family.

Acknowledging that some adolescence-limited delinquents desist later than others, the theory predicted that "variability in age at desistence from crime should be accounted for by the cumulative number and type of ensnaring life events that entangle persons in a deviant life-style" (Moffitt, 1993, p. 691). Many AL men at 26 appeared to suffer such snares that might retard desistence from crime. Though most AL men earned a high school certification, most lost out on higher education. Though the AL men have better jobs than LCP men, many AL men relied on crime for a significant portion of their incomes, echoing ethnographic findings that crime can be too profitable to give up (Fagan & Freeman, 1999). Though the AL men's conviction records were not as extensive as the LCP men's, many AL men believed that their criminal record harms their employment chances, reinforcing legal scholars' plea to the courts to identify AL offenders and give them "room to reform" (Scott & Grisso, 1997). Ominously, many of the AL men had substance-dependence problems.

Why are so many AL men still in trouble past the transition to adulthood? The very name "adolescence-limited" reveals that this much offending by AL men at age 26 was not anticipated by our theory. One possibility is that the theory is fundamentally incorrect in its assertion that the characteristics and experiences distinguishing LCP from AL men in childhood also have consequences for adulthood. It is possible that once a person becomes delinquent he has the same chance as any other delinquent to persist, no matter what his childhood was like prior to offending. However, we retain the theory's view that this is unlikely, because this age-26 follow-up has revealed distinctions between the LCP and AL men that augur greater reform potential for AL men. Consider personality, for example. The LCP men rated significantly worse than the AL men on negative emotionality and callousness, traits in the psychopathic cluster associated with long-term persistence of antisocial behavior (Hare, 1996) even in the face of strong treatment (Rice, Harris, & Cormier, 1992). In contrast, the AL groups' personality profile at age 26 was remarkable mainly for impulsivity, the trait most susceptible to change with adult experience (Roberts & Delvecchio, 2000). Others have shown that delinquents with intellectual and emotional resources like those of the Dunedin AL men's are unlikely to offend as adults (Stattin, Romelsjo & Stenbacka, 1997). We speculate that Dunedin AL men have the capacity to reform, and will do so in future, but for historical reasons they have not yet had the opportunity.

Our expectation that desistance from crime would be well under way by age 26 was based on age–crime curves for cohorts born in the 1930s to 1950s (Blumstein, Cohen, & Farrington, 1988), but these curves may no longer apply. The Dunedin cohort, like other young people born in developed nations after 1970, is experiencing a prolonged and unprecedented maturity gap (Arnett & Taber, 1994). This shift has prompted the contemporary view that true adulthood now begins after age 25, whereas a new developmental stage called "emerging adulthood" occurs after adolescence (Arnett, 2000). This stage is characterized by role-less floundering, in which young people neither perceive themselves to be adults nor choose to occupy any of the adult roles historically favored by people in their twenties (e.g., parenthood, marriage). In New Zealand at the turn of the millennium the mean age of men's first marriage is 29, the mean age men first become the identified father of a child is 31, and jobs are remote because the unemployment rate is 18% for workers under age 24 and 50% for workers lacking high school graduation (Statistics New Zealand cited in Moffitt et al., 2001). This suggests that up to the time they were interviewed at their 26th birthdays, most Dunedin men were still inside the "maturity gap" that (according to the theory) promotes AL offending. Our theory predicted that AL offenders would reform because "when aging delinquents attain the adult privileges they coveted as teens the consequences of illegal behavior shift from rewarding to punishing" (Moffitt, 1993; p. 690). Sampson and Laub (1993) similarly predict that offenders reform because they form bonds to jobs and spouses. Whether privileges or bonds, adulthood's turning points are yet in the future for most of the men in our study. The account of AL crime participation at age 26 advanced in this paragraph is consistent with our theory's argument that adolescence-limited delinquency is "a byproduct of modernization," and its prediction that the strongest predictors of offending by AL individuals should be "attitudes toward adulthood and autonomy, and cultural and historical context" (Moffitt, 1993, pp. 691 and 695). Whether Dunedin AL men are in trouble at 26 because their cohort's maturity gap is prolonged (and the theory is right), or because adult adjustment is not influenced by childhood experience (and the theory is wrong), awaits further follow-up.

IMPLICATIONS FROM THE FINDINGS OF THIS FOLLOW-UP STUDY

The findings from this follow-up must be confirmed by other researchers and extended in our studies using trajectory and growth models (and future follow-ups), before there is a solid evidence base to support detailed recommendations for intervention. For now, our findings from comparisons of the groups in childhood, adolescence, and young adulthood make three suggestions. First, the antisocial trajectory defined by persistent disregard of the rights of others from ages 3 to 26 (and associated with a host of neuro-developmental, family, school, and peer problems) warrants early, sustained, and assiduous intervention to prevent economic failure, mental illness, street violence, and family violence. Second, the antisocial trajectory defined by conduct problems in childhood but only low-level antisocial involvement thereafter also warrants early intervention, mainly to prevent poor economic outcomes. When treating this group, we must keep in mind that whereas their depression, anxiety, and social isolation are undesirable, they may protect against the delinquency and drug use that is otherwise expected. Third, the trajectory defined by postpubertal onset of delinquency clearly warrants intervention, mainly to prevent future acquisitive crimes and in particular, drug- and alcohol-related problems. In other words, effective intervention is needed for antisocial behavior exhibited early or late.

References

Alnaes, R., & Torgersen, S. (1988). The relationship between DSM-III symptom disorders (Axis I) and personality disorders (Axis II) in an outpatient population. *Acta Psychiatrica Scandinavica, 78,* 485–492.
Arnett, J. J. (2000). Emerging adulthood. *American Psychologist, 55,* 469–480.
Arnett, J. J., & Taber, S. (1994). Adolescence terminable and interminable: When does adolescence end? *Journal of Youth and Adolescence, 23,* 517–537.
Bardone, A. M., Moffitt, T. E., Caspi, A., Dickson, N., & Silva, P. A. (1996). Adult mental health and social outcomes of adolescent girls with depression and conduct disorder. *Development and Psychopathology, 8,* 811–829.

Bardone, A. M., Moffitt, T. E., Caspi, A., Dickson, N., Stanton, W. R., & Silva, P. A. (1998). Adult physical health outcomes of adolescent girls with conduct disorder, depression, and anxiety. *Journal of the American Academy of Child & Adolescent Psychiatry, 37*, 594–601.

Blumstein, A., Cohen, J., & Farrington, D. P. (1988). Criminal career research: Its value for criminology. *Criminology, 26*, 1–35.

Bukowski, W. M., Sippola, L. K., & Newcomb, A. F. (2000). Variations in patterns of attraction to same-and other-sex peers during early adolescence. *Developmental Psychology, 36*, 147–154.

Caspi, A., Bem, D. J., & Elder, G. H. Jr. (1989). Continuities and consequences of interactional styles across the life-course. *Journal of Personality, 57*, 375–406.

Caspi, A., & Moffitt, T. E. (1995). The continuity of maladaptive behavior: From description to explanation in the study of antisocial behavior. In D. Cicchetti & D. Cohen (Eds.), *Developmental psychopathology* (Vol. 2; pp. 472–511). New York: Wiley.

Cohen, J. (1988). *Statistical power analysis for the behavioral sciences.* Hillsdale, NJ: Erlbaum.

Fagan, J., & Freeman, R. B. (1999). Crime and work. *Crime and justice: A review of research, 25*, 225–290.

Farrington, D. P., Gallagher, B., Morley, L., St. Ledger, R. J., & West, D. (1988). Are there any successful men from criminogenic backgrounds? *Psychiatry, 51*, 116–130.

Fergusson, D. M., Horwood, L. J., & Nagin, D. S. (2000). Offending trajectories in a New Zealand birth cohort. *Criminology, 38*, 525–552.

Hare, R. D. (1996). Psychopathy: A clinical construct whose time has come. *Criminal Justice and Behavior, 23*, 25–54.

Jeglum-Bartusch, D., Lynam, D., Moffitt, T. E., & Silva, P. A. (1997). Is age important: Testing general versus developmental theories of antisocial behavior. *Criminology, 35*, 13–47.

Kratzer, L., & Hodgins, S. (1999). A typology of offenders: A test of Moffitt's theory among males and females from childhood to age 30. *Criminal Behaviour & Mental Health, 9*, 57–73.

Moffitt, T. E. (1990). Juvenile delinquency and attention-deficit disorder: Developmental trajectories from age three to fifteen. *Child Development, 61*, 893–910.

Moffitt, T. E. (1993). "Life-course-persistent" and "adolescence-limited" antisocial behavior: A developmental taxonomy. *Psychological Review, 100*, 674–701.

Moffitt, T. E. (1994). Natural histories of delinquency. In E. Weitekamp & H. J. Kerner (Eds.), *Cross-national longitudinal research on human development and criminal behavior* (pp. 3–61). Dordrecht: Kluwer Academic Press.

Moffitt, T. E. (1997). Adolescence-limited and life-course-persistent offending: A complementary pair of developmental theories. In T. Thornberry (Ed.), *Advances in criminological theory: Developmental theories of crime and delinquency* (pp. 11–54). London: Transaction Press.

Moffitt, T. E. (2003). Life-course persistent and adolescence-limited antisocial behaviour: A research review and a research agenda. In B. Lahey, T. Moffitt & A.Caspi (Eds.). *The causes of conduct disorder and serious juvenile delinquency.* New York: Guilford.

Moffitt, T. E., & Caspi, A. (2001). Childhood predictors differentiate life-course persistent and adolescence-limited pathways, among males and females. *Development and Psychopathology, 13,* 355–375.

Moffitt, T. E., Caspi, A., Dickson, N., Silva, P. A., & Stanton, W. (1996). Childhood-onset versus adolescent-onset antisocial conduct in males: Natural history from age 3 to 18. *Development and Psychopathology, 8,* 399–424.

Moffitt, T. E., Caspi, A., Harrington, H., & Milne, B. (2002). Males on the life-course persistent and adolescence-limited antisocial pathways: Follow-up at age 26 years. *Development & Psychopathology, 14,* 179–206.

Moffitt, T. E., Caspi, A., Rutter, M., & Silva, P. A. (2001). *Sex differences in antisocial behaviour: Conduct disorder, delinquency, and violence in the Dunedin longitudinal study.* Cambridge, UK: Cambridge University Press.

Moffitt, T. E., Lynam, D., & Silva, P. A. (1994). Neuropsychological tests predict persistent male delinquency. *Criminology, 32,* 101–124.

Nagin, D. S., Farrington, D. P., & Moffitt, T. E. (1995). Life-course trajectories of different types of offenders. *Criminology, 33,* 111–139.

Rice, M. E., Harris, G. T., & Cormier, C. A. (1992). An evaluation of a maximum security therapeutic community for psychopaths and other mentally disordered offenders. *Law and Human Behavior, 16,* 399–412.

Roberts, B. W., & Delvecchio, W. (2000) Consistency of personality across the life-course: A quantitative review of longitudinal studies. *Psychological Bulletin, 126,* 3–25.

Robins, L. N. (1966). *Deviant children grown up.* Baltimore: Williams & Wilkins.

Sampson, R. J. & Laub, J. H. (1993). *Crime in the making: Pathways and turning points through life.* Cambridge, MA: Harvard University Press.

Scott, E. S., & Grisso, T. (1997). The evolution of adolescence: A developmental perspective on juvenile justice reform. *Journal of Criminal Law & Criminology, 88,* 137–189.

Silva, P. A. & Stanton, W. R. (Eds.). (1996). *From child to adult: The Dunedin Multidisciplinary Health and Development Study.* Auckland: Oxford University Press.

Stattin, H., Romelsjo, A., & Stenbacka, M. (1997). Personal resources as modifiers of the risk for future criminality. *British Journal of Criminology, 37,* 198–223.

Tibbetts, S., & Piquero, A. (1999). The influence of gender, low birth weight and disadvantaged environment on predicting early onset of offending: A test of Moffitt's Interactional Hypothesis. *Criminology, 37,* 843–878.

9

A Biocultural Life History Approach to the Developmental Psychobiology of Male Aggression

Carol M. Worthman and Ryan A. Brown

Emory University

New Guinea, early 1930s: "Malikindjin killed her [with sorcery].... That is Malikindjin's way." "But later Malikindjin fell sick [with spirit revenge]. That is because everybody wants vengeance upon him. All who know anything..., they are all agreed."

(narrated case from Bateson, 1958, pp. 64, 67)

Nigeria, early 1940s: "You shouldn't encourage him too much dear. He is too argumentative."

(Soyinka, 1981, p. 55)

Tahiti, early 1960's: "[Shy, *mamahu*, people] can't look you in the eye. They don't seem to get mad easily, but you have to watch out, because if they finally do get mad they are very violent."

(Levy, 1973, p. 286)

Botswana, 1971: "That Besa, something was wrong with his brain! I thought, 'No, this man is a bad one.'" "I thought about how he had hit me and how I didn't like being with a man like that." "Besa was always jealous...."

(Shostak, 1981, p. 226, 225, 309)

INTRODUCTION

Over 50 years ago, Bateson argued strenuously that the concept of individual behavior is vacuous because people act in the context of others' behavior, concluding that social psychology properly should study "the reactions of individuals to the reactions of other individuals" (Bateson, 1958, p. 175). Nonetheless, as the above quotes from his and others' ethnographies suggest, individual differences in behavior are ubiquitous and universally attributed to temperamental differences even as socialization practices are predicated on an equally universal assumption of nurture's role in behavior development. Individual behavior differences continue to be studied intensively, but we lack an overarching explanatory framework for their function and consequences.

Both psychology and behavioral genetics focus on development and variation in social behavior. These traditions have established not only large empirical literatures, but also an expanding theoretical basis. In particular, theoretical accounts have focused on the genetic and ontogenetic bases of variation in social behavior, placed within an adaptationist, evolutionary framework. As Cairns and colleagues noted in a key analysis: "The central questions of social development – from the roots of mother–infant attachment to the plasticity of aggressive behavior – pivot on the relations between genetic and ontogenetic sources of variance" (Cairns, Gariepy, & Hood, 1990). Such investigations in psychology have proceeded independently of parallel empirical and theoretical traditions in the study of social behavior that are also informed by an adaptationist, evolutionary paradigm, namely evolutionary biology, ethology, and anthropology. Yet neither tradition fully engages the role of culture in these matters. Nor do they pursue how extensive individual variation operates *within* human populations, or its implications for understanding adaptation and evolution of social behavior and development.

Our purpose here is to juxtapose and then integrate elements from each tradition to derive an expanded adaptationist, ecological view of behavior development, with particular regard to aggression. We trace the bases of current views that individual differences in behavior such as aggression arise from constitutional differences (temperament), from experiential factors such as rearing practices, and from the coaction of constitution with context. But the power of current integrative nature–nurture models has not yet been brought to bear on the life-course epidemiology of behavior. Specifically, we are interested in how an interactionist model can illuminate the role of culture in human behavior while at the same time drawing greater attention to the significance of individual differences. We seek to demonstrate how production of difference adaptively allows individuals to construct lives but also necessarily allows societies to channel or constrain difference for social purposes.

ADAPTATION ON THE INDIVIDUAL LEVEL

Adaptation Through Development and Microevolution

First, we review models that emphasize the role of person-context coaction in development (Gottlieb, 1991, 1992), and the synergistic action of ontogeny and microevolution in behavior development and adaptation (Cairns et al., 1990). Adaptationist theory was established in psychology by the beginning of the 20th century by Baldwin (1895a, 1895b, 1902), Morgan (1896), and others, and advanced recently by Gottlieb (1991, 1992, 1998), Cairns (Cairns et al., 1990; Cairns, 1976, 2000), and colleagues (Stoff & Cairns, 1996). This tradition addressed population changes in behavior through time rather than individual behavior differences within populations. The key initial concern was to account for regularities in behavior coincident with marked behavioral plasticity. The concurrent rise of empiricism and psychobiology (James, 1890) supported a focus on the individual as the locus of intergenerational adaptation. Briefly, natural within-population variation, particularly ontogenetic plasticity that allows better "fit" with environmental demands, will be differentially represented in the next generation. Consequently, through conventional evolution involving differential fitness, the genetic bases for differential plasticity become prevalent in the population. The process is known in this literature as genetic assimilation. New patterns of behavior development and social interaction stimulated by changing landscapes of social development generate potential for new patterns of social adaptation. In this view, then, individual developmental plasticity in social behavior is the leading edge (or at least requisite condition) for microevolution in social patterns, though the two processes operate in tandem.

The behavioral adaptationist tradition has contributed to models of development by demonstrating the special role of social environment, on theoretical as well as empirical grounds (Gottlieb, 1991, 1998). Such work has converged with multiple lines of evidence from developmental biology that elucidate the pervasive, complex processes of epigenesis, or the coaction of genes and environment that drive ontogeny (Oyama, 2000). From this perspective, development relies on the dynamic interplay of information passed through biological and contextual routes.

Temperament and Adaptability

As the opening quotes indicated, temperamental differences are pervasive. Psychological focus on the individual has pinned the bases of these dispositions to constitutional or innate affective styles and capacities for self-regulation. This approach led to identification of individual differences in *physiological and behavioral reactivity*, the physiologic analogues of temperament. These are among the most commonly cited vulnerability and resilience factors identified by developmental research. The study of temperament and reactivity has used a wide variety of physiological modalities to measure response to external stimuli, including cortisol (HPA axis), catecholamines (SAM axis), gonadal steroids (HPG axis), cardiovascular and hemodynamic response, EEG (central neural reactivity), EMG (local muscular response), eye blink, skin conductance (sympathetically driven sweat gland response), and immune response. Studies have identified group differences in the response properties of these systems for almost every known psychopathological category and axis of temperament. Unusually high reactivity to external stimuli has been associated with risk for internalizing psychopathology (Fox, Schmidt, & Henderson, 2000; Gunnar et al.,

1997; Jemerin & Boyce, 1990; Kagan et al., 1988; Klimes-Dougan, Hastings, Granger, Usher, & Zahn-Waxler, 2001; Scarpa, Raine, Venables, & Mednick, 1997; Stevenson-Hinde & Marshall, 1999), while hyporeactivity to external stimuli is often associated with externalizing psychopathology, including aggression (Bar-Haim, Marshall, & Fox, 2000; Boyce, Goldstein, Adler, & Kupfer., 1999; Gunnar et al., 1997; Kindlon, Tremblay, Mezzacappa, Earls, Laurent, & Schaal, 1995; Magnusson, 1996; Raine, this volume). Increasingly, research on physiological reactivity has focused on the *regulatory properties* of systems, emphasizing that healthy adaptation lies in the ability of systems to respond with appropriate rapidity and intensity, recover when needed, and exhibit dynamic patterns of tonic activation under situations of low ambient stimulation (Brooks-Gunn, Petersen, & Compas, 1995; Calkins & Dedmon, 2000; Donzella, Gunnar, Krueger, & Alwin, 2000; Porges, 1995; Raine et al., 2001; Susman & Ponirakis, 1997; Worthman, 1999b).

Person × Environment Interactions and Contingent Outcomes

Temperamental differences such as reactivity play out against a social background: a substantial body of evidence suggests that the consequences of these dispositions for social competence and adaptation vary widely across social ecologies and are heavily moderated by social relationships. A consistent finding concerning reactivity as a whole is that the valence (positive/negative) and the magnitude of their effects change dramatically across socioecological contexts, study populations, and developmental time. For example, Boyce and coworkers (Boyce et al., 1995) find that higher mean arterial pressure (MAP) reactivity is related to greater physiological health in contexts of low child-care stress, while it is related to *lower* physiological health in high child-care stress environments (Figure 9.1).

Similarly, in his work with rhesus, Suomi (1991) finds that high reactivity is related to higher adult social status in infants who have received good maternal care, while it is associated with *lower* adult social status in infants who have received poor maternal care (Figure 9.2). Recent work by Suomi shows similar person–environment interactions for alleles of the serotonin transporter gene, with each allele producing distinct levels of assertiveness, dependent on the type (maternal vs. peer) and quality (level of positive support) of rearing condition (Suomi, 2000; Suomi, this volume). Similar "crossover" results can be observed in the development of aggression and delinquency (Bronfenbrenner & Ceci, 1994; Caspi & Roberts, 2001; Maughan, 2001; O'Connor & Dvorak, 2001; Rutter et al., 1997; Sameroff, 2000). For instance, Raine and colleagues (Raine, Reynolds, Venables, & Mednick, 1997) report that high skin conductance orienting confers risk for aggressive behavior in low-SES environments, while low skin conductance orienting confers such risk in high-SES environments.

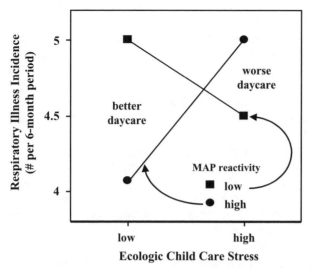

FIGURE 9.1. Moderating effects of child cardiovascular reactivity (assessed by mean arterial pressure, MAP) on relationships of levels of ecologic stress (quality of day care) to incidence of respiratory illness (Boyce et al., 1995).

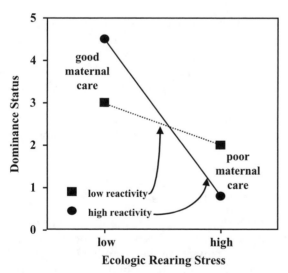

FIGURE 9.2. Moderating effects of infant neurobehavioral reactivity on relationships of ecologic stress (level of maternal competence) to adult social status in rhesus macaques (Suomi, 1991).

Testosterone and Aggression

Multiple findings concerning the relationship between testosterone and aggressive behavior reinforce the need to interpret such results in deep socioecological context. Decades of research have led to the conclusion that this hormone has more to do with striving for social *dominance* than aggression per se (Dabbs, Alford, & Fielden, 1998; Dabbs, Bernieri, Strong, Campo, & Milun, 2001; Mazur & Booth, 1998, 1999; Schaal, Tremblay, Soussignan, & Susman, 1996). Indeed, the many and diverse qualifiers of the relationship between testosterone and aggression, including cortisol level (Dabbs, Jurkovic, & Frady, 1991), IQ (Chance, Brown, Dabbs, & Casey, 2000), social rank (Dabbs & Dabbs, 2000; Mazur & Booth, 1998), and psychopathological diagnosis (Granger, Weisz, McCracken, Kauneckis, & Ikeda, 1994) suggest that individual strategy and capabilities as well as local social context highly determine the linkage (if any) between gonadal steroids and aggressive or violent behavior.

The notion of a direct relationship between one hormone and even a broad behavioral domain has long been surpassed by more sophisticated concepts. Accordingly, testosterone and its metabolites accomplish various roles across development, at different locations in the body, and with several different time courses. One of these roles involves significant neural organization, with developmental peaks pre- and perinatally, as well as during adolescence (De Bellis et al., 2001; Mazur & Booth, 1998; Walker, 2002; Worthman, 1999b). Additionally, developmental studies of relationships between behavioral–psychological profiles and testosterone suggest that patterns of behavior are more likely to influence testosterone than vice versa (Susman, Granger, Murowchick, Ponirakis, & Worrall, 1996; Susman & Ponirakis, 1997). In any case, the behavioral and motivational effects of testosterone are highly subject to modification by the activational state of other hormone and neurotransmitter systems, such as adrenal activity and serotonergic functioning (Blanchard, Sakai, McEwen, Weiss, & Blanchard, 1993; Worthman, 1999b).

The Moderating Effect of Social Relationships

Similar to the "crossover" effects described earlier, recent findings document the moderating effect of social relationships on hormone–aggression interactions. An established study of intact families examined interactions of sons' testosterone with risk behavior and parent–child relationship quality (Booth, Johnson, Granger, Crouter, & McHale, 2003). Where parent–son relationship quality was low, the son's risk behavior correlated positively to his testosterone. Where the relationship quality was high, risk behavior and testosterone were negatively associated. Similarly, a large longitudinal study of adolescent development and psychiatric risk identified a relationship of testosterone to nonaggressive conduct disorder symptoms, but the relationship held only among boys with deviant peers (Rowe, Maughan, Worthman, Angold, & Costello, 2004). Testosterone was linked to *leadership* but not to antisocial behavior among boys who were without deviant peers, suggesting that testosterone is associated with positive social dominance in prosocial conditions. These studies reinforce a view that relationships of testosterone to aggression and antisocial or risk behaviors are potentiated by some social–ecological conditions and buffered by others.

ADAPTATION IN EVOLUTIONARY TERMS

We now throw dynamics of individual psychobehavioral adaptation in evolutionary and life-span relief, introducing a body of theory that originated in evolutionary biology, life history theory. In evolutionary biology, adaptation construes design for capacities that allow the organism to function and reproduce relatively well under the conditions with which it is faced (Reeve & Sherman, 1993). An adaptation also can comprise the phenotype that embodies those capacities. Both senses of adaptation include an ecological dimension. Adaptation, moreover, is relative; it need not be an ideal solution, simply one that does the job better than others. The classic view of adaptation lacked a robust temporal, developmental component, a lacuna addressed by life history theory. In this section, we first discuss life history and its corresponding endocrine architecture, and then turn to niche partitioning as a springboard to integrated evolutionary theories for behavior differences.

Life History

Species are distinguished not only by specific behaviors and morphological features, but also by distinctive life histories (Bonner, 1974; Promislow & Harvey, 1990; Purvis & Harvey, 1995). Life history considers the life course and its architecture as a suite of adaptations that determine how time and energy will be allocated among the basic projects of development, reproduction, and survival. Using cross-taxonomic comparative analysis (Harvey & Pagel, 1991), evolutionary biologists have identified distinctive life history strategies and derived adaptive trade-offs that constrain the evolution of the life course (Charnov, 1993; Stearns, 1992). Trade-offs are conceptually central to this literature. Organisms confront multiple concurrent and competing demands that cannot always be addressed simultaneously; hence, means for prioritization and titration of resource allocation become critical. Accordingly, a life history strategy comprises a set of algorithms that all together optimize the relevant sets of adaptive trade-offs. Aggression and other risky behaviors bear different cost–benefit trade-offs for species that live briefly and breed quickly versus those that live long and breed late. To extend life history analysis to within-species variation, sex differences in the potential reproductive rewards for social dominance weighed against the survivorship cost of aggression likely contribute to sex differences in forms and rates of aggression in humans (Campbell, 1999). Individuals navigating a socioecological context also face such trade-offs and concomitant shifting reward structures, which we will illustrate hereafter.

Neuroendocrine Architecture of Life History and Behavior

Life history comprises a phenotypic suite necessarily produced by a corresponding array of biological, cognitive–behavioral, and temporal processes that operate in dialogue with the set of circumstances encountered by the individual (Finch & Rose, 1995; Ketterson & Nolan, 1992; Worthman, 1999b). Behaviors, such as aggression or caring for young, that carry distinct trade-offs specific to life history strategy are closely regulated, particularly by neuroendocrine mechanisms (Ketterson, Nolan, Cawthorn, Parker, & Ziegenfus, 1996). Comparative study of the actions of testosterone in relation to mating behavior and aggression has demonstrated that hormone–behavior relationships are established through physiologic mechanisms that couple hormones and behavior where the hormones are a salient cue for the behavior, and uncouple them where it is not (Crews, 2002). Furthermore, hormone–behavior interactions can be primed by contextual cues, as exhibited most obviously in seasonal breeders. Thus, in males of some avian species, changes in day length, presence of females, and presence of male territorial competitors stimulate testicular activity. The resultant increased testosterone enhances secondary sex characteristics, competition for territory, and sexual behavior, all necessary for mating success (Wingfield, Hegner, Dufty, & Ball, 1990). While androgen-driven aggressiveness antagonizes pair-bond maintenance and parenting, the trade-off is eased by mechanisms to lower testosterone by interactions with mate, caring for young, and absence of agonistic encounters. Such observations led to the Challenge Hypothesis, which proposes that social context (male–male and male–female interactions along with level of parental care) will shape the ongoing balance between high testosterone (optimal for securing territory and mates) and low testosterone (optimal for parenting) (Wingfield et al., 1990). High levels of testosterone incur social and physical costs, including impaired parenting, decreased stability of social relationships, increased risk-taking, and metabolic changes (Wingfield, Lynn, & Soma, 2001). Indeed, an extensive array of mechanisms have been identified in vertebrates to reduce the psychobiological costs of testosterone.

In sum, an extensive comparative and experimental literature has expanded models of hormone–behavior relationships across the life course to include social dynamics, and suggests the following: (1) Interactions among social context, hormones, and behaviors such as aggression act as important moderators of social relationships and individual life history projects, as in reproduction; and (2) reciprocally, these synergistic effects potentiate responses to salient social contextual cues. Thus, social instability or social threat can be expected to intensify dynamics among testosterone, risk-taking behavior, and aggression at specific points in the life course.

Niche Construction and Multiple Inheritance as Microevolutionary Process

An important component of adaptation, particularly with regard to humans, is the ability to modify environmental forces of natural selection, rather than remain a subject to these forces. Organisms actively select, adjust, construct, and maintain resources and environmental conditions, and thereby exert control over the resource base and circumstances in which they live (Lewontin, 1983). These interventions, or niche construction (Laland, Odling-Smee, & Feldman, 2000; Odling-Smee, Laland, & Feldman, 1996), effectively reorganize the landscape of selective pressures to which the organism is exposed and make it an active agent in its own evolution. Changing selection pressures by selective use and active intervention brings several important consequences. First, niches can be reconstructed through the life course to meet changing needs and capacities. Second, niche construction can, intentionally or inadvertently, affect others' niches. Parental care is a prime positive example, while resource depletion is a negative one. Frequency-dependent selection for behavioral profiles becomes significant, based on the strategies of present and previous members of society. Third, the products of niche construction can be inherited, be it in the literal form of a house, or in less tangible forms such as modified ecosystems. Ecological inheritance (Laland, Odling-Smee, & Feldman, 2001; Laland et al., 2000) adds not only to levels of adaptation, but also to modes of inheritance (in the sense of intergenerational transmission of information or phenotype) beyond genetic or cultural transmission. The twin engines of niche construction and multiple transmission drive both development (life history construction) and microevolution, analogous to Cairns and colleagues' formulation (Cairns et al., 1990).

Niche construction offers two insights about adaptation. Besides complicating views of heritability by demonstrating the role of ecological inheritance (Laland et al., 2000), it highlights the significance of and diversity in life history strategies. Plasticity in and determinants of developmental trajectories in morphology and behavior comprise alternate life history strategies, and form key elements in adaptation and evolution (Stearns & Koella, 1986; West-Eberhard, 1989). The play of alternate life history strategies plus active agency in niche selection and construction establish niche partitioning as a key mechanism for production and accommodation of variation in social development over the life course.

Niche Partitioning and the Socialization of Affect

Humans' wide geographical range and rich cross-cultural variation attest to a substantial capacity for constructing different life histories (Kaplan, Hill, Lancaster, & Hurtado, 2000). Some within-species alternate life history strategies, such as that by sex, are relatively canalized by genetic and epigenetic forces (but see Rhen & Crews, 2002). In the case of humans, development is subject to forces and conditions organized by culture, or the widely shared beliefs, values, and practices prevalent in a community. Through its determination of developmental ecology and the life course, culture underlies the striking capacity for variation in lived experience, behavior, and life course that humans exhibit. Yet even as this diversity is attributable to culture, cultures constrain the life histories of their members, and distinctively manage the human potential within them. Managing psychobehavioral diversity within the population is central to the business of sustaining a workable society while accommodating the construction of coherent, meaningful lives across decades. Orchestrating human psychobehavioral potential involves reinforcing, pruning, canalizing, and producing such variation through the life course, a process that involves the active agency of both individual and social context. This selective–inductive process ideally matches available social niches (roles, statuses, personae) to capacities of individuals through a developmental process that shapes the bio-psycho-behavioral dynamics of the person even as the person shapes society through niche construction. But the process can be fraught, contested, or fail if individual potential and social demand for abilities, opportunities, goals, needs, and perceived values and futures differ too greatly. Match or mismatch in the individual project of survival, sociality, and meaning-making, with prevailing sociocultural conditions of social opportunity, resource allocation, cultural models and values, temporal coherence, and power asymmetries, determines the trajectory and quality of life history, from the view of the individual and of society. This perspective carries us well beyond the "goodness of fit" models in either developmental psychology or evolutionary biology to pose the anthropological question of the role of culture and society in human experience and differential well-being.

Anthropology has a long empirical tradition in the cultural ecology of human development and life history (Boas, 1912; Jessor, Colby, & Shweder, 1996; Mead, 1930; Super & Harkness, 1999; Whiting & Whiting, 1975) that is particularly rich with regard to the role of culture in shaping personality and behavior through the socialization of affect and affect regulation (Bateson, 1958; Benedict, 1934; Briggs, 1998; Harkness & Super, 2000; LeVine, 1974; Mead, 1935; Whiting & Edwards, 1988). Comparative studies have demonstrated cross-cultural differences in forms and rates of aggression, their distribution by sex, and their relationships to child-care practices (Whiting & Edwards, 1988). While documenting population differences, such work has also identified substantial individual behavior differences within cultures. In this ecological view, culture constitutes the context of development (Super & Harkness, 1999) and thereby shapes its course via psychological, behavioral, and biological processes (LeVine, 1990; Worthman, 1999a). Culture moreover defines the ecology within which individuals must function, and thereby determines the consequences for different trajectories of individual development across the life course.

Dynamics of culture, social ecology, and ontogeny may do as much to *promote* variation as they do to enforce similarity. This insight casts a different light on socialization, as reinforcing and producing as much as channeling or narrowing diversity. The following sections explore the cultural ecology of life course development first through a snapshot view in one culture, and then through comparative ethnography.

TEMPERAMENT, TESTOSTERONE, AND LIFE HISTORY: A CASE STUDY OF !KUNG SAN HUNTERS

The adaptationist life history concept of trade-offs is particularly salient for explaining aggressive behavior, by suggesting that perceived present and future distributions of costs and benefits shift the landscape of adaptive value that informs behavior. We explore these issues in data on endocrine physiology, social status, and behavior of !Kung San hunter–gatherers that illustrate the subtleties of adaptive trade-offs around the behavioral biology of aggression.

We lack fine-grained studies of endocrine–behavior dynamics in everyday settings that a rigorous biosocial developmental approach requires (Cairns & Cairns, 1995). Biocultural anthropology pursues such research (Panter-Brick & Worthman, 1999), incorporating techniques of participant observation, attention to social relationships and social dynamics, and a focus on meaning combined with biological measures of function, development, and well-being. A study of !Kung hunters, undertaken by Melvin Konner and Carol Worthman, is an early example of this approach. The principal aim was to examine endocrine correlates of subsistence hunting in a population of foragers, the !Kung San of northwest Botswana. Results and specifics of the study design are described elsewhere (Worthman & Konner, 1987), as are details of !Kung behavior, culture, and ecology (Lee & DeVore, 1976; Shostak, 1981). Here we discuss observations concerning behavioral and endocrine correlates of personality. Discussion of this limited exploratory study is meant to raise points for future investigation, rather than to draw definitive conclusions.

Based on long-term fieldwork with close participant observation of !Kung men and their lives, two field anthropologists (Shostak and Konner) independently rated each participating man on 11 personality and sociobehavioral dimensions: hunting ability, status, aggressiveness, energy, productivity, nuturance, marital stability, husband–wife intimacy, sexual attractiveness, extramarital interest, trance ability (inter-rater CV 4.6%). Morning (7 A.M.) and evening (7 P.M.) serum testosterone was then monitored in eight men for 10 days (before, during, and after a 5-day hunt). During the hunt, level of hunting activity and hunt outcome were scored daily. The date of the study was 1974, when the men of this population were still subsistence hunters.

Trade-offs Among Personality Characteristics: Links to Social Relationships and Productivity

Unsurprisingly, personality ratings were interrelated (Table 9.1), but the configuration of these associations in this small group suggests that men's distinctive sociobehavioral patterns are associated with differences in life history. Social status was strongly and singularly associated with productivity, the man's reliability and capacity as a provider. Also culturally valued, hunting prowess was associated only with aggressiveness. Sexual attractiveness was allied positively to interest in extramarital liaisons, energy, and aggressiveness, but negatively to nurturance and marital stability. Marital stability furthermore correlated directly with nurturance and productivity, and negatively with extramarital interest. Notably, although hunting ability and effort during the hunt correlated positively, ability did not predict overall success during the 5-day hunt. Additionally, energy predicted greater hunting effort and lower hunting success during this brief period. Cultural association of success in big game hunting with reputation as a hunter, combined with greater probability of success while hunting small game, explains the dissociation of hunting reputation from performance over the short run of a 5-day hunt. Sociobehavioral differences among men were associated with positive gains balanced against negative impact in other domains. Hence, constitutional factors that contribute to these differences may be associated with specific social costs and benefits.

Individual Differences in Testosterone Profiles

Population profiles blur the presence and extent of systematic, chronic individual differences in androgen profiles that may arise through numerous sources, such as differences in metabolism, regulatory set points, or receptor populations. Relationships between endocrine profiles and variability

TABLE 9.1. *Intercorrelations of behavior/attitude scores*

	Hunting ability	Status	Aggressiveness	Marital stability	Extramarital interest	Sexual attractiveness	Marital intimacy	Trance ability	Nurturance	Energy
status	0.54									
aggressiveness	0.62*	−0.02								
marital stability	0.17	0.54	−0.60							
extramarital interest	−0.24	−0.30	0.34	−0.82**						
sexual attractiveness	0.29	0.09	0.66*	−0.67*	0.80**					
husband–wife intimacy	−0.07	0.53	−0.28	0.20	0.21	0.09				
trance ability	0.23	0.40	0.03	0.24	0.17	0.43	0.08			
nurturance	−0.25	−0.09	−0.81**	0.77**	−0.60	−0.81**	−0.06	0.05		
energy	0.38	0.19	0.40	−0.43	0.46	0.67*	−0.09	0.19	−0.47	
productivity	0.53	0.85***	−0.18	0.62*	−0.36	−0.02	0.29	0.45	0.26	0.40

Note: Given the small size of the dataset and the consistent pattern of associations, correlations with probability 0.1 are considered significant.

* $p \leq 0.1$; ** $p \leq .05$; *** $p \leq .01$

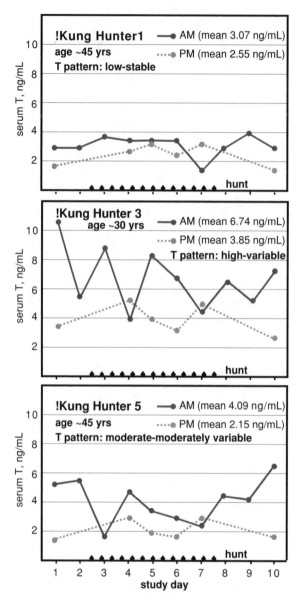

FIGURE 9.3. Contrasting daily testosterone profiles in four !Kung hunters.

across time with behavior and context deserve greater attention. Three distinctive daily testosterone profiles (Figure 9.3) illustrate persistent individual differences in level and variability of testosterone. Variance in hormone levels may exert as much or more influence on cognition than the absolute concentrations themselves.

Testosterone, Attitude, and Behavior

Relationships of testosterone with behavioral and personality assessments are given in Table 9.2. Again, we stress the small size of the sample and the necessarily limited inferences that it supports. Temperament measures did indeed associate with endocrine profiles, particularly those concerning sexual behavior and relationships. Correlates of testosterone values were as follows: (1) negative relationships with nurturance and marital stability, less consistently with status; (2) positive associations with extramarital interest, sexual attractiveness, and more tenuously, aggressiveness and energy; (3) no relationship with hunting ability, productivity, or husband–wife intimacy. These personality scores were associated with levels of testosterone in both the morning and the evening, though more often with the latter. Evening values of testosterone are influenced by activity and affect over the day, which may contribute to the greater frequency of association of P.M. than A.M. testosterone with psychobehavioral scores. Such observations accord with the general point that testosterone levels are a *consequence* of behavior as much or more than they are a cause (Mazur & Booth, 1998, 1999; Zitzmann & Nieschlag, 2001). For instance, our scale for "energetic" globally assesses a man's habitual activity pattern. A man's score on this scale was correlated both with evening testosterone before the hunt, and with levels of hunting activity during the hunt. Further, we observed that hunting activity strongly diminished the diurnal (A.M.-P.M.) decline in testosterone observed in the prehunt period, largely because P.M. values were positively associated with level of hunt activity over the day (Worthman & Konner, 1987). Many studies of hormones and behavior cannot discern directionality in interactions of daily activities, social relationships, and their associated meanings and emotions with the endocrine systems that support them. However, longitudinal designs such as that employed with !Kung hunters do permit discrimination of temporal sequences of behavior-hormone change requisite for strong inference of causality (see also Flinn, 1999).

Testosterone and Social Relationships

Aside from clinical reports, literature on the psychobiology of aggression and its developmental life-course trajectory lacks narrative and descriptive details concerning lives, relationships, and pathways. Even the large Vietnam Veterans study with outcome measures at two decades' remove from intake, does not provide such data although reports present sophisticated analytic models for understanding relationships of hormones and behavior (Booth & Dabbs, 1993; Booth, Johnson, & Granger, 1999a, 1999b). Person-centered pathway approaches to behavior development

TABLE 9.2. *Correlations of sociobehavioral scores and testosterone levels*

	Hunting ability	Status	Aggressiveness	Marital stability	Extramarital interest	Sexual attractiveness	Marital intimacy	Trance ability	Nurturance	Energy
Mean a.m.	-0.34	-0.49	0.32	-0.79**	0.89**	0.48	0.04	-0.20	-0.33	0.39
Mean p.m.	0.06	-0.20	0.76*	-0.93**	0.94***	0.88**	-0.08	0.00	-0.78*	0.64
Mean a.m.-p.m.	-0.62	-0.61	-0.24	-0.40	0.57	-0.06	0.16	-0.37	0.20	0.09
Base a.m.	-0.37	-0.45	-0.02	-0.34	0.52	0.03	0.08	-0.06	0.20	0.11
Base p.m.	0.32	0.02	0.69	-0.70	0.81*	0.89**	-0.13	0.29	-0.58	0.90**
Base a.m.-p.m.	-0.45	-0.37	-0.22	-0.14	0.31	-0.24	0.34	-0.30	0.34	-0.16
Hunt a.m.	-0.13	-0.28	0.51	-0.87**	0.96***	0.68	0.16	-0.23	-0.58	0.57
Hunt p.m.	0.00	-0.22	0.74*	-0.91**	0.92***	0.81*	0.00	-0.08	-0.76*	0.50
Hunt a.m.-p.m.	0.45	-0.48	-0.14	0.58	0.74*	0.26	0.17	-0.44	-0.12	0.53
Post a.m.	-0.53	-0.73*	0.22	-0.76*	0.80*	0.34	-0.24	-0.13	-0.22	0.17
Post p.m.	-0.02	-0.29	0.63	-0.92***	0.87**	0.89**	-0.29	-0.03	-0.83**	0.71
Post a.m.-p.m.	-0.76*	-0.79*	-0.30	-0.28	0.34	-0.27	-0.14	-0.22	0.34	0.29
Activity	0.87**	0.71	0.76*	-0.20	0.27	0.76*	.18	0.39	-0.59	0.74*
Outcome	0.40	-0.28	-0.15	0.14	-0.26	-0.51	0.08	-0.24	0.22	-0.88**

Note: Given the small size of the dataset and the consistent pattern of associations, correlations with probability 0.1 are considered significant.
*$p \leq 0.1$; **$p \leq .05$; ***$p \leq .01$

studied on a population level are needed both to identify key variables determining differential outcomes (Singer, Ryff, & Carr, 1998; Zhao, Brooks-Gunn, McLanahan, & Singer, 2000), and to test theoretical questions about individual and evolutionary adaptation (Cairns et al., 1990). Further, the niche partitioning perspective outlined earlier suggests the importance of context- and culture-specific analyses of niche availability and the processes by which individuals seek or are inducted into them (Laland et al., 2000; Oyama, Griffiths, & Gray, 2001).

The group of !Kung hunters, though small and already adult, captures a social landscape of niches, their psychobehavioral correlates, and concomitant implications for social positionality and life history trajectory. Hunters 8 and 1 (Figure 9.4) represent a contrast in personality and human relationships that illuminates the trade-offs associated with the androgen–psychobehavioral links discussed above. Hunter 8 is low status: he has modest hunting ability, rather low productivity, and is highly aggressive. A "hustler" with high extramarital interest and sexual attractiveness, his marriage consequently is poor, intimacy with wife is low, and nurturance to children similarly low. Despite the high sexual attractiveness and interest in affairs, the actual number of liaisons is low because he is difficult to handle, too intense and aggressive, and indiscreet and jealous. This pattern suggests a trade-off of sexual opportunism against personal relations and parenting. Aggressiveness, moreover, cannot offset weak contributions to subsistence; hence Hunter 8's low status. His evening testosterone averages higher than all other men in all three phases of the study, before, during, and after the hunt; moreover, his morning values also average higher than all but one other man. Together, these observations imply that he chronically maintains high testosterone across the day. This case conforms to Wingfield's Challenge Hypothesis that sustained elevations of testosterone by males to support mating opportunity incur costs to capacity for maintenance of pair bond and nurturance of young (Wingfield et al., 1990).

By contrast, Hunter 1 occupies high status: he has good hunting ability, good productivity, and high assertiveness, but also high nurturance to children, an excellent marriage with good intimacy, and modest sexual attractiveness but no interest in philandering. His testosterone levels are low compared to the other men: mean morning values are lowest and evening values second lowest in the group. Nonetheless, his diurnal variation is absolutely and proportionately the lowest in the group because his testosterone levels are maintained across the day. This case exemplifies the point that low testosterone is not incompatible with high status, and furthermore suggests the importance of age (Hunter 1 was 45 while Hunter 8 was 25 years old). As reported for Western men (Worthman, 1999b), testosterone declined with age in this sample, including morning levels $(t - 3.2, p = .02)$ and evening values $(t - 7.1, p = .001)$, but not diurnal change

(t −1.1, p = 0.3). Relationships and behavior also changed with age in these men: marital stability increased (t 4.6, p < .005), extramarital interest declined (t − .29, p < .05), sexual attractiveness decreased (t − 2.6, p < .05), aggressiveness declined slightly (t − 2.4, p .06), and nurturance and energy tended to decrease (t 2.1, p .1; t − 2.0, p .1). Productivity, status, hunting ability, and intimacy did not change with age. Thus, dual dimensions of age – psychosocial maturation and physical, including endocrine, change – likely operate in tandem to produce the relationships of psychobehavioral patterns with endocrine profiles observed among the men. Again, our sample is too small to allow us to tease these dimensions apart.

Testosterone and Efficacy

Ranked as the second best hunter, Hunter 1 and another man achieved the largest average hunting return during the brief study period by turning to low-risk, low-return hunting after experience of some failure in pursuit of high-risk, high-return big game. Men differed widely in hunting strategy, with concomitant differences in endocrine profiles and attitude scores. Some expended considerably more hunting effort than did others. Significantly, outcome was not related to effort expended, nor was it correlated with score on hunting ability. Dissociation of effort and outcome over the short period of the study appears due to alternate hunting strategies that differ in effort required, probability of success, magnitude of yield, and social rewards. Hunting strategies can be roughly polarized between going for large game, and setting traps for small birds. Individual hunters ranged from near-exclusive pursuit of large game, to mainly trap-setting and opportunistic capitalization on chance encounters or finds. Nearly all men used a mixed strategy, starting out in pursuit of big game but turning to small game and trap-setting when that failed. Notably, the only man who did not employ this strategy was the one rated highest in hunting ability. Of all men on the hunt, he expended the greatest effort and experienced the greatest failure.

   These observations complicate the social–operational definition of a "good hunter." Hunting repute is more closely based on long-term success in achieving the more infrequent and improbable, but massive and impressive, kill. Thus, perceived hunting ability was not associated with short-term hunt success; furthermore, it correlated neither with status, nor productivity. Social status and productivity rest on more than hunting. Other group members, particularly wives, strongly value a track record of daily returns that reflects a man's commitment to ensuring everyday subsistence even as he pursues opportunities for larger game. Hence, productivity was correlated with both social status and marital stability, implying that the capacities involved in pursuit of the mixed subsistence strategy required for consistent, strong productivity were linked to quality of relationships (marriage stability and status), either directly or indirectly, via productivity. The ability to perservere in the face of failure, with its biopsychological underpinnings, can conflict with capacities to be flexible, to attend to and act on cues indicating the need to shift goals and behaviors. Testosterone may modulate the balance between perseveration and goal shifting, or the other way about (Klaiber, Broverman, & Kobayashi, 1967; Klaiber, Broverman, Vogel, Abraham, & Cone, 1971), and it has also been linked to sensation seeking (O'Carroll, 1984). Hunter 1, with high social status, shows low but highly stable levels of testosterone, perhaps reflecting an optimum ability to switch strategies and moderate risk. Low-status Hunter 8 has high and more labile testosterone levels, possibly indicating an inability to switch between tasks and strategies, as well as heavy energy expenditure (perhaps sequences of "gearing up" and defeat), with consequent testosterone lability across the day.

Psychobiology of Behavior, Niche Partitioning, and Life History

The contrasts observed among the eight !Kung hunters, in personality-behavioral styles, social success, and endocrine dynamics, illustrate the operation of alternate life history strategies in men. The alternatives, and their complexity, can be exemplified by two more instances, Hunter 7 and Hunter 5. Hunter 7 (Figure 9.4) has moderately high status. He has outstanding hunting ability with fairly good success, excellent productivity, high aggressiveness but also strong nurturance to children, high level of activity, an excellent marriage though with little intimacy, and good sexual attractiveness but low extramarital interest. Note that, although he is rated the best hunter and put the greatest effort into hunting, he experienced the greatest degree of failure over the course of the study: his hunting strategy aimed at big kills with high unit return but low probability of success per trial. During the 5-day hunt, he persisted in this approach despite failure and defections of the other hunters. His high global score for productivity nonetheless implies that he achieves consistent long-term returns through a high activity level and aggressive drive on an ambitious subsistence strategy. In his case, then, role as excellent hunter is fitted with that as provider–husband by channeling his aggressiveness and energy toward achieving high productivity. The drive to productive goals further intersects with concern for children's and wife's welfare reflected in his nurturance and marriage scores. Ability to channel may also underlie his low extramarital interest despite his sexual attractiveness in a society that tolerates extramarital affairs; absence of such interest definitely enhances marital stability. Another outlet for his high energy and persistence may be trance healing; his excellence in this domain likely enhances his status and nurturance scores.

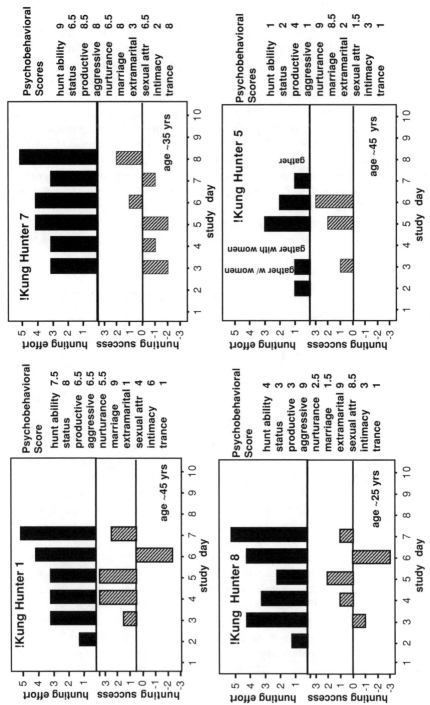

FIGURE 9.4. Personality ratings in relation to hunting effort and success: examples of four !Kung men.

206

The testosterone profile of Hunter 7 is characterized by mean morning levels half a standard deviation below the average for all men, evening values virtually at the sample mean, and low diurnal change in testosterone (three-fourths of a standard deviation below mean). In many respects, testosterone profile for Hunter 7 was quite similar to that for Hunter 1, except that Hunter 7 consistently had slightly higher values. Each had low diurnal variation.

Hunter 5 (Figure 9.4) is the same age as but strongly contrasts with Hunter 1: He has very low status along with abysmal hunting ability and little interest in big game. But he also has fair productivity, no aggressiveness and outstanding nurturance to children, an excellent marriage with fair intimacy, and modest sexual attractiveness but no *overt* extramarital interest. During the hunt, his participation in group pursuit of large game was desultory; he usually faded out as the day progressed or remained in camp altogether, and spent his time making string for bird traps and setting snares, gossiping with women, and playing with children. Remarkably, though he was rated the worst hunter, his cumulative hunt success was the highest over the study period: he pursued a strategy (bird snaring) of low investment, low risk/high probability of return with low unit return. His low involvement in hunting lowered the risk of failure that would detract from his modest successes. Belying his reputation for disinterest in extramarital affairs and lack of sex appeal, three months of bi-daily interviews with the women of this group for a separate concurrent study revealed that number of reported extramarital liaisons with this man was the highest for the entire group. That he was a warm, nonthreatening, readily available, discreet, comfortable nice guy apparently made him an easy choice for women, while his low status, low profile, and hypomacho demeanor neutralized him as an object of jealousy for men. His persona clearly has adaptive advantages for reproductive opportunity, akin to reports in nonhuman primates and other species that alliance with females and nonthreat to males offers a viable life history strategy for males under appropriate circumstances (Daly & Wilson, 1983; Smuts, 1985).

Testosterone profile of Hunter 5 (Figure 9.3) shows a moderate degree of flux across days, but a sharp diurnal variation within days that exceeded any other man's. On average, his testosterone declined by 50% across the day. The marked contrast between this man and Hunter 1 (Figures 9.3, 9.4), in endocrine profiles, behavior, and social status illustrates the power of microniche differentiation and its cumulative social and adaptive consequences (Caspi & Moffitt, 1993). Men of equivalent age who grew up together in a small society, and now live in the same band, their different lives reflect distinctive behavior patterns, emotional–social niches, and corresponding testosterone profiles.

Briefly, the data from !Kung hunters raise the following points about niche partitioning:

1. Large differences in personality and behavioral style exist even in small groups with high pressure for social coherence and cooperation.
2. Personality differences can be linked to important outcomes such as foraging success and reproduction (relationships with women, wife, and children).
3. Niche partitioning creates complementarity and fosters reciprocity. Within-group, psychobiologically grounded diversity of individual personalities permits pursuit of diverse but complementary roles that enhance individual well-being by optimizing daily foraging outcomes through shared returns on mixed strategies. Because returns from hunting are shared across the entire group, differing strategies by individuals are cumulatively risk-minimizing.
4. Some high-status features (best hunter) are not necessarily tied to top social status; moreover, social status or desirability does not always determine evaluations by or behaviors of others (e.g., Hunter 5).
5. Life course development has psychobiological correlates: Men exhibited both endocrine and sociobehavioral changes with age that corresponded to maturational shifts in social roles and relationships (Cairns & Cairns, 2000). Briefly, aggression and hormones have different roles to play at different points of the life course.
6. Reciprocal biosocial dynamics through time construct divergent life courses: Thus, available, tenable social microniches support alternate life history strategies and both induce and accommodate individual variation.
7. No one person can do all things, nor could uniform temperament support the filling of all social niches: personality recognizes and contributes to niche partitioning and social subspecialization, even, or perhaps especially, in small societies.

Our observations suggest that the social landscape has important biological dimensions. Testosterone was associated with aging and its attendant changes in behavior, as well as with an array of psychobehavioral features pertaining to men's relationships, roles, and statuses.

CULTURE AND LIFE HISTORY: COMPARATIVE ETHNOGRAPHY

Understanding of the developmental psychobiology of behavior rests largely on divergent approaches highlighting either endogenous or exogenous factors. The first focuses on the impact of psychobiology (specifically, hormones) on behavior, while the second concerns the impact of experience on psychobiology. This distinction roughly maps on to the literatures on gonadal hormones and behavior, and on stress, respectively. Study of the developmental psychobiology of aggression has adhered substantially to the endogenous model. As reviewed in an earlier section, the literatures on developmental psychobiology of reactivity have found that experience exerts differential impacts on individuals. Further, differential impact is linked to different outcomes for behavior and well-being. Here, we turn to explore an expanded view of exogenous cultural factors and their determinants.

Psychiatry and developmental psychology have examined relationships between psychobehavioral functioning and experience, through either daily stressors of everyday life, or major traumatic events. Adjacent concerns include the impact of social structure (e.g., poverty) on the distribution of both daily stressors and traumatic events (Bronfenbrenner & Ceci, 1994; Costello, Compton, Keeler, & Angold, 2003; Maughan, 2001; Spencer, 2001; Zhao et al., 2000), as well as developmental effects on endocrine and neuroendocrine functioning (Heim, Owens, Plotsky, & Nemeroff, 1997; van der Kolk, 1987; Widom, 1998; Yehuda, 1997). However, surprisingly little is known about how, when, and where the "rubber hits the road" with respect to the structuring, timing, and psychophysiological interpretation of experience by individuals, and the role played by culture and social structure in this process.

A combined *biocultural and life history approach* can help to fill this theoretical and empirical gap, and augment our understanding of the psychobiological development of aggressive behavior. The practices, beliefs, values, and emotional–social landscapes created by cultures define life course options, availability and value of niches, and hence the field of behavior and behavior development. Together, culture and history constitute ecological inheritance, which we identified earlier as a critical component of biocultural adaptation and development (Laland et al., 2000). Besides the impact of child-care and socialization practices along with everyday social ecologies on child emotional–behavioral development, cultures routinely employ ritual interventions. Ritual interventions often are carefully timed and may explicitly target vulnerable developmental periods (Cairns & Cairns, 2000; Worthman, 1998). Most aim directly at identity formation and affective–behavioral regulation, and not infrequently involve emotional or physical violence, mediate trauma, and canalize aggression. As such, ritual furthers the project of niche construction and partitioning. By illustration, the following sections outline a series of generalized biocultural phenomena related to aggression and violence, using examples from the ethnographic and behavioral literature.[1]

---

[1] We are far from being cultural determinists, and fully recognize that stochastic processes play a highly important role in neurobehavioral development, as illustrated by Finch and colleagues (Finch, 1996; Finch & Kirkwood, 2000; Finch & Rose, 1995). However, we maintain that these stochastic processes (and their developmental outcomes) continually interact with the more systematic "work of culture" (*sensu* Obeyesekere, 1990).

Trauma (*Production, Interpretation, Alleviation*)

Many cultures systematically mandate physical and psychological trauma at various points in development. As devices in the constructions of culturally distinctive life courses, rites of passage have been an enduring concern of anthropology, which has documented a wide array of purposive cultural practices (van Gennep, 1960). These include piercing and tatooing at birth, male and female circumcision (sans anesthesia) at a wide variety of ages, maternal separation and mock matricide, long periods of social isolation and psychological terror, food deprivation, ritual scarring, and forced bingeing and purging (Herdt, 1987; Newman & Boyd, 1982; Tuzin, 1982; Worthman, 1993). While brief physical trauma at or near birth has been linked to increased adult stature (Worthman, 1993; Worthman, 1999b), the long-term psychobehavioral effects of ritual terror have been less well-examined. Given the rich literature linking familial abuse to the development of antisocial behavior (Chisholm, 1999; de Zulueta, 1993; Doumas, Margolin, & John, 1994; Dutton, 1999; Lyons-Ruth & Jacobvitz, 1999; Widom & Maxfield, 1996; Zeanah et al., 1999), one would expect significant "downstream" behavioral effects. Indeed, in many societies, such rituals of initiation into manhood are explicitly designed to produce "hot" or aggressive personalities.

The direction and channeling of such experiences involve culture's role in the *interpretation* of trauma. Among traditional New Guinea societies, ritual violence and terror were explicitly designed to expunge female characteristics from male initiates. As their scars heal and their treatment improves, masculine traits are "soothed" into initiates, through a process of verbal and physical pampering made all the more powerful by their juxtaposition with earlier trauma.[2] Synergistic effects of trauma and care help foster not only a physical and psychological dependence on males, but a growing antagonism toward the female gender (Herdt, 1987). Notably, culture plays a role not only in interpreting trauma but also in dissipating and alleviating the psychobehavioral effects of unexpected traumatic events (i.e., natural disasters) (Aldwin, 1994; de Zulueta, 1993; Rousseau & Drapeau, 1998). For example, years of genocidal violence in Uganda have been linked to the development of psychotherapeutic (narrative and collective interpretation) rituals within families (de Zulueta, 1993). As another example, religious asceticism has provided a socially acceptable outlet for the expression of early attachment trauma for certain individuals in Sri Lanka, as well as a way to avoid further victimization in an abusive marriage (Obeyesekere, 1981, 1990).

---

[2] Please note the similarity of this culturally orchestrated process with cycles of "traumatic bonding" in abusive couples, whereby the abused partner is alterately traumatized and pampered, leading to strong psychological (and likely psychobiological) dependence (Bennett, 1991; Painter & Dutton, 1985; van der Kolk & Greenberg, 1987).

Accentuation and Interpretation of Developmental Transition

Periods of neural growth, organization, and pruning (partly prompted through changes in levels of gonadal steroids) offer an easy entry point for cultural rituals to tune the individual psychobehavioral characteristics of its members. This is particularly true during puberty, which is marked by obvious physical changes. As this appears to be a period during which significant structural development is still occurring (Azmitia & Whitaker-Azmitia, 1991; Sowell, Thompson, Tessner, & Toga, 2001) and the actions of gonadal steroids help to develop and reorganize the adolescent brain (Walker, 2002), many cultures "choose" this time to begin elaborate ritual socialization of gender (Caspi & Moffitt, 1993; Herdt, 1987; Shore, 1996; Tuzin, 1982; Worthman, 1999b). For example, the Kikuyu of Kenya traditionally timed clitoridectomy by pubertal stage according to breast development, and age of first emission is strongly related to the initiation of male socialization into manhood (this latter approximation is likely achieved through the observation of subtle behavioral cues) (Worthman, 1993). Through such coordination of cultural practices with physical states, the experience of increasing sexual motivation and competitive urges is set into motion, sculpted, and surrounded by frameworks of interpretation. Meanwhile, the religious and symbolic content experienced at such an early stage (and often in accompaniment with dramatic and novel experiences) provide a framework of understanding and meaning-making that help direct behavioral and coping patterns throughout the life span (Obeyesekere, 1981, 1990). Moreover, animal models suggest that exposure to stress in adolescence can set patterns of neural connectivity (specifically, the balance of serotonergic and vasopressin terminals in the hypothalamus) that make individuals particularly vulnerable to aggressive reactions later in life (Delville, De Vries, & Ferris, 2000; Ferris, 2000).

Behavioral Demands, Expectations, and Sanctions

Beyond concerted efforts to target specific developmental periods, cultural systems also embed more general models and expectations of how men and women in various positions of status "ought" to act when faced with situations that might provoke anger or irritation. Men in many small-scale societies, such as the Sambia and the Kaluli of Papua New Guinea, or the Yanomamo of Amazonia, are not only expected to react with overt confrontation; they are often expected to create situations of overt, competitive confrontation (Herdt, 1982; Newman & Boyd, 1982; Schieffelin, 1976; Tuzin, 1982). Such domains of competition may be given a specific, delimited cultural space, such as oratory battles (Schieffelin, 1976), axe fights (Chagnon, 1968, 1974, 1997), or even collective labor (Herdt, 1982). Societal expectations for male aggressiveness are not equally easy to fulfill for all men, leading to chronic stress for some (Schieffelin, 1985). Individual constitutional differences (whatever their origin) are fodder for another characteristic of cultural systems: the existence of multiple, frequency-dependent social niches, a phenomenon noted by Bateson in his study of the Iatmul of Papua New Guinea (Bateson, 1958, 1987), who recognize and accept both a prototypical "hot" and aggressive male and his "cooler" and more sociable counterpoint. Meanwhile, societies such as the Toraja in Indonesia, who emphasize the internalization and limitation of aggressive or angry emotion, also explicitly recognize strategies for limiting angry display and thereby "staying cool," including dissociative and displacement mechanisms (Hollan, 2000). Finally, cultural systems quite effectively use direct sanctions to control the expression of anger. For example, Fry has documented how display of dramatically different levels of intracommunity violence by two neighboring Mexican communities is set up by the early positive versus negative sanctioning of child "play fighting" (Fry, 1988, 1990).

A BIOCULTURAL VIEW OF THE DEVELOPMENTAL PSYCHOBIOLOGY OF AGGRESSION

As the other chapters in this volume attest, our understanding of behavior development is rapidly growing through empirical research that increasingly supports dynamic, multidimensional models. An expanding body of evidence along with evolving models of behavior development have considerably changed views of the genesis of problem behaviors, including aggression. Specifically, the nature and significance of individual–environment interactions in ontogeny, the impact of social ecology and gender, and the necessity of a life-span, life-history view have all claimed a place in emerging views of the development of social behavior and its related psychobiology. But the value of individual differences and capacity for development of such differences has not received attention by literatures focusing on adjustment or competence. We have marshaled theoretical and empirical evidence to suggest that individual difference in behavior plays adaptive roles, both for individuals who must get a life, and for the crucial social necessity to fill social niches, harness human capacities, and support the essential project of constructing sustainably meaningful, coherent life histories. Adaptive value emerges from niche partitioning, or the carving up of possible life histories around the available landscapes of social and material resource availability. Such partitioning occurs through the active efforts of individuals, agents of socialization, and cultural systems in which they are embedded. This agency results in niche construction, which is the modification of environments of rearing and function. Thus, these environments both shape ontogeny and determine the value or consequences of its outcomes.

Building upon insights gained in the comparative anthropological study of life history and its cultural ecology, we place the study of aggression in the context of: (1) individual life history trajectories that negotiate complex human relationships, and (2) cultural systems and institutions that determine social opportunities and demands throughout the life-span. The human capacity for psychobehavioral diversity is realized by contingent coaction among genetic diversity, environmental heterogeneity, and life-span ontogeny. Such coaction operates through a cultural, social, and physical context dynamically shaped by purposive efforts of individual, socializing, and cultural agents. Hence, the forms, prevalence, and individual costs or benefits of aggression lie in intersections of developmental psychobiology with cultural and social ecology of risk and benefit. Forms of aggression that some societies seek to expunge are fostered in others; prevalence varies accordingly, as does the relationship of individual constitutional differences to outcomes and context. Hence, a constitutional difference expressed as reactivity or irritability can be a valuable basis for adult assertiveness, status seeking, and productivity, whereas the same difference can be detrimental under other circumstances or social microecologies. Capacity for diverse outcomes, within individuals and populations, is maintained evolutionarily by heterogeneity of adaptive landscapes (in terms of costs and benefits of phenotypes) and their variation through time (Reeve & Sherman, 1993).

In sum, biocultural production and adaptive value of psychobehavioral variance within and among populations merits closer attention in the comparative study of behavior development. This expanded view has two components: (1) coaction of individual and society and the resultant person-specific microecology of rearing and function, understood through time; and (2) feed-forward impact of culture and history on the dynamics of person–environment coaction by shaping understandings, intentions, resources, and opportunities, and thus behaviors and their sequelae, understood at the population level. Quantitative and qualitative comparative research is needed to delineate the relationships of structural and historical factors to individual variation in behaviors and life histories.

References

Aldwin, C. M. (1994). *Stress, coping, and development: An integrative perspective.* New York: Guilford Press.

Azmitia, E. C., & Whitaker-Azmitia, P. M. (1991). Awakening the sleeping giant: Anatomy and plasticity of the brain serotonergic system. *Journal of Clinical Psychiatry,* (52 Suppl.), 4–16.

Baldwin, J. M. (1895a). *Mental development in the child and the race: Methods and processes.* New York: Macmillan.

Baldwin, J. M. (1895b). A new factor in evolution. *American Naturalist, 30,* 441–451, 536–553.

Baldwin, J. M. (1902). *Development and evolution.* New York: Macmillan.
Bar-Haim, Y., Marshall, P. J., & Fox, N. A. (2000). Developmental changes in heart period and high-frequency heart period variability from 4 months to 4 years of age. *Developmental Psychobiology* 37(1), 44–56.
Bateson, G. (1958). *Naven, a survey of the problems suggested by a composite picture of the culture of a New Guinea tribe drawn from three points of view* (2nd ed.). Stanford, CA: Stanford University Press.
Bateson, G. (1987). *Steps to an ecology of mind: Collected essays in anthropology, psychiatry, evolution, and epistemology.* Northvale, NJ: Aronson.
Benedict, R. (1934). *Patterns of culture.* Boston: Houghton Mifflin.
Bennett, L. (1991). Adolescent girls' experience of witnessing marital violence: A phenomenological study. *Journal of Advanced Nursing, 16,* 431–438.
Blanchard, D. C., Sakai, R. R., McEwen, B., Weiss, S. M., & Blanchard, R. J. (1993). Subordination stress: Behavioral, brain, and neuroendocrine correlates. *Behavioural Brain Research, 58*(1–2), 113–121.
Boas, F. (1912). *Changes in bodily forms of descendants of immigrants.* New York: Columbia University Press.
Bonner, J. T. (1974). *On development. The biology of form.* Cambridge, MA: Harvard University Press.
Booth, A., & Dabbs, J. M., Jr. (1993). Testosterone and men's marriages. *Social Forces, 72,* 463–477.
Booth, A., Johnson, D. R., & Granger, D. A. (1999a). Testosterone and men's depression: The role of social behavior. *Journal of Health & Social Behavior, 40*(2), 130–140.
Booth, A., Johnson, D. R., & Granger, D. A. (1999b). Testosterone and men's health. *Journal of Behavioral Medicine, 22,* 1–19.
Booth, A., Johnson, D. R., Granger, D. A., Crouter, A. C., & McHale, S. (2003). Testosterone and child and adolescent adjustment: The moderating role of parent–child relationships. *Developmental Psychology, 39,* 85–98.
Boyce, W. T., Chesney, M., Alkon, A., Tschann, J. M., & Adams, S., Chasterman, B., et al. (1995). Psychobiologic reactivity to stress and childhood respiratory illnesses: Results of two prospective studies. *Psychosomatic Medicine, 57*(5), 411–422.
Boyce, W. T., Goldstein, L. H., Adler, N. E., & Kupfer., D. J. (1999). Social dominance and preschool morbidities; A developmental anlage of SES effects on health? *Annual Meeting of the American Psychosomatic Society.*
Briggs, J. L. (1998). *Inuit morality play: The emotional education of a three-year-old.* New Haven, CT: Yale University Press.
Bronfenbrenner, U., & Ceci, S. J. (1994). Nature-nurture reconceptualized in developmental perspective: A bioecological model. *Psychological Review, 101*(4), 568–586.
Brooks-Gunn, J., Petersen, A. C., & Compas, B. E. (1995). Physiological processes and the development of childhood and adolescent depression. In I. M. Goodyer (Ed.), *The depressed child and adolescent: Developmental and clinical perspectives* (pp. 81–110). Cambridge, U.K.: Cambridge University Press.
Cairns, R., Gariepy, J.-L., & Hood, K. (1990). Development, microevolution, and social behavior. *Psychological Review, 97,* 49–65.

Cairns, R. B. (1976). The ontogeny and phylogeny of social behavior. In M. E. Hahn & E. C. Simmel (Eds.), *Evolution and communicative behavior* (pp. 115–139). New York: Academic Press.

Cairns, R. B. (2000). Developmental science: Three audacious implications. In L. R. Bergman & R. B. Cairns (Eds.), *Developmental science and the holistic approach* (pp. 49–62). Mahwah, NJ: Lawrence Erlbaum Associates.

Cairns, R. B., & Cairns, B. D. (1995). Social ecology over time and space. In P. E. G. H. Moen, Jr. (Ed.), *Examining lives in context: Perspectives on the ecology of human development* (pp. 397–421). Washington, DC: American Psychological Association.

Cairns, R. B., & Cairns, B. D. (2000). The natural history and developmental functions of aggression. In A. J. Sameroff & M. Lewis (Eds.), *Handbook of developmental psychopathology* (2nd ed. pp. 403–429). New York: Kluwer Academic/Plenum Publishers.

Calkins, S. D., & Dedmon, S. E. (2000). Physiological and behavioral regulation in two-year-old children with aggressive/destructive behavior problems. *Journal of Abnormal Child Psychology, 28*(2), 103–118.

Campbell, A. (1999). Staying alive: Evolution, culture, and women's intrasexual aggression. *Behavioral & Brain Sciences, 22*, 203–214.

Caspi, A., & Moffitt, T. E. (1993). When do individual differences matter? A paradoxical theory of personality coherence. *Psychological Inquiry, 4*(4), 247–271.

Caspi, A., & Roberts, B. W. (2001). Personality development across the life course: The argument for change and continuity. *Psychological Inquiry, 12*, 49–66.

Chagnon, N. A. (1968). *Yanomamo, the fierce people.* New York: Holt Rinehart and Winston.

Chagnon, N. A. (1974). *Studying the Yanomamo.* New York: Holt Rinehart and Winston.

Chagnon, N. A. (1997). *Yanomamo* (5th ed.). Fort Worth: Harcourt Brace College Publishers.

Chance, S. E., Brown, R. T., Dabbs, J. M., Jr., & Casey, R. (2000). Testosterone, intelligence and behavior disorders in young boys. *Personality & Individual Differences, 28*(3), 437–445.

Charnov, E. (1993). *Life history invariants: Some explorations of symmetry in evolutionary ecology.* Oxford: Oxford University Press.

Chisholm, J. S. (1999). *Death, hope and sex: Steps to an evolutionary ecology of mind and morality:* New York: Cambridge University Press.

Costello, E. J., Compton, S., Keeler, G., and Angold, A. (2003). Relationships between poverty and psychopathology: A natural experiment. *Journal of the American Medical Association 290*, 2023–2029.

Crews, D. (2002). Diversity and evolution of hormone–behavior relations in reproductive behavior. In J. B. Becker, S. M. Breedlove, D. Crews, M. M. McCarthy (Eds.), *Behavioral endocrinology* (pp. 223–288). Cambridge, MA: MIT Press.

Dabbs, J. M., & Dabbs, M. G. (2000). *Heroes, rogues, and lovers: Testosterone and behavior.* New York: McGraw-Hill.

Dabbs, J. M., Jr., Alford, E. C., & Fielden, J. A. (1998). Trial lawyers and testosterone: Blue-collar talent in a white-collar world. *Journal of Applied Social Psychology, 28*(1), 84–94.

Dabbs, J. M., Jr., Bernieri, F. J., Strong, R. K., Campo, R., & Milun, R. (2001). Going on stage: Testosterone in greetings and meetings. *Journal of Research in Personality*, 35(1), 27–40.

Dabbs, J. M., Jr., Jurkovic, G. J., & Frady, R. L. (1991). Salivary testosterone and cortisol among late adolescent offenders. *Journal of Abnormal Child Psychology*, 19, 469–478.

Daly, M., & Wilson, M. (1983). *Sex, evolution, and behavior* (2nd ed.) Belmont, CA: Wadsworth.

De Bellis, M. D., Keshavan, M. S., Beers, S. R., Hall, J., Frustaci, K., Masalehdan, A., et al. (2001). Sex differences in brain maturation during childhood and adolescence. *Cerebral Cortex*, 11, 552–557.

de Zulueta, F. (1993). *From pain to violence: The traumatic roots of destructiveness*. London: Whurr Publishers.

Delville, Y., De Vries, G. J., & Ferris, C. F. (2000). Neural connections of the anterior hypothalamus and agonistic behavior in golden hamsters. *Brain, Behavior & Evolution*, 55(2), 53–76.

Donzella, B., Gunnar, M. R., Krueger, W. K., & Alwin, J. (2000). Cortisol and vagal tone responses to competitive challenge in preschoolers: Associations with temperament. *Developmental Psychobiology*, 37(4), 209–220.

Doumas, D., Margolin, G., & John, R. S. (1994). The intergenerational transmission of aggression across three generations. *Journal of Family Violence*, 9(2), 157–175.

Dutton, D. G. (1999). Traumatic origins of intimate rage. *Aggression & Violent Behavior*, 4(4), 431–447.

Ferris, C. F. (2000). Adolescent stress and neural plasticity in hamsters: A vasopressin–serotonin model of inappropriate aggressive behaviour. *Experimental Physiology*, 85 Spec No, 85S–90S.

Finch, C., & Rose, M. (1995). Hormones and the physiological architecture of life history evolution. *The Quarterly Review of Biology*, 70(1), 1–52.

Finch, C. E. (1996). Commentary: Biological bases for plasticity during aging of individual life histories. In D. Magnusson (Ed.), *The lifespan development of individuals: Behavioral, neurobiological, and psychosocial perspectives: a synthesis* (pp. 488–511). Cambridge, UK: Cambridge University Press.

Finch, C. E., & Kirkwood, T. B. L. (2000). *Chance, development, and aging*. New York: Oxford University Press.

Flinn, M. V. (1999). Family environment, stress, and health during childhood. In C. Panter-Brick & C. M. Worthman (Eds.), *Hormones, health, and behavior: A socioecological and lifespan perspective* (pp. 105–130). Cambridge, UK: Cambridge University Press.

Fox, N. A., Schmidt, L. A., & Henderson, H. A. (2000). Developmental psychophysiology: Conceptual and methodological perspectives. In J. T. Cacioppo & L. G. Tassinary (Eds.), *Handbook of psychophysiology* (2nd ed., pp. 665–686). New York: Cambridge University Press.

Fry, D. P. (1988). Intercommunity differences in aggression among Zapotec children. *Child Development*, 59(4), 1008–1019.

Fry, D. P. (1990). Play aggression among Zapotec children: Implications for the practice hypothesis. *Aggressive Behavior*, 16(5), 321–340.

Gottlieb, G. (1991). Experiential canalization of behavioral development: Theory. *Developmental Psychology, 27,* 4–13.

Gottlieb, G. (1992). *Individual development and evolution: The genesis of novel behavior.* New York, Oxford University Press.

Gottlieb, G. (1998). Normally occurring environmental and behavioral influences on gene activity: From central dogma to probabilistic epigenesis. *Psychological Review, 105,* 792–902.

Granger, D. A., Weisz, J. R., McCracken, J. T., Kauneckis, D., & Ikeda, S. (1994). Testosterone and conduct problems. *Journal of the American Academy of Child & Adolescent Psychiatry, 33*(6), 908.

Gunnar, M. R., Tout, K., de Haan, M., Pierce, S., & Stansburg, K. (1997). Temperament, social competence, and adrenocortical activity in preschoolers. *Developmental Psychobiology, 31*(1), 65–85.

Harkness, S., & Super, C. M. (2000). Culture and psychopathology. In A. J. Sameroff & M. Lewis (Eds.), *Handbook of developmental psychopathology* (2nd ed., pp. 197–214). New York: Kluwer Academic/Plenum Publishers.

Harvey, P. H., & Pagel, M. D. (1991). *The comparative method in evolutionary biology.* Oxford: Oxford University Press.

Heim, C., Owens, M. J., Plotsky, P. M., & Nemeroff, C. B. (1997). The role of early adverse life events in the etiology of depression and posttraumatic stress disorder. Focus on corticotropin-releasing factor. In R. Yehuda & A. C. McFarlane (Eds.), *Psychobiology of posttraumatic stress disorder. Annals of the New York Academy of Sciences* (Vol. 821, pp. 194–207). New York: New York Academy of Sciences.

Herdt, G. H. (1982). *Rituals of manhood: Male initiation in Papua New Guinea.* Berkeley: University of California Press.

Herdt, G. H. (1987). *The Sambia: Ritual and gender in New Guinea.* New York: Holt Rinehart and Winston.

Hollan, D. (2000). Culture and dissociation in Toraja. *Transcultural Psychiatry, 37*(4), 545–559.

James, W. (1890). *The principles of psychology.* New York: Holt.

Jemerin, J. M., & Boyce, W. T. (1990). Psychobiological differences in childhood stress response: II. Cardiovascular markers of vulnerability. *Journal of Developmental & Behavioral Pediatrics, 11*(3), 140–150.

Jessor, R., Colby, A., & Shweder, R. A. (Eds.). (1996). *Ethnography and human development: Context and meaning in social inquiry.* Chicago: University of Chicago Press.

Kagan, J., Reznick, J. S., Snidman, N., Gibbons, J., & Johnson, M. O. (1988). Childhood derivatives of inhibition and lack of inhibition to the unfamiliar. *Child Development, 59*(6), 1580–1589.

Kaplan, H., Hill, K. R., Lancaster, J., & Hurtado, A. M. (2000). A theory of human life history evolution: Diet, intelligence, and longevity. *Evolutionary Anthropology, 9,* 156–185.

Ketterson, E. D., & Nolan, V. (1992). Hormones and life histories: An integrative approach. *American Naturalist, 140,* S34–S62.

Ketterson, E. D., Nolan, V., Cawthorn, M. J., Parker, P. G., & Ziegenfus, C. (1996). Phenotypic engineering: Using hormones to explore the mechanistic and functional bases of phenotypic variation in nature. *Ibis, 138,* 70–86.

Kindlon, D. J., Tremblay, R. E., Mezzacappa, E., Earls, F., Laurent, D., & Schaal, B. (1995). Longitudinal patterns of heart rate and fighting behavior in 9- through 12-year-old boys. *Journal of the American Academy of Child and Adolescent Psychiatry* 34(3), 371–377.

Klaiber, E. L., Broverman, D., & Kobayashi, Y. (1967). The automatization cognitive style, androgens, and monoamine oxidase. *Psychopharmacologia, 11*, 320–336.

Klaiber, L., Broverman, D., Vogel, W., Abraham, G., & Cone, F. (1971). Effects of infused testosterone on mental performances and serum LH. *Journal of Clinical Endocrinology, 32*, 341–349.

Klimes-Dougan, B., Hastings, P. D., Granger, D. A., Usher, B. A., & Zahn-Waxler, C. (2001). Adrenocortical activity in at-risk and normally developing adolescents: Individual differences in salivary cortisol basal levels, diurnal variation, and responses to social challenges. *Development & Psychopathology, 13*(3), 695–719.

Laland, K. N., Odling-Smee, J., & Feldman, M. W. (2000). Niche construction, biological evolution, and cultural change. *Behavioral & Brain Sciences, 23*(1), 131–175.

Laland, K. N., Odling-Smee, F. J., & Feldman, M. W. (2001). Niche construction, ecological inheritance, and cycles of contingency. In S. Oyama, P. E. Griffiths, & R. D. Gray (Eds.), *Cycles of contingency: Developmental systems and evolution* (pp. 117–126). Cambidge, MA: MIT Press.

Lee, R. B., & DeVore, I. (Eds.). (1976). *Kalahari hunter-gatherers: Studies of the !Kung San and their neighbors.* Cambridge, MA: Harvard University Press.

LeVine, R. A. (1974). *Culture and personality: Contemporary readings.* Chicago: Aldine.

LeVine, R. A. (1990). Enculturation: A biosocial perspective on the development of self. In D. Cicchetti & M. Beeghly (Eds.), *The self in transition: Infancy to childhood. The John D. and Catherine T. MacArthur foundation series on mental health and development* (pp. 99–117). Chicago: University of Chicago Press.

Levy, R. L. (1973). *Tahitians. Mind and experience in the Society Islands.* Chicago: University of Chicago Press.

Lewontin, R. C. (1983). Gene, organism, and environment. In D. S. Bendall (Ed.), *Evolution from molecules to men* (pp. 273–285). Cambridge, UK: Cambridge University Press.

Lyons-Ruth, K., & Jacobvitz, D. (1999). Attachment disorganization: Unresolved loss, relational violence, and lapses in behavioral and attentional strategies. In J. Cassidy & P. R. Shaver (Eds.), *Handbook of attachment: Theory, research, and clinical applications* (pp. 520–554). New York: Guilford Press.

Magnusson, D. (1996). The patterning of antisocial behavior and autonomic reactivity. In D. M. Stoff and R. B. Cairns (Eds.), *Aggression and violence: Genetic, neurobiological, and biosocial perspectives* (pp. 291–308). Mahwah, NJ: Lawrence Erlbaum.

Maughan, B. (2001). Conduct disorder in context. In J. Hill & B. E. Maughan (Eds.), *Conduct disorders in childhood and adolescence.* (pp. 169–201). New York: Cambridge University Press.

Mazur, A., & Booth, A. (1998). Testosterone and dominance in men. *Behavioral & Brain Sciences, 21*(3), 353–397.

Mazur, A., & Booth, A. (1999). The biosociology of testosterone in men. In D. D. Franks & T. S. Smith (Eds.), *Mind, brain, and society: Toward a neurosociology of emotion, Vol. 5. Social perspectives on emotion* (pp. 311–338). Stamford, CT: JAI Press.

Mead, M. (1930). *Growing up in New Guinea: A comparative study of primitive education.* New York: W. Morrow.

Mead, M. (1935). *Sex and temperament in three primitive societies.* New York: W. Morrow.

Morgan, C. L. (1896). *Habit and instinct.* London: Arnold.

Newman, P. L., & Boyd, D. J. (1982). The making of men: Ritual and meaning in Awa male initiation. In G. R. Herdt (Ed.), *Rituals of manhood: Male initiation in Papua New Guinea* (pp. 239–285). Berkeley, CA: University of California Press.

Obeyesekere, G. (1981). *Medusa's hair: An essay on personal symbols and religious experience.* Chicago: University of Chicago Press.

Obeyesekere, G. (1990). *The work of culture: Symbolic transformation in psychoanalysis and anthropology.* Chicago: University of Chicago Press.

O'Carroll, R. E. (1984). Androgen administration to hypogonadal and eugonadal men: effects on measures of sensation seeking, personality and spatial ability. *Personality & Individual Differences, 5,* 595–598.

O'Connor, B. P., & Dvorak, T. (2001). Conditional associations between parental behavior and adolescent problems: A search for personality–environment interactions. *Journal of Research in Personality, 35*(1), 1–26.

Odling-Smee, F. J., Laland, K. N., & Feldman, M. W. (1996). Niche construction. *American Naturalist, 147,* 641–648.

Oyama, S. (2000). *The ontogeny of information: Developmental systems and evolution* (2nd ed.). Durham, NC: Duke University Press.

Oyama, S., Griffiths, P. E., & Gray, R. D. (Eds.). (2001). *Cycles of contingency: Developmental systems and evolution.* Cambridge, MA: MIT Press.

Painter, S. L., & Dutton, D. (1985). Patterns of emotional bonding in battered women: Traumatic bonding. *International Journal of Women's Studies, 8*(4), 363–375.

Panter-Brick, C., & Worthman, C. M. (Eds.). (1999). *Hormones, health, and behavior: A socio-ecological and lifespan perspective.* New York: Cambridge University Press.

Porges, S. W. (1995). Orienting in a defensive world: Mammalian modifications of our evolutionary heritage. A polyvagal theory. *Psychophysiology, 32,* 301–318.

Promislow, D., & Harvey, P. H. (1990). Living fast and dying young: A comparative analysis of life history variation among mammals. *Journal of the Zoological Society of London, 220,* 41–437.

Purvis, A., & Harvey, P. H. (1995). Mammal life-history evolution – a comparative test of Charnov's model. *Journal of Zoology, 237,* 259–283.

Raine, A., Reynolds, C., Venables, P. H., & Mednick, S. A. (1997). Biosocial bases of aggressive behavior in childhood: Resting heart rate, skin conductance orienting and physique. In A. B. P. A. Raine (Ed.), *Biosocial bases of violence. NATO ASI series: Series A: Life sciences* (Vol. 292, pp. 107–126). New York: Plenum Press.

Raine, A., Venables, P. H., Dalais, C., Mellingen, K., Reynolds, C., & Mednick, S. A. (2001). Early educational and health enrichment at age 3–5 years is associated with increased autonomic and central nervous system arousal and orienting at age 11 years: Evidence from the Mauritius Child Health Project. *Psychophysiology, 38*(2), 254–266.

Reeve, H. K., & Sherman, P. W. (1993). Adaptation and the goals of evolutionary research. *Quarterly Review of Biology, 68,* 1–32.

Rhen, T., & Crews, D. (2002). Variation in reproductive behaviour within a sex: Neural systems and endocrine activation. *Journal of Neuroendocrinology, 14,* 517–531.

Rousseau, C., & Drapeau, A. (1998). The impact of culture on the transmission of trauma: Refugees' stories and silence embodied in their children's lives. In Y. Danieli (Ed.), *International handbook of multigenerational legacies of trauma. The Plenum series on stress and coping* (pp. 465–486). New York: Plenum Press.

Rowe, R., Maughan, B., Worthman, C. M., Angold, A., & Costello, E. J. (2004). Testosterone, conduct disorder and social medicine in boys: Pubertal development and biosocial dominance. *Biological Psychiatry 55,* 546–552.

Rutter, M., Dunn, J., Plomin, R., Simonoff, E., Pickles, A., Maughan, B., et al. (1997). Integrating nature and nurture: Implications of person–environment correlations and interactions for developmental psychopathology. *Development & Psychopathology, 9*(2), 335–364.

Sameroff, A. J. (2000). Developmental systems and psychopathology. *Development and Psychopathology, 12,* 297–312.

Scarpa, A., Raine, A., Venables, P. H., & Mednick, S. A. (1997). Heart rate and skin conductance in behaviorally inhibited Mauritian children. *Journal of Abnormal Child Psychology, 106*(2), 182–190.

Schaal, B., Tremblay, R. E., Soussignan, R., & Susman, E. J. (1996). Male testosterone linked to high social dominance but low physical aggression in early adolescence. *Journal of the American Academy of Child & Adolescent Psychiatry, 35*(10), 1322–1330.

Schieffelin, E. L. (1976). *The sorrow of the lonely and the burning of the dancers.* New York: St. Martin's Press.

Schieffelin, E. L. (1985). Anger, grief, and shame: Toward a Kaluli ethnopsychology. In G. M. White & J. Kirkpatrick (Eds.), *Person, self, and experience* (pp. 168–182). Berkeley, CA: University of California Press.

Shore, B. (1996). *Culture in mind: Cognition, culture, and the problem of meaning.* New York: Oxford University Press.

Shostak, M. (1981). *Nisa, the life and words of a !Kung woman.* Cambridge, MA: Harvard University Press.

Singer, B., Ryff, C., Carr, D., & Magee, W. J. (1998). Linking life histories and mental health: A person centered strategy. In A. Rafferty (Ed.), *Sociological methology* (pp. 1–51). Washington, DC: American Sociological Association.

Smuts, B. B. (1985). *Sex and friendship in baboons.* New York: Aldine.

Sowell, E. R., Thompson, P. M., Tessner, K. D., & Toga, A. W. (2001). Mapping continued brain growth and gray matter density reduction in dorsal frontal cortex: inverse relationsships during postadolescent brain maturaiton. *Journal of Neuroscience, 21,* 8819–8829.

Soyinka, W. (1981). *Aké.* New York: Aventura.

Spencer, M. B. (2001). Resiliency and fragility factors associated with the contextual experiences of low-resource urban African-American male youth and families. In A. E. Booth & A. C. E. Crouter (Eds.), *Does it take a village?: Community effects on children, adolescents, and families* (pp. 51–77). Mahwah, NJ: Lawrence Erlbaum Associates.

Stearns, S. (1992). *The evolution of life histories.* New York: Oxford.

Stearns, S. C., & Koella, J. C. (1986). The evolution of phenotypic plasticity in life-history traits: Prediction of reaction norms for age and size at maturity. *Quarterly Review of Biology, 40*(5), 893–910.

Stevenson-Hinde, J., & Marshall, P. J. (1999). Behavioral inhibition, heart period, and respiratory sinus arrhythmia: An attachment perspective. *Child Development, 70*(4), 805–816.

Stoff, D. M., & Cairns, R. B. (Eds.). (1996). *Aggression and violence: Genetic, neurobiological, and biosocial perspectives.* Mahwah, NJ: Lawrence Erlbaum Associates.

Suomi, S. (1991). Early stress and adult emotional reactivity in rhesus monkeys. In G. Bock & J. Whelan (Eds.), *The childhood environment and adult disease* (pp. 171–188). Chichester, UK: Wiley.

Suomi, S. J. (2000). A biobehavioral perspective on developmental psychopathology: Excessive aggression and serotonergic dysfunction in monkeys. In A. J. Sameroff, M. Lewis, & S. M. Miller (Eds.), *Handbook of developmental psychopathology* (2nd ed., pp. 237–256). New York: Kluwer Academic/ Plenum Publishers.

Super, C. M., & Harkness, S. (1999). The environment as culture in developmental research. In S. L. Friedman & T. D. Wachs (Eds.), *Measuring environment across the life span: Emerging methods and concepts* (pp. 279–323). Washington, DC: American Psychological Association.

Susman, E. J., Granger, D. A., Murowchick, E., Ponirakis, A., & Worrall, B. K. (1996). Gonadal and adrenal hormones. Developmental transitions and aggressive behavior. *Annals of the New York Academy of Sciences, 794,* 18–30.

Susman, E. J., & Ponirakis, A. (1997). Hormones–context interactions and antisocial behavior in youth. In A. Raine, P. A. Brennan, D. P. Farrington, & S. A. Mednick (Eds.), *Biosocial bases of violence.* New York: Plenum Press.

Tuzin, D. F. (1982). Ritual violence among Ilahita Arapesh: The dynamics of moral uncertainty. In G. R. Herdt (Ed.), *Rituals of manhood: Male initiation in Papua New Guinea* (pp. 321–355). Berkeley, CA: University of California Press.

van der Kolk, B. A. (1987). The psychological consequences of overwhelming life experiences. In B. A. van der Kolk (Ed.), *Psychological trauma* (pp. 1–31). Washington, DC: American Psychiatric Press.

van der Kolk, B. A., & Greenberg, M. S. (1987). The psychobiology of the trauma response: Hyperarousal, constriction, and addiction to traumatic reexposure. In B. A. van der Kolk (Ed.), *Psychological trauma* (pp. 63–89). Washington, DC: American Psychiatric Press.

van Gennep, A. (1960). *The rites of passage.* Chicago: University of Chicago Press.

Walker, E. F. (2002). Adolescent neurodevelopment and psychopathology. *Current Directions in Psychological Science, 11*(1), 24–28.

West-Eberhard, M. J. (1989). Phenotypic plasticity and the origins of diversity. *Annual Review of Ecology and Systematics, 20,* 249–278.

Whiting, B. B., & Edwards, C. P. (1988). *Children of different worlds: The formation of social behavior.* Cambridge, MA: Harvard University Press.

Whiting, J. W. M., & Whiting, B. (1975). *Children of six cultures: A psycho-cultural analysis.* Cambridge, MA: Harvard University Press.

Widom, C. S. (1998). Childhood victimization: early adversity and subsequent psychopathology. In B. P. Dohrenwend (Ed.), *Adversity, stress, and psychopathology* (pp. 81–95). New York: Oxford University Press.

Widom, C. S., & Maxfield, M. G. (1996). A prospective examination of risk for violence among abused and neglected children. In C. F. Ferris & T. Grisso (Eds.), *Understanding aggressive behavior in children. Annals of the New York Academy of Sciences* (Vol. 794, pp. 224–237). New York: New York Academy of Sciences.

Wingfield, J. C., Hegner, R. E., Dufty, A. M., & Ball, G. F. (1990). The challenge hypothesis – theoretical implications for patterns of testosterone secretion, mating systems, and breeding strategies. *American Naturalist, 136,* 829–846.

Wingfield, J. C., Lynn, S., & Soma, K. K. (2001). Avoiding the "costs" of testosterone: ecological bases of hormone–behavior interactions. *Brain, Behavior & Evolution, 57*(5), 239–251.

Worthman, C. M. (1993). Biocultural interactions in human development. In M. E. Pereira & L. A. Fairbanks (Eds.), *Juvenile primates: Life history, development, and behavior* (pp. 339–358). New York: Oxford University Press.

Worthman, C. M. (1998). Adolescence in the Pacific: A biosocial view. In G. H. Herdt & S. C. Leavitt (Eds.), *Adolescence in Pacific Island societies* (pp. 27–54). Pittsburgh: University of Pittsburgh Press.

Worthman, C. M. (1999a). Emotions: You can feel the difference. In A. L. Hinton (Ed.), *Biocultural approaches to the emotions. Publications of the Society for Psychological Anthropology* (pp. 41–74). New York: Cambridge University Press.

Worthman, C. M. (1999b). Epidemiology of human development. In C. Panter-Brick & C. M. Worthman (Eds.), *Hormones, health, and behavior: A socio-ecological and lifespan perspective* (pp. 47–104). New York: Cambridge University Press.

Worthman, C. M., & Konner, M. J. (1987). Testosterone levels change with subsistence hunting effort in !Kung San men. *Psychoneuroendocrinology, 12,* 449–458.

Yehuda, R. (1997). Sensitization of the hypothalamic–pituitary-adrenal axis in post-traumatic stress disorder. In R. Yehuda & A. C. McFarlane (Eds.), *Psychobiology of posttraumatic stress disorder. Annals of the New York Academy of Sciences* (Vol. 821, pp. 57–75). New York: New York Academy of Sciences.

Zeanah, C. H., Danis, B., Hirshberg, L., Benoit, D., Miller, D., & Heller, S. S. (1999). Disorganized attachment associated with partner violence: A research note. *Infant Mental Health Journal, 20*(1), 77–86.

Zhao, H., Brooks-Gunn, J., McLanahan, S., & Singer, B. (2000). Studying the real child rather than the ideal child: Bringing the person into developmental studies. In L. R. Bergman, R. B. Cairns, L.-G. Nilsson, L. Nystedt (Eds.), *Developmental science and the holistic approach* (pp. 393–421). Mahwah, NJ/London: Lawrence Erlbaum Associates.

Zitzmann, M., & Nieschlag, E. (2001). Testosterone levels in healthy men and the relation to behavioural and physical characteristics: facts and constructs. *European Journal of Endocrinology, 144,* 183–197.

PART III

GENE–ENVIRONMENT INTERACTIONS

10

Toward an Integrative Account of the Development of Aggressive Behavior

Kathryn E. Hood
The Pennsylvania State University

To the memory of Robert B. Cairns (1933–1999)

"The reader who wants to study the best work on aggression in the second half of the 20th century will find most of it in the works of Bob Cairns."

Tremblay 2000 p. 138

Toward an integrative understanding of behavioral development, one sufficient to address how complex behaviors emerge over the course of development, the field of developmental psychobiology has advanced in recent years to transcend dichotomous views of cause and effect or nature versus nurture. Beyond parsing the stuff of life into genetic or environmental sources, contemporary theorists are likely to envision three-dimensional interactive webs, lifelines or fabrics of intertwined strands, recursive fractal forms, and dialectical transformations across levels of organization as conceptual models for aspects of developmental processes (Cairns, 1996; Gottlieb, 1998; Hood, 1995; Lerner, 1998; Michel & Moore, 1995; Thelen & Smith, 1998). Whether these models are generative in revealing new properties of specific developmental domains is an active question. For present purposes, they bring an expanding range of issues to the research agenda for a multidisciplinary approach to the study of development. A consideration of aggressive behavior as enfolded within a dynamic developmental manifold may contribute to the goal of a fully integrative account. This is the present project.

A critical issue for proceeding is how to construe the ubiquitous and continuous bidirectional flow of actions that comprise social interchanges. Social environments affect individual development even as individuals

I wish to thank Gilbert Gottlieb for his valuable comments on an early version of this article. Support from the Center for Developmental Science at UNC-Chapel Hill, National Institutes of Mental Health, the Penn State College of Health and Human Development, and the Department of Human Development and Family Studies is gratefully acknowledged.

choose and shape their changing social environments. Two issues, the inevitable embedding of individuals within social contexts and the construction or interpretation of social contexts by individuals, complicates the analysis of developmental process. Even richly elaborated descriptive accounts of individuals and their circumstances, which can be immeasurably valuable for constructing theory, are refractory to analysis in that they typically fail to distinguish among historical/cultural, social, psychological, and biological factors that may be active in specific settings. Correlation and probability-based methods of analysis are useful to describe discrete clusters, embedded and hierarchical clusters, and succession of events over time. In bidirectional or multidirectional sets of relationships, path models offer accounts that fit, along with alternative models that also fit, highlighting the most salient components among those measured as part of a process. Important research using these methods has substantially addressed human aggressive behavior in the major longitudinal studies of Cairns & Cairns (1994), Moffitt, Caspi, Rutter, & Silva (2001), Magnusson (1988), and Tremblay (2000), among others.

The complementary approach is to mount an experimental design. Comparative methods of study using strong controlled and randomized designs can achieve considerable analytical power. Using animal subjects allows for an expansion of the time scale to include studies of life span, multigenerational, and microevolutionary processes. Although the advantages of analytic power are considerable, limits on the generalization of comparative findings provide the counterbalancing factor. Generalizations between relatively close species, such as mice and rats, must be tested, and many strains of mice are variously distinct in social and nonsocial behaviors. That said, studies of animals may give important insights and yield novel questions about the roles of aggressive expression in social relationships, and these often can be directly tested in humans. A comparative approach has been useful in untangling experiential and biological influences in health and behavior (Brunelli & Hofer, 2001; Cacioppo, Berntson, Sheridan, & McClintock, 2000; Kehoe & Shoemaker, 2001), clinical problems (see the special issue of *Hormones and Behavior*, volume 44, edited by Lederhendler, 2003) and aggressive development (Hood, 1996; Miczek, 2001).

Selective breeding is a particularly interesting experimental manipulation because of its ancient origins in the domestication of nonhuman animals, as well as the increased powers harnessed by humans through that process. To briefly review, there is general agreement that the unit of selection is the phenotype of the organism as a whole, in selective breeding and in natural selection. The process of selection is directed in relationship to a particular context, on the farm (for travel, a light fleet horse, but for grinding corn, a placid strong horse) or in the forest (changes in seeds with corresponding changes in beaks of the finch). The further point, made most elegantly by Lewontin (1983), is that organisms are active in choosing and shaping contexts: conspecifics, habitats, diets, and mates. The rapid pace of change over the course of a few generations of selective pressure is remarkable, defying the adage that evolution creeps along imperceptibly. Especially, selection can operate by fine-tuning the rate of development, speeding up to get a larger animal faster (as in commercially raised chickens), or slowing down to prolong juvenile exploration and learning (as in contemporary humans). Because selection operates on the manifested phenotype, it is a holistic operation resulting in a lineage with intended or adaptive changes, often accompanied by other manifest or latent, unidentified characteristics. These may be correlated characters with functional relationships to the criterion for selection, or they may co-occur by accident. Response to selective breeding has been studied with diverse species and with regard to various criteria for selection: social and nonsocial behaviors, size, color, emotional behaviors and reactivity, responses to drugs, maze learning, sensory, physiological, and reproductive characteristics.

A valuable example of such a study is the developmental analysis of Brunelli and Hofer (2001). In order to better understand the development of anxiety disorders in humans, they implemented selective breeding for high or low vocalization during a mild stressor (emotional reactivity) at an early stage of life, in infant rats. The effect of selective breeding for an infantile trait was to alter developmental timing in both lines, with an increased rate of development in the low-reactive line and a decreased rate of development in the high-reactive line. These developmental changes occurred rapidly within three generations of selection, with no evidence of maternal behavioral contributions to pup reactivity in a cross-fostering design (Brunelli, Hofer, & Weller, 2001). Much later in the life span, adult rats that were high and low reactors showed high and low anxiety-like behaviors, respectively, in the elevated plus maze, a test of exploratory behavior (Dichter, Brunelli, & Hofer, 1996).

In the study of aggressive behavior, an extended series of reports originates from the work of Robert B. Cairns. That foundational program of research provides the main focus of this review. Contributions from the Cairns laboratory are remarkable in two areas: a developmental analysis of selective breeding effects in mice, and a landmark longitudinal study of human aggressive development over two generations (e.g., Cairns & Cairns, 1994). Both areas of study are ongoing, providing a multifaceted approach to the understanding of developmental and intergenerational processes related to aggressive expression. The animal studies support investigations of behavior and physiology over the course of selective breeding, for hormones, neurotransmitters, and immune system functioning. The early environment of maternal care as well as social experience with conspecifics have been shown to mediate social and aggressive expression over the course of development.

Related studies from other laboratories are regrettably given short shrift here but deserve full examination for their special merits. The early work of Lagerspetz and Lagerspetz (1971) produced selectively bred lines of mice for high and low aggression with findings that importantly correspond with those from the Cairns group. Sandnabba (e.g., 1996) continues to actively investigate these lineages. Van Oortmerssen independently derived mice that were selectively bred for fast or slow attack (Van Oortmerssen & Bakker, 1981), with research continuing in related biobehavioral domains (Sluyter, Van Oortmerssen, & Koolhaus, 1996).

THE DYADIC INTERCHANGE AS A UNIT OF ANALYSIS

In accord with the precedence of T. C. Schneirla (1957) and Z.-Y. Kuo (1967, 1970), Cairns represents social behavior as a continuous dynamic process, a patterned, rhythmic series of actions, a reciprocal exchange of initiatives and responses in the interchange they construct together. In mice, the elements of exchange are several highly organized, discrete, species typical behavioral forms that occur as correlated reactions between individuals. These may show individual bias in responses to the social stimulation provided by the other. In particular, Cairns' model depicts individuals as embedded in a dyadic social exchange (Figure 10.1: Cairns, 1996). The arrow of

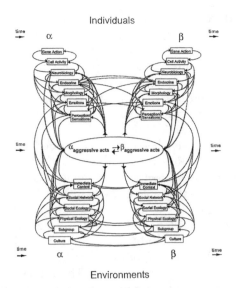

FIGURE 10.1. Schematic representation of two interacting individuals (alpha and beta) within the systems of relationships that have been empirically demonstrated in studies of mice. Arrows represent directionality of time and relationships among factors. Solid lines represent well-established findings, and broken lines represent occasional findings. For citations related to each relationship, see Cairns (1996).

time goes forward, but this figure whirls as the exchange unfolds. Multiple levels of influence can alter the social interchange, including internal (biological) and external (environmental, social) factors. In the figure, the lines and arrows linking levels represent empirical demonstrations of factors that act at other levels of organization to influence aggressive expression within the dyad. Notice that there are no direct connections between genes and behavior. All genetic effects are mediated through other systems that themselves are regulated through elaborate feedback loops. The strongest effects on the aggressive exchange are within the dyad, the social actions of the partner, which also are functions of individual and shared influences at multiple levels.

A unique aspect of Cairns' representation is that he posits the social dyad as the unit of analysis. In the constellation of factors that influence the exchange, horizontal links occur across the dyad at multiple levels: behavioral, endocrine, emotions, immediate context, physical ecology, subgroup, and culture. Vertical links represent relatively independent individual factors, with bidirectional effects at every step. These are integrated within individuals (genetic, cellular, and neurobiological activities, morphology, sensations and perceptions) and within embedded social networks and ecologies of the individual. (Also see the representation of bidirectional levels of influence in Gottlieb, 1991.)

The model resembles a whirlwind, which may characterize energetic aggressive interchanges in particular. Cairns' model implies that stability is itself dynamic, in that stability is maintained by damping responses to disturbances, so that "Even seemingly stable ... behaviors ... reflect a continuing adaptation to internal and external change" (Cairns, 1979, p. 5).

The sequential analysis of interchanges during dyadic encounters is useful, for example, in characterizing individual differences in social reactivity (Cairns & Hood, 1983, p. 338 ff.; Cairns, Hood, & Midlam, 1985). The dyad also can be the unit of analysis in sequential analyses using specific forms of dyadic exchanges (alpha attacks – beta defends) occurring in discrete 5-second intervals. In catastrophe analyses, these exchanges show a nonlinear organization of state transitions for selectively bred mice, but not for mice from the control lines (Hood, Molenaar, & Rovine, in progress).

DEVELOPMENT AS A DEPENDENT VARIABLE

To study aggressive behavior, it must occur reliably and at reasonably high rates. Cairns was among the first to show how to create these conditions among normally peaceable mice. Social experience was not required, but rather the absence of social experience. After 2 weeks of isolation housing, male mice are more likely to fight vigorously and repeatedly in a dyadic social test. An analytical set of studies (Cairns, 1973; Cairns & Scholz, 1973) identified the mediating factor: increased reactivity to tactile stimulation, sniffing and grooming by the test partner, after a week of social isolation.

At least this was true for some males. To further increase the occurrence of fighting by males to levels sufficient for study, Cairns began what turned into an extensive investigation of selective breeding effects on aggression. In two breeding series, starting with outbred ICR mice from different suppliers for each series, within one to four generations, selective breeding for high aggression in one line, and for low aggression in the other line, produced significant line differences in behavior (Cairns, MacCombie, & Hood, 1983; Cairns, Gariépy, & Hood, 1990). The rapidity of selection effects was a surprise. Despite the intent to produce highly aggressive males, the significant change that was produced occurred in the line of low-aggressive males. Low-aggressive line males (with low variability in scores) are significantly different from the foundation stock in each of the breeding series, while the high-aggressive line males (with more variability in scores) show no change from the foundation stock (Figure 10.2). Other selective breeding series also show rapid differentiation of the low line, for

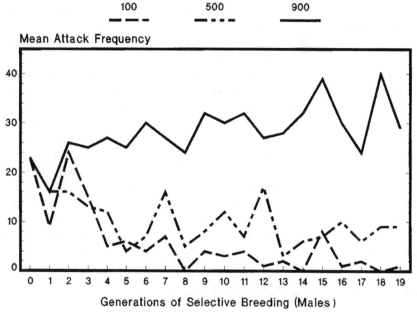

FIGURE 10.2. Selective breeding effects on aggressive behavior in the second series, with generations 12–19 representing descendants of animals brought to Penn State in 1984. 100 refers to the low-aggressive line, 500 refers to the control line, and 900 refers to the high-aggressive line. Selective breeding continued through the 30th generation. Penn State lines were maintained by line breeding in following generations to the present (48th generation).

aggressive behavior (Lagerspetz & Lagerspetz, 1971; van Oortmerssen & Bakker, 1981) and initially, for ultrasonic vocalization (Brunelli & Hofer, 2001; Hofer, Shair, Masmela, & Brunelli, 2001). How are these selective breeding effects realized over generations? In the "developmental–genetic analysis" proposed by Cairns, the expectation was that changes in developmental patterns would play a role in producing selective breeding effects (Cairns, 1976). Changes in developmental patterns might occur through an acceleration of rate of development (progenesis) or a retardation of rate of development (neoteny). If neoteny is the agent of change, one would expect to see youthful characteristics retained longer in the life span over successive generations. Adult characteristics may (or may not) make a delayed appearance. In this mouse model, aggressive behavior typically appears at pubertal maturation, about 35 days of age for a mouse.

Two aspects of the selective breeding protocol were critical for the analysis: age and housing conditions. The age at which selection of males for breeding was made in every generation was young adulthood: days 45 to 64. The criterion for selection was based on aggressive behavior in a 10-minute social-dyadic test, implemented after at least 24 days of isolation housing. Other social behaviors were not considered in selecting males (and their sisters) for breeding. Also notable is that heritability coefficients were never reported in this series of studies, and there was no speculation about single genes or specific gene complexes controlling aggression. Rather, the phenomenon of selective breeding effects was subjected to a range of social–developmental conditions to determine the generality of selection effects or, alternatively, the constraints on expression of social–behavioral changes.

The Developmental–Genetic Analysis

In the first step of the developmental–genetic analysis (Cairns et al., 1983), comparisons of the developmental profile of aggressive expression in the first and fourth generations of animals (in the second of the two breeding series) were made using one-time behavioral assessments of four male siblings assigned to testing at different ages. Because brothers show a relatively high intraclass correlation for aggressive behavior in the dyadic test ($r = .3$ to $.5$; Cairns & Hood, 1983), this "co-sibial" design preserved family differences while avoiding repeated test effects. By the fourth generation of selective breeding (Figure 10.3C), line differences are significant at every age after puberty, that is, as soon as aggressive behavior emerges in the behavioral repertoire after sexual maturation (age 30 to 35 days). However, differences are most clear in young adulthood, the age at which the selection criterion was applied.

The second step of the analysis consists of a comparison of developmental profiles in the first generation and the fourth generation of selective

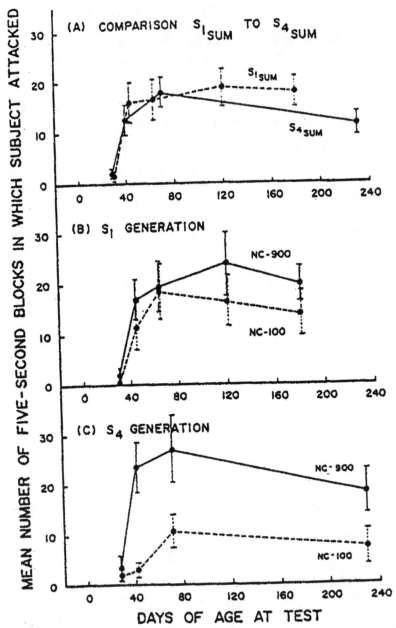

FIGURE 10.3. The developmental–genetic analysis proceeds by comparing the similar overall developmental profiles of two generations, S1 and S4 (A), and then by comparing line differences in developmental profiles within each generation, S1 (B) and S4 (C). Line differences are found in S4 (C) (Cairns et al., 1990).

breeding (S1 and S4 in Figure 10.3). For this comparison, the high and low lines in each generation were combined to show the average score at each age for each generation. Those two generations were compared to assess the presence of intergenerational changes in general developmental rate. Figure 10.3A shows that the two generations are similar. In Figure 10.3B, the failure of the two lines in the S1 generation to differentiate is apparent: No line differences obtain at any age. In Figure 10.3C, the S4 generation, differentiation appears as a flattening of the developmental profile in the low line, so that aggressive behavior fails to appear until later in the life span, well after day 42. This pattern is consistent with the process of neoteny, a prolonged retention of juvenile characteristics. Aggressive behavior is not abolished in the low line: It is delayed. This result supports Cairns' interpretation that developmental and genetic forces can collaborate in producing microevolutionary change (as originally suggested by Gavin DeBeer, 1958). Changes in behavior due to selective breeding (or natural selection, in the wild) may result from alterations in the timing of normative developmental sequences.

In an important confirmation of this finding, Gariépy, Bauer, and Cairns (2001) applied growth curve models to examine changes in developmental patterns over generations, extending the analysis to the 13th generation of selective breeding. Hierarchical linear modeling procedures were applied to assess changes in growth curves among brothers within litters within lines over generations 1, 4, and 13. The investigators replicated neotenous changes in the low-aggressive line. In addition, selective breeding effects are largely complete by the fourth generation, with no evidence for acceleration of the development of attacks in the high-aggressive line. Interestingly, both repeated test effects and the effects of social versus isolation housing on aggressive expression are stable over generations, implying that sensitivity to social experience is not altered by continued selective breeding in these lines, from the foundation stock to the 39th generation (for example, Figure 10.4: Hood, unpublished data).

Selective breeding has correlated effects in another behavior system that is enhanced after isolation housing: freezing, or prolonged tonic immobility in response to tactile stimulation by the partner. Freezing behaviors are typical of very young animals and were not part of the criterion for selective breeding. The remarkable finding was that the low-aggressive line showed elevated rates of freezing throughout the life span, and continued to increase over generations, well after changes in aggressive expression had stabilized (Gariépy, Hood, & Cairns, 1988). Thus, in the low-aggressive line only, freezing responses were retained longer in the life span, and at higher rates, successively through the 13th generation. Socially isolated males from the selectively bred lines are equally reactive to tactile stimulation from a social partner's sniffing and grooming, but they respond in different ways: fighting or freezing.

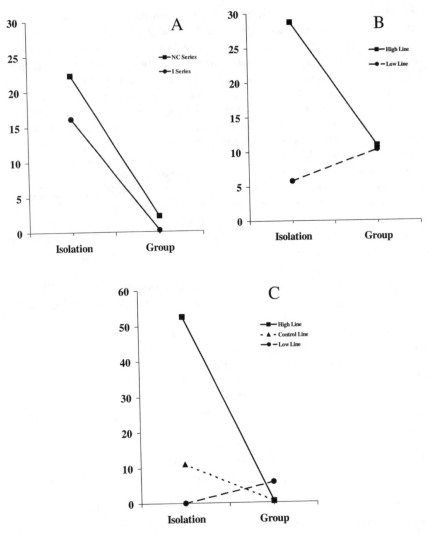

FIGURE 10.4. (A) Attack frequency in a 10-minute test after isolation housing or group housing in the foundation lines for the selective breeding series. The "I Series" began in at Indiana University. The "NC Series" began at the University of North Carolina; these are progenitors of the present colonies. (B) Selectively bred males from the fifth generation are tested after isolation or group housing. (C) Selectively bred males from the 39th generation at Penn State are tested after isolation or group housing, including the comparison control line bred without selection for behavior. At Penn State, selective breeding continued through 30 generations, followed by line breeding.

Understanding Developmental–Genetic Processes

Evidence from the developmental–genetic analyses to date offers a new interpretation of microevolutionary change: that changes in developmental timing, "heterochronic changes can be experimentally manipulated and mapped out systematically over generations," and also that "heterochronic changes may have their origins in the plasticity of the epigenetic process." (Gariépy et al., 2001, p. 933). Cairns (1993) explained how this might come about:

What seem to be Lamarkian outcomes may be achieved through non-Lamarkian mechanisms because the same behavioral outcomes can be addressed through different routes in two time frames. Parallel and mutually supportive behavioral modifications may be rapidly mobilized in ontogeny and evolution by separate processes that act upon the same behavioral components. Evolutionary modifications may occur, developmental accommodations may occur, or both may occur simultaneously. The effects of individual experience upon behavior may look to be heritable when, in fact, the transgenerational effects are mediated through conventional mechanisms of genetic selection and assortative mating. . . .

This bias across generations may arise through one of several channels, including: (a) the biological conditions that give rise to the adoption of the [new] behavior; (b) the contexts preferred by the descendants which, in turn, increase the likelihood of the behavior; or (c) the stimulus properties of descendants that promote certain experiences that lead to adoption of the behavior. These experiences *do not* include the direct genetic transmission of the results of individual experience. Nonetheless, the same behavioral outcome generated in ontogeny can be generated in phylogeny through processes that are appropriate to time-units of microevolution and the phenomona of genetic transmission. . . . It has only been recently discovered how fast an alignment may be produced between experiential mechanisms and genetic mechanisms. Special concepts of cross-generational transfer, whereby experiences act directly on the genome, become superfluous. (pp. 67–69, emphasis in original)

Cairns continues in that discussion to credit Lloyd Morgan, who proposed these possibilities in 1902 as "coincident variation." Similar themes are important in the work of Gilbert Gottlieb (1992), while evidence on "nongenomic transmission" of maternal behavioral tendencies and offspring outcomes supports their feasibility (Denenberg & Rosenberg, 1967; Francis, Diorio, Liu, & Meaney, 1999; Levine, 2001; Liu et al., 1997). Whether these intergenerational similarities can result in differences that persist without the support of the new environment remains to be seen. For an extended discussion of the historical, empirical, and theoretical foundations for this view of the "dual genesis of behavior in evolutionary adaptations and developmental accommodations," see Cairns, Gariépy, and Hood (1990); Cairns and Hood (1983); Gottlieb (1992; and Waddington, 1957). In a similar mode of analysis, Hofer et al. (2001) find heterochrony to underlie their selective breeding process, producing high levels of pup ultrasounds at age 10 days through neoteny (with increased ultrasounds appearing over generations at *earlier* ages also, at ages 3 and 7 days). This group also finds changes due to progenesis, accelerated behavioral maturation with cessation of infantile calls, and correspondingly low levels of ultrasounds at age 10 days in the low line.

Consequent studies in the laboratories at UNC – Chapel Hill and at Penn State followed Cairns et al.'s (1990) further propositions: (1) Changes in aggressive behavior may reflect physiological changes in general developmental rate. (No line differences were found in males' age at onset of puberty: Hood, unpublished data.) (2) Changes in aggressive behavior may be correlated with changes in other behavior systems. (Freezing, behavioral immobility, is negatively associated with aggressive behavior, over development and over generations; Gariépy, Hood, & Cairns, 1988, and in the Lagerspetz lines; Sandnabba, 1996.) (3) Age and experience may be sufficient to eliminate presumed genetic effects in social behavior. (Age effects interact with social or isolation housing: Hood & Cairns, 1989.) (4) These effects may not generalize to interactions in different ecological settings, or in longer behavioral assessments (confirmed by Berg & Hood, unpublished data; Gariépy, 1995). (5) Female behaviors may be similar to those of their male siblings. (High-line females are more aggressive: Hood, 1988; Hood and Cairns, 1988; similar results obtain with the Lagerspetz lines; Sandnabba, 1993.) Together, these studies extend the domains under which selective breeding effects have been assessed for "organism by experience by development" interactions.

GENOTYPE–ENVIRONMENT INTERACTIONS AS
DEVELOPMENTAL PLASTICITY

The concept of genotype–environment interaction implies an interdependence of individual (genetic) and contextual factors in the expression of an outcome of interest. The very existence of environments that qualify genetic effects was denied by some behavior geneticists until recent findings forced a reconsideration. Failures to confirm some behavioral outcomes across laboratories, even under the best of controlled conditions and using genetically identical mice (e.g., Crabbe, Wahlsten, & Dudek, 1999) has resurrected the issue forcefully. Happily, one investigator's source of error is another investigator's opportunity. G × E interactions are grist for the developmental-genetic analysis, with a focus on the proviso that age or developmental stage may interact with genetic and environmental/ experiential factors to produce a G × E × D interaction. Higher order interactions such as these may point to openings in the developmental timetable where new behavioral adaptations can emerge.

Housing and Social Experience Effects

Cairns' early demonstration of isolation housing effects was replicated in both of the foundation lines used for selective breeding (Figure 10.4A). Only after isolation housing were significant levels of aggressive behavior observed in these foundational males. The comparison was repeated with the selectively bred lines to show a G × E interaction: Significant line differences in the fifth generation obtain only after isolation housing. High-line males reared in groups are identical to low-line males in the dyadic test (Figure 10.4B). In the 39th generation, again the pattern obtains, with the control line intermediate to the selectively bred lines (Figure 10.4C). Using a selection procedure that includes isolation housing has created line differences – but they are manifest only under the exact conditions established during the process of selective breeding.

Recent research using an early handling paradigm (Gariépy, Rodriguiz, & Jones, 2002) shows that handling effects in these lines also depend on postweaning social or isolation housing, as well as social or nonsocial conditions of testing. (Also see the section on neurotransmitters, below.)

Age-Related Interactions

In the first round of investigations (Cairns et al., 1983), isolation-reared males with their first test at different ages show developmental patterns that vary by line (Figure 10.5). When tests are repeated for each male, the lines converge. After repeated tests, males show no line difference at age 235: Low-line males are equally quick to attack as high-line males. By contrast, males tested for the first time at that age *do* show significant line differences. In this design, age-related changes are evident when housing conditions exclude social experience. In first tests conducted over the life span, increased readiness to attack obtains for both lines with increased age.

Housing and Age-Related Interactions

Confirmatory findings in the S5, S6, and S9 generations are based on both dyadic tests and intruder tests in the home cage, with isolation-reared and group-reared males from 46 to 200 days of age (Hood & Cairns, 1989). Generally, only isolate males show line differences. However, a striking inversion in developmental expression of effects is seen after continuous group housing, with no line difference in males at age 46 (the age of selection) and an emergence of high levels of attacks much later in life in high-line males. Repeated test effects are not as powerful for group-reared males, in that repeated longitudinal tests and first tests in late life produce identical results (compare to Figure 10.5).

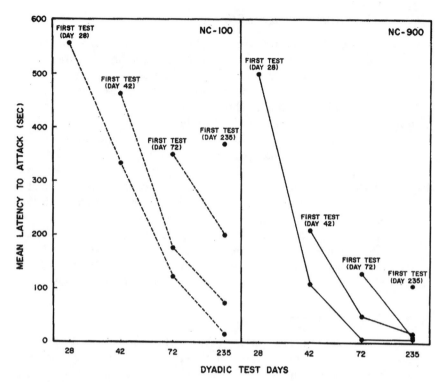

FIGURE 10.5. "Genotype" by experience by development interactions are evident in mean latency to attack (in seconds) in the low-aggressive (left panel) and the high-aggressive (right panel) selectively bred lines as a function of the age at which the first dyadic test was given. Each curve represents a longitudinal test series, with groups beginning at different ages (Cairns, Gariépy, & Hood, 1990).

Spontaneous aggressive exchanges in long-established groups of same-line males (age 200 days) were given a close examination. Over 7 days of observation, no line differences were found in attack frequency or total duration of spontaneous attack sequences. However, line differences were found in the organizational pattern over time, with more frequent bouts of shorter duration, occurring more consistently over the 7 days of observation in the high-aggressive line. By contrast, when these same males later were moved into new groups with unfamiliar males and observed for 10 minutes, robust and predictable line differences were observed: High-aggressive males attacked faster and more frequently (Hood & Cairns, 1989). Gariépy (1995) reports a parallel outcome using male–female groups, with the additional finding of a time effect: In trials of longer duration, line differences in males disappear after 30 or 40 minutes (also corroborated by Berg and Hood, unpublished data).

In summary, the more we look, the more we find interactions that open up the effects of selective breeding for new responses to specific environments. The possibility that these may suffice to perpetuate favorable responses links transgenerational developmental accommodations with processes of evolutionary change. Also notable is that what varies is not the ethological form of the behavior under selection pressure, but the frequency and latency parameters of its occurrence, its intensity, and patterns of occurrence over hours and days. Low-line males' attacks, when they occur, have the form of high-line attacks, with similar precursor movements, behavioral components, and interactional sequences. From this perspective, the result is that after 30 generations of selective breeding, the behavior itself shows no change, but the conditions under which it occurs have changed immensely.

BIOLOGICAL ASPECTS OF GENOTYPE–ENVIRONMENT INTERACTIONS

What are the biological components, substrates, or consequences of selective breeding effects on aggression? At the genetic level, little is known about these outbred lines of mice except that transmission is autosomal. This deduction is based on the finding that females resemble their brothers in aggressive behavior, although selection was based entirely on the behavior of males. When females are tested appropriately, for example, in tests of maternal behavior, female line differences in maternal aggression are more pronounced than line differences in males (Hood & Cairns, 1989).

Hormones

Selected hormonal systems have been plumbed, with mainly negative results (but see the later discussion on responses to immune stimulation). Although female aggressive behavior varies over the ovulatory cycle in these mice (Hood, unpublished data), for males neither testosterone nor corticosterone response patterns distinguishes the selectively bred lines at rest (Gariépy & Rodriguiz, 2002; Hood & Jones, in progress). However, after brief social encounters with novel male conspecifics, high-aggressive line males which are likely to attack show higher corticosterone than low-aggressive line males which are likely to freeze upon social contact (Hood & Jones, in progress). When introduced to nonsocial novel environments, low-line adult males showed higher corticosterone responses than high-line males. However, low-line males that had a handling experience as neonates, or that were reared in social groups, showed attenuated corticosterone responses to the novel environment (Gariépy & Rodriguiz, 2002).

Neurotransmitters

Of the several neurotransmitter systems that have been studied in these lines of mice, two systems are of interest: the dopamine system, a highly localized neural system that is implicated in the initiation of behavioral actions, and the GABA (gamma-aminobutyric acid) system, a diffuse and ubiquitous neural system that modulates or inhibits neurotransmission in other neural systems.

Studies by Gariépy and colleagues on changes in the dopamine system show that dopamine patterns in the limbic system depend on both selective breeding and social experience. Line differences consist of lower levels of dopamine and more dopamine receptors (in nucleus accumbens and caudate nucleus) in isolate-reared low-line males compared to high-line males. In the low-aggressive line, isolation housing fails to produce the increase in D1 receptor density (in caudate-putamen) that is found in isolation-reared high-line males. Moreover, the increase in high-line males after isolation housing is reversible by changing housing conditions to group rearing (Gariépy, Gendreau, Mailman, Tancer, & Lewis, 1995). Both lines show increased D1 receptors in response to early handling stimulation (Gariépy et al., 2002).

These findings indicated the usefulness of an experimental manipulation of the dopamine system. Dopamine activation (through administration of a D1 receptor-specific agonist) of isolation-reared males disrupts typical social behaviors in both lines, due to treatment-related increases in social reactivity (kicking, jumping, and vocalizing to social stimulation). The same treatment produces no effects on behaviors in group-reared males from each line (Gariépy, Gendreau, Cairns, & Lewis, 1998; Lewis, Gariépy, Gendreau, Nichols, & Mailman, 1994; Gariépy, Lewis, & Gendreau, 1996 also see the chapter by Gendreau and Lewis, this volume.) The dopamine system appears to mediate isolation-reared subjects' sensitivity to social stimulation, which is a product of both line and social experience. Turning up the dopamine system to very high levels elevates social reactivity preemptively, with startle responses in the low-line and active evasion in the high-line isolation-reared males (Gariépy & Rodriguiz, 2002).

To investigate the GABA system in these lines, measures of naturally occurring GABA system activity as well as receptor density assays and experimental manipulations of the GABA system were carried out (Weerts, Miller, Hood, & Miczek, 1992). The GABA-α, receptor complex contains a binding site for benzodiazepines (anxiety-reducing agents such as Valium) that facilitates GABA binding and activity. Treatment with benzodiazepines generally reduces aggressive behavior in humans and animals. In naive males from the selectively bred lines, GABA-α receptor density shows line differences, with high, moderate, and low levels of binding in the low, control, and high lines, respectively (in cortex, hypothalamus, and hippocampus). Endogenous receptor functioning (GABA-dependent chloride uptake) also shows high, moderate, and low levels of functioning in the low, control, and high lines, respectively. Increasing GABA function with benzodiazepine treatment alters social behaviors in unexpected patterns: decreased aggression accompanied by increased social exploration in the high line, and no changes in the low-aggressive line. The low line shows high endogenous levels of GABA activity, whereas augmentation of GABA functioning in the high line causes their social behaviors to converge with the typical pattern of low-line males.

These findings are of particular interest because measures of receptor binding density and activation at the neuronal membrane (chloride uptake) are more direct indicators of system effects than measures of neurotransmitter levels and turnover rates. What is lacking is the test of GABA system reactivity after group housing or repeated testing. Whether the GABA system is involved in genotype–environment interactions is unknown at present. However, studies are in progress to determine the extent of line differences in anxiety (Hood & Quigley, in progress) and social behaviors, with GABA agonist and inverse agonist agents administered in each line (Hood & Dacal, in progress).

GABA mediated responses to alcohol show sex differences, line differences, and housing effects (Reed, Hood, Cortes, & Jones, 2001). Most affected are low-aggressive line females reared in isolation, which are slowest to acquire tolerance to a standard dose of alcohol. This outcome points to low-line females as uniquely susceptible to behavioral disruption, a finding that will be expanded in observations of maternal behavior.

In a converse approach to this question, using a mouse model, selective breeding for sensitivity to a GABA inverse agonist (β-CCM) proceeded rapidly (Chapoutier, Launay, Venault, Breton, Robertoux, & Crusio, 1998), with associated changes in aggressive behavior that conform to the pattern we have found in our selectively bred lines (Guillot, Sluyter, Crusio, & Chapoutier, 1999). These convergent findings support the expectation that GABA system functioning modulates aggressive expression in particular and that it may serve as a system for behavioral modulation in multiple domains.

Immune System Function

Strong replication is found in various models of immune response implemented in the laboratories at UNC and Penn State that the high line is more reactive to immune system stimulation than the low line. Higher levels of response are found in high-aggressive line males and females, in spleen weight, corticosterone production and CRF (Granger et al., 1997), natural killer cells, interleukin-2, interleukin-6, and interferon production

(Granger, Hood, & Banta, submitted; Petitto, Lysle, Gariépy, & Lewis, 1994).
Housing conditions do not alter these responses (Petitto et al., 1999).

Does immune system stimulation cause short-term or long-term changes in social behavior? Are some types of individuals more susceptible to the effects of this type of stressor? Early studies demonstrated that injection of an immune stimulant sufficient to induce a transient flulike state causes more extreme physiological responses, including corticosterone response, in the high line. In dyadic tests 24 hours after injection, both lines show increased freezing and decreased social exploration, with reduced aggression in the high-aggressive line (Granger et al., 1997). Immune stimulation during the neonatal period (age 5 or 6 days) also causes changes in adult social behaviors, with increased reactivity in both lines, and in the high line, decreased aggression and increased freezing. Changes in reactivity are associated with changes in CRF in the high line, but not in the low line (Granger, Hood, Ikeda, Reed, & Block, 1996).

Developmental questions about how this early experience could affect behaviors much later in life led to two main hypotheses. A physiological pathway of direct effects of immune system products specifies a cascade of physiological effects including alterations in stress-response thresholds in the HPA axis, which would be manifested in social–behavioral responses to a novel conspecific. The most credible alternative pathway is through alterations in maternal behaviors during and after the induction of a brief (1-day) pup illness. Maternal behaviors have been shown to mediate the development of HPA stress-response thresholds in rat pups (Liu et al., 1997). It seems credible that developmentally acquired levels of stress reactivity may play a role in the expression of aggression during socially stressful encounters.

MATERNAL MEDIATION OF NEONATAL STRESSORS

Cairns' intergenerational studies necessarily raise the issue of dyadic mediation through the embedded reciprocities of early dam–pup interactions. We investigated the possibility of line differences in maternal mediation using a reciprocal cross-fostering design (Hood, Dreschel, & Granger, 2002). Early social interactions among dams and litters were observed in undisturbed litters, and after one of two stressors, an intraperitoneal injection of saline to all pups in the litter, or an injection of LPS to all pups. LPS is a lipopolysaccharide cell fragment that stimulates the immune system to mimic the effects of a transient illness. We were interested in the possibility that maternal behavior (licking of pups, in particular) would provide a nongenomic pathway for intergenerational transmission of behavioral phenotypes (as in Liu et al., 1997; Francis, Diorio, Liu, & Meaney, 1999).

In the reciprocal cross-fostering design, we designated dams from the three selectively-bred lines to receive foster pups from the control line. In the complementary component of the design, pups from the three lines were cross-fostered to control-line dams. The design provides these comparisons for analysis:

1. Selectively bred dams (high or low line) reared with neutral (control line) pups reveal effects of dam-line behaviors on pups.
2. Selectively bred pups (high or low line) reared with neutral (control line) dams reveal pup-line effects on early social interactions and later social development.
3. Neutral dams rearing neutral foster pups (control line) provide comparison groups.
4. Administration of a stressor (immune stimulation by LPS injection, compared to saline controls) reveals effects of pup stress on early social relationships and later social development within each cross-fostering condition.

Analyses are presently available from the first and third groups: three types of dams reared with foster control-line pups (Hood, Dreschel, & Granger, 2002). For the present discussion, we will consider exploratory comparisons of these results to parallel studies of dams rearing their own pups in the selectively bred and control lines (Granger, Hood & Dreschel, 2001). Of many findings, including line differences in maternal behaviors, we focus here on one particular configuration: patterns of social development in pups that are related to maternal behaviors in the first week of life.

Maternal Effects on Adult Social Development

The finding of line-specific patterns of dam and pup line effects in the cross-fostering study are of particular interest, suggesting that pup and dam behaviors tend to shape social development in complementary directions. These result from inextricably embedded, age-limited, and specialized interactions of dams and neonates. They exemplify Cairns' proposal that the analysis of dyadic interactions may yield unique perspectives on processes that underlie social development. Three summary statements indicate the most salient patterns in the series of observations of early dam–pup interactions, and the social-developmental outcomes of pups grown into young adults, 40 days later.

(1) *Low-aggressive line dams* produce young males with *decreased social exploration* (sniffing or grooming during a 10-minute dyadic encounter with a novel same-age male), compared with those reared by control-line dams. This dam–line effect holds for low-line pups, and also for fostered control-line pups that are stressed, that is, LPS treated, compared to controls (Granger, Hood, Dreschel, Sergeant, & Likos, 2001; Hood et al., 2002, Tables 2 and 4). Low-line females are most sensitive to disruption. After

LPS injections and return of pups to the dam, observed maternal behaviors were extremely ineffective, with long latency to retrieve pups and more time off-nest.

(2) Control-line pups that are stressed by LPS in early life show opposite outcomes as adults, compared to saline-treated controls, depending on their dam's line of descent. *Control-line dams* produce young males with *increased social exploration*; In contrast, *low-line dams* produce young males with *decreased social exploration* (Hood et al., 2002). Control-line dams are unflappable, with little disruption of maternal care. High levels of licking of LPS-treated pups correlates with lower levels of later aggressive behaviors by young males.

(3) *High-aggressive line dams* uniquely produce effects on aggressive behavior – but not other social behaviors – even when rearing fostered control-line pups. High-line dams rearing LPS-stressed pups from their own line or fostered pups from the control line produce young males with *decreased aggressive behavior* (attacks with wrestling and biting), compared to saline-treated controls (Granger et al., 2001; Hood et al., 2002). High-line dams are moderately disruptable, and again high licking of LPS-treated pups correlates with lower levels of later aggressive behaviors by young males.

These dam–pup patterns appear to be enacted through behaviors related to the intimate early environment of lactation and mutual stimulation by pups and dams, with different elements of maternal behavior predicting pup outcomes in the different dam lines. The puzzle of how aggressive behaviors in control-line pups are altered by maternal behaviors of high-aggressive dams is addressed by dams' high levels of licking directed at stressed pups (and in control-line dams as well, although to a lesser extent). Direct measures of stress reactivity (as in Liu et al. 1999) would be useful in assessing the mode through which effective maternal moderation of offspring social behavior occurs.

The particularity of these developmental pathways strikes a similar chord to the observation of Hofer et al. (2001, pp. 237–238), that individual rat pups in their selectively bred lines showed idiosyncratic developmental pathways that did not conform to group means. These parallel outcomes suggest that a variety of processes are in play within each group of animals. However, a cross-fostering study by the same group, using rat pups selectively bred for high or low levels of vocalizing at age 10 days, showed no maternal effects (Brunelli et al., 2001).

Selective Breeding Effects on Dam–Pup Relationships?

These empirical outcomes suggest a fresh perspective on the origins of selective breeding effects. The patterns of dam and pup outcomes in our findings to date are consistent with the possibility that selective breeding (and natural selection) may operate on multiple levels, including the level of *relationships* among dams and pups. Such a possibility would imply that selection pressure for dam behavior operates within the context of relevant pup characteristics, and vice versa. Dam and pup characteristics such as intensity of stimulation provided to the other, and response threshold to stimulation provided by the other, may vary in different interactional domains of dam–pup relationships: lactation, manual and oral stimulation, temperature regulation, vocalization, maintenance of the nest, and the pup huddle. To ascertain how selection for relationships would manifest in any specific setting calls for exquisite observational discipline and exacting manipulation of pup and dam properties.

It is further remarkable that individual differences in dam behaviors among the low-line dams, whose maternal behavior typically is *most* disrupted by pup LPS treatment, produced significant effects in the next generation. For those low-line dams with maternal responsiveness that was *not* disrupted by pup illness, *increased maternal responsiveness* is related to *more social exploration* by foster offspring as adults. Even within this high-risk group of low-line dams, individual competencies are effective in preserving more favorable outcomes for pups. By contrast, no correlations were found between maternal changes in responsiveness and social exploration in litters reared by control or high-line dams (Hood et al., 2002).

These interpretations reflect the intriguing proposition by Gottlieb and Halpern (2002) that the most likely level for the realization of causal effects in development resides in relationships among variables, rather than in variables themselves. Accordingly, selective breeding effects for social outcomes might most effectively operate on the social milieu, the interindividual relationships that constitute a developmental context in which the social outcome is likely to emerge. This possibility is illustrated by our confirmation of the reports (Liu et al., 1997; Francis et al., 1999) that maternal licking provides a pathway for intergenerational effects on behavior. In our study, high maternal licking is correlated with lower aggression in control-line adults that had been foster reared, but only for those reared with control-line dams or high-line dams, that is, dams from lines in which aggressive behavior is likely to occur. In these lines, maternal behaviors such as licking may be fine-tuned to modulate the later aggressive expression of their own offspring (Hood et al., 2002).

IMPLICATIONS FOR THE UNDERSTANDING OF AGGRESSIVE BEHAVIOR

It is tempting to redraw the Cairns model of developmental synthesis (Figure 10.1) using only the empirical findings garnered to date from these multiple avenues of investigation of the Cairns lines of mice. However, that would be premature. New investigations with these animals are under way to support the realization of the Cairns model as a fully contextualized bidirectional dyadic exchange, including specific identified genes as embedded in and reactive to elements at other levels of the coactional system, changing over development and over generations of selective pressure. In our future studies, we do not expect to find that one key factor, such as a gene or a set of genes, tilts the balance to cause aggressive behavior. Testosterone is not the key; rather it is social experience that alters testosterone and corticosterone response levels in these males. Brain metabolism in high-aggressive line males shows high levels of dopamine (for initiation of action), and low levels of GABA system modulation – but only after social isolation. Adaptation in the transition from isolation to a social context occurs within an hour: high-aggressive line males become appropriately prosocial, and low-aggressive line males become well able to fight. A coordinated assembly of genetic, neuro-hormonal, and behavioral factors constitute the critical surround of social beings over generations, and this is transmuted, partly through maternal-offspring interactions, to change – not aggressive behavior itself, but the conditions under which it occurs, and the age at which it appears.

The study of aggressive behavior in humans has expanded to encompass these issues, including distinctions among different forms and meanings of related behaviors. Physical aggression, as distinct from verbal aggression and from other forms of antisocial behavior, offers particular predictive value for longitudinal outcomes (Tremblay, 2000). With a more differentiated analysis of circumstances and outcomes related to specific forms of aggression, more incisive results become available, such as the intriguing finding from Pulkinnen's (1993) distinction of forms of aggressive expression among girls. Close inspection (by factor analysis) of teachers' ratings revealed that in 8-year-old children, girls with higher levels of facial aggression attained higher levels of education in later life. Early verbal and physical aggression by girls did not relate to positive outcomes (Pulkinnen, 1993). This suggests that conceptualizations of aggressive expression might usefully include normative social responses in support of self-development. Moreover, the normative patterns and meanings of aggression are not fixed across time and place. The developmental analysis of Cairns and Cairns (1994) explicitly proposes that "The properties of the construct of 'aggression' change over development. At each developmental stage, the construct reflects the social judgments of society, the social attributes of researchers, and the social constructions of the self" (p. 278). In this sense, aggression is in the eye of the beholder: even physically aggressive children are likely to view their own actions as defensive rather than aggressive (Cairns & Cairns, 1994).

A recent finding of genotype–environment interaction in the development of aggression in humans (Caspi et al., 2002) is remarkable both for its scientific value and for the social implications that were appended to the result. An identified genetic variant that decreases monoamine oxidase activity is related to the development of aggressive and antisocial behavior, but only for those children subjected to early stress through familial maltreatment. The closing remark in that report suggests that pharmacological treatments may be at hand for children in abusive families. From another perspective, one might recommend an ecological approach: reducing familial maltreatment through social interventions that are presently available. Social interventions that have reduced harm from tobacco use (in the U.S.) and bullying can inform those efforts.

The emerging analysis of multi-level dynamics in human development includes genetic, neural, hormonal, organ systems functioning, behavior, contexts for behavior, and developmental effects such as the setting of response thresholds. Appropriate metaphors are most useful at this stage. Cairns notably remarked that "Behavioral processes are more akin to brain metabolism than brain structure." (1993, p. 64) With respect to the emerging complexities of brain functioning, this serves as a caution indeed. However, Cairns also proposed that by fully taking into account the complexities of behavioral development, its simplicity ultimately will be revealed. The intellectual lineage that Cairns has carried forward proposes that the active organism and the manifold of relevant environmental opportunities provide both stability and openings for "fresh adaptations" throughout the life span (also see Gottlieb, 2003; Hood, 1995; Michel & Moore, 1995.)

Articulation of the features that are open to these changes and the factors and forces that bring them about will constitute the field of developmental science as it was first proposed by Robert B. Cairns (1979; Cairns, Elder & Costello, 1996).

References

Brunelli, S. A. & Hofer, M. A. (2001). Selective breeding for an infantile phenotype (isolation calling): A window on developmental processes. In E. Blass (Ed.), *Developmental psychobiology, Vol. 13, Handbook of behavioral neurobiology*. New York: Kluwer.

Brunelli, S. A., Hofer, M. A., & Weller, A. (2001). Selective breeding for infant vocal responses: A role for postnatal maternal effects? *Developmental Psychobiology, 38*, 221–228.

Cacioppo, J. T., Berntson, G. G., Sheridan, J. F., & McClintock, M.K. (2000). Multilevel integrative analyses of human behavior: Social neuroscience and the complementing nature of social and biological approaches. *Psychological Bulletin, 126*, 829–843.

Cairns, R. B. (1973). Fighting and punishment from a developmental perspective. In J. K. Cole & D. D. Jensen (Eds.), *Nebraska Symposium on Motivation* (Vol. 20, pp. 59–124). Lincoln: University of Nebraska Press.

Cairns, R. B. (1976). The ontogeny and phylogeny of social interactions. In M. E. Hahn & E. C. Simmel (Eds.), *Communicative behavior and evolution*. New York Academic Press.

Cairns, R. B. (1979). *Social development: The origins and plasticity of social interchanges.* San Francisco: Freeman.

Cairns, R. B. (1993). Belated but bedazzling: Timing and genetic influences in social development. In G. Turkewitz & D. A. Devenny (Eds.) *Developmental time and timing.* Hillsdale, NJ: Erlbaum Associates.

Cairns, R. B. (1996). Aggression from a developmental perspective: Genes, environments, and interactions. In M. Rutter (Ed.), *Genetics of criminal and antisocial behavior, Ciba Foundation Symposium No. 194* (pp. 45–60). London: John Wiley & Sons.

Cairns, R. B., & Cairns, B. D. (1994). *Lifelines and risks: Pathways of youth in our time.* Hemel Hempstead (UK): Harvester Wheatsheaf and New York: Cambridge University Press.

Cairns, R. B., Elder, G. H. Jr., & Costello, E. J. (1996). (Eds.), *Developmental science.* New York: Cambridge University Press.

Cairns, R. B., Gariépy, J.-L., & Hood, K. E. (1990). Development, microevolution, and social behavior. *Psychological Review, 97,* 49–65.

Cairns, R. B., & Hood, K. E. (1983). Continuity in social development: A comparative perspective on individual difference prediction. In P. B. Baltes & O. G. Brim, Jr. (Eds.), *Life-span developmental psychology: Vol. 5.* New York: Academic Press.

Cairns, R. B., Hood, K. E., & Midlam, J. (1985). On fighting in mice: Is there a sensitive period for isolation effects? *Animal Behaviour, 33,* 166–180.

Cairns, R. B., MacCombie, D. J., & Hood, K. E. (1983). A developmental–genetic analysis of aggressive behavior in mice: I. Behavioral outcomes. *Journal of Comparative Psychology, 97,* 69–89.

Cairns, R. B., & Scholz, S. D. (1973). On fighting in mice: Dyadic escalation and what is learned. *Journal of Comparative and Physiological Psychology, 85,* 540–550.

Caspi, A., McClay, J., Moffitt, T. E., Mill, J., Martin, J., Craig, I. W., Taylor, A., & Poulton, R. (2002). Role of genotype in the cycle of violence in maltreated children. *Science, 297,* 851–854.

Chapoutier, G., Launay, J.-M., Venault, P., Breton, C., Robertoux, P. L., & Crusio, W. E. (1998). Genetic selection of mouse lines differing in sensitivity to a benzodiazepine receptor inverse agonist. *Brain Research, 787,* 85–90.

Crabbe, J. C., Wahlsten, D., & Dudek, B. C. (1999). Genetics of mouse behavior: interactions with lab environment. *Science, 284,* 1670–1672.

DeBeer, G. (1958). *Embyros and ancestors* (3rd ed.). London: Oxford Universtiy Press.

Denenberg, V. H. & Rosenberg, K. M. (1967). Nongenetic transmission of information. *Nature, 10,* 459–550.

Dichter, G. S., Brunelli, S. A., & Hofer, M. A. (1996). Elevated plus-maze behavior in adult offspring of selectively bred rats. *Physiology and Behavior, 60,* 299–304.

Francis, D., Diorio, J., Liu, D. & Meaney, M. (1999). Nongenomic transmission across generations of maternal behavior and stress responses in the rat. *Science, 286,* 1155–1158.

Gariépy, J.-L., Bauer, D. J., & Cairns, R. B. (2001). Selective breeding for differential aggression in mice provides evidence for heterochrony in social behaviors. *Animal Behaviour, 61,* 933–947.

Gariépy, J.-L., Gendreau, P. L., Cairns, R. B., & Lewis, M. H. (1998). D_1 dopamine receptors and the reversal of isolation-induced behaviors in mice. *Behavioural Brain Research, 95,* 103–111.

Gariépy, J.-L., Gendreau, P. L., Mailman, R. B., Tancer, M., & Lewis, M. L. (1995). Rearing conditions alter social reactivity and D1 dopamine receptors in high- and low-aggressive mice. *Pharmacology, Biochemistry, and Behavior, 51*, 767–773.

Gariépy, J.-L., Hood, K. E., & Cairns, R. B. (1988). A developmental–genetic analysis of aggressive behavior in mice: III. Behavioral mediation by heightened reactivity or immobility? *Journal of Comparative Psychology, 102*, 392–399.

Gariepy, J.-L., Lewis, M. H. & Cairns, R. B. (1996). Genes, neurobiology, and aggression: Time frames and functions of social behaviors in adaptation. In D. M. Stoff & R. B. Cairns (Eds.), *Aggression and violence: Genetic, neurobiological, and biosocial perspectives*. Mahwah, NJ: Erlbaum.

Gariepy, J.-L. & Rodriguiz, R. (2002). Issues of establishment, consolidation, and reorganization in biobehavioral adaptation. *Brain and Mind, 3*, 53–77.

Gariépy, J.-L., Rodriguiz, R. M., & Jones, B. C. (2002). Handling, genetic and housing effects on the mouse stress system, dopamine function, and behavior. *Pharmacology, Biochemistry, and Behavior, 73*, 7–17.

Gottlieb, G. G. (1991). Experiential canalization of behavioral development: Theory. *Developmental Psychology, 27*, 4–13.

Gottlieb, G. (1992). *Individual development and evolution: The genesis of novel behavior.* New York: Oxford University Press

Gottlieb, G. (1998). Normally occurring environmental and behavioral influences on gene activity: From central dogma to probabilistic epigenesis. *Psychological Review, 105*, 792–802.

Gottlieb, G. (2003). On making behavioral genetics truly developmental. *Human Development, 46*, 337–355.

Gottlieb, G., & Halpern, C. T. (2002). A relational view of causality in normal and abnormal development. *Development and Psychopathology, 14*, 1–15.

Granger, D. A., Hood, K. E., & Dreschel, N. (2001). Developmental effects of early immune stress on aggressive, socially reactive, and inhibited behaviors. *Development and Psychopathology. 13*, 597–608.

Granger, D. A., Hood, K. E., Ikeda, S. C., Reed, C. L., & Block, M. L. (1996). Neonatal endotoxin exposure alters the development of social behavior and the hypothalamic–pituitary–adrenal axis in selectively bred mice. *Brain, Behavior, and Immunity, 10*, 249–259.

Granger, D. A., Hood, K. E., Ikeda, S. C., Reed, C. L., Jones, B. C., & Block, M. L. (1997). Effects of peripheral immune activation on social behavior and adrenocortical activity in aggressive mice: Genotype–environment interactions. *Aggressive Behavior, 23*, 93–105.

Guillot, P. V., Sluyter, F., Crusio, W. E., & Chapoutier, G. (1999). Mice selected for differences in sensitivity to a benzodiazepine receptor inverse agonist vary in intermale aggression. *Neurogenetics, 2*, 171–175.

Hofer, M. A., Shair, H. N., Masmela, J. R., & Brunelli, S. A. (2001). Developmental effects of selective breeding for an infantile trait: The rat pup ultrasonic isolation call. *Developmental Psychobiology, 39*, 231–246.

Hood, K. E. (1988). Female aggression in [albino ICR] mice: Development, social experience, and the effects of selective breeding (*Mus musculus*). *International Journal of Comparative Psychology, 2*, 27–41.

Hood, K. E. (1995). Dialectical and dynamical systems of approach and withdrawal: Is fighting a fractal form? In K. Hood, G. Greenberg, & E. Tobach (Eds.), *Behavioral development: Concepts of approach-withdrawal and integrative levels, Vol. 5, The T. C. Schneirla Conference Series* (pp. 19–76). New York: Garland.

Hood, K. E. (1996). Intractable tangles of sex and gender in women's aggressive behavior: An optimistic view. In D. M. Stoff & R. B. Cairns (Eds.). *Aggression and violence: genetic, neurobiological, and biosocial perspectives* (pp. 309–335). Mahwah, NJ: Erlbaum.

Hood, K. E., & Cairns, R. B. (1988). A developmental–genetic analysis of aggressive behavior in mice: II. Cross-sex inheritance. *Behavior Genetics, 18,* 605–619.

Hood, K. E., & Cairns, R. B. (1989). A developmental–genetic analysis of aggressive behavior in mice: IV. Genotype-environment interaction. *Aggressive Behavior, 15,* 361–380.

Hood, K. E., Dreschel, N. A., & Granger, D. A. (2002). Maternal behavior changes after immune challenge of neonates with developmental effects on adult social behavior. *Developmental Psychobiology, 42,* 17–34.

Kehoe, P. & Shoemaker, W. (2001). Infant stress, neuroplasticity, and behaivor. In E. M. Blass (Ed.). *Developmental Psychobiology. Vol. 13, Handbook of Behavioral Neurobiology.* New York: Kluwer Academic/Plenum.

Kuo, Z. Y. (1967). *The dynamics of behavior development: An epigenetic view.* New York: Random House. Second edition (1976). *The dynamics of behavior development: An epigenetic view.* New York: Plenum.

Kuo, Z. Y. (1970). The need for coordinated efforts in developmental studies. In A. Aronson, E. Tobach, D. S. Lehrman, & J. S. Rosenblatt (Eds.) *Development and evolution of behavior: Essays in memory of T. C. Schneirla* (pp. 181–193). San Francisco: W. H. Freeman.

Lagerspetz, K., & Lagerspetz, K. Y. H. (1971). Changes in the aggressiveness of mice resulting from selective breeding, learning, and social isolation. *Scandinavian Journal of Psychology, 12,* 241–248.

Lederhendler, I. (2003). (Ed.) Aggression and violence: Perspectives on integrating animal and human research approaches. *Hormones and Behavior (Special Issue), 44.*

Lerner, R. M. (1998). Theories of human development: contemporary perspectives. In W. Damon (Series Ed.) & R. M. Lerner (Vol. Ed.), *Handbook of child psychology: Vol.1. Theoretical models of human development.* New York: Wiley.

Levine, S. (2001). Primary social relationships influence the development of the hypothalamic – pituitary – adrenal axis in the rat. *Physiology & Behavior, 73,* 255–260.

Lewis, M. H., Gariépy, J.-L., Gendreau, P., Nichols, D. E., & Mailman, R. B. (1994). Social reactivity and D_1 dopamine receptors: Studies in mice selectively bred for high and low levels of aggression. *Neuropsychopharmacology, 10,* 115–122.

Lewontin, R. C. (1983). The organism as the subject and object of evolution. *Scientia, 118,* 63–82.

Liu, D., Diorio, J., Tannenbaum, B., Caldji, C., Francis, D., Freedman, A., et al. (1997). Maternal care, hippocampal glucocorticoid receptors, and hypothalamic–pituitary–adrenal responses to stress. *Science, 277,* 1659–1662.

Magnusson, D. (1988). Individual development from an interactional perspective: A longitudinal study (Vol.1) In D. Magnusson (Ed.), *Paths through Life.* Hillsdale, NJ: Erlbaum.

Michel, G. F. & Moore, C. L. (1995). *Developmental psychobiology: An interdisciplinary science.* Cambridge, MA: MIT Press.

Miczek, K. (2001). Research on animal aggression: Emerging successes for understanding determinants of human violence. In E. M. Blass (Ed.). *Developmental Psychobiology. Vol. 13, Handbook of Behavioral Neurobiology.* New York: Kluwer Academic/Plenum.

Moffitt, T. E., Caspi, A., & Silva, P. (2001). Sex differences in antisocial behaviour: conduct disorder, delinquency, and violence in the Dunedin longitudinal study. New York: Cambridge University Press.

Petitto, J. M., Gariépy, J.-L., Gendreau, P. L., Rodriguiz, R., Lewis, M. H., & Lysle, T. (1999). Differences in NK cell function in mice bred for high and low aggression: Genetic linkage between complex behavioral and immunological traits? *Brain, Behavior, and Immunity, 13,* 175–186.

Petitto, J. M., Lysle, D. T., Gariépy, J.-L., & Lewis, M. H. (1994). Association of genetic differences in social behavior and cellular immune responsiveness: Effects of social experience. *Brain, Behavior, and Immunity, 8,* 111–122.

Pulkinnen, L. (1993). The path to adulthood for aggressive girls. In K. Bjorkqvist & P. Niemela (Eds.) *Of mice and women: Aspects of female aggression.* New York: Academic Press.

Reed, C. L., Hood, K. E., Cortes, D. A., & Jones, B. J. (2001). Genetic–environmental analysis of sensitivity and acute tolerance to ethanol in mice. *Pharmacology, Biochemistry, and Behavior, 69,* 461–467.

Sandnabba, N. K. (1993). Female aggression during gestation and lactation in two strains of mice selected for isolation-induced intermale aggression. *Behavioural Processes, 30,* 157–164.

Sandnabba, N. K. (1996). Selective breeding for isolation-induced aggression in mice: Associated responses and environmental influences. *Behavior Genetics, 26,* 477–488.

Schneirla. T. C. (1957). The concept of development in comparative psychology. In D. B. Harris (Ed.). *The concept of development.* Minneapolis: University of Minnesota Press.

Sluyter, F., van Oortmerssen, G. A., & Koolhaus. J. M. (1996). Genetic influences on coping behaviour in house mouse lines selected for aggression: Effects of the Y chromosome. *Behaviour, 133,* 117–128.

Thelen, E. & Smith, L. B. (1998). Dynamic systems theories. In W. Damon (Series Ed.) & R. M. Lerner (Vol. Ed.). *Handbook of child psychology: Vol. 1. Theoretical models of human development.* New York: Wiley.

Tremblay, R. E. (2000). The development of aggressive behaviour during childhood: What have we learned in the past century? *International Journal of Behavioural Development, 24,* 129–141.

Van Oortmerssen, G. A., & Bakker, Th. C. M. (1981). Artificial selection for short and long attack latencies in wild *Mus musculus domesticus. Behavior Genetics, 11,* 115–126.

Waddington, C. H. (1957). *The strategy of the genes.* London: Allen & Unwin.

Weerts, E. M., Miller, L. G., Hood, K. E., & Miczek, K. A. (1992). Increased GABA$_A$ – dependent chloride uptake in mice selectively bred for low aggressive behavior. *Psychopharmacology, 108,* 196–204.

11

How Gene–Environment Interactions Shape the Development of Impulsive Aggression in Rhesus Monkeys

Stephen J. Suomi

National Institute of Child Health & Human Development,
National Institutes of Health, DHHS

INTRODUCTION

Professor Robert B. Cairns was a giant in the field of developmental science. His theoretical vision and his empirical rigor and persistence drove a lifelong research and academic career that uniquely helped shape this emerging, dynamic interdisciplinary field. He was a remarkable teacher, researcher, and scholar who profoundly influenced countless students and colleagues and whose legacy will long be with us.

I first got to know Bob Cairns during a mutual stint at the Center for Interdisciplinary Studies (ZIF) at the University of Bielfeld in Germany during the fall and winter of 1977–78. We were both at the ZIF as part of a 9-month-long program entitled "Early Development in Animals and Man" organized by the late ethologist Professor Dr. Klaus Immelmann, who had brought together a group of prominent researchers, representing a wide range of disciplines, who studied developmental phenomena both in humans and in a variety of other mammalian and avian species. I had known about Bob Cairns and his research since my very first days in graduate school at the University of Wisconsin – at that time Jim Sackett was telling all the graduate students at the Primate Laboratory about this guy in Indiana who hauled sheep to his lab in back of his station wagon in order to run studies that demonstrated the power of contiguity conditioning in establishing social bonds. The unusual program at the ZIF not only enabled me to hear Bob discuss his own research in considerable detail and elaborate extensively on his general philosophy of science first-hand, but also provided a wonderful opportunity to get to know him on a personal basis rather than as merely a name in the literature. We ultimately wrote a chapter together (along with Jim Sackett and Arnold Sameroff) for the ZIF proceedings volume (Sackett, Sameroff, Cairns, & Suomi, 1981), and we also began a long and gratifying period of mutual exchanges of new ideas, finds, and insights.

When Bob Cairns arrived at the ZIF back in 1977 he was in the middle of writing his classic text on social development (Cairns, 1979). In the course of our mutual discussion he talked for hours on end about some of the basic concepts concerning developmental processes he was highlighting in this groundbreaking book – concepts that most developmental researchers today largely take for granted, but which at that time seemed almost revolutionary in nature. First and foremost was his view that focusing on individuals was at least as important for understanding developmental process as was focusing on specific variables thought to influence development, the approach favored by most mainstream developmental psychologists at the time. Cairns passionately argued that developing organisms were not merely passive recipients of various environmental inputs but instead were active, purposeful participants in the shaping of their own developmental trajectories. In his view, they were continuously involved in dynamic, reciprocal interactions with their respective environments throughout the whole of their ontogeny. Moreover, Cairns posited that developmental processes *within* each individual were similarly dynamic and interactive with one another. Emotional, social, and cognitive features of an organism did not develop in isolation of one another, nor were they independent of biological systems that were simultaneously emerging in each individual. Furthermore, building on previous notions put forward by Kuo (1967) and other epigenetically oriented developmental theorists, he argued that the contribution of genetic and environmental factors in shaping individual developmental trajectories were neither exclusive nor independent of one another, but rather were thought to interact in dynamic fashion throughout the whole of development.

The basic principles that Cairns ascribed for developmental processes in general had several important implications for carrying out research in this area. First, focusing on individuals as they developed essentially required the use of prospective longitudinal research designs rather than the typical parametric cross-sectional experiments in vogue at the time. Although clinical researchers had long focused on studying individuals, most of their investigations were retrospective in nature. Prospective longitudinal studies, in contrast, enabled one to document and assess developmental changes as they were occurring in the individual. Second, acknowledging that the cognitive, social, emotional, and biological changes unfolding during development were not independent of one another provided a compelling rationale for collecting data encompassing multiple levels of analysis at the same or comparable points of time for each individual under study. Third, thorough experimental study of potential gene–environment interactions would ultimately require manipulation of both sets of factors in one way or another – and because direct experimental manipulation of either genes or environments was never ethical and seldom practical for most, if not all studies involving humans, prospective longitudinal experiments investigating gene–environment interactions would have to be designed and carried out with animal rather than human subjects.

When Bob Cairns left the ZIF and returned to North Carolina, he began two major programs of research that he would continue for the rest of his life. Both programs were centered on understanding factors that influenced the development and expression of aggressive behavior throughout ontogeny, and both were conceived and conducted in the spirit of pursuing the basic developmental principles he had so eloquently laid out in his speaking and writing while at the ZIF. The first, carried out in collaboration with his wife Beverly, was a long-term prospective longitudinal study in which large numbers of children were observed, tested, and interviewed annually from early childhood, through adolescence, and into adulthood. The second major research program, carried out in collaboration with Jean-Louis Gariépy, Kathryn Hood, and others, utilized different strains of mice that had been selectively bred over several generations and reared in a variety of carefully controlled postnatal environments. Both programs of research, each described more thoroughly elsewhere in this volume, have continued to make important contributions to our knowledge regarding the development of aggression to this day.

In the late 1980s J. D. Higley, the late Markku Linnoila, and I began our own long-term program of research investigating the development of aggression and its possible biological underpinnings in rhesus monkeys. The initial impetus for this research came from several human clinical studies that were reporting a strong association between unusually violent aggressive behavior and apparent deficits in central serotonergic functioning, as indexed by cerebrospinal fluid (CSF) concentrations of the primary central serotonin metabolite 5-hydroxyindoleacetic acid (5-HIAA). Violent individuals were consistently found to have abnormally low CSF 5-HIAA concentrations, whether they were children who were unusually aggressive toward peers and hostile toward their mothers (Kruesi et al., 1990); children who tortured animals (Kruesi, 1989); children and adolescents with disruptive behavior disorders (Kruesi et al., 1990); offenders convicted of violent aggressive acts and/or property damage (Linnoila et al., 1983); men with personality disorders having extreme scores for aggression, irritability, hostility, and psychopathic deviance on standardized tests (Brown, Linnoila, & Goodwin, 1990; Linnoila, 1988); men expelled from the Marines for excessive violence and psychopathic deviance (Brown, Goodwin, Ballenger, Goyer, & Major, 1979); suicide victims (Mann, Arango, & Underwood), or sons of men arrested for violence and arson (Linnoila, DeJong, & Virkkunen). Accordingly, we carried out a preliminary cross-sectional study utilizing a sample of rhesus monkeys varying in age, gender, and early rearing history and, consistent with the extant human data, we found a striking *inverse* relationship between levels of intense physical aggression and 5-HIAA concentrations both between and within each age–sex class (Higley, Suomi, & Linnoila, 1990). Given the results of those analyses, we decided to embark on a major program of study to further investigate this inverse relationship and factors that might contribute to it. In designing and carrying out this research program we were very much influenced by the basic theoretical and methodological principles that Bob Cairns had taught me a decade earlier.

SPECIES-NORMATIVE DEVELOPMENT AND THE REGULATION OF AGGRESSION IN RHESUS MONKEYS

Ethologists have long argued that social aggression serves important adaptive functions, having been largely conserved over mammalian evolutionary history. Being capable of engaging in aggressive attack and defense in the service of protecting self, family, and friends from predators and competitors seems crucial for the survival of the individual and the maintenance of any social group across successive generations. However, excessive and/or inappropriate aggression by any individual has the potential of destroying the very social fabric that binds the group together. If the group is to maintain its social cohesion over time, the expression of aggression must therefore be regulated, that is, individual group members must come to know which social stimuli merit an aggressive response and which do not, and for those that do, to what degree, and for how long. Indeed, learning how and when to avoid an aggressive encounter and when and how to end it once begun may be at least important as learning how and when to start or respond to an aggressive act (Suomi, 2000).

The development of proficiency in the regulation of aggression appears to be especially important for rhesus monkeys and other advanced primates who live in communities that are well defined in terms of both kinship relationships and social dominance hierarchies. In their natural habitats rhesus monkeys typically reside in large, distinctive social groups (termed "troops") composed of several female-headed families, each spanning three or more generations of kin, plus numerous immigrant adult males. This pattern of social organization derives from the fact that rhesus monkey females stay in their natal troop for their entire lives, whereas virtually all rhesus monkey males emigrate from their natal troop around the time of puberty, usually in their fourth or fifth year, and then join other troops (Lindburg, 1971). The troops are also characterized by multiple social dominance relationships, including distinctive hierarchies both between and within families, as well as a hierarchy among the immigrant adult males. For those males, relative status seems to be largely a function of one's ability to join and maintain coalitions, especially with high-ranking females (Berard, 1989). Indeed, the dominance status of any particular rhesus monkey within its troop depends not so much on how big and strong it is but rather who its family and friends are – and the latter is clearly dependent on the development of complex social skills during ontogeny.

Rhesus monkey infants spend virtually all of their first month of life in physical contact with their biological mother, during which time they form a strong and enduring specific attachment bond with her. In their second month of life, they begin exploring their immediate physical and social environment, using their mother as a "secure base" to support such exploration (cf. Suomi, 1995), and they also begin interacting with other troop members, especially peers. In subsequent months play interactions with peers increase dramatically in both frequency and complexity and thereafter remain at high levels until puberty. Aggression first appears in a young monkey's behavioral repertoire around 6 months of age, typically in the context of rough-and-tumble play (Symonds, 1978). Sham-biting, hair-pulling, wrestling, and other forms of physical contact are basic components of rough-and-tumble play directed toward peers, occurring with increasing frequency among males in the second half of their first year of life and, in fact, becoming their predominate form of play behavior throughout the juvenile years. Although some form of virtually all of the basic physical components of adult aggressive exchanges can be seen in these rough-and-tumble play bouts, the intensity of such interactions is usually quite controlled and seldom escalates to the point of actual physical injury – if it does, the play bout is almost always terminated immediately, either via adult intervention or by one or more of the participants backing away themselves. The importance of these peer play bouts for the regulation of aggression becomes apparent when one considers that rhesus monkey infants reared in laboratory environments that deny them regular access to peers during their initial months inevitably exhibit excessive and socially inappropriate aggression later in life (cf. Suomi & Harlow, 1975).

The onset of puberty is associated with major life transitions for both males and females, involving not only major hormonal alterations, pronounced growth spurts, and other obvious physical changes, but also major social changes for both genders. Males experience the most dramatic social disruptions: when they leave home they sever all social contact not only with their mother and other kin but also with all others in their natal social troop. Virtually all of these adolescent males soon join all-male "gangs," and after several months to a year most of them then attempt to join a different troop, usually composed entirely of individuals largely unfamiliar to the immigrant males (Berard, 1989). The process of natal troop emigration is exceedingly dangerous for adolescent males – the mortality rate from the time they leave their natal troop until they become successfully integrated into another troop can approach 50%, depending on local circumstances (e.g., Dittus, 1979). Recent field studies have identified and characterized striking variability in both the timing of emigration and the basic strategies followed by these males in their attempts to join other established social groups.

Adolescent females, by contrast, never leave their maternal family or natal troop. Puberty for them is instead associated with increases in social activities directed toward maternal kin, especially when these young females begin to have offspring of their own. Indeed, the birth of a new infant (especially to a new mother) often has the effect of bringing extended family members closer both physically and socially and, coincidentally, providing a buffer from external threats and stressors for mother and infant alike. These females' ties to both family and troop are facilitated throughout adulthood by appropriate regulation of aggression; conversely, these ties can be compromised whenever such emotional regulation goes awry (Suomi, 1999).

INDIVIDUAL DIFFERENCES IN THE REGULATION OF AGGRESSION

While the basic developmental sequence just outlined is characteristic of most rhesus monkeys growing up both in the wild and in captive social groups, there are nevertheless substantial differences among individuals in the precise timing and relative ease with which they make major developmental transitions, as well as how they manage the day-to-day challenges and stresses that are an inevitable consequence of complex social group life. In particular, my colleagues and I have identified a subgroup of individuals, comprising approximately 5–10% of the population, who appear to have problems regulating their aggressive behavior. These monkeys appear to be unusually impulsive, insensitive, and overly aggressive in their interactions with other troop members. Impulsive young monkeys, especially males, often are unable to moderate their behavioral responses to rough-and-tumble play initiations from peers, frequently escalating initially benign play bouts into full-blown, tissue-damaging aggressive exchanges (Higley et al., 1992). Not surprisingly, most of these males tend to be avoided by peers during play bouts, and as a result they become increasingly isolated within their own social group. In addition, they appear unwilling (or unable) to follow the "rules" inherent in rhesus monkey social dominance hierarchies. For example, they may directly challenge a dominant adult male, a foolhardy act that can result in serious injury, especially when the juvenile refuses to back away or exhibit submissive behavior once defeat becomes obvious. Impulsive juvenile males also show a propensity for making dangerous leaps from treetop to treetop, sometimes with painful outcomes (Mehlman et al., 1994).

We have found that overly impulsive and aggressive monkeys, male and female alike, consistently exhibit deficits in their central serotonin metabolism, as reflected by chronically low CSF 5-HIAA concentrations. Laboratory studies have shown that these deficits are apparent in the initial weeks of life and tend to persist throughout development for those individuals, even as CSF 5-HIAA concentrations generally decline with increasing age in all subjects, as noted previously. Moreover, individuals who have chronic deficits in serotonin metabolism are also likely to exhibit relatively poor state control and visual orienting capabilities during early infancy (Champoux, Suomi, & Schneider, 1994), poor performance on delay-of-gratification tasks during childhood (Bennett et al., 1999), and disrupted sleep patterns (Zajicek, Higley, Suomi, & Linnoila, 1997) as adults. Overly impulsive and aggressive adolescents and young adults also tend to consume excessive amounts of alcohol when placed in a "happy hour" experimental paradigm daily over a period of several weeks (Higley, Hasert, Suomi, & Linnoila, 1991). Finally, in several independent studies, we have shown that individual differences in 5-HIAA concentrations are highly heritable among monkeys of similar age and comparable rearing background (Higley et al., 1993; Lorenz et al., submitted).

We now know from prospective longitudinal field studies that the long-term prognosis for aggressive young rhesus monkey males with low CSF 5-HIAA concentrations who grow up in free-ranging environments is not very promising. Ostracized by their peers and frequently attacked by adults of both genders, most of these young males are physically driven out of their natal troop prior to 3 years of age, long before the onset of puberty (Mehlman et al., 1995). They generally lack the social skills to be able to join another troop; indeed, they even seem unable to join all-male gangs. Consequently, most of these males become solitary, and almost all of them die or are killed within a year, long before reaching reproductive maturity (Higley et al., 1996).

Given the finding that individual differences in CSF 5-HIAA concentrations appear to be highly heritable and the additional finding that most male rhesus monkeys with unusually low CSF 5-HIAA concentrations perish prior to puberty, how could it be that 5–10% of rhesus monkeys living in wild populations apparently maintain chronically low CSF 5-HIAA concentrations? Three possible explanations readily come to mind. One possibility might be that the few males with low CSF 5-HIAA who do survive to adulthood sire a disproportionately large number of offspring (the so-called "silver bullet" hypothesis). Recent field observations suggest that this hypothesis is exceedingly unlikely. In point of fact, the low CSF 5-HIAA males who do survive tend to be actively avoided by most females. On the rare occasions in which consort behavior with a female actually occurs, those males tend to engage in fewer mounts per copulatory sequence (rhesus monkeys are serial mounters), are less likely to ejaculate before the sequence is terminated, and have a lower probability of inseminating the females when they do ejaculate than do other males in the population (Mehlman et al., 1997).

A second, perhaps more plausible possibility is that the propensity for developing chronically low central serotonin metabolism, as well as excessive impulsive aggressiveness, is passed on to the next generation of rhesus monkeys primarily through the female rather than the male genome. Young female rhesus monkeys with low 5-HIAA concentrations are indeed impulsive, aggressive, and tend to be generally incompetent socially (Westergaard et al., 2003). Unlike males, however, they are not expelled from their natal troop but instead remain in their respective families for the rest of their lives. Moreover, they engage in relatively normal reproductive behavior, and they clearly produce and rear offspring – offspring who therefore may well be at some genetic risk for having low CSF 5-HIAA concentrations and developing poor impulse control and excessive aggressiveness themselves.

Evidence for a third possible mechanism for cross-generational transmission of deficits in serotonergic functioning and associated behavioral difficulties comes from recent studies of maternal behavior in captive rhesus monkey groups. We have found that females with chronically low CSF 5-HIAA concentrations tend to exhibit significant abnormalities in their maternal behavior, often resulting in the development of insecure and/or disorganized attachment relationships with their infants. Other recent data suggest that infants who develop the least secure attachment relationships with their mothers are also the most likely to develop deficits in serotonin functioning (cf. Suomi, 1999b). Thus, an alternative possible means of cross-generational transmission of the propensity to have chronically low CSF 5-HIAA concentrations and associated behavioral problems may be via aberrant maternal care, or other forms of social stimulation, that offspring might experience during development. According to this view, the mother's behavior toward offspring may be more relevant than her genes for cross-generational transmission of these phenomena. Of course, these two potential pathways are not necessarily mutually exclusive (Suomi & Levine, 1998).

EFFECTS OF EARLY PEER REARING

Although the findings from both the field and laboratory studies cited earlier indicate that differences among rhesus monkeys in their CSF 5-HIAA concentrations and their regulation (or lack thereof) of impulsive aggression tend to be quite stable from infancy to adulthood and are at least in part heritable, this does not mean that they are necessarily fixed at birth, immune to subsequent environmental influence. To the contrary: An increasing body of evidence from studies from our own and several other laboratories has demonstrated that patterns of behavioral development, neuroendocrine responsiveness, and neurotransmitter metabolism alike can be modified substantially by certain early social experiences, particularly those involving early attachment relationships.

Among the most compelling evidence for such experiential influences comes from studies of rhesus monkey infants raised with peers instead of their biological mothers. In these studies infants typically have been permanently separated from their biological mothers at birth; hand-reared in a neonatal nursery for their first month of life; housed with same-aged, like-reared peers for the rest of their first 6 months; and then moved into larger social groups containing both peer-reared and mother-reared age mates. During their initial months, peer-reared infants readily establish strong social bonds with each other, much as mother-reared infants develop attachments to their own mothers (Harlow & Harlow, 1969). However, because peers are not nearly as effective as typical monkey mothers in providing a "secure base" for exploration, the attachment relationships that these peer-reared infants develop are almost always "anxious" in nature. As a result, while peer-reared monkeys show completely normal physical and motor development, their early exploratory behavior tends to be somewhat limited, they seem reluctant to approach novel objects, and they tend to be shy in initial encounters with unfamiliar peers (Suomi, 1999b).

Even when peer-reared youngsters interact with their same-age cage-mates in familiar settings, their emerging social play repertoires are usually retarded in both frequency and complexity. One explanation for their relatively poor play performance is that their peer partners have to serve both as attachment figures and as playmates, a dual role that neither mothers nor mother-reared peers have to fulfill. Another obstacle to developing sophisticated play repertoires faced by peer-reared monkeys is that all of their early play bouts involve partners who are basically as incompetent as themselves. Perhaps as a result, peer-reared youngsters typically drop to the bottom of their respective dominance hierarchies when they are subsequently housed with mother-reared monkeys their own age (Higley et al., 1996).

Early peer-rearing has another long-term developmental consequence for rhesus monkeys – it tends to make them more impulsive and aggressive. Peer-reared males initially exhibit overly aggressive tendencies in the context of juvenile play; as they approach puberty, the frequency and severity of their aggressive episodes typically exceed those of their mother-reared cohorts. Peer-reared females tend to groom (and be groomed by) others in their social group less frequently and for shorter durations than their mother-reared counterparts, and, as noted earlier, they usually remain at the bottom of their respective dominance hierarchies. The differences between peer-reared and mother-reared age mates in aggression, grooming, and social dominance are maintained throughout the preadolescent and adolescent years (Higley et al., 1996). Peer-reared monkeys also consistently show lower CSF concentrations of 5-HIAA than their mother-reared counterparts. These group differences in 5-HIAA concentrations appear well before 6 months of age, and they remain robust at least throughout adolescence and into early adulthood (Higley & Suomi, 1996). Additionally, peer-reared adolescent monkeys as a group consume larger amounts of alcohol under comparable ad libitum conditions than their mother-reared age mates (Higley et al., 1991). They also rapidly develop a greater tolerance for alcohol, and this tendency appears to be associated with differences in serotonin turnover rates (Higley et al., in press) and with differential serotonin transporter availability (Heinz et al., 1998). Thus peer-reared monkeys exhibit the same general tendencies that characterize excessively impulsive and aggressive mother-reared rhesus monkeys, not only behaviorally but also in terms of decreased serotonergic functioning.

GENE–ENVIRONMENT INTERACTIONS

Studies examining the effects of peer-rearing and other variations in early rearing history (e.g., Harlow & Harlow, 1969), along with the previously cited heritability findings, provide compelling evidence that *both* genetic and early experiential factors can affect a monkey's capacity to regulate expression of aggression, as well as its serotonergic functioning. Do these factors operate independently, or do they interact in some fashion in shaping individual developmental trajectories? Ongoing research capitalizing on the discovery of polymorphisms in one specific gene – the serotonin transporter gene – suggests that gene–environment interactions not only occur but also can be expressed in multiple forms.

The serotonin transporter gene (5-HTT), a candidate gene for impaired serotonergic function (Lesch et al., 1996), has length variation in its promoter region that results in allelic variation in 5-HTT expression. A "short" allele (LS) confers low transcriptional efficiency to the 5-HTT promoter relative to the long allele (LL), raising the possibility that low 5-HTT expression may result in decreased serotonergic functioning (Heils et al., 1996), although evidence in support of this hypothesis in humans has been decidedly mixed to date (e.g., Furlong et al., 1998). The 5-HTT polymorphism was first characterized in humans, but it also appears in largely homologous form in rhesus monkeys and some other primates but, interestingly, not in other mammalian species (Lesch et al., 1997).

In collaboration with K. P. Lesch at the University of Wuerzburg, we utilized polymerase chain reaction (PCR) techniques to characterize some of our mother-reared and peer-reared monkeys with respect to their 5-HTT polymorphic status. The genotypic analyses revealed that the relative frequency of subjects possessing the LS versus the LL allele did not differ significantly between these two rearing groups, an expected finding given that those monkeys had been randomly assigned to their respective rearing conditions at birth. Because we had previously collected extensive observational data and biological samples from these monkeys throughout development, it was possible to examine a wide range of behavioral and physiological measures for potential 5-HTT polymorphism main effects and interactions with early rearing history. Analyses completed to date suggest that such interactions are widespread and diverse.

For example, Bennett et al. (2002) found that CSF 5-HIAA concentrations did not differ as a function of 5-HTT status for mother-reared subjects, whereas among peer-reared monkeys individuals with the LS allele had significantly lower CSF 5-HIAA concentrations than those with the LL allele. One interpretation of this interaction is that mother-rearing appeared to "buffer" any potentially deleterious effects of the LS allele on serotonin metabolism. Barr et al. (in press) reported a similar buffering effect with respect to aggression: High levels of aggression were found in peer-reared monkeys with the LS allele, whereas mother-reared LS monkeys exhibited low levels that were comparable to those of both mother- and peer-reared LL monkeys. A somewhat different form of gene–environment interaction was suggested by the analysis of alcohol consumption data: whereas peer-reared monkeys with the LS allele consumed more alcohol than peer-reared monkeys with the LL allele, the reverse was true for mother-reared subjects, with individuals possessing the LS allele actually consuming *less* alcohol than their LL counterparts (Bennett, Lesch, Heils, & Linnoila, 1998). In other words, the LS allele appeared to represent a risk factor for excessive alcohol consumption among peer-reared monkeys but a protective factor for mother-reared subjects. Finally, Champoux et al. (2002) examined the relationship between early rearing history and serotonin transporter gene polymorphic status on measures of neonatal neurobehavioral development during the first month of life and found further evidence of maternal "buffering." Specifically, infants possessing the LS allele who were being reared in the laboratory neonatal nursery showed significant deficits in measures of attention, activity, and motor maturity relative to nursery-reared infants possessing the LL allele, whereas both LS and LL infants who were being reared by competent mothers exhibited normal values for each of these measures.

In sum, the consequences of having the LS allele differed dramatically for peer-reared and mother-reared monkeys: Whereas peer-reared individuals with the LS allele exhibited deficits in measures of neurobehavioral functioning during their initial weeks of life and high levels of aggression, reduced serotonin metabolism, and excessive alcohol consumption as adolescents, mother-reared subjects with the very same allele developed normal early neurobehavioral functioning, regulation of aggression, and serotonergic functioning and reduced risk for excessive alcohol consumption. Indeed, it could be argued on the basis of these findings that having the "short" allele of the 5-HTT gene may well lead to psychopathology among monkeys with poor early rearing histories but might actually be adaptive for monkeys who develop secure early attachment relationships with their mothers.

The implications of these recent findings are considerable with respect to the potential for cross-generational transmission of these biobehavioral characteristics, in that the attachment style of a monkey mother is typically "copied" by her daughters when they grow up and become mothers themselves (Suomi, 1999b). If similar buffering is indeed experienced by the next generation of infants carrying the LS 5-HTT polymorphism, then having had their mothers develop a secure attachment relationship with their own mothers when they were infants themselves might well provide the basis for a non-genetic means of transmitting its apparently adaptive consequences to that new generation of monkeys.

SUMMARY AND COMMENTARY

This chapter has summarized a program of research investigating the development of impulsive and excessive aggression in a subgroup of rhesus monkeys. It described how aggression is typically socialized during the infant and juvenile years and contrasted this developmental pattern with that of the subgroup of individuals who consistently exhibit such aggression, as well as other behavioral manifestations of impulsivity and consistent deficits in a measure of central serotonin metabolism. These biobehavioral patterns emerge early in development, are maintained through puberty if not beyond, and are at least in part heritable. Male monkeys who develop these patterns in nature seldom survive beyond puberty, whereas females developing parallel patterns of inappropriate aggression and serotonergic dysfunctioning usually survive to bear and rear offspring, unfortunately often in less than optimal fashion. Early rearing experiences can clearly influence the development of these biobehavioral patterns, even those with demonstrated heritability. Indeed, it appears that genetic and early experiential factors can and do interact to shape individual developmental trajectories. In particular, being reared by a competent mother appears to somehow protect offspring at genetic risk for developing problems in behavioral and biological functioning when reared in less socially supportive settings.

The program of research outlined in this chapter clearly reflects the theoretical approaches and methodological strategies for studying developmental processes and outcomes that I first heard Bob Cairns articulate and promote so elegantly and persuasively a quarter century ago. Although our initial study reporting an association between high levels of aggression and low CSF 5-HIAA concentrations in rhesus monkeys was cross-sectional in nature (Higley, Suomi, & Linnoila, 1990), it was only when we began employing prospective longitudinal research designs encompassing much of the life span of our subjects that we were able to fully appreciated how robust and developmentally stable this inverse relationship was from infancy to adulthood. Moreover, by taking Bob Cairns' oft-stated advice to collect data representing multiple levels of analysis from the same individuals over the same general time frame, we were able to characterize the striking associations between deficits in serotonergic functioning and a host of neurobiological, behavioral, socio-emotional, and motivational characteristics. Finally, our initial decision to use rhesus monkeys to investigate a phenomenon first recognized in the human clinical literature allowed us to manipulate certain independent variables (e.g., early rearing history) and to measure a wide range of dependent variables (e.g., repeated CSF sampling) that would be problematic at best in any human study – and ultimately allowed us to test basic developmental hypotheses involving gene–environment interactions directly and rigorously.

My colleagues and I plan to continue our investigations of gene–environment interactions and how they might influence individual developmental trajectories throughout the life span of our rhesus monkey subjects. We are especially interested in characterizing potential interactions between polymorphisms in the 5-HTT gene and differences in early rearing history over a wider range of measures of biobehavioral functioning than we have been able to study to date, as well as looking at potential gene–environment interactions involving other candidate genes whose polymorphisms are either homologous or functionally similar in humans and rhesus monkeys. We are also interested in better understanding the actual biological mechanisms underlying these interactions, addressing specific questions regarding how environmental events might be regulating gene expression at the molecular level. Finally, we are interested in documenting and characterizing the ways – both genetic and nongenetic – in which certain biological and behavioral characteristics are transmitted from one generation to the next. Although we fully recognize that rhesus monkeys are clearly *not* furry little humans with tails but rather members of another (albeit closely related) species, we sincerely believe that there will likely be some general principles emerging from our research with rhesus monkeys that can enhance our understanding of the role of gene–environment interactions in human development. It is a view that I am certain Bob Cairns would endorse, because he is the one who first taught it me.

References

Barr, C. S., Newman, T. K., Becker, M. L., Parker, C. C., Champoux, M., Lesch, K. P., et al. (in press). Early experience and rh5-HTTPLR genotype interact to influence social behavior and aggression in nonhuman primates. *Genes, Brain, and Behavior*.

Bennett, A. J., Lesch, K. P., Heils, A., &. Linnoila, M. (1998). Serotonin transporter gene variation, CSF 5-HIAA concentrations, and alcohol-related aggression in rhesus monkeys (*Macaca mulatta*). *American Journal of Primatology, 45,* 168–169.

Bennett, A. J., Lesch, K. P., Heils, A., Long, J., Lorenz, J., Shoaf, S. E., et al. (2002). Early experience and serotonin transporter gene variation interact to influence primate CNS function. *Molecular Psychiatry, 17,* 118–122.

Bennett, A. J., Tsai, T., Hopkins, W. D., Lindell, S. G., Pierre, P. J., Champoux, M., et al. (1999). Early social rearing environment influences acquisition of a computerized joystick task in rhesus monkeys (*Macaca mulatta*). *American Journal of Primatology, 49,* 33–34.

Berard, J. (1989). Male life histories. *Puerto Rican Health Sciences Journal, 8,* 47–58.

Brown, G. L., Goodwin, F. K., Ballenger, J. C., Goyer, P. F., & Major, L. F. (1979). Aggression in humans correlates with cerebrospinal fluid amine metabolites. *Psychiatry Research, 1,* 131–139.

Brown, G. L., Linnoila, M., & Goodwin, F. K. (1990). Clinical assessment of human aggression and impulsivity in relation to biochemical measures. In H. M. Van Praag, R. Plutchik, & A. Apter (Eds.), *Violence and suicidality: Perspectives in clinical and psychobiological research* (pp. 184–217). New York: Bruner/Mazel.

Cairns, R. B. (1979). *Social Development: The origins and plasticity of social exchanges.* San Francisco: Freeman.

Champoux, M., Bennett, A. J., Lesch, K. P., Heils, A., Nielson, D. A., Higley, J. D., et al. (2002). Serotonin transporter gene polymorphism and neurobehavioral development in rhesus monkey neonates. *Molecular Psychiatry, 7,* 1058–1063.

Champoux, M., Suomi, S. J., & Schneider, M. L. (1994). Temperamental differences between captive Indian and Chinese–Indian hybrid rhesus macaque infants. *Laboratory Animal Science, 44,* 351–357.

Dittus, W. P. J. (1979). The evolution of behaviours regulating density and age-specific sex ratios in a primate population. *Behaviour, 69,* 265–302.

Furlong, R. A., Ho, L., Walsh, C., Rubinsztein, J. S., Jain, S., Pazkil, E. S., Eaton, D. F., & Rubinsztein, D. C. (1998). Analysis and meta-analysis of two serotonin transporter gene polymorphisms in bipolar and unipolar affective disorders. *American Journal of Medical Genetics, 81,* 58–63.

Harlow, H. F., & Harlow, M. K. (1969). Effects of various mother–infant relationships on rhesus monkey behaviors. In B. M. Foss (Ed.), *Determinants of infant behaviour* (Vol. 4). London: Methuen, pp. 15–36.

Heils, A., Teufel, A., Petri, S., Stober, G., Riederer, P. Bengel, B., & Lesch, K. P. (1996). Allelic variation of human serotonin transporter gene expression. *Journal of Neurochemistry, 6,* 2621–2624.

Heinz, A., Higley, J. D., Gorey, J. G., Saunders, R. C., Jones, D. W., Hommer, D., et al. (1998). *In vivo* association between alcohol intoxication, aggression, and serotonin transporter availability in nonhuman primates. *American Journal of Psychiatry, 155,* 1023–1028.

Higley, J. D., Hasert, M. L., Suomi, S. J., & Linnoila, M. (1991). A new nonhuman primate model of alcohol abuse: Effects of early experience, personality, and stress on alcohol consumption. *Proceedings of the National Academy of Sciences, USA, 88,* 7261–7265.

Higley, J. D., Hommer, D., Lucas, K., Shoaf, S., Suomi,S. J., & Linnoila, M. (in press). CNS serotonin metabolism rate predicts innate tolerance, high alcohol consumption, and aggression during intoxication in rhesus monkeys. *Archives of General Psychiatry.*

Higley, J. D., Mehlman, P. T., Taub, D. M., Higley, S., Fernald, B., Vickers, J. H., et al. (1996). Excessive mortality in young free-ranging male nonhuman primates with low CSF 5-HIAA concentrations. *Archives of General Psychiatry, 53,* 537–543.

Higley, J. D., Mehlman, P. T., Taub, D. M., Higley, S. B., Vickers, J. H., Suomi, S. J., & Linnoila, M. (1992). Cerebrospinal fluid monoamine and adrenal correlates of aggression in free-ranging rhesus monkeys. *Archives of General Psychiatry, 49,* 436–441.

Higley, J. D., & Suomi, S. J. (1996). Reactivity and social competence affect individual differences in reaction to severe stress in children: Investigations using nonhuman primates. In C. R. Pfeffer (Ed.), *Intense stress and mental disturbance in children* (pp. 3–58). Washington, DC: American Psychiatric Press.

Higley, J. D., Suomi, S. J., & Linnoila, M. (1990). Parallels in aggression and serotonin: Consideration of development, rearing history, and sex differences. In H. van Praag, R. Plutchik, & A. Apter (Eds.), *Violence and suicidality* (pp. 245–256). New York: Bruner/Mazel.

Higley, J. D., Suomi, S. J., & Linnoila, M. (1996). A nonhuman primate model of type alcoholism?: Part 2: Diminished social competence and excessive aggression correlates with low CSF 5-HIAA concentrations. *Alcoholism: Clinical and Experimental Research, 20,* 643–650.

Higley, J. D., Thompson, W. T., Champoux, M., Goldman, D., Hasert, M. F., Kraemer, G. W., et al. (1993). Paternal and maternal genetic and environmental contributions to CSF monoamine metabolites in rhesus monkeys (*Macaca mulatta*). *Archives of General Psychiatry, 50,* 615–623.

Kruesi, M. J. (1989). Cruelty to animals and CSF 5-HIAA. *Psychiatry Research, 28,* 115–116.

Kruesi, M. J., Rapoport, J. L., Hamburder, S., Hibbs, E., Potter, W. Z., Lenane, M., et al. (1990). Cerebrospinal fluid monoamine metabolites, aggression, and impulsivity in disruptive behavior disorders of children and adolescents. *Archives of General Psychiatry, 47,* 419–426.

Kuo, Z.-Y. (1967). *The dynamics of behavioral development: An epigenetic view.* New York: Random House.

Lesch, K. P., Bengel, D., Heils, A., Sabol, S. Z., Greenberg, B. D., Petri, S., et al. (1996). Association of anxiety-related traits with a polymorphism in the serotonin transporter gene regulatory region. *Science, 274,* 1527–1531.

Lesch, L. P., Meyer, J., Glatz, K., Flugge, G., Hinney, A., Hebebrand, J., et al. (1997). The 5-HT transporter gene-linked polymorphic region (5-HTTLPR) in evolutionary perspective: alternative biallelic variation in rhesus monkeys. *Journal of Neural Transmission, 104,* 1259–1266.

Lindburg, D.G. (1971). The rhesus monkey in north India: An ecological and behavioral study. In L. A. Rosenblum (Ed.), *Primate behavior: Developments in field and laboratory research* (Vol. 2, pp. 1–106). New York: Academic Press.

Linnoila, M. (1988). Monoamines ands impulse control. In J. A. Swinkels & W. Blijeven (Eds.), *Depression, anxiety, and aggression* (pp. 167–172). Houten, The Netherlands: Medidact.

Linnoila, M., DeJong, J., & Virkkunen, M. (1989). Monoamines, glucose metabolism, and impulse control. *Psychopharmacy Bulletin, 25*, 404–406.

Linnoila, M., Virkkunen, M., Scheinin, M., Nuutila, A., Rimon, R., & Goodwin, F. K. (1983). Low cerebrospinal fluid 5-hydroxyindoleacetic acid concentration differentiates impulsive from nonimpulsive violent behavior. *Life Sciences, 33*, 2609–2614.

Lorenz, J. G., Long, J. C., Linnoila, M., Goldman, D. A., Suomi, S. J., & Higley, J. D. Genetic and other contributions to alcohol consumption in a nonhuman primate: a nonhuman primate model 10 years later. *Submitted for publication.*

Mann, J. J., Arango, V., & Underwood, M. E. (1990). Serotonin and suicidal behavior. *Annals of the New York Academy of Science, 600*, 476–485.

Mehlman, P. T., Higley, J. D., Faucher, I., Lilly, A. A., Taub, D. M., Vickers, J. H., et al. (1994). Low cerebrospinal fluid 5-hydroxyindoleacetic acid concentrations are correlated with severe aggression and reduced impulse control in free-ranging primates. *American Journal of Psychiatry, 151*, 1485–1491.

Mehlman, P. T., Higley, J. D., Faucher, I., Lilly, A. A., Taub, D. M., Vickers, J. H., et al. (1995). CSF 5-HIAA concentrations are correlated with sociality and the timing of emigration in free-ranging primates. *American Journal of Psychiatry, 152*, 901–913.

Mehlman, P. T., Higley, J. D., Fernald, B. J., Sallee, F. R., Suomi, S. J., & Linnoila, M. (1997). CSF 5-HIAA, testosterone, and sociosexual behaviors in free-ranging male macaques during the breeding season. *Psychiatric Research, 72*, 89–102.

Sackett, G. P., Sameroff, A. S., Cairns, R. B., & Suomi, S. J. (1981). Continuity in behavioral development: Theoretical and empirical issues. In K. Immelmann, G. W. Barlow, L. Petrinovich, & M. Main (Eds.), *Behavioral development: The Bielefeld interdisciplinary project.* New York: Cambridge University Press, pp. 395–431.

Suomi, S. J. (1995). Influence of Bowlby's attachment theory on research on non-human primate biobehavioral development. In S. Goldberg, R. Muir, & J. Kerr (Eds.), *Attachment theory: Social, developmental, and clinical perspectives* (pp. 185–201). Hillsdale, NJ: Analytic Press.

Suomi, S. J. (1999a) Conflict and cohesion in rhesus monkey family life. In M. Cox & J. Brooks-Gunn (Eds.), *Conflict and cohesion in families.* Mahway, NJ: Lawrence Erlbaum, pp. 283–299.

Suomi, S. J. (1999b). Attachment in rhesus monkeys. In J. Cassidy & P. R. Shaver (Eds.), *Handbook of attachment: Theory, reserarch, and clinical applications* (pp. 181–197). New York: Guilford Press.

Suomi, S. J. (2000). A biobehavioral perspective on developmental psychopathology: excessive aggression and serotonergic dysfunction in monkeys. In A. J. Sameroff, M. Lewis, & S. Miller (Eds.), *Handbook of developmental psychopathology* (pp. 237–256). New York: Plenum Press.

Suomi, S. J., & Harlow, H. F. (1975). The role and reason of peer friendships. In M. Lewis & L. A. Rosenblum (Eds.), *Friendships and peer relations* (pp. 310–334). New York: Basic Books.

Suomi, S. J., & Levine, S. (1998). Psychobiology of intergenerational effects of trauma: evidence from animal studies. In Y. Daniele (Ed.), *International handbook of multigenerational legacies of trauma.* New York: Plenum Press, pp. 623–637.

Symonds, D. (1978). *Play and aggression: A study of rhesus monkeys.* New York: Columbia University Press.

Westergaard, G. C., Suomi, S. J., Chavanne, T., Houser, L., Hurley, A. C., Cleveland, A., et al. (2003). Physiological correlates of aggression and impulsivity in free-ranging female primates. *Neuropsychopharmacology, 28,* 1045–1055.

Zajicek, K., Higley, J. D., Suomi, S. J., & Linnoila, M. (1997). Rhesus macaques with high CSF 5-HIAA concentrations exhibit early sleep onset. *Psychiatric Research, 77,* 15–25.

CONCLUSION

12

Synthesis and Reconsiderations of the Psychobiology of Aggressive Behavior: A Conclusion

Elizabeth J. Susman

The Pennsylvania State University

David Stoff

National Institute of Mental Health

INTRODUCTION

The expression that time changes everything could be no more true than in the case of the integration of human biology and aggressive behavior. Earlier perspectives concerning the integration of biology and behavior were riddled with ideas of determinism and the preponderance of nature over nurture. Biological processes were viewed as causal agents in behavior. Current perspectives view biology and behavior as evolving in dynamic interaction throughout ontogeny (Lerner, 2002; Magnusson, 1999; Magnusson & Stattin, 1998; Susman, Dorn, & Schiefelbein, 2003; Susman & Rogol, 2004). These perspectives suggest that levels of existence, from the molecular and genetic to the macro social levels, co-dependently produce the uniqueness of individuals.

The chapters in this volume attest to how the decline in the perennial debate about nature and nurture has facilitated the acceptance of new theoretical and empirical developments on biological parameters of aggressive behavior. First, the chapters show that explaining a complex human behavior, such as aggression, now is not the purview of any one disciplinary perspective. Throughout the history of the study of development, philosophers and scientists have been devotees of either a biological or a social perspective on the causes of aggressive and criminal behavior. In the past few decades, a clear distinction existed between biological, behavioral, and social science perspectives on aggression. The prevailing view was that biologists search for universals to explain human behavior and differences among species. In contrast, behavioral and social scientists focus on social processes and search for individual differences among persons.

The opinions expressed herein are the views of the authors and do not necessarily reflect the official position of the National Institute of Mental Health or any other part of the U.S. Department of Health and Human Services or The Pennsylvania State University.

These single disciplinary approaches to development are now viewed as impoverished and inaccurate (Hinde, 1987). Integrated perspectives on the ontogeny of aggressive behavior operate under the assumption that development proceeds simultaneously on multiple biological and behavioral levels, and that therefore, scientific endeavors also should reflect integration across disciplines. Second, integration across levels of analysis and models based on multilevel paradigms has enabled developmental scientists to construct well-articulated integrative models of the development of aggression.

Historically, the concept of development was synonymous with biological change (e.g., Harris, 1957; Schneirla, 1957). The revival of these earlier models is enriched by consideration of multiple processes and mechanisms as well as issues of plasticity and bidirectionality. For instance, Raine, Brennan, & Farrington (1997) present a bidirectional model that integrates genetics, environment, biological and social-risks and protective factors, biosocial interactions, and violence. Third, the development of biobehavioral models and theories has led to increasing specificity and sensitivity of assessments. The method of assessing aggressive behavior and its correlates traditionally was a questionnaire or observational assessment. Assessments of risk for and actual aggressive behavior currently are of greater specificity and sensitivity than in the past and include multiple questionnaire measures of aggressive concepts, hormones, genes, neurotransmitters, and functional and structural magnetic resonance imaging. In addition, new statistical methods enable investigators to test sophisticated multilevel hypotheses about the course and consequences of aggressive behavior (Broidy et al., 2003). In brief, the consequence of these three advances is that research now is based on multilevel theories, multiple levels of assessment, dynamic interactions across levels, and sophisticated multivariate statistical models.

PLASTICITY, BIDIRECTIONALITY, AND GENETICS

The following discussion of the chapters is organized around the three concepts discussed in the Stoff and Susman chapter: plasticity, bidirectionality, and genetics. The related concepts are intertwined, but for purposes of pointing to advances in research, the chapters will be considered within these three concepts.

Plasticity

The concept of plasticity evolves from the potential for change that exists across the life span of the developing human (Lerner, 1998). Plasticity is the antonym for the presupposition of limits on individual development. The potential for change is thought to exist because of the dynamic irrevocable connections between an individual and the environment (Lerner, 2002).

Plasticity exists throughout the lifetime in the form of either functional or structural changes (Brim & Kagan, 1980). Contemporary theorists emphasize *relative* as opposed to infinite plasticity across the life span (Lerner, 1998). Relative plasticity implies that across the lifetime, intraindividual development is constrained; all developmental modifications are not possible and all possible variations are not desirable (Brandtstaedter, 1998). Development and systematic change have constraints imposed both from endogenous (e.g., genetic) and exogenous constraints (e.g., cultural norms and sanctions). Therefore, the study of plasticity involves observation of the history of dynamic organism–context interactions or the fusion of nature and nurture (Lerner, 1998). Plasticity is a feature neither of nature nor of nurture but is inherent in the fusion of nature and nurture. The features of nature generally considered are psychophysiological, neurotransmitter, hormone, brain structure and function, obstetrical risks, birth complications, hormones, neurotransmitters, and toxins. In almost all cases, these biological dimensions interact with the social factors of family, neighborhood, and community environment to influence the degree of plasticity exhibited by organisms.

Raine discusses plasticity in relation to the interaction of biological and behavioral processes. Specifically, Raine's discussion entails the importance of considering gene–environment interactions. The study of interactions has lagged behind the biology-direct effects model of antisocial behavior. Equally relevant is the case of the individual–environment interaction and antisocial behavior: A benign or inattentive environment moderates plasticity in a biological factor to result in a greater amount of aggressive behavior. In contrast, a teratogenic biological factor interacting with an adverse environment does not always lead to more aggressive behavior or criminality. This perspective is referred to as social push wherein children lack social factors that ordinarily would push or predispose them toward antisocial behavior. The case for the importance of social factors is noted in the instance in which social and antisocial variables are the independent variable and biological functioning is the outcome factor. In this case, social factors likely moderate the antisocial–biological relationship.

A historical question has been how much relative plasticity is there among levels of analysis. By nature, degree of plasticity may not be apparent in the short run. Raine addresses this question by examining the interactions between biological and social levels of analysis in the study of childhood aggression. Raine suggests that the antisocial child with a biological risk, as an adult, may seek opportunities to commit deviant behaviors outside the environs of a stable home and community. Thus, the biological factor becomes highly plastic, and rather than the more distal social cause, in this case, traveling to a high-crime neighborhood, the biological factor could be considered an interactive influence on antisocial behavior.

Raine also presents information on the importance of considering brain plasticity in adulthood. His research has indicated that violent offenders exhibit reduced functioning of the prefrontal cortex (Raine, Stoddard, Bihrle, & Buchsbaum, 1998). However, deprivation of the home environment moderated prefrontal cortex functioning and violent behavior. Deprived murders showed relatively good prefrontal functioning whereas nondeprived murders showed significantly reduced prefrontal functioning. These findings suggest that factors other than the home environment moderate criminal behavior. Raine's concluding paragraphs stress the importance of considering interactions to move the field forward.

Plasticity or the brain's capacity to adapt and change in response to environmental stimulation was appreciated by scientists even before the advent of molecular biology, according to Gendreau and Lewis. They cite William James' perspective on plasticity suggesting that the brain is composed of a structure weak enough to be influenced but strong enough not to be totally yielding to environmental stimuli. James' hypotheses have been confirmed by experiments with subhuman primates as well as in less complex organisms such as *Drosophila*. One of the first experiments to demonstrate the influence of the environment on brain plasticity showed that early monocular deprivation in kittens led to persistent functional alteration in visual cortex neurons (Wiesel & Hubel, 1965). In their chapter, Gendreau and Lewis present persuasive contemporary evidence on the effects of the environment on plasticity in the dopamine system and subsequent social behavior. By administration of a dopamine agonist, the frequency and intensity of isolation-induced aggressive behavior was altered in 20 generations of mice. Multiple other studies show the effects of maternal separation and isolation experiments on social behavior. Although the exact mechanism is not definitively established, Gendreau and Lewis suggest that variations in social experience and related alterations in the dopaminergic system mediate long-term social and emotional functioning. These alterations are moderated by when they occur in the life cycle, otherwise referred to as sensitive periods of brain development.

Very little is known about the effects of attachment, maternal deprivation, and isolation on the dopamine system in humans. In contrast, an extensive literature documents the effects of maternal deprivation and isolation on social and emotional development in humans. In addition, alterations in dopamine and dopamine receptors and transporters are known to be related to aberrant behaviors in humans. The next logical step in research on brain plasticity is to combine research on insecure and attachment loss dopamine with the structural and functional aspects of brain development. New imaging technologies will enable scientists to assess brain structure–function and outcomes associated with attachment loss and early experiences.

In an animal model, Ferris and colleagues addressed this important problem of plasticity of brain development related to the effects of early experience (social subjugation) on neurobiological systems. Ferris is convincing in his presentation of how experiences evoke long-term changes on both the serotonergic and vasopressin system. Golden hamsters were exposed to social subjugation, in a resident intruder model, and also were exposed to alcohol during adolescence. Adolescent hamsters exposed to social subjugation exhibited unique neurobiological and behavioral outcomes compared to adult animals. Male golden hamsters were exposed daily to aggressive adults and later tested for offensive aggression as young adults. Adolescent hamsters with a history of social subjugation show a typical conditioned defeat fleeing reaction, as is also true of socially subjugated adult male hamsters. What is unique about the socially subjugated adolescents is that when confronted by a smaller, weaker intruder they are exceedingly aggressive. The aggressive behavior may reflect either a fear response or an offensive move in anticipation of further subjugation.

The Ferris chapter additionally addresses two other aspects of the neurobiology of aggression: serotonin (5-HT) and vasopressin (AVP). Simultaneously assessing 5-HT and AVP is important as both are implicated in aggressive behavior. This multidimensional approach is innovative as biosocial research generally considers a single biological substance. Five-HT and AVP play opposing roles in aggressive behavior with serotonin reducing aggressive behavior and vasopressin increasing aggressive behavior. AVP has a stimulatory effect on the HPA stress axis (Gibbs, 1986), whereas serotonin is associated with low stress. Therefore, 5-HT may reduce stress-related aggressive behavior and AVP may exaggerate aggressive behavior in human as well as in lower mammals.

In summary, plasticity in both the serotonergic and AVP systems related to dominance was demonstrated in an animal model. Social subjection in early development and aggressive behavior and atypical 5-HT and AVP in adulthood is an example of how brain function is molded by the contexts of early daily life. The Ferris golden hamster animal model of early experience and later aggressive behavior is an excellent paradigm for developing hypotheses about the effects of early child abuse and early traumatic experiences on brain development in humans. Human model studies will benefit from linking early life experience and 5-HT in later ages, as low 5-HT may be a predictable outcome of adverse early trauma and an adult risk for aggressive behavior.

Graber and colleagues discuss the issue of plasticity in relation to the range of functioning at puberty. A key principle underlying the range of behavior at puberty is that plasticity in brain development and neural connections continues throughout the life span and that plasticity is core to individual differences in development. Plasticity in pubertal processes is reflected in the timing of puberty and, hence, individual differences in hormone and growth processes. Puberty is initiated primarily through the expression of genes related to structural and functional changes: growth, increases in hormones, and reproductive capability (Bourguignon & Plant, 2000). Experiences and behavior also affect the timing of puberty (see review by Susman et al., 2003). Plasticity in the timing of pubertal development is considered to result from a combination of genetic and experiential factors, but the interaction of genes and environment has yet to be addressed.

Plasticity in the timing of puberty imposes implications for the adjustment of adolescents as being earlier or later is associated with poor adjustment (Susman & Rogol, 2004). As suggested by Graber and others, timing of puberty is related to both internalizing and externalizing problems, with earlier timing being more likely to be associated with both sets of problems. Of note is that the effects of timing of puberty on depression are maintained into adulthood (Graber, Lewisohn, Seeley, & Brooks-Gunn, 1997; Stattin & Magnusson, 1989). The Graber and colleagues' findings on the long-term effects of plasticity in timing of puberty and related behavior problems provide an excellent model for future research on early plasticity in biological development and antisocial behavior throughout the life span. Overall, Graber and colleagues set, as a future task, understanding when and why the range of timing and behavior problems develops: the essential task of virtually all biosocial research in development.

Bidirectionality

Bidirectionality is concerned with issues of the embeddedness of evolution and ontogeny, of consistency and change, and of the role developing persons play in their own development (Lerner, 1987). The arguments surrounding bidirectionality in biology–social context causality derive from the controversy about the evolutionary development of humans. In general, modern anthropologist agree that the social functioning of humanoids is reciprocally related to the evolution of the human brain (Lerner, 2002). Embeddedness involves the reality that the phenomena of human life exist at multiple levels of being: innerbiological, individual–psychological, social networks, community, societal, cultural, and the larger physical ecology and historical context (Hinde, 1987; Lerner, 1987; Lerner & Foch, 1987; Susman, 1998; Susman & Rogol, 2004). Contexts of development include historical events, family, peers, and the multiple social institutions that surround the developing individual. Bidirectionality also implies that the levels of biological, psychological, and social functioning are not independent; rather, the processes at one level influence and are influenced by the processes at other levels. With reference to aggressive and violent behavior, each act is reciprocally influenced by biological and psychological processes embedded in the contexts of development.

Fields provides multiple examples of how levels of analysis, from the cultural to the neurotransmitter level, mutually influence each other to eventuate in the ultimate violence against self, suicide. The premise underlying her work is that cultural norms, arising from the social context about the lack of touching, are causally implicated in the triad of depression, aggressive behavior, and suicide. Lack of touching can lead to problems of attachment and brain abnormalities. The thesis is that affective and behavioral dimensions associated with touching are related to multiple biological systems, specifically brain functioning, based on EEG-documented abnormalities, and neurotransmitter systems. The serotonergic, dopaminergic, and catecholamine systems have been linked to aggressive and violent behavior. High dopamine is expected to lead to aggressive behavior, low norepinephrine to underinhibited behavior, and low serotonin to poor impulse control, high aggression and perhaps suicide.

One of the most robust findings linking suicide and neurotransmitters is that low serotonin is linked to both high impulsivity and suicide (Brown et al., 1982). Recent molecular-level biological lines of evidence suggest that a partly genetically controlled serotonergic dysfunction is involved in the pathogenesis of suicide (Ono et al., 2002). These studies implicate both pre- and postsynaptic polymorphisms [e.g., 5HT2A receptor gene polymorphism, A1438G (Ono et al., 2002)] and receptors [e.g., HTR1B (Sanders, Duan, & Gejman, 2002)] in violence. Findings from a future generation of studies on the molecular biology of the serotonergic system will likely illuminate future treatment of both affective and externalizing disorders.

The hypothalamic–pituitary–adrenal (HPA) axis is also implicated in suicide. Field cites evidence showing that adrenal gland weight is significantly higher in suicide victims. The tropic characteristics of the adrenal gland may be a result of hypercortisolism involved in depression (Chrousos & Gold, 1992). In brief, Field presents a bidirectional model with implications for intervention showing that massage therapy effects lead to increases in serotonin and decreases in aggressive behavior, decreases in cortisol and depression, and decreases in right posterior EEG activity. Bidirectional biobehavioral models such as the one proposed by Field have enlightened prevention and intervention efforts.

Sex differences in bidirectional influences between early aggression and socialization are the foci of the Zahn-Waxler and Usher chapter. The focus on early aggression is unique as it allows for establishing bidirectionality in socialization and aggressive behavior in the establishment of life-span persistent deviant behavior. Findings are presented that indeed support the role of socialization in modulating early aggressive behavior. Proactive parenting predicted positive change in children who showed early onset of aggressive, antisocial behaviors. Zahn-Waxler and colleagues earlier had demonstrated that negative parenting diminished children's empathy over time, whereas positive parenting that included warmth, modeling prosocial behavior, and use of firm, clear explanations about others' feelings of distress after experiencing harm (Robinson, Zahn-Waxler, & Emde, 1994) diminished aggressive behavior. These examples of social–contextual influences provide support for the essential nature of considering bidirectional multiple levels of analysis in the development of aggressive behavior: The aggressive child influences parenting behavior that, in turn, elicits parenting styles that either increase or decrease aggressive child behavior.

Adding the biological level of analysis reminds the reader of the inadequacies of considering only a two-level, child behavior–parenting bidirectional model of aggressive behavior. Zahn-Waxler and Usher show that aggressive children do not consistently demonstrate attenuation of electrodermal activity, basal level heart rate, or cortisol level that has been demonstrated in adults (e.g., Raine, Venables, & Mednick, 1997). Specifically, there was no evidence of underarousal of autonomic nervous system functioning in aggressive boys or girls. However, a subgroup of children who overtly expressed anger showed a pattern of attenuation in heart rate, high vagal tone, and large autonomic nervous system (ANS) changes. This pattern of hypoarousal in cortisol is consistent with recent findings regarding cortisol hypoarousal in girls with conduct disorder diagnoses but not with conduct disorder and depression (Pajer, Gardner, Rubin, Perel, & Neal, 2001).

The pattern of gender differences identified throughout the Zahn-Waxler and Usher findings convincingly shows the importance of differences in bidirectionality based on chromosomal and phenotypic sex. Zahn-Waxler and Usher's findings also provide illustrative evidence of the essential need to dismiss arguments as irrelevant regarding what is a biological and what is a contextual cause of aggressive behavior.

The issue of bidirectionality takes on another dimension when considering the developmental passage from deviant to nondeviant behavior during childhood, adolescence, and young adulthood. Moffitt and Caspi verify that some individuals show no adjustment problems across childhood, adolescence, and young adulthood. In contrast, those with adjustment problems can be classified into various taxonomies based on the continuity or discontinuity in pathways of adjustment problems. Three broad groups of individuals are considered in their discussion: life course persistent (LCP), adolescence-limited (AL), and early problems and then recovery. However, after following the recovered group to age 26, what had appeared to be a recovered group in adolescence proved to be a misnomer, as 25% of the age 26 group engaged in illegal behavior. Thus, the direction of adjustment problems was multidirectional over the life course; adjustment problems, recovery, and then adult adjustment problems and deviance.

The bidirectional relationship between period of development and recovery from deviance, we speculate, is a function of the intimate links between an individual's biological and psychological characteristics and the contexts in which the individual is operating. This interpretation of the importance of social context is supported by the finding that a portion of the recovered group was unlikely to be involved with drugs, which Moffitt and Caspi suggest is the most social among the problems behaviors assessed. The men who did not get involved with drugs were social isolates, had difficulty making friends, and were unlikely to get married. However, the stability of the deviant behavior in the LCP group suggests that the context of development may minimally influence patterns of deviant behavior, as the changing contexts inherent in development did not deter some individuals from deviance. Instead, an early pattern of deviance persisted across development. One could argue that the neurobiological dysfunctions that characterized some children set in motion a pattern of vulnerabilities that were not moderated by important social contexts and life transitions.

The pattern of early adjustment followed by recovery and then relapse mimics what was referred to by Cairns as "correlated constraints." This concept refers to the notion that certain behaviors are constraining in relation to the development of other behaviors (Cairns & Rodkin, 1998). The action of correlated constraints in development brings order, organization, and continuity to developmental processes despite the inevitable fluidity in contexts, persons, relationships (Cairns & Rodkin, 1998), and biological processes.

Worthman and Brown present a unique perspective on both plasticity and bidirectionality in the psychobiology of aggression. Their model is derived from an expanded adaptationist, ecological view of aggressive behavior and development. The combined perspective of biology, ethology, and anthropology adds depth and breath for understanding the integration of biological and behavioral processes and aggressive behavior. The Worthman and Brown perspective is consistent with the concept of embeddedness described above. This perspective assesses, in detail, the *life experiences* of the individual as context for understanding variations in biological processes and social behavior. Individuals are viewed as active organisms that participate in niche selection and construction as a means of adapting to contextual challenges in the process of ontology. With recognition of the importance for adaptation by active environmental selection and modification, two insights were stimulated: Views of heritability are made more complex by demonstrating the role of ecological inheritance and the significance of diversity in life history. The history of aggression is placed in the context of individual life histories that considers complex human relationships and cultural institutions that determine social opportunities and challenges throughout the life span.

Creatively woven into this perspective is the view of niche partitioning and the role of biological attentional and arousal regulating systems in such partitioning.

Worthman and Brown discuss adaptation at the individual level in evolutionary terms, as opposed to the species level. By integrating individual and cultural and physical evolution, the study of biosocial processes is taken to a new level by linking temperament, testosterone, and life history. Referred to as biocultural anthropology, testosterone and behavior are considered in an often-called-for multimethod and multidimensional approach: participant observation, attention to social relationships and social dynamics, a focus on meaning with biological processes of function, development, and well-being. These multiple ways of gaining information about a range of functioning in individuals is conceptually parallel with Magnusson's (1999) notion of holism or Susman's notion of developmental integration (Susman & Rogol, 2004).

The idea of adaptation at the individual level should not be construed as a passive response to environmental demands as could be interpreted from traditional Darwinism suggesting that all changes, at a species level, are a result of environmental demands. Rather, adaptation with reference to aggressive behavior connotes an active process of changing behavior to overcome environmental constraints by evolving a new set of behaviors, or by changing the environment to fit with current functioning.

Genetics

Genes no longer are considered purely deterministic influences on development. Instead they are viewed as interactive with the environment, with the environment being an essential element for the gene to be expressed. Furthermore, genes are not static influences but shift with development (Rowe, 1999). In brief, genes, the individual and the environment consistently are in a state of dynamic interaction.

Hood extends this notion in the context of Cairns' (1979) model of the integrated influence of genetic and contextual influences and modern holistic metamodels of development. The intellectual lineage for Cairns was that of T. C. Schneirla (1957) who proposed that the study of a behavioral pattern must begin with the biosocial organization of the individual, the structure of its group, and the nature of the interchanges in which behavior occurs. By necessity genes influence the biosocial organization of the individual, and the social organization of an individual influences genetic expression.

The Cairns approach, as discussed by Hood, captures the essence of development through a multilevel integration of genetic, social (behavioral), and contextual levels of analysis. Genes are viewed as not directly influencing development; rather, genes themselves are mediated through other systems and relevant feedback loops. The integration of genes, behavior, and context is illustrated in the case of dyadic interaction in selectively bred mice. In low- and high-line aggressive mice, selective breeding across four generations did not eliminate aggressive behavior; instead, aggressive behavior was developmentally delayed in the low-aggressive mice. When considering two additional levels of functioning, the immune system and the environment, further qualifications were added to the genetics of aggressive behavior. In a cross-fostering study of pups exposed to immune function stress, dam–pup similarity was the most striking finding in the absence of clear low- versus high-line aggressive differences and developmental pathways. The similarity in dams and pups appeared to be mediated by the quality of social dyadic interaction characterized by contact and licking. The conclusion is that selective breeding may operate on multiple levels, including the level of relationships between dams and pups. An important lesson learned from the Hood work is that the plasticity of social patterns does not preclude an influence by heredity, but rather that there is an isomorphism between genetic and behavioral units across time.

The combined influence of genes and environment is further demonstrated in Suomi's chapter based on research with rhesus monkeys. He suggests that ethologists posit that social aggression serves an adaptive function (at least in subhuman species) as species must protect self, family, and friends from predators and competitors to ensure survival across generations. At the same time, excessive aggression can destroy the social strands that hold the group together. Thus, individuals within the group through the process of social integration must learn when to respond with aggression and when to avoid such displays. As in humans, some rhesus monkeys fail to develop regulatory processes to control aggression. These aggressive group members are expelled from their nuclear family group, exhibit less successful reproductive strategies, exhibit low serotonin levels, and die younger than their less aggressive group mates. Furthermore, Suomi and colleagues showed that a short allele (LS) on the serotonin transporter gene (5-HTT), a gene implicated in impaired serotonergic functioning, was associated with low cerebrospinal fluid (CSF) serotonin (5-HIAA) in peer-reared but not mother-reared monkeys. In addition, the LS allele was a risk for excessive alcohol consumption among peer-reared monkeys compared to the long allele (LS) monkeys. The reverse was true for mother-reared subjects with individuals possessing the LS allele consuming less alcohol: the LS allele had a protective effect. These innovative findings of gene–environment interactions in rhesus monkeys parallel the findings of gene–environment interactions in the case of child abuse and serotonin system genes (Caspi et al., 2002). With regard to humans, fostering attachment and positive parenting in early development may override genetic influences on aggressive behavior.

THE FUTURE: INTEGRATION

What We Now Know

As demonstrated by the chapters in this volume, significant progress has been made in understanding the interface among the biology, experiences, and contexts of aggressive and violent behavior. Advances include the identification of patterns of attenuation (low) or amplification (high) of hormone levels, heart rate, 5-HT, and AVP and other processes linked to aggressive behavior. Patterns of continuity and discontinuity of aggressive behavior from childhood to young adulthood, and the role of early experience, were described in relation to differences in neuropsychological, neurotransmitter, and social context parameters. Sex differences in biosocial parameters of aggressive behavior also were noted. Given these varied and rich new findings, how can these advances provide a platform for the next generation of research on aggressive behavior and violence? Three principles are advanced for guiding future research: (1) Models and theories of aggression will consider the multilevel and dynamic nature of aggressive behavior. (2) Measures will assess multiple levels of analysis. (3) Translation of biosocial findings will yield implications for new prevention and intervention strategies.

Models and Theories

The theoretical frameworks just discussed are hallmarks of the acknowledged importance of integrated biological, psychological, and social–contextual perspectives on development. These theoretical perspectives are consistent with an integration metamodel suggesting that processes of development can only be understood by considering the multiple systems that simultaneously function at multiple levels of development, from the genetic, molecular, and cellular levels to the whole-organism and societal level (Susman & Rogol, 2004). The complexity of integrating these multiple levels of analysis necessarily requires longitudinal large-scale studies combined with advanced computer technologies. This may not necessarily always be the case, as hypothesis-driven, small-scale studies to establish mechanisms at specific levels of analysis are critically important to carry out in the early phases of research. What is critical to acknowledge in single-level studies is to link the phenomenon of interest to levels above and below, or hypothesized distal levels, to the targeted level. For instance, the quality of neighborhoods is known to affect the incidence of crime, but as discussed above, not all individuals in bad neighborhoods become criminals. Distal psychological and biological characteristics may lead criminals to actively seek out neighborhoods in which to commit crimes. Thus, it is critical for scientists to acknowledge the limitations imposed by one-level studies as well as to acknowledge the contribution of mediators and moderators at other levels of analysis.

To develop innovative theory-derived whole-organism hypotheses, scientists from different disciplines must establish collaborations so as to productively maximize integration of knowledge across levels of analysis. The animal model of early subjugation, employed by Ferris, is illustrative of how the findings of scientists working at a neurotransmitter mechanism level can provide a model for scientists attempting to identify social etiological factors in outcomes. At the same time, sociologist–criminologists are likely to have findings that support the experience of social subjugation in the pathway to deviance. Given the collective wisdom derived from both animal and human model studies, clearer hypotheses about the etiology of aggression are likely to emerge.

Integrated Models

Based on current theories of the development of aggressive behavior, future models are likely to be characterized by holistic thinking. (See Magnusson, 1999.) Holistic models are representative of ideas proposed earlier in this chapter suggesting that biological processes depend upon and simultaneously are dependent on the psychological and social–contextual levels of functioning. Consistent with the holistic interactionism perspective, Susman & Rogol (2004) suggest integration models that view the merging of levels of functioning. A fundamental premise of an integration model is that development proceeds through integration rather than compartmentalization of psychological, biological, and contextual processes. An integrated model does not imply that all aspects of an individual are considered simultaneously. Rather, the developmental integration model, as is the case for the developmental–contextual and holistic models, acts as a guide for selecting constructs and measures that are hypothesized to be dynamically related.

Within an integrated model, developmental processes are accessible to systematic, scientific inquiry since they occur in a specific way within organized structures and are guided by specific principles (Magnusson, 1999). An example of an integration model is the inclusion of the influence of early experiences, early adverse child-rearing, nature of the social context, and later adolescent aggressive behavior with the inclusion of biological processes across time. Each of these constructs and processes is considered bidirectional and integrated over time. That is, change at a serotonergic neurotransmitter level is integrated with change in family and peer interactions.

Methods and Measures

The methods and measures required to carry out integrated levels of research may be as problematic to develop as the problems and hypotheses. Behavioral and social scientists rely almost exclusively on questionnaires and interviews to study aggressive behavior. Behavior observational studies are rare outside the childhood age period. Methods that accompany integrated models might include the clustering methods developed by Bergman and colleagues (Bergman, Magnusson, & El-Khouri, 2003) and discussed herein by Worthman. These methods include multiple characteristics of individuals that then yield profiles for groups of individuals. Furthermore, these avenues of assessment could be merged with established methods or person-oriented approaches and include qualitative data, systematic observations, in-depth verbal assessments of concurrent affect, cognition and contextual characteristics (e.g., family functioning), brain imaging, and genotyping. Such an integrated multimethod approach could yield information about the integration of amygdala functioning and reported emotions, especially anger, an important risk for aggressive behavior as discussed in the chapter by Zahn-Waxler and Usher. The amygdala has been the focus of neuroscientists studying emotions, stress, and memory; however, these neurobiological studies have not been integrated with qualities of the person in context.

Translation of Biosocial Findings

The question is often asked: "What does biology have to do with prevention of aggressive behavior or interventions to reduce aggressive behavior?" An outmoded perspective on biological processes was that biology cannot be changed, and therefore, knowing the relationships between biology and behavior did not yield implications for prevention or intervention. Given the advances in understanding mechanisms of aggression, specifically the effect of behavior and emotions on genes, neurotransmitters, hormones, and immune functioning, a more appropriate question is: "How can biology be ignored in the prevention of aggressive behavior?" Importantly, new theoretical orientations point out the continuous and dynamic interactions among biological, psychological, and contextual processes (Cairns, 1979; Gottlieb, 1998; Hinde, 1987; Lerner, 2002; Magnusson, 1999; Magnusson & Stattin, 1998; Susman et al., 2003; Susman & Rogol, 2004). Finally, biological processes require an environment in which to be expressed, with the most obvious example of genes requiring a specific environment in which to be translated into proteins. Overall, biological processes should be considered variables that enrich rather than complicate developmental models of aggression.

Prevention

The literature documents that attenuation of arousal is a reliable risk factor for antisocial behavior (see Raine, 2002; Susman & Pajer, 2004). Indices of attenuation include low resting heart rate (Raine, 2002) and low cortisol (e.g., Moore, Scarpa & Raine, 2002; Pajer et al., 2001; Susman,

Dorn, Inoff-Germain, Nottelmann, & Chrousos, 1997) and low serotonin (see Ferris and Suomi chapters). Animal model studies of aggressive behavior are instructive as well in identifying new risk factors indicating the desirability of prevention. For instance, Ferris cites findings showing that "abused" hamsters were physically aggressive against others and had lower serotonin than nonabused animals. Similarly, children who have been physically abused are considered at risk for mental health problems such as depression and, to a lesser extent, aggressive behavior. Serotonin is lower in physically aggressive human males as well. Thus, children with low cortisol, low resting heart rate, who have been abused, and/or have low serotonin may benefit from prevention programs. However, these biological processes should be considered along with a comprehensive psychological and behavioral assessment prior to making decisions about whether or not prevention efforts are indicated.

In contemporary prevention research, there is not necessarily an isomorphism between the structure of risk and the structure of prevention programs, although the former informs the latter. Therefore, prevention programs to reduce aggressive behavior of necessity will not be oriented to only one aspect of psychological functioning or behavior (Coie, 1996). It follows that singling out one specific biological substance or process is not consistent with quality prevention science. The next generation of prevention studies will benefit from including biological indices with the aim of answering the question of whether programs designed to prevent antisocial behavior also change biological processes, such as heart rate, serotonin, or cortisol. Changing these biological parameters, in turn, may prevent further aggressive behavior. An additional point to be communicated to those responsible for social policy, with regard to preventing violence and imposing sanctions, is that a genetic risk does not always lead to crime. As discussed in the Hood chapter, genes require an environment in which to be expressed: A good family environment may significantly change the risk for antisocial behavior.

The timing of prevention programs also is informed by biological research. Recent research on the biology of puberty indicates that prevention efforts should be initiated at a younger age than in the past, given that hormone changes precede physical maturational changes by months or years. Given that hormone changes affect brain development, emotion and behavior changes may occur 2 to 3 years before the manifestations of puberty are obvious or anticipated by parents and teachers.

A goal of prevention is to find a period in development when prevention efforts have some hope of success (Coie et al., 1993). An example of the age-appropriate preventive effort is intervening to prevent the rise in adolescent behavior problems. Body self-awareness, parental monitoring, and emotion recognition programs are especially important to implement early in puberty. Emotions are related to pubertal hormones (Brooks-Gunn

& Warren, 1989; Susman et al., 1997), and antisocial children have difficulty with emotion recognition (Coie, 1996). The emotional understanding and self-control skills program (PATHS) (Greenberg & Kusche, 1993), a component of Fast Track (Bierman, 1997), may be efficacious in preventing aggression in early maturers. The unique feature of a prevention intervention that includes information about pubertal-hormone effects is that the intervention would include emotion recognition related to hormone changes as well as teaching children how their bodies will change (body self-awareness) and the implications of these changes for interactions with peers and family. Thus, interventions to prevent a rise in aggressive behavior at puberty are likely to be most efficacious if they begin prior to puberty, especially in the group of children at higher risk for aggressive behavior, such as those with early-onset antisocial behavior (Moffitt, 1993; Loeber et al., 1993).

Interventions

The points raised regarding prevention are equally appropriate for considering the implications of understanding psychobiological processes and efficacy of interventions to reduce aggressive behavior. Given the dynamic interaction between individual psychological, biological, and contextual processes, the ideal intervention program would target all these processes simultaneously. Given that biology, psychology, and contextual processes are dynamically integrated, a key questions is whether interventions to reduce aggression and violence also change biological risk factors. Important to note is that early interventions to reduce aggressive behavior can change biological functioning as well as behavior. Raine and colleagues (Raine et al., 2001) showed that early educational and health enrichment was associated with long-term increases in psychophysiological orienting and arousal. Changing these characteristics in the early years may lead to less hypoarousal and enhancement of attention to environmental cues, therefore increasing empathetic responding to others. In conclusion, scientists currently stand at the entrance to a scientific haven for establishing the bidirectional dynamic effects of interventions to reduce the risk for aggressive behavior and changes in brain development, hormone levels, heart rate, and neurotransmitters.

References

Bergman, L. R., Magnusson, D., & El-Khouri, B. M. (2003). *Studying individual development in an interindividual context: A person-oriented approach.* Mahwah, NJ: Lawrence Erlbaum Associates.
Bierman, K. L. (1997). Implementing a comprehensive program for the prevention of conduct problems in rural communities – the Fast Track experience. *American Journal of Community Psychology, 25*, 493–514.

Bourguignon, J. P., & Plant, T. M. (2000). *The onset of puberty in perspective.* Amsterdam: Elsevier.

Brandtstaedter, J. (1999). The self in action and development: Cultural, biosocial, and ontogenetic bases of intentional self-development. In R. Lerner & J. Brandtstaedter (Eds.), *Action & self-development: Theory and research through the life span.* (pp. 37–65). Thousand Oaks, CA, US: Sage Publications, Inc.

Brim, O. G., & Kagan, J. (Eds.) (1980). *Constancy and change in human development.* Cambridge, MA: Harvard University Press.

Broidy, L. M., Nagin, D. S., Tremblay, R. E., Bates, J. E., Brame, B., Dodge, K. A., et al. (2003). Developmental trajectories of childhood disruptive behaviors and adolescent delinquency: A six site, cross-national study. *Developmental Psychology, 39,* 222–245.

Brooks-Gunn, J., & Warren, M. P. (1989). Biological and social contributions to negative affect in young adolescent girls. *Child Development, 60,* 40–55.

Brown, G. L., Ebert, M. H., Goyer, P. F., Jimerson, D. C., Klein, W. J., Bunney, W. E., et al. (1982). Aggression, suicide, and serotonin: Relationships to CSF amine metabolites. *American Journal of Psychiatry, 139,* 741–746.

Cairns, R. B. (1979). *Social development: the origins and plasticity of social interchanges.* San Francisco: Freeman.

Cairns, R. B., & Rodkin, P. C. (1998). Phenomena regained: From configurations to pathways. In R. B. Cairns, & L. R. Bergman (Eds.), *Methods and models for studying the individual* (pp. 245–265). Thousand Oaks, CA: Sage.

Caspi, A., McClay, J., Moffitt, T. E., Mill, J., Martin, J., Craig, I. W., et al. (2002). Role of genotype in the cycle of violence in maltreated children. *Science, 297,* 851–854.

Chrousos, G. P., & Gold, P. W. (1992). The concepts of stress and stress system disorders. *Journal of the American Medical Association, 267,* 1244–1252.

Coie, J. D. (1996). Prevention of violence and antisocial behavior. In R. S. Peters & R. J. McMahon (Eds.), *Preventing childhood disorders, substance abuse, and delinquency* (pp. 1–18). Thousand Oaks, CA: Sage Publications.

Coie, J. D., Watt, N. F., West, S. G., Hawkins, J. D., Asarnow, J. R., Marksman, H. J., et al. (1993). The science of prevention: A conceptual framework and some directions for a national research program. *American Psychologist, 48,* 1013–1022.

Gibbs, D. M.. (1986). Vasopressin and oxytocin: Hypothalamic modulators of the stress response: review. *Psychoneuroendocrinology, 11,* 131–140.

Gottlieb, G. (1998). Normally occurring environmental and behavioral influences on gene activity: From central dogma to probablistic epigenesis. *Psychological Review, 105,* 792–802.

Graber, J. A., Lewisohn, P. M., Seeley, J. R., & Brooks-Gunn, J. (1997). Is psychopathology associated with the timing of pubertal development? *Journal of the American Academy of Child and Adolescent Psychiatry, 36,* 1768–1776.

Greenberg, M. T., & Kusche, C. A. (1993). *Promoting social and emotional development in deaf children: The PATHS Project.* University of Washington Press: Seattle, WA.

Harris, D. B. (Ed.) (1957). Problems in formulating a scientific concept of development. In *The concept of development: An issue in the study of human behavior* (pp. 3–14). Minneapolis: University of Minnesota Press.

Hinde, R. A. (1987). *Individuals, relationships and culture: Links between ethology and the social sciences.* New York: Cambridge University Press.

Lerner, R. M. (1987). A life-span perspective for early adolescence. In R. M. Lerner & T. T. Foch (Eds.), *Biological–psychological interactions in early adolescence* (pp. 1–34). Hillsdale, NJ: Erlbaum.

Lerner, R. M. (1998). Theories of human development: contemporary perspectives. In W. Damon (Ed.), *Handbook of child psychology* (pp. 1–24). New York: John Wiley & Sons, Inc.

Lerner, R. M. (2002). *Concepts and theories of human development*, Mahwah, NJ: Lawrence Erlbaum Associates.

Lerner, R. M., & Foch, T. T. (Eds.) (1987). *Biological–psychological interactions in early adolescence*. Hillsdale, NJ: Erlbaum.

Loeber, R., Wung, P., Keenan, K., Giroux, B., Stouthamer-Loeber, M., & van Kammen, W. B. (1993). Developmental pathways in disruptive child behavior. [Special issue]. *Development & Psychopathology, 5*, 103–133.

Magnusson, D. (1999). Holistic interactionism: A perspective for research on personality development. In L. A. Pervin & O. P. John (Eds.), *Handbook of personality: Theory and research* (pp. 219–247). New York: Guilford.

Magnusson, D., & Stattin, H. (1998). Person–context interaction theories. In W. Damon, & R. M. Lerner (Ed.), *Handbook of child psychology: Vol. 1. Theoretical models of human development* (pp. 685–759). New York: Wiley.

Moffitt, T. E. (1993). Adolescence-limited and life-course-persistent antisocial behavior: a developmental taxonomy. *Psychological Review, 100*, 674–701.

Moore, T., Scarpa, A., & Raine, A. (2002). A meta-analysis of the serotonin metabolite 5-HIAA and antisocial behavior. *Aggressive Behavior, 28*, 299–316.

Ono, H., Shirakawa O., Kitamura, N., Hashimoto, T., Nishiguchi, N., Nishimura, A., et al. (2002). Tryptophan hydroxylase immunoreactivity is altered by the genetic variation in postmortem brain samples of both suicide victims and controls. *Molecular Psychiatry, 7*, 112–732.

Pajer, K., Gardner, W., Rubin, R., Perel, J., & Neal, S. (2001). Decreased cortisol levels in adolescent girls with conduct disorder. *Archives of General Psychiatry, 58*, 297–302.

Raine, A. (2002). Biosocial studies of antisocial and violent behavior in children and adults: a review. *Journal of Abnormal Child Psychology, 30*, 311–326.

Raine, A., Brennan, P. J., & Farrington, D. P. (1997). Biosocial bases of violence: Conceptual and theoretical issues. In A. Raine, D. Farrington, P. Brennan, & S. A. Mednick (Eds.), *Unlocking crime: The biosocial key* (pp. 1–20). New York, Plenum.

Raine, A., Stoddard, J., Bihrle, S., & Buchsbaum, M. (1998). Prefrontal glucose deficits in murderers lacking psychosocial deprivation. *Neuropsychiatry, Neuropsychology, and Behavioral Neurology, 11*, 1–7

Raine, A., Venables, P. H., Dalais, C., Mellingen, K., Reynolds, C., & Mednick, S. A. (2001). Early educational and health enrichment at age 3–5 years is associated with increased autonomic and central nervous system arousal and orienting at age 11 years: Evidence from the Mauritius Child Health Project. *Psychophsiology, 38*, 254–266.

Raine, A., Venables, P. H., & Mednick, S. A. (1997). Low resting heart rate at age 3 years predisposes to aggression at age 11 years: Evidence from the Mauritius child health project. *Journal of the American Academy of Child & Adolescent Psychiatry, 36*, 1457–1464.

Robinson, J. L., Zahn-Waxler, C., & Emde, R. N. (1994). Patterns of development in early empathic behavior: environmental and child constitutional influences. *Social Development, 3*, 125–145.

Rowe, D. (1999). Introduction to the special section on behavioural genetics. *International Journal of Behavioral Development, 23*, 289–292.

Sanders, A. R., Duan, J., & Gejman P. V. (2002). DNA variation and psychopharmacology of the human serotonin receptor 1B (HTR1B) gene. *Pharmacogenomics, 3*, 745–62.

Schneirla, T. C. (1957). The concept of development in comparative psychology. In D. B. Harris (Ed.), *The concept of development* (pp.78–108). Minneapolis: University of Minnesota Press.

Stattin, H., & Magnusson, D. (1989). The role of early aggressive behavior in the frequency, seriousness, and types of later crime. *Journal of Consulting and Clinical Psychology 57*, 710–718.

Susman, E. J., (1998). Biobehavioural development: An integrative perspective. *International Journal of Behavioral Development, 22*, 671–679.

Susman, E. J., Dorn, L. D., Inoff-Germain, G., Nottelmann, E. D., & Chrousos, G. P. (1997). Cortisol reactivity, distress behavior, behavior problems, and emotionality in young adolescents: A longitudinal perspective. *Journal of Research on Adolescence, 7*, 81–105.

Susman, E. J., Dorn, L. D., Schiefelbein, V. (2003). Puberty, sexuality, and health. In R. M. Lerner, M. A. Easterbrooks, & J. Mistry (Eds.) *The comprehensive handbook of psychology, Vol. 6: Developmental psychology.* (pp. 295–324). New York: Wiley.

Susman, E. J., & Pajer, K. (2004). Biology–behavior integration and antisocial behavior in girls. In K. Bierman & M. Puttallz (Eds.), *Aggression, antisocial behavior and violence among girls: A developmental perspective* (pp. 23–47). New York: Guilford.

Susman, E. J., & Rogol, A. (2004). Puberty and psychological development. In R. M. Lerner & L. Steinberg (Eds.), *Handbook of adolecent psychology* (pp. 15–44). New York: John Wiley & Sons.

Wiesel, T. N., & Hubel, D. H. (1965). Extent of recovery from the effects of visual deprivation in kittens. *Journal of Neurophysiology, 28*, 1060–1072.

Author Index

Subject Index